Out of Order, Out of Sight

Out of Order, Out of Sight

Volume II: Selected Writings in Art Criticism 1967–1992

Adrian Piper

The MIT Press
Cambridge, Massachusetts
London, England

This book was set in Meta by Graphic Composition, Inc. and was printed and bound in the United States of America.

Library of Congress Cataloging-in-Publication Data

Piper, Adrian, 1948–
Out of order, out of sight / Adrian Piper.
p. cm.
Contents: v. 1. Selected writings in meta-art 1968–1992 — v. 2. Selected writings in art criticism 1967–1992.
Includes bibliographical references and index.
ISBN 0-262-16155-9 (v. 1 : alk. paper). — ISBN 0-262-16156-7 (v. 2 : alk. paper)
1. Piper, Adrian, 1948– . 2. Artists — United States — Biography. 3. Art — Philosophy. 4. Art criticism — United States. I. Title.
N6537.P5A2 1996
700'.92 — dc20 95-24490
CIP

In memory of my parents, Olive Xavier Smith Piper and Daniel Robert Piper

Contents

List of Illustrations ix
Foreword by Robert Storr xi
Acknowledgments xxiii
Introduction: Some Very FORWARD Remarks xxv

I. Art Criticism 1967–1970
Conceptualizing Conceptual Art 1

1. A Defense of the "Conceptual" Process in Art (1967) 3
2. Idea, Form, Context (1969) 5
3. Three Models of Art Production Systems (1970) 13

II. Art Criticism 1973–1983
Art-World Politics 15

4. In Support of Meta-Art (1973) 17
5. A Political Statement (1973) 29
6. A Proposal for Pricing Works of Art (1975) 31
7. Cheap Art Utopia (1976) 33
8. Arty and Illiterate in Berlin (1978) 35
9. Critics' Delight (1979) 41
10. Some Thoughts on the Political Character of This Situation (1980) 43
11. Ideology, Confrontation, and Political Self-Awareness (1981) 47
12. Performance and the Fetishism of the Art Object (1981) 51
13. Power Relations within Existing Art Institutions (1983) 63

III. Art Criticism 1984–1992
Art-World Practice and Real-World Politics 91

14. Performance: The Problematic Solution (1984) 93
15. An Open Letter to Donald Kuspit (1987) 107
16. Ways of Averting One's Gaze (1988) 127
17. A Paradox of Conscience (1989) 149
18. The Triple Negation of Colored Women Artists (1990) 161
19. Goodbye to Easy Listening (1990) 175

20. Notes on the White Man's Burden: Multiculturalism and Euroethnic Art Criticism at the Millennium (1991) 183
21. Brenson on Quality (1991) 189
22. Government Support for Unconventional Works of Art (1992) 201
23. The Logic of Modernism (1992) 209
24. Two Kinds of Discrimination (1992) 215

Adrian Piper: A Biography 261
Index 291

Illustrations

1. *What It's Like, What It Is #3* (1991). Environmental installation with lights, mirrors, four videodisks, and music soundtrack. Photo by Scott Frances/Esto. Collection of the artist. xx
2. Donald Judd, *Untitled* (1967). Lacquered galvanized iron, 14½″ × 76½″ × 25½″. Courtesy Donald Judd Estate. 9
3. Eva Hesse, *Repetition Nineteen* (first edition) (1968). Plaster, each 10″ × 7″ × 7″. The Museum of Modern Art, New York, Gift of Charles and Anita Blatt, 1969. © The Estate of Eva Hesse. 9
4. Steve Reich, *Pendulum Music* (May 1969; Paula Cooper Gallery, Whitney Museum [two performances]). Two pendulum microphones. Performance documentation photo. Courtesy Steve Reich/Nova Scotia College of Art and Design Press. 10
5. Robert Smithson, *Asphalt Rundown* (1969; Rome, Italy). Earthwork. Courtesy John Weber Gallery. 10
6. Sol LeWitt, *Forty-Nine Three-Part Variations on Three Different Kinds of Cubes* (1967–1970). Painted steel, each 4½′ × 1½′ × 1½′. Courtesy John Weber Gallery. 11
7. Hanne Darboven, *Untitled Drawing* (1968). Pen, graph paper, two pages, 8½″ × 11″. Courtesy Wadsworth Atheneum. 11
8. Vito Acconci, *Points, Blanks Way* (1969; Paula Cooper Gallery). Telephoned and announced information. Courtesy Barbara Gladstone Gallery. 12
9. *Area Relocation Series* (1969). Written language in *The Village Voice,* Gallery Guide, May 29, 1969. Collection of the artist. 12
10. *An Open Letter from Adrian Piper* (1981). Photocopied form letter dropped from original "Art of Conscience" catalog, 8½″ × 11″. Collection of the artist. 45
11. *Kuspit Extermination Fantasy* (1987). Pencil drawing for *Real Life* magazine cover, 9″ × 12″. Courtesy John Weber Gallery, collection University of Colorado at Boulder Art Museum. 106
12. *Kuspit Strangulation Fantasy* (1987). Pencil drawing, 9″ × 12″. Courtesy John Weber Gallery, collection University of Colorado at Boulder Art Museum. 119
13. *Vanilla Nightmares #16* (1987). Charcoal drawing on double page of *New York Times* Calvin Klein ad, 28″ × 22″. Courtesy John Weber Gallery, collection of the artist. 131
14. *Why Guess? #2* (1989). Color photo: two identical enlarged photographs, each approx. 34″ × 36″, one with silkscreened text. Photo by *Ebony* magazine. Courtesy John Weber Gallery, collection of the artist. 147
15. *Ur-Mutter #2* (1989). Color photo: Enlarged photo, 23″ × 40″, with silkscreened text. Photo by Peter Turnley/Black Star. Courtesy John Weber Gallery, collection of the artist. 160

16. *Free #2* (1989). Color photo: Two enlarged newspaper photos with silkscreened texts: 48½″ × 30″ and 37¼″ × 52½″. Photos by Klanwatch Archive/*The New York Times*; Gerard Martineau/*The Washington Post.* Courtesy John Weber Gallery, collection of the artist. 179
17. Sol LeWitt, *Forty-Nine Three-Part Variations on Three Different Kinds of Cubes* (1967–1970). Painted steel, each 4½′ × 1½′ × 1½′. Courtesy John Weber Gallery. 208
18. *Out of the Corner* (1990). Video installation: seventeen video monitors, sixteen with subtitled texts, music soundtrack, sixty-four framed photographs, each 9″ × 12″. Courtesy John Weber Gallery, collection Whitney Museum. 208
19. *The Grid* (1989). Detail: Pencil, transparent tape, graph paper, 11¹⁄₁₆″ × 8″. Courtesy Paula Cooper Gallery, collection Peter Soriano. 259

Foreword by Robert Storr

This book is about the education of an artist. The story it tells takes place against the background of the last quarter century, and that background increasingly becomes the foreground as the narrative proceeds. It is the tale of the artist's passage from the hypothetical objectivity of disinterested aesthetics to the complex subjectivity of someone whose global view is consciously qualified by an ever increasing awareness of her fluid but finally inescapable "specialness." Whether the rule in force is social, sexual, artistic, or intellectual, Adrian Piper is repeatedly the exception not only by birthright or as a result of her actions or ideas but by dint of her undeterable will to explain the reasons for and ramifications of her position. Autobiography, therefore, plays a significant part in this composite record, and throughout there are flashforwards and flashbacks that link particular moments of recognition or judgment to their specific context, whether it be periods of private introspection, the seasons of taste in the art world, or the years of social conflict in the nation during the last two-and-a-half decades.

By narrative, however, I also mean the gradual unfolding of ideas as if their sequence indicated the steps toward an intellectual destiny in significant ways independent of pressing personal circumstances. The heart of the matter here is the tension between the implicit freedom of thought of and the explicit constraints placed upon the thinker. Ultimately, given the character and convictions of its author, these pages emphasize a conditional license to speculate over and above experienced limits on that promise. When Piper reports on the world as it is, with its settled opinions and unsettled accounts, she speaks, despite all evidence to the contrary, as if that world were open to rational change. Cultural and political knots can be untied, she argues, if only one goes about it as systematically as one would unscrambling an abstract philosophical conundrum. This, then, is a mid-life memoir of a mind at work on the hopeful prospect that reason will prevail over prejudice because that latter is too costly and ignoble and the former too amazing and efficient to neglect.

Piper has divided this collection into two parts, in accordance with her separation of her written work into two functional types: meta-art, which describes and analyses her actual aesthetic practice, and art criticism, which addresses the situation and issues that surround it. Each of these sections begins at the same moment in the late 1960s. Those were the early days of conceptualism during which Piper recalls being so intoxicated by pure ideas that even her fellow celebrants worried for her. So heady was that time, indeed, that it is still hard to avoid a slight contact high from the vertiginous prospects disclosed to the imagination by pure objective inquiry freed from any obligation to make objects. Sol LeWitt's "Sentences" and "Paragraphs on Conceptual Art" sounded the call to which Piper answered with an ardent curiosity, confident quirkiness, and methodological exactitude unique even then. She was ripe for the intellectual challenge, and more committed than she yet knew to applying the lessons of this apprenticeship to new problems. The chapters of this book devoted to the conceptual movement at its founding thus have an emerging you-are-there quality that make them among the essential documents as well as the most closely observed critiques of the subject yet to see print.

Unlike most of her downtown colleagues, Piper traced the loosely scattered intellectual threads of conceptualism all the way back to their philosophical roots. While others borrowed paradigms from various academic disciplines and used them approximately or metaphorically—anthropology, geology, mathematics, linguistics, and cybernetics were then the favorite hunting grounds for artists—Piper felt compelled to master analytic thinking on its own terms, becoming an academic philosopher in the process. Retrospectively, this decision and the scholarship it required explains the high standards she sets for other kinds of cross-cultural intercourse. When, for example, she complains of the modernist art historians' capricious or ethnocentric interpretation of non-Western art, she does so from the position of someone who knows what it means to fully immerse oneself in a field of study before claiming expertise. Her respectful appreciation of colleagues who have paid a similar price for the right to address the problems of artistic method and meaning—Robert Farris Thompson on African traditions or Michael Brenson on the relativity of aesthetic quality—stems from that preparation.

Piper's education prompted her to become an educator. Among the many roles she has played in her professional life—theoretician, writer, studio practitioner, performer, provocateur—all relate to this primary vocation. It was the least common of choices for artists of her generation. If they taught at all, most of them did so to sustain an aesthetic endeavor that eschewed didacticism of any kind. Contrary to that norm, and to its historical art-for-art's-sake justification, Piper has mounted a spirited and articulate defense of the didactic mode. In essence she has revived the classical ideal, that, as well as please, art should, without qualm or dessemblance, instruct. Furthermore, she is quick to remind us, all art carries a message whether or not the maker admits to the purposefulness of its formulation and delivery or the recipients recognize their desire for it and its full effects upon them. The pleasures Piper offers are of a very particular order, and while offering them, she deliberately withholds those which the public habitually expects. Enlivened with tart anecdote and accented by lapidary American usage, the dryness of her verbal or visual presentation is a carry-over from philosophical practice and exhibits her delight in clarity while attesting to her hope that others will see the beauty of logic and the artfulness of the linguistic restraint its expression requires.

At the same time, Piper's declarative style creates a superficially neutral setting against which her humor and her fervor are plainly apparent. Early on there was a deliberate absurdity to many tasks she set herself—riding on a bus with a cloth stuffed into her mouth, for instance—but the aim was always to learn something, as well as to show something to others by example. When she eventually turned her attention to broad questions of cultural assimilation and resistance, she tackled the problem with an equally keen sense for the liberating effects of planned incongruity. After all, when something doesn't fit and the desire to *make* it fit or make it go away takes over, an all-too-human awkwardness almost inevitably intrudes and sunders what remains of everyone's best attempt to keep up appearances. Piper thus presented a series of participatory lecture-demonstrations to diagram the physical grammar of ethnic stereotypes. Modernist revampings of American Bandstand or Soul Train, in their own self-satirical pedagogic fashion, these class-parties fulfilled the old dramatic imperative of balancing organized catharsis with heightened understanding. Never before, it is safe to say, have Funkmaster George Clinton and mastermind Immanuel Kant had equal part in inspiring a work of art. And if you were present at such a disco-discourse and missed the fun, then you missed the point, since Piper's critical view of the contemporary scene hinges precisely upon the enforced separation of individual imaginative engagement and communal activism.

In this ritual and others, Piper casts the artist as an agent of social change. Contrary to the romantic schematizing of that other teacher, Joseph Beuys, Piper seeks to clear away the mental and moral cobwebs that cloud our tangled involvements with one another and our relationship to ourselves. Central to that mission is the assumption of full responsibility for one's acts and attitudes. In that she recalls Allan Kaprow as well, for in addition to pioneering the situational performance genres she practices, Kaprow was the first contemporary artist-writer to announce that the time had come for artists to act on their own behalf in every dimension of their creative lives. Gone, he argued, were the days of bohemian aloofness and the special dispensations and protections that went with that status. The modern artist was a man-of-the-world, he declared, and must behave as such. Granted, Kaprow excluded politics from the artist's mandates qua artist, and, granted, he neglected to say what it might mean to be a woman of or in the world. Nevertheless, it was he who most forcefully made the case for reconceiving the artist's role as that of the savvy and self-reliant producer, disseminator, and interpreter of his or her own work.

Piper has vigorously attended to all these tasks. Art criticism is chief among them because it sets the stage for the rest, by describing the art-world infrastructure and rhetoric that determine the fate of ideas launched into the public domain. Despite the commonplace perception that artists act and critics react, Piper joins a long list of writer-practitioners who have provided much of the basic and most reliable literature on modern and contemporary art. And like her dual-role colleagues such as Allan Kaprow and the late Donald Judd, she is not the least bit indulgent toward the run-of-the-mill taste-makers and trend-followers in the press. For example, "Critics' Delight," her generic fill-in-the-blanks review with its "overheard telephone conversation" sequel mockingly parrots the prompted enthusiasm of gallery goers and vacuous catchphrases of their professional guides. "Goodbye to Easy Listening" neatly skewers the modernism-lite of 1980s appropriation, and longer essays, such as "Power Relations within Existing Art Institutions," "Ways of Averting One's Gaze," and "The Triple Negation of Colored Women Artists," deal in depth with the omissions and evasions that account for the consistent marginalization of cultural and political dissent.

In the critical realm, taking responsibility for one's work may mean asserting control even at the cost of alienating those who distort the work while ostensibly explicating and promoting it. Piper's rebuttal of Donald Kuspit's aborted catalog text for her 1987 retrospective at the Alternative Museum is a classic of its rare kind. These days *very* few artists publicly take powerful commentators to task for their hidden agendas or blatant errors. Being a "difficult" artist can ruin one's chances at success; being marginalized with nothing to lose frees the mind and the tongue. Accordingly, having one's text "reviewed" by its unrestrained subject is a critic's nightmare, but then, like all nightmares, as Piper's down-to-the-screws dismantling of Kuspit's theses show, the worst horrors are pure products of the dreamer's repressed fantasies. In Kuspit's case they center upon his need to reimpose the antiquated notion of the artist as a helplessly eloquent neurotic incapable of higher thought, and the critic as a superior intellectual being who organizes the spasmodic insights of creative individuals into overarching theories.

The lethal precision with which Piper completes her mission is in line with the similar care with which she disposes of other types of analytic sloppiness. Exposing the thin veneer of Kantianism behind which Greenbergian formalism hid its contradictions, Piper answers with her own interpretation of the aesthetic and ethical implications of Kant's philosophy, emphasizing his procedural rigor over his aesthetic predispositions. She takes an equally tough stance with regard to Greenberg's postmodernist heirs, particularly those who have traded in his hegemonic concept of the mainstream for speculations on "otherness" that nevertheless ignore what artists outside the mainstream do or say. Neither forgetting nor forgiving such lapses, Piper notes that even as she attacked the myopia of traditional art history, Rosalind Krauss announced at a 1983 symposium that she doubted there was any unrecognized African-American art of quality because if it didn't bring itself to her attention, it probably didn't exist. Such statements are recalled and worth recalling because the sentiments expressed are widespread even though seldom enunciated with such embarrassing candor. Self-protective ignorance about and disdain for things outside our ken is the taproot of institutional prejudice.

No kinder to doctrinaire self-righteousness than she is to latent chauvinism, Piper flatly condemns ideology in all its forms, including that of the scholastic Left, since the objectivity she advocates is incompatible with preordained truths. In lieu of axiomatic beliefs Piper offers a method of investigation and synthesis. An aesthetic empiricist on the order of John Dewey, whose words introduce her essay "Talking to Myself," Piper aims to break the closed circuit of art-for-art's-sake and reintegrate art into life. Rather than invoke the premodern past by inventing futuristic cathedrals, as Utopian modernists often did, Piper wants to live more completely in the present by diffusing art into the atmosphere of daily existence. "Unobtrusively insinuating art into nonart situations really interests me," she wrote of her early conceptual projects. "I like the idea of doing away with all discrete forms, and letting art lurk in the midst of things."

As her meta-art essays explain, Piper's initial research focused on determining the spatial and temporal coordinates that differentiate ordinary objects from each other. Following this, she devised behavioral crucibles that pushed her to the limits of self-analytical detachment. Historical conditions snapped her back. "When you are drunk on abstract conceptual metaphysics—in my case, the representational limits of infinity and dimensionality—sociopolitical transactions of power simply do not exist. It never occurred to me that these events had anything to do with my actual gender or racial identity. . . . My objecthood became my subjecthood." The turning point was 1970, which witnessed the bitter fragmentation of the civil rights and black power movements, the expansion of the Vietnam War into Cambodia, the shooting of students at Kent State and Jackson State by "the forces of order," and the birth of the women's movement. It also saw the temporary closing of City College, where Piper had begun her undergraduate studies in philosophy. All these events caused her to step out into the streets and to step back from the art world even as she was being pushed away by the growing realization, shared by many of her cohorts, that "the aesthetic value of our work has come to be tailored for an educated leisure class whose politics we frequently abhor and of whose financial manipulations we are often the victim."

Breaking away from the near solipsism of her previous attempts to explore consciousness by personifying states of total dispassionate isolation, Piper altered her strategy and developed a series of alter egos to be used as social probes. Her point of departure was to assert the full prerogatives of a persona whose characteristics of omniscience and omnipotence were a model inherent in her formal education but clearly not a legacy meant for her in the "real world." Savoring its irony, she described her position as follows:

> *I personally have the deep-seated, optimistic sense of entitlement of an upper-middle-class het WASP male. . . . I always have, and there's nothing I can do about it . . . to have that sense on this particular planet is to have no bounded sense of self at all, since all of one's subjective tastes, prejudices, and impulses are equated with objective truth. It presumes that what one believes and perceives to be the case just simply is the case. It expresses one's thoughts in categorical declaratives without appending intentional operators. Expressing one's thoughts in this way simultaneously expresses an exquisite comfort and familiarity with the essential course and character of the universe. I am skeptical of this attitude, but I revel in it too.*

Refusing to relinquish the privileges of the dominant culture into which she was educated, Piper speaks in universals precisely in order to reveal the intrinsic partiality of any claim to that perspective. In the ordinary course of affairs the minute an African-American woman addresses the world in that manner, she is said to be remarkable. And at the same time her status is called into question as if she had been schooled or was pretending to be something she was not. As if, in short, she was performing a part. This, of course, supposes that Caucasian men who adopt this tone do so "naturally," that is, without pretense or special training. The obvious but conveniently overlooked falseness of this supposition is precisely what Piper holds up to our scrutiny by her gambit. Again turning the tables on herself and her environs, her next step was to create a black counterpart of the "upper-middle-class het WASP male." This so-called Mythic Being was the vehicle for a series of documented performances and published works in 1973–74, in which Piper impersonated a hip black man with Afro and attitude, and so exposed the nerve of racial and gender stereotypes implicit in his invention. "The Persona is my opposite in every conceivable respect. He and I are the complements," Piper commented in her in-progress evaluation of the project, tacitly acknowledging the symbiosis of fearful projection and latent identification that exist between any two antitheses.

Piper's own old diary entries provided the mantra-like dialogue for the street-wise character whose posture she assumed, further complicating the interplay of the dichotomous male-female and active-passive aspects that were the essence of "His" nature. Like the displacement of personality and the telltale cross-dressing in the photo-tableaux of Cindy Sherman, and the reassignment of texts and confusion of authorial authenticity associated with the fables of Jorge-Luis Borges, whose doppelganger protagonist Pierre Menard "writes" Don Quixote in something of the same way Piper's Mythic Being ventriloquized her own private musings, Piper's performance was prototypical of much that is called postmodern. With its layering of words and appropriated images, Piper's phototext piece *This is Not the Documentation of a Performance* (1976) also anticipated the whole genre of graphic political montage to which Barbara Kruger and others turned in the 1980s. In this same general vein, Piper's 1988 three-footnote exegesis of one line from George Gershwin's *Porgy and Bess* is perhaps the most elegant textual deconstruction of recent years. Certainly it is the deftest parsing of the racial and racist syntax of that opera to be found in five manuscript pages.

At the basis of Piper's role playing is the understanding that her "natural" self belongs nowhere unambiguously on either side of this nation's racial divide. A light-skinned woman of African-American descent, she "passes" in white society without intending to, and as a result has been involuntarily privy to its concealed bias. "I am the racist's nightmare," Piper has declared, "the obscenity of miscegenation. I am a reminder that segregation is impotent. . . . I am the alien interloper, the invisible spy in the perfect disguise who slipped past the barricades in an unguarded moment. . . . Frequently I provoke hostility in those whose social comfort requires my conformity to stereotyped social categories. . . . I must be prepared to disabuse them, in order to avoid serious and irreversible misunderstandings. . . . In part my work stems from a compulsion to embody, transform, and use these experiences in constructive ways, in order not to feel trapped and powerless."

Among the devices she has used to disabuse the secret bigots of her acquaintance were the calling cards she printed to hand out on occasions when someone unguardedly let slip a racist remark in her presence. Addressed "Dear Friend" and relentlessly polite in the phrasing of their rebuke, these cards identify their author as black and apologize for the discomfort her presence may have caused the card's recipient, pinning the offender down like a specimen. In this as in other pieces, such as the video-installation *Cornered* (1988) where she patiently lectures her audience on the deceptiveness of skin-tone-based assumptions of ethnic origin, Piper's style is aggressively well mannered, as though she believed that ingrained prejudice could be corrected by following the proper etiquette. She is not so naive as that, of course, but her tactic invokes a standard of civility and of rationality commonly used against those who protest inequities by smug conservatives. So doing, she defies the "right-minded" and "well-behaved" to acknowledge and abandon their racism and thereby live up to their own professed code of conduct. Modulating resentful confrontation with exemplary courtesy, Piper holds up a sharply focused mirror to racial blindness, reminding those who discover their own likeness in its enhanced reflection, "You know better."

Faced by so blunt a demand, many will seek escape. To close the exits, Piper had compiled a diagnostic litany of denials by means of which people hide from their own fear and avoidance of those alien to them, and this catalog of reflex reactions forms the basis for many of her more recent installations. Implicit in the way she frames the encounter between art lovers and the ethnic or cultural object of their conscious anxiety and perhaps unconscious hostility is Piper's awareness that the majority of viewers—but by no means all—will be educated middle-class, outwardly liberal and probably white. The minute they enter into contact with her ambiguously archetypal black surrogates—are they menacing or peaceful, angry or self-possessed?—she has that equivocal public squarely in her sights. "I am particularly interested," she has said, "in grappling with the 'Who, me?' syndrome that infects the highly select and sophisticated audience that typically views my work." The creator of environments where that audience must confront not only fictive others but their shadow-selves, Piper set the conditions for holding the public to the letter of the social contract they have theoretically endorsed. "I want viewers of my work to come away from it with the understanding that racism is not an abstract, distant problem that affects all those poor, unfortunate other people out there. It begins between you and me, right here and now, in the indexical present."

Piper's blunt ethical exigency is consistent with her aesthetic literalism. Her early conceptual phase and her more recent emphasis of social praxis are linked by the exhaustive approach and the consistent series of decisions that resulted in her transformation from thinking cipher to active catalyst. Applying the principle inherent in Sol LeWitt's complete diagramming of all the fragmentary permutations of the cube, an exercise that demonstrated the intricacy and eccentricity of the geometrically obvious, Piper has set about documenting all the absurd dimensions and perverse reconfigurations of our obviously illogical social structure. It is not necessary that one concur with all aspects of her assessment to benefit from her examination of the variables. Excluding the debater's points and rhetorical questions that might be raised against Piper's arguments in an effort to deflect its focus on our most painful national reality, there are many ways to differ with parts of what she says. It is possible to join in her dismay at the present state of affairs without believing, as she does, that artistic probity is so intimately connected to the personal morality of the artist—good art "happens" to bad people—or without sharing her faith in art as a tool for change. Modernism incorporates a long roster of reactionaries and boasts a short list of direct progressive achievements. Despite her extensive proofs and polemics, however, Piper does not demand or expect complete agreement. Nor does she propose a cure-all for our collective ills. "I cannot, of course, describe in any way what a correct response to racism would look like. . . . I wanted to identify well-known, knee-jerk unacceptable responses—not prescribe the politically correct one." Instead, she demands political coherence, preferring realism to abstract virtue. The control she exerts is to keep the inquiry on track and to keep the participants honest about the compromises and ambivalence implicit in their varying situations. In matters of race, no one sees the picture whole and no one stands at safe distance.

An installation Piper created in 1991 at the Museum of Modern Art made that plain. It consisted of a square room, banked with stair-like bleachers centering on a boxy pillar. Illuminated by dozens of naked lightbulbs, every surface in the room was painted a hard, dazzling white. Around the wall at the top of the stairs ran a continuous mirror, and on the four facets of the column at the same level as the mirrors were set video monitors that showed the head of a young African-American man. Staring straight out but often blinking uncomfortably as he spoke the words, the man listed and denied a string of racial slurs. "I am not horny," he said, "I am not smelly, I am not shiftless," and so on until, unable to utter another, he fell silent and turned his head away into shadow. It was never certain from his demeanor to whom these lines were being spoken, to himself reflected on all the surrounding walls or to the casual listener who walked into the space. Nor, if it was the latter, was there any clear indication who the man thought he was addressing, whites or blacks or both. In actuality, people of every description and, presumably, every social experience and political opinion could and did wander into his hearing during the course of the exhibition, and in so doing they found themselves simultaneously confronted by the man's presence, the presence of a random mixture of their fellow citizens, and their own mirror image. Under laboratory conditions, in short, they took their uneasy place in a disparate community and listened to the shaming and shameful phrases that have divided it for generations.

There was another kind of tension in the room as well, for as harsh as his words were and as unsettling their effect upon the public was, the chamber itself exuded an uncanny peacefulness and order. This was by design, inasmuch as the entire environment had been based on the serene geometric structures typical of minimal and conceptual sculpture of the 1960s. Those objects were the products of wholly disinterested abstract thought. Encased in one such module Piper's video protagonist was the product of another set of abstractions. Juxtaposing pure formal rationality and crude verbal caricature, an ideal expression of human capacity and the vile denigration of a man's worth, a detached state of mind and a restricted state of being. Piper forced her audience to come to terms with the coincident incommensurability of two symbolic codes, one transcendent, the other all too recognizably down and dirty.

1.
What It's Like, What It Is #3 (1991). Photo by Scott Frances/Esto. Collection of the artist.

That dual awareness is the core of Piper's philosophical and aesthetic problem, and she fully intends for us to understand that it is our problem too. Having started out to explore the further reaches to which logic and language could take her, Piper was brought up short by the one set of variables she had taken for granted: her sex and her race. The lure of infinity could not overcome these tethering facts, and the final realization of such limits provoked a psychic split she eloquently describes in her 1987 essay "Flying":

> *Abstraction is flying. Abstracting is ascending to higher and higher levels of conceptual generalization; soaring back and forth, reflectively circling around above the specificity and immediacy of things and events in space and time. . . . Abstraction is also flight. It is freedom from the immediate spatiotemporal constraints of the moment; freedom to plan the future, recall the past, comprehend the present from a perspective that incorporates all three; freedom from the immediate boundaries of concrete subjectivity, freedom to imagine the possible and transport oneself into it; freedom to survey the real as a resource for embodying the possible; freedom to detach the realized object from oneself more and more fully as a self-contained entity. . . . Abstraction is a solitary journey through the conceptual universe, with no anchors, no cues, no signposts, no maps, no foundations to cling to.*

"Swooping and swerving crazily through the uncharted sky," she continues, "I plummeted back to earth where I landed with a jolt." The weight that bore her down was what others saw and refused to see in her.

> *Each of these responses—fear, fantasy, mistrust, anger, confusion, ignorance—obstructs my self-transcendence, my ability to lose myself temporarily in the other, in the world, in ideas. These are the barriers that my art practice reflects, because they are the ones that keep me grounded. . . . I am no longer drunk on abstract theory, because the sobering facts press in on my daily life too insistently. . . . So partly by choice, partly by accident of my birth and position in society, I am cornered, hemmed in, somewhere in the basement of the building, preparing to crash my way out. My art practice is a reflecting mirror of light and darkness, a high sunny window that holds out to me the promise of release into the night.*

The last sentence in this extraordinary passage recalls the ironic image with which Ralph Ellison opens *The Invisible Man,* his seminal novel of race in America. In order to make himself visible to himself in refuge from a society that ignores his existence except as a type, Ellison's African-American hero surreptiously taps into underground power cables and fills his cellar retreat with dozens upon dozens of electric lamps. Piper also sheds revealing light on the obscured issues of racial identity—her installation at the Museum of Modern Art was in that regard a further play to Ellison's trope, which made any and all comers starkly visible to themselves and each other—however, in the basement of the metaphorical building from which she prepares to crash her way out, she aspires not only to reach the high sunny window but fantasizes release into the night. In the dialectic of black and white, even as she seeks enlightenment, Piper sees in the dark and hungers for darkness's familiar and enveloping embrace.

Yet another voice echoes in Piper's writing. It is that of Langston Hughes, who asked, "What happens to a dream deferred?" Although favored by intellect and circumstance, Piper poses the same question in her own name as well as in that of African-Americans as a group, for so long as her flights of fancy, or anyone's, are checked by overt and covert prejudice, the dream of freedom is still deferred no matter what economic or social improvements have been made meanwhile. The great privilege whites in this society widely enjoy is seldom having to think about their color; the abiding burden of blacks is never being allowed to forget theirs. That inequality, like all others that form the chains of racial constraint, is of such long standing that it is hard to believe that it will ever be completely undone. The perennial deferment of the dreams of African-Americans is the tragic dimension of the American Dream. Tragedy is the consequence of an essential flaw in human nature, and in its classical context such flaws and the distortions of character they cause can never be rectified but must play themselves out to their bitter end. Against tragedy's inexorable course, noble resignation is the best that can be hoped for. This, then, is the backdrop for Piper's seemingly quixotic devotion to logic as an antidote to myth. She is not prepared to accept defeat; and neither will she permit her deferred dreams—which Hughes likened to a raisin in the sun—to sugar over and rot or explode. Instead she maintains that the cruel givens of the collective situation in which we involuntarily share are not the work of the fates but the direct result of our illusions. If it is not entirely within the grasp of logic to change the world, changing consciousness, which is the locus and origin of our crippling misperceptions, is. To have a passion for reason like Piper's, therefore, is to have a passionate need for reason to show the way out of an impasse. That is the *agon* of this book, the denouement of which is still unwritten. In it, however, Piper tells us how far she has come and how far ahead there still is to go. And know it or not, like it or not, she reminds us, we are her traveling companion.

Robert Storr

Acknowledgments

I am grateful to Arlene Raven for offering me the opportunity to compile this material, originally intended for a volume in the UMI Press series of which she was the editor. Mary Schmidt Campbell recently remarked that many African-American artists have archives of their work because they are worried about being eradicated from the annals of mainstream art history. Despite some recently increased visibility, I share that worry—the down side of having lived most of my artistic life to date on the margin. I still often read articles or reviews that discuss my peers in groups defined by formal strategies, historical moments, or topical concerns and notice my own name missing. Then I feel relegated to the ghostly, the supernatural, like a disembodied spirit hovering around, hoping that some warm body will suddenly develop ESP. Perhaps the readers of these volumes will.

I would also like to thank Patricia Failing, whose efforts at an earlier stage in the evolution of this work kicked it decisively into shape. Roger Conover's initiative, enthusiasm, fortitude in negotiations, and patience in the production process are largely responsible for the final emergence of these two volumes into the light of day. Without Jenya Weinreb's careful and wise editing of the manuscript, and her willingness to extend extra help during some periods that were personally very difficult for me, this project would have taken much longer and looked very much the worse. I am indebted to her not only for her skill and patience but also for her good humor in hard times. Melissa Vaughn shepherded these volumes through the production process and provided the wise counsel, detailed information, and fortitude I needed to remain on track. Jeannet Leendertse's design expertise, and willingness to share it above and beyond working hours, taught me to appreciate the aesthetic requirements of these volumes as art objects in their own right. The intelligence and skill in each of these contributions will be evident in the end result; and render it highly unlikely that I will have to make a sincere effort to kill anyone.

Finally I would like to thank Deborah Rindge and Grace Lee for transcribing onto disk most of the material in these two volumes; the John Weber Gallery for providing many of the illustrations; and Mike West, John Robertson, Bernard DeMartini, and the staff at Campbell Photo and Printing for handling with sensitivity the conceptually and visually difficult material that always enters into my work, extending credit where necessary to get it done; and communicating respect and support for the creative process.

Introduction: Some Very FORWARD Remarks

This two-volume selection of my writings of the past twenty-five years chronicles two simultaneous processes: first, the process of my learning to think clearly about my work, and second, the process of my gaining critical distance from my role as an artist and socially embedded being. These two processes are not conceptually unrelated: I don't think that it is possible either to think clearly about one's work if the more general cultural and sociopolitical ramifications of making it are ignored, or to write convincingly about such general ramifications while ignoring one's own creative contributions to them. To describe the first process, I coined the term *meta-art* in 1972 to describe a kind of writing an artist may do about her work that examines its processes and clarifies its sociopolitical context and conceptual presuppositions from the first-person perspective (see "In Support of Meta-Art" [1973] in volume II). I have found this kind of writing to be extremely helpful in situating my work in the intellectual and interpretative context in which I think it is best understood. This exercise has been particularly useful at those art-historical junctures when prevailing critical trends have been unaware of, or unresponsive to, my interests and concerns as an artist. Writings in volume I of this selection, on meta-art, therefore focus on the presuppositions and conditions surrounding particular works I did that I needed to explicate in order to clarify what I was doing and why, at times when the preoccupations and resources of contemporary art criticism offered no fertile insights I could use for this purpose.

The second process results in generalized but politically self-aware art criticism, that is, art criticism informed by an understanding of one's own cultural and sociopolitical role in relation to the object of one's criticism. An art critic does not also have to make art in order to practice this kind of art criticism. She has only to recognize her own creative processes of writing criticism as a response to a socially and culturally conditioned object or situation—a response that is worthy and deserving of scrutiny to the same degree that an artist scrutinizes her processes of making art, that is, from the meta-art perspective. So this brand of art criticism is incompatible with the myth that the critic may impersonally efface herself and her subjectivity in order more accurately to deliver objectively valid pronouncements about the criticized object. In "Power Relations within Existing Art Institutions" (1983), volume II, I argue that artists need the politically informed art-critical perspective in order to retain control over the public meaning and material fate of their work. Selections in volume II, on art criticism, therefore consist of this kind of writing. It is grounded in my practice as a working artist but extrapolates from that practice to more general and theoretical arguments of a critical nature.

These two processes are, in my case, also causally related: Although I have always found it easier to think more clearly about matters relatively remote from my personal situation, I did not feel motivated to think about the art context in general terms until after I was compelled to think in personal terms about my own work and position in it. At first, in the late 1960s, this meant struggling to define my work and articulate my ideas in relation to a general context—the art-historical context of first-generation conceptual art—that was receptive but inchoate, and that as yet lacked a shared vocabulary for explicating the ideas and concepts that I was investigating. I remember all too clearly the tongue-tied frustration of futilely searching for words and concepts in which to explain, even to the most sympathetic listener, what I was doing in my work and why. This inarticulation is perhaps most clearly expressed in "Space, Time, Language, Form" (1968), volume I, ably and patiently edited by Mary Peacock, and "Letter to Terry Atkinson" (1969), volume I. It was one of the factors that motivated me to return to school to study philosophy. Later, in the early 1970s, as I found reason—in my own work and personal situation as a colored[1] woman artist—to question and then repudiate the general values and practices that defined mainstream contemporary art, my resulting distance from them enabled me to think more clearly about my own processes and presuppositions. And this, in turn, furnished the distance I needed in order to begin thinking about those values and practices more critically from a general perspective.

Thus the two volumes divide this selection of writings into these two methodological groups, of meta-art and art criticism. Within each volume, the writings are arranged chronologically. In volume I, the writings are dated according to when the work was produced; in volume II, the writings are dated according to when the essay was written, and are grouped thematically according to concerns I detect in each stage of my own development. These themes are to be found in both volumes within each chronological period. So the two volumes can be read methodologically, that is, first with a focus on the meta-art writings and thus on particular works, and second with a focus on the art-critical writings and thus on theory; or else they can be read thematically, comparing entries in the first volume to entries in the second within each chronological period heading, in order to explore the relations between practice and theory in each period.

In volume I, of meta-art writings about my work, the entries are arranged chronologically by date of the work discussed. In some cases I wrote about the work several years after the work itself was executed, and in some cases I have made yet further revisions for this project. In these cases the voice is clearer, and more de-

1.
For an explanatory note on my use of this term, see note 1 of "The Triple Negation of Colored Women Artists," volume II.

tached and informed by temporal distance and political awareness. In volume II, of more generalized art criticism and theory, my allegiance to the voice of objective universality is a constant (as befits such an allegiance). I regard earlier conceptual concerns as incorporated into later ones rather than repudiated.

Both of these processes have had a great influence on my work. In the late 1960s, my work was abstract, general, systematic, and formalistic. The more my habits of *thought* about my work, my situation, and the art context inclined in this direction (as the result of my increasing involvement with analytic philosophy), the more concrete, political, and confrontational *the work itself* became, and the more it issued from an understanding of my own sociopolitical position. It seemed that the more clearly and abstractly I learned to think, the more clearly I was able to hear my gut telling me what I needed to do, and the more pressing it became to do it. At this point I detect no mediation (that is, obfuscation) of theory at all between my own creative impulses and my observing awareness of them. Although these impulses are far from immediately transparent to me, they always become accessible if I ignore deadlines and demands and allow them to emerge at their own pace. I now know to reject out of hand ideas for work that are unconnected to my own standpoint, or that are generated by my tendency to cook up abstract political analyses that neglect scrutiny of my own role or involvement in the issue. I don't believe work that fails to speak *from* me can successfully speak *to* anyone else. This form of aesthetically direct speech can be distressing to viewers who seek the contemplation of objects in order to escape from people.

The union of the personal with the political often makes such work seem excessively confrontational or didactic to some viewers. I think this is because art functions for me as not only a medium of exploration but also a medium of communication between me and the viewer. The idea that art may actually attempt to communicate something to a viewer is historically a commonsense concept. But it has been lost in a contemporary-art context that has been cowed into self-censorship by threats of political censorship and the withdrawal of public and private funds for controversial or unconventional works of art. A great deal of artwork that has been produced in this country during the past few decades bears comparison with literature produced in Eastern Europe under communism: It is sly, cynical, subtle, understated, and noncommittally open to a broad range of interpretations from the innocuous (for an unschooled public) to the provocative (for the cognoscenti). I discuss these values in "Goodbye to Easy Listening" (1990), volume II). They are characteristic of art produced in a climate of fear—of institutional or governmental or corporate retaliation—under any regime. So when a viewer comes across a work that attempts not only to say something clearly and without circumlocution but to say it *directly to that particular viewer,* it is not surprising that some viewers may feel attacked, or buttonholed, or lectured.

When artists in a repressive society choose to market their work to survive economically, they have to produce that work with one eye to the stifling and punitive requirements of institutional legitimation. This often produces Easy Listening art that offends no one and challenges no one. And then its public grows unused to art as an experience of active engagement with, or dialogue about, controversial issues. I believe that my work is perceived to have this confrontational and didactic character, in part because I have chosen an unrelated day job, to which I am also committed, as my means of economic survival. Because my survival does not depend on selling my artwork, I am free in my work to do whatever I want and say whatever I want to whomever I want, regardless of their political clout or social status or institutional power within the art world (see "Porgy" [1988], volume I).

The trade-off is, first and foremost, the double dose of exhaustion that every single working mother experiences in working two jobs, each of which requires the energy and creativity that others expend on one. Second, I sacrifice greater professional recognition, institutional legitimation, and market demand for my work. I know what I would have to do—how I would have to act and what kind of work I would have to make—in order to obtain more of these benefits, and I am simply not willing to do it. These are trade-offs I am more than willing to make in return for the freedom of doing and saying what I want, and they are trade-offs I have often had the opportunity to reaffirm. Under these circumstances I feel I have—with the help of long-standing supporters who have recently ascended to positions of institutional power—done surprisingly well professionally. None of my many complaints are on *that* score.

Yet I feel increasingly concerned and responsible for those supporters of my work who, for having supported, promoted, exhibited, or written about it, have been professionally punished by losing their funding, their professional status, their jobs, or their voice in the community. This has now happened on eight or nine separate occasions, and invariably the pattern is the same: The person—in most cases either young or privileged or an idealistic white male or all three—is hired to a position of institutional power and falsely believes that this professional advancement is an expression of institutional empowerment for her or his progressive values and ideas, when in fact it is an expression of institutional judgment that this person is best suited to promote and protect the institution's own—usually conservative—agenda under a progressive guise. So the person acts to realize her or his ideals by promoting my work; is then punished, demoted, silenced, or fired on the basis of some spurious and unrelated charge; tries to defend herself or himself against that charge, or convince the institution that its charge was mistaken—unsuccessfully, of course; and only gradually comes to understand that those who control the institution perceive my work—often rightly—as an attack on their class interests and will not permit or empower anyone, no matter how highly credentialed or authoritative, to imperil those interests by giving it the institution's legitimation.

I find it increasingly difficult to watch these friends and supporters go through the shock, disbelief, anger, humiliation, and cynical disillusionment attendant on this process of enlightenment; and to witness the spectrum of ways in which they are punished for supporting my work, from the economic to the professional to the psychological to the moral. What is more difficult is that it is impossible to warn them in advance that they are embarking on a dangerous course in allying themselves with my work, because they never believe me. They can't conceive that the work could be that threatening to anyone else, because it isn't to them; or their sense of their own entitlement, legitimation, and professional mission is so strong that they cannot believe others would dare to strip them of it; or their view of the institution and those who control it is benign in the way it must be for those of us who are still inclined to take others at their word; or they don't realize how precariously their own class interests balance against their progressive convictions. That is, they do not see that in protecting itself by suppressing my work, the institution is very often also protecting people *like them* from having to relinquish the class privileges that go with racism—the very privileges that enabled them to advocate my work publicly in the first place. They do not see that in the eyes of the institution, their support for my work flouts and belittles the power the institution conferred on them to do that. By promoting my work, they treat the power and privileges of their own position in the institutional hierarchy as ultimately dispensable (because dispensing with privilege is what it would mean to implement a nonracist society). In this sense it is not surprising that the institution feels betrayed by what it perceives as their defection. As though anyone should suppose that these public statements of institutional policy, issued as press releases, were to be taken seriously!

Of course, each time, I go through this process of disillusionment with them, because in each case I secretly hope that they will prove me wrong. But they almost never do.

Compiling the material for these volumes has been a process of self-discovery. For one thing, it has given me insight into my deep-seated, optimistic sense of entitlement—the sense of entitlement of an upper-middle-class heterosexual WASP male, the pampered only son of doting parents. This sense is expressed implicitly in my work and, I think, more clearly and overtly in the writings that constitute these volumes. To have that sense on this particular planet is to have no bounded sense of self at all, because all of one's subjective tastes, prejudices, and impulses are equated with objective truth. To have that sense is to presume that what one believes and perceives to be the case just simply is the case. One expresses one's thoughts in categorical declaratives without appending intentional operators, as though they communicated simple matters of fact. This manner of expression conveys an exquisite comfort and familiarity with the essential course and character of the universe. Although I am skeptical of this attitude, I prize it, too. I am much more skeptical of an epistemological stance that denies that the experience of racism, misogyny, or homophobia can be anything more than an ungrounded or fractured subjective perception.

Many of the early chapters in these volumes express my white male's sense of entitlement unself-consciously. These chapters are written in the objective voice. They are reasonable, tolerant, modest, and dogmatic. They are touchingly naive in their unspoken assumption that the world of art ideas is there to be mined and ordered by my intellect. They express the undifferentiated and prereflective abstract consciousness of the infant whose world is a nipple available on demand. This is the voice of objective universality. It is the voice of innocent, humble authority. With very few qualifications, and in spite of the ways in which my work has evolved, it expressed ideas in which I continue to believe.

When very young children talk in the objective voice, we are indulgent because they are young. When actual upper-middle-class het WASP males, the pampered only sons of doting parents, talk in this voice, we listen—warily—because often they certainly seem to know what they are talking about (the nipple has not yet been withdrawn). But when a young colored woman talks in this voice, she is apt to get put in her place, very quickly and very rudely. How long it takes her to *learn* her place is a different story. That depends on the strength and tenacity of her sense of entitlement.

In preparing these volumes, I have come to realize that my sense of entitlement and allegiance to the objective voice has been tenacious indeed. Reading through the early material for inclusion elicited long-dormant memories of events that scarcely registered at the time. While romping in the theoretically fertile but disorganized universe of conceptual art in the late 1960s, and implicitly thinking of myself as the next *enfant terrible* of the art world, I was being systematically marginalized: by one major art magazine editor who disinvited an article (by Scott Burton) upon learning that its subject was a woman and a student; by another who disinvited an essay by me upon learning that its author was a woman and a student; by critics and curators who stopped promoting my work when they discovered I was a woman (heaven only knows where I would have ended up had my name been Shirley or Belinda[2]) and colored; and by dealers and promoters who thought my true destiny was to be an outstandingly creative gallery receptionist. In those days, conceptual art was a white macho enclave, a fun-house refraction of the Euroethnic equation of intellect with masculinity. Christine Kozlov and I were the only women admitted, and we were perceived as mascots. In the "Conceptual Art and Conceptual Aspects" catalog (1970), she is listed as "C. Kozlov." I often wonder where she is now.

Some of the more theoretically inclined men of that group defined conceptual art in terms of its purported relation to analytic philosophy. They later claimed to have rejected this affiliation because of analytic philosophy's oppressive institutional structure within the academy. I saw their rejection differently. As I began to study analytic philosophy more seriously and carve my own path into the academy, I recognized that the linguistic practices of some of these "analytic" artists were dismissed by the academic philosophers from whom they claimed to derive inspiration. And I saw that they would have needed to acquire a great deal more advanced training in technical skills of logic and semantics in order to pursue their artistic investigations in the philosophy of language. They said that they repudiated analytic philosophy for political reasons. To me it looked as though they repudiated it because it was too demanding. And the more completely I embraced it, the more decisively they repudiated me and it as well.

I didn't realize I was being marginalized. I didn't realize it, first, because this interpretation of the events (the flirtatious and derogatory remarks, the articles and interviews that were never published, the invitational shows from which I was excluded) was simply inconceivable, unthinkable to me at that time. When you are drunk on abstract conceptual metaphysics—in my case, the concrete representational limits of infinity and dimensionality—sociopolitical transactions of power simply do not exist. Second, the events in any case coincided with my own increasing

2.
Sherrie, Laurie, Cindy, Jenny, Nancy! Who could have dreamed in those days that major art-world movers and shakers would ever have such names? It would have seemed ridiculous, incongruous, oxymoronic.

alienation from the promotional art market and considered choice to distance myself from it. My choice to do street performances outside the limits of the art world, and my isolated performance forays into the psychosexual terrain of street people, the homeless, and third-world masculinity, fully determined the art world's fading enthusiasm for my work. It never occurred to me that these events had anything to do with my actual gender or racial identity.

Third, I didn't realize I was being marginalized because the effort was in any case impotent to affect the trajectory of my creative development. Sol LeWitt had been generous with inspiration and support for my work. Vito Acconci had published my first conceptual work in his *0 to 9* magazine. John Weber and Paula Cooper had been the first dealers ever to show my work, and Lucy Lippard the first to curate it. My subsequent gallery and museum exposure in the late 1960s and early 1970s seemed fortuitous, an unbidden gift I eventually felt free to decline. It didn't dawn on me then that this exposure would have ceased in any case, and for good, when my gender and racial identity became known. At the time it seemed that the universe simply cooperated in my decision to drop out. This unself-conscious presumption of inner harmony with the external universe is a typical expression of the sense of entitlement of the upper-middle-class het WASP male, the pampered only son of doting parents. I know it well.

I drew my emerging political analysis of the art world, and my awareness of my own sociopolitical role in it, from the real-world politics I encountered upon leaving its sheltered confines; for the art world by itself offered no resources for thinking clearly, concretely, and analytically about these issues. Despite all the attention to theory and political analysis that has characterized the more progressive segments of the art world in recent years, I continue to see a paucity of such resources. There are no forces *within the art world itself* for personally galvanizing the arbiters and inhabitants of prevailing art institutions to a greater political self-awareness of their roles, actions, and decisions. The ideological indoctrination of the art world—through techniques of recognition and passive censorship, rewards and exclusion in art schools, the media, and institutional and market practices—is just too pervasive.

Those of us who are fortunate enough to gain and bring to bear such insight on our art practice draw it from external sources. We are the tour guides who venture—or are pushed—out into the field, and then return to infuse our art products with cultural—not just aesthetic—significance. We draw cultural significance from outside the boundaries of the art world into it, may be briefly noticed by it, before our findings are appropriated by the mainstream and we are then pushed back outside it again, to forage for new infusions of cultural reference, derived from our personal experiences on the edge, that supply the art world its next art-historical fix.

Meanwhile mainstream artists replicate, permutate, and ennervate those references, slowly wringing them of cultural significance, making them institutionally palatable to paranoid and socially repressive institutions, turning the aesthetic experience of them into Twenty Questions, a gimmicky, low-brow name-that-form game show of cultural hide-and-seek, repackaging and swathing them in layers of obscurity, of increasingly veiled and muffled meanings with the pellucid recognition of which a sophisticated and culturally informed aesthetic experience ought to begin. For us it is easy to detect the tinny squeak of superficial, bad-faith theorizing on the part of those sheltered denizens who lack such roots in personal external experience, or who ignore them when venturing out onto the shifting and unstable terrain of abstract generality.

I have now been perched on the outer edge of the art world for twenty-five years, with only very occasional fifteen-minute forays into the center (these forays begin after I've been outside the mainstream long enough for it to forget who I am, and end—quickly—after I've been inside long enough for it to remember). During this time I have twice witnessed the art world's response to direct and confrontational infusions of external cultural significance. In the early 1970s, women artists, most of them white, insistently and vocally made their concerns and presence felt to already safely ensconced white women critics and curators, in a rash of group shows and articles on "Women Artists." And in the late 1970s young white women artists entered the inner sanctum. But these artists were almost never those who had participated in the earlier feminist movement. Oh, no! For you see, there was no connection between that earlier application of political pressure and the art world's acknowledgment of these younger women artists. They're just good artists, that's all! Similarly, in the late 1980s, colored artists made their presence felt, in a similar rash of group shows and articles on "Black Artists." And in the early 1990s, younger colored artists—almost never any of those named in these earlier shows or articles—are entering the white mainstream in record (which is not to say large) numbers. Because they're just good artists, that's all!

Just as an institutionally repressive and self-censoring art world responds to socially controversial subject matter in art by disregarding or disowning it, that same mainstream art world responds to externally infused cultural significance by ignoring it, then pretending to discover or create it; and by choosing among its candidates for mainstream visibility those who are untainted by its prior campaign of marginalization.[3] That way it can repeatedly regenerate itself parasitically, with a clean slate from which the past is erased, without ever acknowledging responsibility for having perpetrated the injustices it now in effect repairs. It prefers to conceive itself as moved solely by pristine aesthetic imperatives, in order to muffle the by now quite insistent pangs of a bad conscience.

You know how unpleasant and boring it is to be around people who have a bad conscience. They can't afford to acknowledge or discuss anything interesting, for fear that it might lead inadvertently to the taboo topic, so their conversation is relentlessly shallow; and they're always trying to compensate by dragging you down to their level with extravagant displays of coziness, so they won't feel so bad. These are not unintelligent people. But they are weighted down by an intolerable burden—the burden of their own unacknowledged past bad behavior—and they are inviting you to help them shoulder the load. Unless you are motivated by selfless compassion or single-minded self-interest to suppress your feeling of nausea and collude, self-exile to the margins may well seem the only viable strategy for creative survival.

So my ostracism and flight from the art world, and subsequent battles in the real world, were without question the best and most important events I could have experienced for the enrichment of my work. They gradually taught me who I am and brought me to a bounded sense of self, from the undifferentiated esoteric realm of pure form. They revealed inner and outer resources it had never occurred to me I had, let alone could draw on in my work. Like spending a year in Europe between college and graduate school for the upper-middle-class het WASP male, the pampered only son of doting parents, an extended period of external sociopolitical engagement should be a requirement of every art student's education. Suffering deepens one's character. It also teaches one who one is, and what it really means, in truly objective, world-historical terms, to be an upper-middle-class het WASP male, the pampered only son of doting parents.

3.
Nevertheless I predict that colored artists as a group are going to have a much harder time of it than white women artists did, because there are so few of their own already safely ensconced in the Euroethnic mainstream to pull them in. Nothing is more persuasive than the sight of a former mainstream conservative hardliner who sheds her colonized ideology and advocates for her sisters as eloquently as she formerly argued against them. White women artists had those advocates in formerly conservative white women critics and curators; colored artists, with very few exceptions, do not. Unlike white women artists, we have no one among our own "on the inside" to invite us in. We are the eternal gatecrashers of the great, ongoing Euroethnic party.

There are many advantages to learning who you are, and even more to retaining your white male's sense of entitlement without actually being a white male. For example, being punished for asserting your ideas leads reflexively—if you are as deeply attached to the ideal of objective universality as I am—to scrutinizing their veracity, as a matter of course, and epistemic insecurity is a tactical advantage in the competition for truth, a personal extension of methodological skepticism. Whatever survives that scrutiny is all the more impervious to future attack. Also, epistemic insecurity enhances critical discrimination. You win absolute conviction in the objective validity of your ideas, while differentiating yourself from those who are trained to declaim their ideas with absolute conviction. You learn tact. And you find you can experience the epistemic confidence of an upper-middle-class het WASP male, the pampered only son of doting parents, without sharing the same unsatisfactory epistemology. You learn firsthand the meaning of solipsism.

Finally, you earn the riches and satisfactions of interiority, the blessed, invaluable side effect of repeatedly thwarted communication. Not for such as me the luxuries of repression, absent-mindedness, or inchoate thought sublimated into impulsive or irresponsible behavior. These stopgap measures are designed for relatively minor episodes of self-censorship, within the walls of a friendly private club that rejoices in the abstract theoretical sleepwalking of its members. For those of us still applying to get in, such indulgence in response to the coercive requirement of massive self-censorship could cost us our lives, our sanity, or at least the linings of our stomachs. So instead we *consider* what we see but are prevented from voicing. We take it into our selves, we muse on it and analyze it; we scrutinize it, extract its meaning and lesson, and record it for future reference. Our unspoken or unacknowledged contributions to discourse infuse our mental lives with conceptual subtlety. We become deep, perceptive, alert, and resourceful.

It seems to me now that the writings in these two volumes are best understood as evolving expressions of a coerced, reflective interiority that develops in response to my increasing grasp of the point: that I am not, after all, entitled simply to externalize my creative impulses in unreflective action or products, because, being merely a foreign guest in the private club in which I entertain, my self-confident attempts at objective communication with my audience would be permanently garbled, censored, ridiculed, or ignored, were it not for a critical and discursive matrix that I—with effort—eventually supply. This matrix permeates with intended meaning the vacuum of silence, speechlessness, and suspicious withdrawal that often spreads outward around my work (this is how I am reminded of my overnight visitor's status). To the extent that the voice of intended meaning is the only voice in the vacuum, it becomes epistemologically equivalent to objective meaning, which reinforces my commitment to that ideal. To the extent that the voice of intended meaning is answered by voices of perceived meaning—to the extent, that is, that my work sparks the beginnings of actual communication—it gradually fashions a reciprocal social and cultural space in which my concerns have currency, a space through which I can navigate as an artist, a person, and a social agent among others. Thus my writing feeds my white male's sense of entitlement even as it locates me as a subject relative to an audience. And this enhances my confidence, my epistemic insecurity, my interiority. The system is complete and self-sustaining.

I. **Art Criticism 1967–1970:** *Conceptualizing Conceptual Art*

1. A Defense of the "Conceptual" Process in Art

Written in 1967 and previously unpublished.

I am very much aware of the thorniness (at this late date!) of using words like "detached" or "objective" in relation to an artist's work or attitude about his work. I've often attempted to plow through people's protests about the vulgarity of an artist's non-involvement in his work supposedly implied in the use of such terms. However, that is not at all what those words mean to me; on the contrary—I think that a greater total involvement in one's work is possible when one attempts to be objective than when one does not. I have found that the limitations imposed by decisions based on my personal "tastes" are absolutely stifling. Choices made through the criteria of subjective likes and dislikes are to me nothing more than a kind of therapeutic ego-titillation that only inhibit further the possibility of sharing an artistic vision (as if it weren't difficult enough a thing to do as it is).

Besides, I really believe that truly good art is always made of broader stuff than the personality of the artist. Think of all the hangups Cézanne had that he managed to transcend in his work! I don't mean to imply that great artists of the past necessarily knew and consciously strove for this kind of objectivity—I don't presume to know whether they did or not—but I think that the mere fact of their work's ability to affect us on any level is an indication that they attained and shared this breadth of vision. The new terminology—"cool," "rational," "reductive" art—simply corroborates my opinion that the necessity for this transcendence of subjectivity has been recognized, and that attempts are being made to facilitate the process.

To me, people who complain about the "antihumanism" of conceptual art are missing the point. Any kind of objectivity—whether it is in the formulation of a concretized system, a rational decision-making method, conceptual clarity—can serve only to facilitate the final emergence, in as pure a form as possible, of the artistic idea, which is almost always basically intuitive in nature. It is only when one subordinates the original intuition to the subjective distillations and limitations of one's own personality that one need be finally confronted with a kind of mirror image of one's egoistical conflicts as an end product.

I think that the best thing an artist can do for his creative development is allow his intuitions as full an actualization as possible—unhampered by ultimately unavoidable limitations of personality and material. This is not to say that I think the best and purest form of art exists in the depths of the psyche—I believe very strongly in the necessity of the physical realization of an idea: First, I am convinced that the final, concretized form of an idea is its true existence, in that it is then subject only to the physical laws of the deterioration of material form and no longer to the inevitable inconsistencies and fluctuations of the only-human artistic mind; second, if there exists any ultimately objective reality of an idea at all (and I can't give any opinion as to whether there does or not), I'm sure it can exist only as a total additive vision in which everyone participates, and toward this end there must necessarily be a physical form that everyone can perceive and formulate a vision *of*. I have found that the best way for me to deal with my own subjective limitations is in the process of conceptual formulation.

Concerning the question of form and materials, I attempt to disregard both as potential conceptual material in themselves, because they seem to present me with limitations as rigorous and stifling as the psychological ones. What I mean is that the possible number of forms and the possible number of materials seem to have been as completely exhausted as newly discovered inspirational material as the possible number of unique psychological make-ups, given our societal environment as a whole.[1]

Only the intuitive is truly unlimited. I see all art as basically an intuitive process, regardless of how obliquely it has been dealt with in the past. Within this context, I think "conceptual art" is the most adequate way of liberating the creative process so that the artist may approach and realize his work—or himself—on the purest possible level.

1.
Again, this is not to say that everyone is psychologically (in the Freudian sense) the same, but merely that given these environmental conditions, the possible psychological reactions to these conditions are finite and predictable, and thus psychological-symbolist art interests me only on a limited subjective level.

2. Idea, Form, Context

Written in 1969 and previously unpublished.

Idea

1. Good ideas are necessary and sufficient for good art.

2. A good idea is too broad in scope to be stated directly; it can be implied only in a given set of conditions. A well-constructed set of conditions allows great breadth of implication in a direction defined by the idea.

3. There are two basic kinds of art idea: ideas that use life conditions (such as physical forces, concrete material, or sensory phenomena), and ideas that use ideas or theories about life conditions (such as physics, Gestalt psychology, philosophy, geometry, math). Both kinds of idea are inherent in a work, but the predominance of one leads the viewer to infer the other.

4. The first kind of art idea reorganizes specific life conditions to form a unique, artificial entity that takes its place in life as a new condition among existing conditions. Responding to this kind of idea usually involves adapting the new life condition into an existing perspective, relating it to past experience, learning to feel comfortable with it. One is required to reason inductively from the new life condition to an existing perspective or idea about that condition. By doing this, the experience is situated in one's consciousness.

5. The second kind of art idea reorganizes specific ideas about existing life conditions to form a unique, artificial entity that takes its place as a new perspective on life conditions among existing perspectives; it adds to the sum total of ideas about life, rather than to life itself. Responding to this kind of idea usually involves adapting an existing life condition to a new perspective; redefining past experience in light of it; learning to feel *un*comfortable with it. One is required to reason inductively from the existing life condition to a new or unfamiliar idea about that condition. By doing this, the implications of the (or any) familiar life conditions are broadened in one's consciousness.

6. The first kind of idea has the effect of broadening one's range of life conditions; the second, the effect of broadening one's perspective. The first adds to reality; the second adds to mind. Reality adds to mind inductively; mind adds to reality deductively.

Form

1. Form is separate from, but necessary for, the realization of an idea.

2. The function of form is to communicate as much of an idea as possible, to eliminate those aspects of a given set of conditions that are irrelevant to the idea, and to retain only those aspects that clarify the idea. Ideally, an idea should have no form at all. With no perceptual energy filtered out in the process of communication, apprehension of the set of conditions and its implications would then have total impact on the understanding.

3. The less a form is intrinsically interesting, the more suitable it is as a communicative medium. Concrete visual and spatial forms are intrinsically interesting. They embody their own perceptual character and communicate their own perceptual significance; they indiscriminately convey the chaos inherent in any situation, thus obscuring or nullifying the possibility of apprehending the idea. (Chaos as an idea can be conveyed with complete clarity in a nonconcrete form.)

4. Forms that traditionally convey information about things external to themselves, such as spoken or written language, records, tapes, slides, films, television, photographs, maps, or diagrams, are interesting only insofar as what they refer to is interesting. They eliminate irrelevant aspects of a set of conditions by simply not referring to them. They need have little intrinsic interest if they are used in a traditional, nonexperimental way. They are thus more suitable for conveying an idea.

Context

1. Context is separate from, but necessary for, presenting a realized idea.

2. An artificial context is unimportant in an idea that deals directly with life conditions.[1] A work of this nature is itself a unique life condition. It remains an adjunct to reality; art of, but separate from, any set of familiar life conditions (those of the home, gallery, or outdoor environment).

1.
See "Idea," number 4.

3. An artificial context is important for presenting the kind of art idea that deals with ideas about life conditions.[2] The context must present an existing life condition in a way that emphasizes and broadens its implications beyond the routine pattern in which it normally occurs.

4. The form of this kind of idea should be adapted to the artificial context used. This further minimizes the significance of the form and allows maximum control in conveying the idea.

5. In an event context, both time and space factors are controlled. Forms that control both time and space factors include films, television, sometimes slides, and sometimes spoken language. These forms are thus most easily adaptable to the event context.

6. In a spatial context (such as a gallery or outdoor environment), the space factor is controlled. Forms that may control the space factor alone include diagrams, maps, photographs, and slides. Gallery contexts also, however, control the time factor in a more subtle way. The adaptability of these forms to the gallery context may therefore be questioned.

7. In an aural information context (telephone, radio, loudspeaker), the time factor alone is controlled. Forms that control the time factor alone include tapes, records, and sometimes spoken language. These forms are thus most easily adaptable to an aural information context.

8. Books, folders, and other similarly unsituated sets of information control neither the time nor the space factor. Forms that control neither the time nor the space factor include written language, maps, diagrams, and photographs. These forms are thus most easily adaptable to an unsituated information context.

9. Any context is an existing life condition that normally occurs in a routine pattern. The information presented in an artificial context may therefore convey something about that context itself as an existing life condition. When this is the case, the artificial context becomes a member in the set of conditions that supports the idea. The idea may then be completely based on ideas about life conditions and may not manipulate reality in any way.

2.
See "Idea," number 5.

Idea, Form, Context

1. The major premises of the preceding three articles can be restated in the following ways:

   a. Idea: [The existence of an] idea is necessary and sufficient for [the existence of] art; idea is equivalent to art.[3]

   b. Form: [The existence of] form is necessary but not sufficient for [realizing an] idea; [realizing an] idea is sufficient but not necessary for [the existence of] form. [The existence of] idea is not equivalent to [the existence of] form.[4]

   c. Context: [The existence of] context is necessary but not sufficient for form [through which an idea has been realized]; form [through which an idea has been realized] is sufficient but not necessary for [the existence of] context. [The existence of] form is not equivalent to [the existence of] context.[5]

2. From these premises, this conclusion follows:

   [The existence of] context is necessary but not sufficient for [conveying an] art idea; [conveying an] art idea is sufficient but not necessary for [the existence of] context.[6] [Conveying an] art idea is not equivalent to [the existence of] context. From this argument taken as a whole, both form and context are shown to be secondary considerations; necessary but not sufficient for art. The primary consideration in art is idea.

3. However, the relative importance of form and context in an idea are factors by which the general nature of certain ideas may be determined.

3.
See "Idea," number 1.

4.
See "Form," number 1.

5.
See "Context," number 1.

6.
Some conditions in which [conveying an] art idea is sufficient but not necessary for [the existence of] context are discussed in "Context," number 9.

4. When form is important and context unimportant, the idea is generally formal[7] in nature.

2.
Donald Judd, *Untitled* (1967). Courtesy Donald Judd Estate.

3.
Eva Hesse, *Repetition Nineteen* (first edition) (1968). The Museum of Modern Art, New York, Gift of Charles and Anita Blatt, 1969. © The Estate of Eva Hesse.

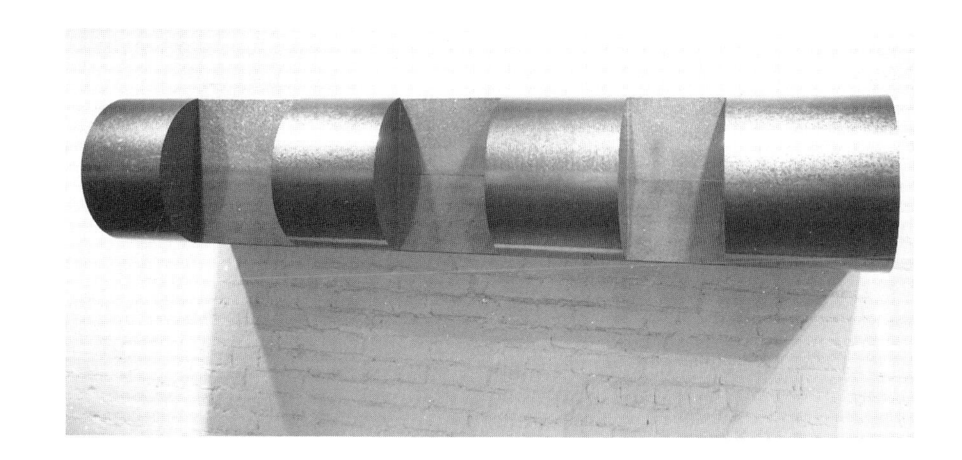

7.
The term *formal* is used as a convenient method of summarizing the ideas discussed in "Form," number 3, and "Context," number 2.

5. When both form and context are important, the idea is generally environmental[8] in nature.

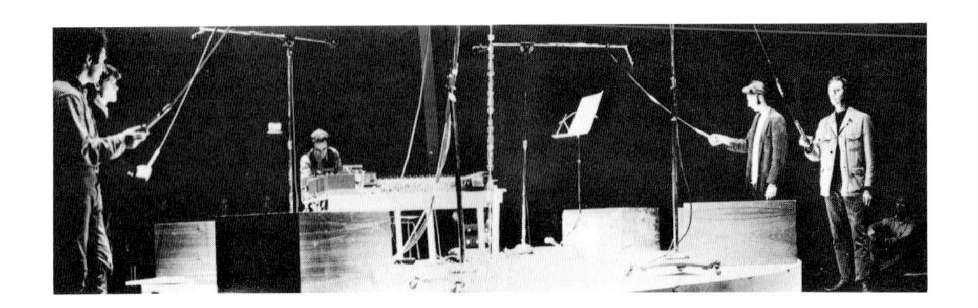

4.
Steve Reich, *Pendulum Music* (May 1969; Paula Cooper Gallery, Whitney Museum [two performances]). Courtesy Steve Reich/Nova Scotia College of Art and Design Press.

5.
Robert Smithson, *Asphalt Rundown* (1969; Rome, Italy). Courtesy John Weber Gallery.

8.
The term *environmental* is used as a convenient method of summarizing the ideas discussed in "Form," number 3, and "Context," number 3.

6. When both form and context are unimportant,[9] the idea is generally conceptual after the aesthetic developed in the work of Sol LeWitt.[10]

6.
Sol LeWitt, *Forty-Nine Three-Part Variations on Three Different Kinds of Cubes* (1967–1970). Courtesy John Weber Gallery.

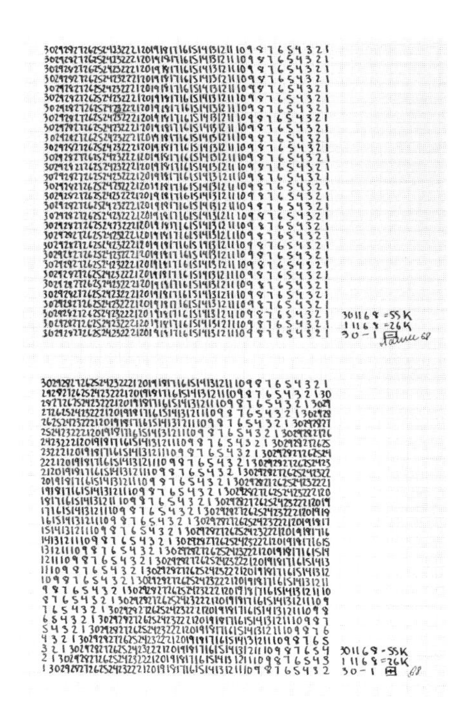

7.
Hanne Darboven, *Untitled Drawing* (1968). Courtesy Wadsworth Atheneum.

9.
As discussed in "Form," number 2, and "Context," number 2.

10.
See Sol LeWitt, "Paragraphs on Conceptual Art," *Artforum* 5, no. 10 (Summer 1967), pp. 79–83.

7. When form is unimportant and context important, the idea is generally ideal[11] in nature.

Vito Acconci
Points, Blanks, 1969
Paula Cooper Gallery, 96 Prince Street, New York City
June 13, 1969; 7:30 PM

Project Description

- At 7:30, the start of the evening's program, I am at 100th Street and Broadway, about 100blocks away from the gallery.
- I walk down Broadway, to the gallery; approximately ever 10 minutes, I call the gallery and reported where I was.
- Between the other performances, an announcement is made; "At (time), while walking to the gallery, Vito Acconci called and said he was at (place)."

Realization

- While the other performances were being carried out, in the larger room, the phone could be heard from the smaller room.
- Phone calls were made at the following times and places:
  7:31 - Broadway and 100th Street (NE)
  7:42 - Broadway and 90th Street (NE)
  7:51 - Broadway and 84th Street (SE)
  8:05 - Broadway and 76th Street (SW)
  8:20 - Broadway and 68th Street (NE)
  8:31 - Broadway and 60th Street (SE)
  8:42 - Broadway and 55th Street (NE)
  8:50 - Broadway and 50th Street (NE)
  9:01 - Broadway and 42nd Street (NE)
  9:10 - Broadway and 35th Street (SE)
  9:20 - Broadway and 28th Street (NW)
  9:30 - Broadway and 20th Street (SW)
  9:38 - Broadway and 12th Street (NE)
  9:47 - Broadway and 4th Street (SE)
- I reached the gallery about four minutes after the evening's program ended.

the village VOICE, *May 29, 1969*

art

Continued from preceding page

autobiographical. If one reports one's reactions to a work of art—or to life—rather than describing or analyzing, it is one's sensitivity and one's truthfulness that determines the worth of this confession.

But back to the panel discussion. First of all the panelists did not arrive at the appointed time. Charlotte Moorman filled in the gap by sitting on the stage all wrapped up in pink cloth, as was her cello. By 9 o'clock I began to think that the bastards had really done it and that the rascals were not going to arrive at all. I toyed around with the idea and felt comfortable with it and felt it appropriate given the announced topic, so at 9.05, when they began filing in, I was a little disappointed. It was an incestuous panel, just as this is, I suppose, an incestuous column. The panel: David Bourdon (Life magazine), was the moderator and was joined by Ultra Violet, Brigid Polk (of Cock-book fame), Walter Gutman, John de Menil, Gregory Battcock, Lil Picard, and Andy Warhol, who was introduced by Bourdon as a young man impersonating a rather well-known artist. Throughout Andy did not say a word, but occasionally used his Polaroid. To make a long story short, thanks to Bourdon's cool and sometimes cruel wit, everything was light-hearted and fairly entertaining. At one point Brigid took off her blouse. Gregory exposed his cock to Warhol's camera, forgetting that those in the balcony could see what was going on and began shouting "How big is it?"

This was the third in a series of panels organized or disorganized by Jill and, yes, the topic "The

Galleries

NUMBER 7
Compiled By
LUCY LIPPARD
PAULA COOPER
96/100 PRINCE ST.
Thurs., Fri., Sat.: 11-6 & By Appt

IRVING Thru Mid-June
KATZENSTEIN
paintings
GREEN MOUNTAIN GALLERY
17 PERRY ST. (Cor. 7 Ave.)

Sandi Thru June 8
GROSS
THE MERCER GALLERY
215 Thompson St. (nr. Bleecker)

The area described by
the periphery of this
ad has been relocated
from Sheridan Square
New York, N.Y.
to (your address) .
--area relocation #2
A. Piper

OPPORTUNITY FOR ARTISTS
To exhibit in SUMMER FESTIVAL
FALL EXHIBITIONS. All media
Call or write.
LYNN KOTTLER GALLERIES
3 E. 65th St., N.Y.C. RE 4-3491
est. 1949

PORNOMETRY
NAGLE
opening June 3 to June 14
Lowe Gallery Hudson Guild 441 26 St.

DORSKY 867 MADISON
MICHAEL BIGGER
20 MAY — 15 JUNE

1969
NUDES
Wickersham Gallery
959 Madison Ave. at 75th St.

THE JUDSON GALLERY
presents
THE BLACK EXPERIENCE
THRU BLACK ART
May 30th thru June 30th
Sun. thru Fri. 1-7 p.m.
Sat. 1-10 p.m.
239 THOMPSON STREET

HOWARD WISE
50 W 57
T.V.
as a
creative
medium

RENA
MANDELBAUM
SPECTRUM
1043 MADISON

WEISBURD
"BOXED ENVIRONMENTS"
825 SEVENTH AVENUE AT 53rd
CHELSEA
MONDAY — FRIDAY

MICROFOCUS AND SURREAL OBJECTS
Liba Bayrak, Gene Gregan, Carol Heineman and John Weichsal, with Martin Gray, Kathrine Korn, Geoff Hendricks, Helen Yrisarry and Darya Panesoff
May 24th — June 8th — Saturdays & Sundays — 11-5
GAIN GROUND, 246 W 80 (BROADWAY) 877-8584

Howard Through June 20
KOTTLER
Mad Plates From the Decalcomaniac
Lee Nordness Galleries
236 E. 75 St.

RALPH & SYLVIA MASSEY
CHAPMAN SCULPTURE GALLERY
922 Madison at 73rd
Opening Today

BRUCE NAUMAN HOLOGRAMS,
VIDEO TAPES & OTHER WORKS
LEO CASTELLI 4 E. 77, NEW YORK

ART
NOUVEAU
an exhibition
assembled by
PAUL MAGRIEL
Through June 15

903 Madison Avenue
At 72nd Street

2nd Annual
Outdoor Art Show

8.
Vito Acconci, *Points, Blanks Way* (1969; Paula Cooper Gallery). Courtesy Barbara Gladstone Gallery.

9.
Area Relocation Series (1969). Collection of the artist.

8. When the considerations of form and context are of secondary importance to an art idea, the relative importance of form and context are elements by which the nature of the art idea may be analyzed.

11.
The term *ideal* is used as a convenient method of summarizing the ideas discussed in "Idea," number 5, "Form," numbers 2 and 4, and "Context," numbers 3–9.

3. Three Models of Art Production Systems

First published in the catalog *Information* (New York: Museum of Modern Art, 1970); out of print.

Key:

(*I*) = df. any sensory, intellectual, or otherwise experiential information input.

(*C*) = df. any active consciousness that discriminates, qualifies, adds to, interprets, alters, and utilizes (*I*).

(*P*) = df. the product (e.g., thought, action, idea, object, event, etc.) of (*I*) → (*C*). An art product (P_a) is defined as any product (*p*) that is presented in an art context.

→ = df. is transformed into

System I:

(*I*)→(*C*)→(P_a)

(P_a) is a separate and final stage in the production process. (P_a) has a physical and/or temporal existence that is qualified by and external to (*I*)→(*C*).

System II:

(I)→(C;P_a)←

(P_a) is a final stage within the domain of (*C*). (P_a) properly has internal existence only, which is conveyed through external communication forms, such as language, plans, photos, and so on.

System III:

(*I*;P_a)↔(*C*)

(P_a) is any particular (*I*) condition. (P_a) has a physical and/or temporal existence, which is unqualified but recognized and distinguished by (*C*).

In each of the above systems, (*I*)→(*C*) is antecedent, (*P*) or (P_a) a transitive consequent. Other models may be constructed using the same four components in varying functional positions.

This exposition uses System II.

II. Art Criticism 1973–1983:

Art-World Politics

4. In Support of Meta-Art

First published in *Artforum* 12, no. 2 (October 1973), pp. 79–81.

I would like to make a case for a new occupation for artists. This occupation might exist as part of, alongside, or instead of the art itself. If it existed as part of or alongside the art, it might have the effect of giving the art a perspicuous and viable interpretation, support, or framework, although I don't see this as its intention. If, on the other hand, it were to replace the art, well and good. We could then add it as a nascent appendage to the field, and spend hours of discussion and many kilocalories deciding upon its status and implications. I will call the occupation I have in mind "meta-art." To establish something of its character, I will first give a loose account of what I mean by the term. Then I will try to sharpen the definition somewhat by contrasting it with other activities for which it might be mistaken, namely, art and art criticism. Finally I will attempt to justify the contention that we need such a thing.

1.

By "meta-art" I mean the activity of making explicit the thought processes, procedures, and presuppositions of making whatever kind of art we make. Thought processes might include how we hypothesize a work into existence: whether we think subliminally and suddenly have it pop into consciousness fully formed; or reason from problems encountered in the last work to possible solutions in the next; or get "inspired" by seeing someone else's work, or a previously unnoticed aspect of our own; or read something, experience something, or talk; or find ourselves blindly working away for no good reason; or any, all, or other processes of this kind.

Procedures might include how we come by the materials we use; what we do in order to get them; whom we must deal with, and in what capacity; what kinds of decisions we make concerning them (aesthetic, pecuniary, environmental, etc.); to what extent the work demands interactions (social, political, collaborative) with other people, and so on. In general, by procedures I mean what we *do* to realize the work as contrasted with how and what we *think*.

Whereas getting at thought processes and procedures is largely a matter of perspicuous description of what is immediately available, getting at presuppositions is not. Here there are many possible methods, all having to do with analysis of some kind. One might be what Kant called the method of "regressive proof," which he used in the *Critique of Pure Reason*. Such an analysis would consist in beginning with the fact of the work itself, and from its properties inferring backward to the conditions necessary to bring it into existence. Luckily there is no need to insist that such conditions be transcendental. They might just as easily be social, psychological, political, metaphysical, aesthetic, or any combination thereof. Still another kind might be based on a loosely construed Hegelian method, in which the work is treated as thesis, an antithesis is posited, and a synthesis arrived at which in turn becomes thesis. The resulting dialectic attempts to specify the work with respect to the system of which it is a part. A third might be some variety of formal or informal psychological analysis: Freudian, Jungian, Reichian, and so on, in terms of which we would try to make clear our subjective assumptions about the world.[1] Clearly there are others. We might do induction on the dreams we've been having, conduct ultimately *ad hominem* arguments with friends about the nature of art, and so on.

The distinctions among the above are not intended to be sharply drawn. Generally what is required in meta-art is that we stand off and view our role of artist reflectively; that we see the fact of our art making as itself a discrete state or process with interesting implications worthy of pursuit; that we articulate and present these implications to an audience (either the same as or broader than the art audience) for comment, evaluation, and feedback.

2.

It might happen that the results of such an occupation alongside the art would feed back into and change the art: Like everything else, it might become grist for the mill of art making. Or, as I suggested, it might replace the art. By this I mean that one might come to spend all one's time reflecting on the thought processes, procedures, and presuppositions of making art, using the impulse to make art as itself grist for the mill of reflection. I will consider the possibility of making meta-art a vocation in order to clarify some of the differences between art and meta-art, offer some suggestions about what our identity as "artist" consists in, and argue that meta-art is specifically a job for artists.

1.
For some examples in this and other fields from an observer's standpoint, see Anthony Storr, *The Dynamics of Creation* (New York: Atheneum, 1972); Ernst Kris, *Psychoanalytic Explorations in Art* (1952; reprint, New York: Schocken Books, 1964); Bruce Mazlish, ed., *Psychoanalysis and History* (New York: Universal Library, 1971); C. Hanley and M. Lazerowitz, eds., *Psychoanalysis and Philosophy* (New York: International Universities Press, 1970); Rosemary Mayer, "Performance and Experience," *Arts* (December–January), 1973, pp. 33–36. Evaluations of some of these efforts—predominantly negative, and justifiably so—include Robert Coles, "Shrinking History Part 1," *New York Review of Books*, February 22, 1973, pp. 15–21; Emmet Wilson, Jr., review of *Psychoanalysis and Philosophy*, ed. Charles Hanley and Morris Lazerowitz, *The Journal of Philosophy* 70, no. 5 (March 8, 1973), pp. 128–134.

An artist's impulse to make art issues in a product that is in a sense opaque. That is, an artist doesn't work to revise the world or the structure of society (except in the broadest sense of adding a new entity or event to it) by doing social or political work, teaching, medicine, and so on. Nor does he or she offer supportive labor, such as driving a cab, administrating a business, and so on. Nor contribute to the general sum of human knowledge by making a scientific discovery, doing anthropological research, and so on. Nor improve the environment (although this may be a peripheral effect of the work or its location), as do the industrial arts, interior decorating, fashion, architecture, and so on. These descriptions may be, and often are, used to justify the existence of the work, but they don't describe the character of the work. In saying that art is opaque, I want to suggest that it is a unique, concrete example and epitome of something, the referents and implications of which are not fully accessible. But probable referents may include the artist's personality, aesthetic preoccupations, the current sociopolitical climate, and so on. The vocational role of artist differs from other vocational roles in the artist's impulse to epitomize experience in the fruits of labor.

A.

Although I've suggested some possible referents of a work of art (I deliberately ignore the question of which are intended and which are not), it is in the nature of the work that listing its possible referents can neither fix nor exhaust the significance it has for us: It seems that only repeated and excessive contact can do that. The claim that the work is unique implies this. That is, if there is just one, then its "meaning" cannot be successfully rendered in language. Words, excluding proper names, must have *general* application if they are to have any. The relation of an artwork to other facts in the world is epistemologically analogous to that between a proper name and the sentence in which it occurs: For all the "meaning" or information a proper name gives us, it may as well be an ellipsis. An artwork is similarly nongeneralizable and nonfunctional. Though one can describe its physical (that is, spatiotemporal) presence the way one can describe the alphabetical and phonetic structure of a proper name, the significance of the work eschews analysis. The uniqueness of it as a fact in the world makes it inarticulable and therefore inscrutable. This is just to say that it is an aesthetic, rather than an epistemic, object.

B.

The activity of making art is similar in character to the work itself. It is opaque in the sense that we can't seem to rationalize the impulse to epitomize our experience. We can *justify* it in terms of the effects of the work, but I doubt if we would claim as an explanation of *motive* the wish to edify, beautify, propagandize, and so on, as one might explain one's motive for being a social worker by one's concern for society. There is no rational explanation for the art-making activity any more than there is for the existence of the work. Similarly, the uniqueness of the activity is determined by the uniqueness of the work: We don't, indeed can't by definition, go through the same process each time we make a work. And this reinforces the opacity of the activity. It determines its degree of invulnerability to conceptual elucidation for exactly the same reasons as the work itself.

C.

But ultimately, the opacity of the activity is determined by the opacity and uniqueness of the artist as person. People in general are this way: If we tire of someone, it's usually not because we really think the person diaphanous but because those qualities we do know are the only ones we seem to be able to elicit, and *those* bore us. We tire of the person long before we exhaust the range of predicates that characterize him or her. From this it follows that there can be no *reason* for a person's existing (as distinguished from the cause of someone's existing). I can try to explain the *way* I live, but not the *fact* of my living.

So far I've tried to define the inscrutability of the artist in terms of the essential aesthetic qualities of opacity and uniqueness. But an artist epitomizes a wider range of influences, which is accessible only to the artist and not the artwork or art audience. The nature of the work is determined partially by sociopolitical and aesthetic influences on the artist, partially by the agency of the artist—which is, I have argued, itself opaque in the previous sense. But the artist per se, as a social and aesthetic being with a vocational role defined in relation to the rest of society, is determined *not* by the agency of anyone else but only by a broader and more subtle spectrum of undeterminable forces. These include the social, political, psychological, physiological, aesthetic, philosophical, and so on. This is simply to accept the truism that art reflects the society in which it is made, and then to reason that likewise the artist surely must, and must do so even more. The defining of oneself as an artist and the process of making art—that is, the thoughts, procedures, and presuppositions—are an organic barometer of societal pressures, customs, and assumptions in a broader sense than the art itself can encompass.

The argument has been that artwork, activity, and artist are essentially homogeneous. The last can be seen as active and more complex, but generically similar to the first. But the differences between them are important for my definition of meta-art. One is that the nature of art is necessarily aesthetic and not epistemic, while an artist is both of these and more. An artist is aesthetic in his or her personhood; in being unique, particular, uncategorizable, inscrutable, ultimately opaque. But we are also conceptualizing, discursive, cognitive creatures. And to the extent that we can successfully analyze, identify, and ascribe properties to ourselves, we forfeit that aesthetic quality and become what might be called "epistemically transparent": We can be known.

This implies a second difference. Whereas an artwork is always a third-person object which we can never penetrate, an artist has privileged access to himself or herself: We can know *ourselves.* If the foregoing suggestion that both artworks and artists are opaque in the way I have described is accepted, then these differences imply that only the referents of the latter can be successfully, if incompletely, articulated.

Because art, making art, and being an artist are generically related, the character of the genus is immediately accessible only to the artist, both aesthetically and epistemically. But although we can have an aesthetic experience by making and looking at art, we can't thereby know anything in the conceptual or discursive sense; I have argued that it is in the nature of the aesthetic that we can't. Further, I have argued that any attempt to unpack the object through conceptual analysis will be at the least problematic and ultimately unsuccessful. If we want to articulate anything, it must be by appeal to our epistemological abilities, and not to the aesthetic experience.

Meta-art is generically related to art, art activity, and being an artist. The impulse to meta-art is unfathomable in the way the impulse to art is; meta-art is unique in just the way art-making activity is, and for the same reasons; its subject matter is, like both of these, immediately accessible to artists. But unlike art and art making, meta-art is not completely opaque because its tools are the discursive, conceptualizing, cognitive abilities of the artist. Doing meta-art presupposes immediate and privileged access to the impulse, the activity, and the emergence of the art. It is all of a piece with these, but in addition requires an epistemic self-consciousness about them, namely, viewing ourselves as the aesthetic objects we are, then elucidating as fully as possible the thoughts, procedures, and presuppositions that so define us.

3.

Obscuring the distinction between meta-art and art criticism has resulted in the conceptions of the artist as superstar, as financial con artist, as political satrap, as public relations expert. But it makes a difference whether we describe our own machinations and the motives and presuppositions behind them, or whether these machinations are revealed or imputed to us by a critic. The interviews in *Avalanche* attempt to circumvent or simply ignore this problem by allowing artists to speak for themselves. But this mode of self-representation is not immune to the problem of misrepresentation encountered in third-person discourse. The point I want to press is that it is one thing to handle the referents of art*works* in the third-person case, or try to educe them from the work: art itself can't, after all, protest that it is being misunderstood. But to handle artists this way is more often than not to make of them unpleasantly stylized biographical objects. This then creates near-inviolable prejudices, which blind us to any genuine attempts to penetrate past the formal properties of the work for a framework in which to understand it. Artists almost always complain about the way they come off in such articles or interviews, the best intentions of the critic notwithstanding. Because they are clearly not averse to having the material revealed in the first place, the implication is that artists should take the means of revelation into their own hands.

One way of emphasizing the distinction between meta-art and art criticism is by looking at the focal point of each. For a meta-artist the focal point is oneself as object, and the process by which one realizes a work. For an art critic the focal point is, generally speaking, the work alone. The artist is of interest only to the extent that he or she contributes to a better understanding of the work. This has certain implications in the matter of evaluation, all of which turn on the concern of art criticism with art history, however broadly this is understood.

Art history is the history of things, not people. To analyze and apply aesthetic standards of evaluation has been, until recently, to place a particular work within the context of others like it, both past and present. The significance of the work comes from giving it a position relative to the coherent framework of art history, on which the very language of art criticism is based.[2]

Moreover, art history is the history of a certain *kind* of entity: an entity that has performed at various times a decorative, illustrative, or propagandistic service, but the essential definition of which does not depend on criteria of utility. Most re-

2.
I had to put in "until recently" after reading a passage in an article by John Perreault, "Art," *The Village Voice,* March 1, 1973: "Although escapist art has its place, I much prefer the art that makes me remember the news and remember myself. By news, I don't mean this or that disaster, but the condition of public and personal disaster, teasing me and waking me with what I am most likely to forget: my physicality, the complexity of my sensory system and my thoughts, my mortality." Perreault is, as far as I know, the first to broach the possibility of using an essentially subjective humanistic response as a critical tool. This "critical subjectivity" preserves the general character of aesthetic response, unlike the "I-don't-know-much-about-art-but-I-know-what-I-like," "It-just-makes-me-feel-good," "I-could-do-that-if-I-tried," brand of subjective humanistic response.

cently, art history is at least the history of entities with significant capital power. The account of an artwork at any particular time in recent art history is at least (and sometimes only) the account of its financial history and value to contemporaneous and future collectors, and our historical distance from it is directly proportional to its capital—and (perhaps therefore) aesthetic—value in our eyes. Buying, selling, collecting, and showing art is the means by which recognition by a public is ensured, thus the means by which the critical availability and possible immortality of the work are also ensured. These activities consist primarily in financial speculation and investment. Typically, the capitalist system is centered around the work; it provides for the artist only secondarily and often poorly.

This means that what the critic evaluates (and thus prescribes for more discriminating aesthetic consumption) has already been evaluated and prescribed for by someone else, not aesthetically but financially. Not only has the work been filtered once, but the initial filter—the art speculator—thereby determines the scope, financial status, and cultural education of the less general viewing audience, including the critic: The works that broadly compose the art world at different times are the works that have been preserved and evaluated by those rich and educated enough to do so. From these, the critic (the role of which presupposes a greater cultural education and therefore an at least comparable financial security) further delimits the scope of objects to be included in the annals of art history, in the process of critical evaluation. That is, the speculator and then the critic are successive *steps* in the process of rarefying the scope of objects included in the art establishment, and thus in art history.

The same kinds of determinants that circumscribe which artworks are accessible to critics are also those that, in a different but related way, circumscribe which people become artists. It is one thing for a person to be given a broad, liberal, cultural education with the financial security that presupposes, and *then* decide to starve for the sake of art; it is unlikely that a person given little or no education, subject to various forms of social oppression, and living in poverty for the first third of his or her life would make the same decision. It is in fact more likely that such a person would choose a vocation that offered at least a minimum amount of financial security. Thus the very existence of the work presupposes the filtering out of certain sociological and psychological pressures.

Because monetary, social, and psychological pressures determine the scope of entities that compose art history, the scope of art criticism is circumscribed by these pressures. Further, the fact that art criticism is concerned with the artwork precludes concern with its own presuppositions. For the presuppositions and pressures that delimit art history also delimit the role of the critic: The artwork and thus the critic presuppose many of the same societal conditions, filters, forces. This means that the critic cannot criticize these conditions and pressures within the framework of criticism without threatening the edifice on which his or her status depends. This is a consequence of the fact that art history is not coextensive with, but a subset of, history. The critic's concern must be with the aesthetic properties of the work, and not with any broader ramifications it may have.

Because the focal point of meta-art is on the artist *qua* artist, it simultaneously accommodates all those broader referents that support the art (including its cultural, financial, and social status), while circumventing the requirements of cultural anthropology to account for an entire social context. Although the values will be social, ethical, philosophical, political, as well as aesthetic, the meta-artist need merely explicate his or her particular condition in order to suggest the condition of the society.

The contrast I have tried to bring out supports a description of meta-art as artistic in its concerns, epistemological in its method, humanistic in its system of values.

4.

My strategy in justifying the claim that we are in need of something like meta-art will be to elaborate on suggestions I have already made, and also to conflate argument with facts. The claim might be reformulated as a question: Why do artists need to do anything besides make art?

I characterized meta-art as a cognitive, self-conscious process that attempts to elucidate the broad scope of referents which together define the art-making process over and above the art. I contended that such an elucidation would include its social, political, philosophical, and psychological, as well as aesthetic, components; and that consequently—because we are social beings—the system of values would be humanistic. Right now, our system of values centers around the aesthetic; the relative isolation of artist from the rest of society is accepted as status quo. And we think that this part is all right: Didn't romanticism demonstrate the necessarily asocial temperament of the true artist? And didn't it demonstrate as an exigency the role of the artist as pariah? We take a covert, perverse pride in our maverick status. But we ignore the repercussions of it by enclosing ourselves in the language, associations, and interactions of the art world. And we then operate under the implicit assumption that the value of our art is somehow directly proportional to our ability to maintain this art-world context as an enclave in the midst of society.

But broaching the topic of the recondite nonutility of the product provokes a barrage of defense. We point to the improvement of the environment through art (which is placed in parks and plazas, and then defaced by a public not sufficiently educated or sophisticated to appreciate its aesthetic value); to the didactic psychological value of art, through which we are taught to broaden our range of expectations about the world (but which are not only determined and delimited by the expectations of art speculators, critics, and the most recent art "movement," but indeed superseded by the unpredictable and incomprehensible actions of prominent political figures); to the necessity of satisfying our basic aesthetic proclivities.

I think none of this will do, because as things stand, the work of art *is* functionless. While it does indeed affect us, annoy us, stimulate us, "remind us of who we are," it has no function that can't be performed as well by architecture, Gestalt psychology, or popular culture. As I claimed earlier, there are many valid justifications of the effects of the work from the position of spectator. But because these justifications are generally not the same as our *intentions,* they are not sufficient to justify or explain our activity. And if we accept the assumptions about the necessary utility of the work, our defensiveness is compounded by the fact that for whatever reason, the impulse to make art compels artists whether the product has discernible utilitarian value or not. It would, on analogy, be difficult to conceive of a psychologist feeling irrationally driven to conduct T-group events after finding that the entire enterprise had been rendered categorically useless by applied pharmacology.

The work per se is without pragmatic value, and this is as it should be. If we are going to justify the activity, it can't and shouldn't be by reference to the product of our labor, but to ourselves as conscious and responsible agents. It is not the art but our role as artist that needs analysis.

Of course I want to press the argument that art activity is a great deal more than a gratuitous game. The argument is, however, that its value encompasses more than its aesthetic alone, mainly because the aesthetic as such is significant, indeed available, only to a very small, highly educated segment of the population. It is in the nature of what artists do to be prescriptive of particularly aesthetic experience. But the value of artists' activity can't rest only on the aesthetic value of the work, because these values are arcane with respect to social values in ways they have not been in the past, and in ways the artist in fact is not with respect to society. I don't mean to imply that aesthetic values were ever the same as social values in the broad sense, but just that artists' activity has been more obviously formative of social values and more ensconced in the social matrix than it now seems to be (witness, for example, the role of religious art in the Catholic Counter-Reformation). Now, there is an implicit but sharply drawn distinction between the aesthetic and the social: Any suggestion that the two are related is met with ridicule, imputations of a social realist sensibility, and so on. I want to suggest that the distinction is valid when drawn specifically between the products of art activity and the products of other forms of labor: We would probably go mad, or at least get bored, if all the *entities* that confronted us were useful. But the distinction is invalid when drawn between artists and other workers: What we *do* as artists is useful because our activity epitomizes the social currents of this society, just as art activity of the Catholic Counter-Reformation served to prescribe the religious currents of its society.

An art*work* thus has a necessary aesthetic value: That is, it is an enigmatic exemplar, unique and permanently opaque in its significance for us. But the aesthetic by definition presupposes the social and cultural conditions that make it possible. I have argued that the attempt to educe sociological or epistemological referents from the work itself is, at this point in history, futile. These conditions can be found not in the product of the activity but in the agent of it. This is just to repeat that artists are more than aesthetic beings. The art-making *activity* has a necessary pragmatic value because it reveals society in a way that can and needs to be articulated. It reveals society to itself because we are social beings. Doing meta-art explicates the character of and reasons for making art in ways the art itself cannot and should not be expected to do.

I think we need to assert the didactic social value of making art now, just because it is in question; because we are losing our audiences to political rallies, losing our governmental support to military defense, thinning our own ranks by defections to social work and politics. Somehow our isolation, our social kinkiness, seems less and less acceptable or meaningful. Similarly, the aesthetic value of our work has come to be tailored for an educated leisure class whose politics we frequently abhor and of whose financial manipulations we are often the victim, and whose own ranks have been decimated by the genuine pangs of conscience that make concerned rich people give their money to Cesar Chavez rather than artists.

I said earlier that the values of meta-art were humanistic in character. I meant to contrast this with the narrowly aesthetic values of art, and then argue that aesthetic values alone were in fact never sufficient to explain or justify making art, when viewed in its broader social context. Our basic aesthetic proclivities may indeed be real enough; but curiously, they barely develop, if at all, in the face of poverty, overcrowding, fifth-rate education, or job discrimination. Having aesthetic proclivities presupposes gratification of survival needs, and the more we are hit by the social and political realities of the suffering of other people, the more the satisfaction of aesthetic proclivities seems a fatuous defense of our position.

In elucidating the process of making art on a personal level, meta-art criticizes and indicts the machinations necessary to maintain this society as it is. It holds up for scrutiny how capitalism works on us and through us; how we therefore live, think, what we do as artists; what kinds of social interactions we have (personal, political, financial); what injustices we are the victim of, and which ones we must inflict on others in order to validate our work or our roles as artist; how we have learned to circumvent these, if at all, that is, how highly developed we have had to become as political animals; what forms of manipulation we must utilize to get things done; what compromises we must make in our work or our integrity in order to reach the point where such compromises are no longer necessary; whether, given the structure of this society, there can be such a point.

This is not to say that the justification for meta-art is social indictment alone. It can also be an epistemic tool for discussing the work on a broader basis, which includes the aesthetic. But ultimately the justification of meta-art is social, because it is concerned with artists, and artists are social: We are not exempt from the forces or the fate of this society.

5. A Political Statement

Written in 1973 and first published in *Art-Rite* 6 (Summer 1974); out of print.

Power is bad for the lining of the stomach. Financial success causes overweight and heart trouble. Art-world parties are bad for the liver. Galleries cause headaches and blood-sugar attacks. Dealers cause dislocation of the jaw. Critical reviews cause digestive upsets and emphysema. Competition between fellow artists for any of the above is a known carcinogen.

6. A Proposal for Pricing Works of Art

First published in *The Fox* 1, no. 2 (1975); out of print.

I. The proposal is that exchange value be identical to production value. Production value equals the sum of

i. Retail cost of materials used.

ii. Labor cost.

Labor is a function of actual work-hours, that is, time engaged in thinking about, planning, and/or physically producing work. This can be computed either on an hourly or a weekly basis, according to whether or not the artist orders his or her art production time along the lines of a full-time, "nine-to-five"-type job (that is, with regular hours spent per day per week at the office, studio, library, factory, etc.). In either case, this amount should not exceed the wage or salary scale of an average blue- or white-collar civil service worker (the ABW).

iii. Residual living expenses.

This is intended to accommodate those artists who cannot think about or do art full time, for financial or health reasons. Because the labor cost in such cases will be less than the ABW, a supplementary means of self-support is suggested in the following formula:

$$\text{(1) (ABW} - \text{labor cost)} = \text{residual living expenses}$$

iv. Secondary labor costs.

This supplements (ii), if necessary. It provides for special accommodations expenses such as needed long-term materials, working space, tools, equipment, and so on. Ideally these should be provided by government or community agencies, just as work space and adequate equipment are provided for other civil service workers. In this case (iv) would not be a factor in the production value of a work at all. But realistically assuming that, at present, the buyer of a work stands in the employer role relative to the artist, let

$$\text{(2)}\ \frac{\text{Special accommodations expenses}}{\text{Total number of work-hours/week}} = \text{Secondary labor costs,}$$

to be charged with labor costs (ii) on a fractional basis per work sold until special accommodations are paid for.

II. Production value is a necessary condition of aesthetic value.

i. Although the translation of production value into aesthetic value cannot itself be computed on a monetary basis, the aesthetic value of a work clearly has its prior production, or material history, as a necessary component. This is just to observe that a work of art is at least a created artifact, and the economics of its production contributes to important aesthetic facts about it.

ii. This suggests the possibility of incorporating the computed production value of the work into the work itself, for example, by inscribing it somewhere in the work. It might, for example, appear as part of the work, or be added to the artist's signature, date of completion, or title of the work. Provided that (I.) is adopted, this inscription could function analogously to the date of completion of the work: It could be recognized as binding on the buyer as a condition of sale of the work, and accorded the same kind of significance as relevant aesthetic information about the work. This would prevent any fluctuation in the market value of the work, because the exchange value of the work (= production value) would then be constant.

III. Exchange value is not a sufficient condition of aesthetic value.

i. This just reminds us that the degree of our aesthetic appreciation of a work of art is not supposed to depend on how much one must pay for it. In fact, it is theoretically not supposed to be influenced by the price of the work at all. It may be less obvious that the aesthetic value we accord a work is also supposed to be independent of how much one may contemplate selling it for.

ii. (III.i) could be proved false by one possible set of consequences of adopting this proposal. That is, it might happen that because under this program neither the artist nor the dealer nor the buyer stands to make a substantial profit on works of art, interest in producing and acquiring art might die out. Art, as well as art-as-speculation and art-as-investment security, might disappear. This would demonstrate that exchange value *is* a sufficient condition of aesthetic value; that the increased economic availability of art is directly antithetical to its perceived aesthetic desirability; and thus that the production of art depends on a capitalist economy after all.

iii. On the other hand, adoption of this proposal might not have these consequences. It might happen that such a program facilitated producing art as a modest means of self-support for more artists by making it more economically accessible to more people. If this program, voluntarily undertaken, turned out to be a valid mode of survival for artists, it would both demonstrate the truth of (III.i) and, more important, bring out more clearly the de facto viability of conceiving artists as workers rather than as constituting a privileged class. It might also make possible a greater solidarity with other workers.

7. Cheap Art Utopia

First published in *Art-Rite* 14 (Winter 1976–77), pp. 11–12; out of print.

Suppose art were as accessible to everyone as comic books? as cheap and as available? What social and economic conditions would this state of things presuppose?

1. It would presuppose a conception of art that didn't equate spatiotemporal uniqueness with aesthetic quality. People would have to be able to discriminate quality in art without the trappings of preciousness, such as the gilt frame, the six-figure price tag, the plexiglass case, the roped-off area around the work, etc.

2. It would presuppose a different economic status for artists. Because art would be cheap and accessible, artists could no longer support themselves by receiving high prices for their work. Their situation would be comparable to that of writers, for whom first editions, original manuscripts, and the like play virtually no economic role during their own lifetime.

3. Therefore art dealers would bear much the same sort of economic relationship to artists that agents bear to writers: perhaps just as symbiotic (we should no longer fool ourselves into thinking of the relationship as parasitic), but not nearly as lucrative an enterprise as art dealing is now. Economically, artists' and art dealers' profits would diminish proportionally.

4. Because artists' revenue would depend more on volume of sales than on making a killing on the yearly masterpiece, artists would gradually feel increasingly disposed to make their work palatable or relevant to a larger segment of society than that which now constitutes the art world. Some would equate this increased popularity (literally) with a decline in aesthetic quality; these individuals would become bitter, dogmatically elitist, and would comfort themselves with the thought that their work represented the last bastion of aesthetic integrity. Others would find that this state of things no longer fueled their images of themselves as rare and special persons, and so would desert art for flagpole sitting.

5. Artists would get feedback on their work from this larger segment of society, and no longer just from the relatively small, highly educated percentage of the population that have the leisure and developed aesthetic inclination to frequent museums and galleries and read art magazines. This would be a particularly unpleasant experience for those artists whose work requires for its appreciation the advanced cultural education on which it currently feeds.

6. The social role of art critics would be invested with greater responsibility because they would be legislating aesthetic standards (as they always do in fact) for a much larger audience, the political and economic orientation of which would be very different from that of the current art audience.

7. It would be easier for more artists to publicize their work without going through the political process of selection now required (that is, where you went to art school, whom you know, where you live, whether you've gotten "written up" and by whom and where, whom you've slept with, where you hang out, etc.). So new, aesthetic standards would have to evolve in order to discriminate mediocre from first-rate work, rather than the standard of simply having been sifted through this process itself. Also, people would actually have to develop these new standards themselves instead of leaving all the hard work to critics, because there would not be enough famous critics to pass judgment on all the work.

8. The social responsibility of artists would increase proportionally with that percentage of the population the work affected. Some artists would meet this challenge by becoming more conscious of, and exerting more control over, the social implications of their work. Others would get scared and retreat to the old "Don't-ask-me-I-just-make-the-stuff-God-works-through-me" routine. Still others would run for president.

Distributing art in books would make it as cheap and accessible as comic books. And that would change a lot of things.

8. Arty and Illiterate in Berlin

Written in October 1978 and previously unpublished.

I go to get my luggage after getting off the plane at Berlin Airport and the porter asks me for my passport. He examines it very closely and asks me what I am doing here and how long I plan to stay. I tell him. He scrutinizes me very closely and then nods and dismisses me. I reflect on how oddly authority is delegated at German airports. I notice, on the other hand, that no one examines the contents of my luggage. I reflect on all I could have smuggled in if it had occurred to me.

The cab driver, who loads my luggage and unloads it again after a long drive to the Goethe-Institut, returns the tip I attempt to give him, gesturing that it is far too much. 'Bye! he says lightly in English, as he drives off. To me he communicates the sentiment, Good luck, American sucker, you're going to need it.

I move into a Studentenheim in a run-down, predominantly Turkish neighborhood near the Berlin Wall. Almost everyone looks a little like me and is friendly, only a bit surprised when it comes out that I don't speak Turkish. On Kudamm, Berlin's main drag, on the other hand, nobody looks anything like me. And they don't get friendly until it comes out that I don't speak Turkish but am instead an American. They they get *very* friendly.

When Mahmet, my Turkish friend from the Studentenheim, and I get into an argument about Hans-Martin Schleier and the Baader-Meinhof gang, I notice that he intends as a reproach the observation that I really think I have something to say. But not before I've responded, stupidly, that obviously I must, as I've just said what I thought. Later I see that power relations between men and women in Germany are played out both more subtly and more overtly than in the States, in the realm of language and spoken conversation at least as much as that of the division of labor. I think to myself that it's not fair that German can be spoken so gutturally. Men get to boom, while women can only twitter. By the time some of my male German friends are writing to me in the States explaining their theories of conversational etiquette — actually the etiquette of listening — long after my first year in Germany is over, I no longer find anything to remark on in this.

Nevertheless my most unforgettable encounter is with Fritz, a stolid and taciturn doctor whose Schwabische peasant origins inflect his manner and appearance as well as his speech. He is very Teutonic and very proud. He invites me to visit him at his home. After dinner he grunts, Nun hören Sie 'was besonders, and proceeds to play his absolutely superb collection of black American funk, soul, and rhythm-and-blues music, the best and most complete selection I've ever heard anywhere, which he's been taping from American Armed Forces Radio for the last ten years. I am dazzled, awestruck by his cultural reach.

Dogs are brought everywhere: on the subways, shopping, to fancy restaurants. Most of the people who own them, like most of the people in Berlin, are very old.

I run every day in a nearby park on the Lunarstraße, and the old people who walk their dogs there take great pleasure in letting them loose as I run past. The dogs snap at my heels and bark loudly. I scream, Ihren Hund, Bitte! But the old people smirk and pretend not to understand.

Train fare on Berlin's U-Bahn works on the honor system: You buy a ticket good for a period of weeks to your destination and pass freely back and forth through the turnstyles. No one checks to see that you've paid enough, or have a ticket at all. But on random occasions (actually about once every two weeks, according to my calculations), the doors of the subway car close behind a uniformed officer who shouts, Fahrkarten, Bitte! and then goes through the car systematically examining everyone's tickets. Anyone who fails to show one is loudly berated, shamed before the other passengers, and escorted off the train at the next station. I notice how much these gentlemen enjoy their jobs. Much later, after many deepening acquaintances and friendships with German men and women, I marvel at how genuinely creative some of them can be with this kind of thing.

Propriety sometimes transforms first into friendship, then intimacy, then emotional upheaval, during an evening spent drinking beer at a Kneipe, where strangers sit together at the same tables without violating one another's privacy until and unless both subtly indicate their willingness to make contact. This convention really is very subtle, next to which singles-bar behavior in the States seems modeled on that of raiding police who kick in the door with heavy boots after scarcely a knock. I cultivate my ability to navigate through this convention, but it is not easy at the beginning. I am paranoid about being picked up and so excessively standoffish, or don't know how or where to draw the line at the depth of confidences I am willing to hear or values I am willing to discuss, and so find myself observing with horror, at the end of the evening, the spectacle of my new friend weeping into his beer, or pounding his fist on the table and raising his voice. I gradually come to understand that, in the matter of psychological intimacy, *I* must decide the limits, or there will be none; none at all. In Germany I make some of the deepest friendships I have ever had, and more quickly than I ever have. To my surprise, they are lasting.

The elderly German woman who cleans the Studentenheim befriends me, invites me to her house for dinner. She is patient with my halting German and we have a nice conversation, except that she refuses to discuss the past. It's not just the topic of World War II that causes her to fall silent. She won't talk about *anything* related to the history of her country or city, either near or distant in time. Afterward she introduces me to her granddaughter Hannelore and encourages me to tutor Hannelore in English. These pleasant sessions come to an end when they realize that I speak American English rather than British English. At a party, an Englishwoman tries to explain to me how humiliating, how personally devastating it is for her to be mistaken for an American. I try to be sympathetic.

I learn to endear myself to people by making a joke out of my linguistic incompetence and acting friendly, helpless, and as though my continual gaffes in the German language are my most favored sources of amusement, talking heatedly, for example, about whether the jailhouse guards shit (*geschissen*) terrorists Raspe and Baader rather than whether they shot (*geschossen*) them. Everyone likes this particular mistake very much. I learn fast, on many levels. I make friends quickly; my German friends are tolerant, especially the men. But they seem to become less tolerant as my fluency increases. This puzzles me at first.

The dada show, a part of the "Tendenz der Zwanzigen Jahre" exhibit that is taking place simultaneously in four major Berlin museums, is breathtakingly good. I feel like a real grownup again because I don't need to speak German in order to recognize just how good it is. But I curse in frustration at not being able to understand the recorded audio monologues made by the likes of Schwitters and Duchamp, and others whose names I don't recognize. The nonsense, the frenetic, sometimes frantic playfulness of the work is immediately conveyed. I stay so long that I get a blinding headache, something I promised myself long ago that I'd never let happen again, not for any art exhibit.

The surrealism show is irritating because it is so poorly hung and lit, and because I have to wait in line for two hours to see it. I won't allow a sweet-looking old couple to maneuver their way into line ahead of me. You folks look pretty *gesund* to me, I mutter to myself. And besides, I'm the one with fallen arches. . . . They turn to look at me with a mixture of puzzlement and contempt. They probably think I'm Turkish. Inside the paintings are hung too close together and one above the other right up to the ceiling, and there aren't enough Magrittes. Also I've had a bad time getting through Berlin on this particular day with my winning pidgin German. And although I'm awed by the immense quantity and quality of this work, and by the ways in which surrealism developed in Germany, I've had it with lengthy historical explanations I can't understand, of the cultural context of work I find fascinating to look at. It occurs to me that I haven't looked at oil paintings of any kind for about ten years.

The very best exhibit in Berlin—in fact, one of the best I've ever seen—is called "Wem Gehört die Welt?" (Who Owns the World?) It's a show of leftist political posters, books, films, and graphics of the twenties and thirties. It shows how clearly they already knew what was going to happen and how they tried frantically to stop it, to educate people, to put up a battle against the increasing flow of Nazi campaign propaganda. At the same time the view is bleak, pessimistic; it depicts, sardonically, the situation as it is, and not what it could be. They have already given up the attempt to provide an alternative vision of society. They want only to fight what it is turning into. The work is strong and simple, expressive of a real political urgency that I don't fully understand. I am forced to acknowledge that these artists perceived something about their world that we are failing to perceive about ours.

The contemporary German work that I see in small galleries is disappointing. Lots of perfectly executed hard-edge quasi-minimalism, predictably bare of content. One exhibit of heads and torsos made out of steel machine parts. Kinky.

Then I decide to venture into East Berlin, after having peered out of the windows of the U-Bahn, often enough, at the interiors of East Berlin subway stations that are sealed and guarded by armed guards stationed in them to prevent East Berliners from jumping onto the trains to escape to the West. This time I go aboveground, stopping at the Haus am Checkpoint Charlie, the small museum documenting the history of the wall that divides East and West Berlin. It is right next to the entrance into East Berlin for tourists and non-Germans and seems like a good place to get prepared for my East-bloc country experience. It isn't. I am moved to tears by the photo narrative account of the first days during which the wall was erected; by the total incomprehension and disbelief of the citizens of Berlin that this was really happening; and by the ingenuity and insanity of those who tried, successfully or unsuccessfully, to escape. At the same time I fully realize that I am in part being taken in by an extremely effective propaganda campaign, and that the issue is not as simple as the West Germans make it look.

There is a competition of proposed artists' murals to be painted on the sides of the houses that face directly into East Berlin from the West Berlin side. They are figurative, symbolic, stirringly full of idealism: sunrises; men, women, and children walking arm in arm together; a partially destroyed wall over which people climb to embrace each other. The most realistic is also the most effective: a painting of the wall as it is, with people observing each other from observation decks on opposite sides of the wall. These artists don't care much about aesthetic innovation. They want to get a message across to people who need to have it, to be effective in changing things. I wonder what it must be like to feel that way about one's art.

East Berlin is impressive and tragic. The magnificent buildings and monuments, the broad streets with ornate street lamps underline the fact that this was once the center of the city. But it is too quiet, and there is grass growing out of all the cracks in the sidewalks and buildings, and the people don't match the place. There are no advertisements or neon signs, relatively few people, and fewer cars. The not-yet-rebuilt city is a monument to war and makes West Berlin's half-destroyed Kaiser-Wilhelm-Gedächtniskirche look like a poor imitation of a Claes Oldenburg lipstick. In West Berlin, the hegemonic effects of the Marshall Plan obscure the many and deep-seated cultural and social differences between Americans and Germans: Everything is displayed, advertised, renovated, rebuilt, lined with neon and rock music. In East Berlin, all of that is absent. The people are subdued, react to me as to a stranger, and eye my Levi blue jeans. The guard that I found so easy to lower in the Kneipen in West Berlin is up permanently and concretely, like the Wall, between me and my hosts in East Berlin. In East Berlin, I don't need to search out the areas of cultural dissonance between us. The quest is rather for the safe topic of conversation that will allow both of us to relax. On my first visit I commit the faux pas of asking, in a book store, for Kant's collected works. The proprietor answers coldly that Marx is available in numerous editions.

The standing exhibit of official East German art at the Volkspalast is awful, embarrassing, incompetent, painful to look at. All figurative, all symbolic, I take it, of the inevitably successful struggle to overcome world imperialism and of the march toward communism. I feel the frustrations of artists fighting to show even the slightest formal inventiveness—disruption of narrative time and space, odd colors and proportions in depicting human subjects—against seemingly insurmountable odds. But with one exception—a delicate, quasi-photo-realist painting of a family walking in the country with a busy industrialized city in the background called *Guten Tag*—it is a losing battle. The art is uniformly stiff, provincial, unimaginative. This is not what I want socialist art to look like. This is not what socialist art does look like.

The state of official East German art is in some ways even more expressive of the bleakness and repression the East Germans must feel than the depressed faces of the people themselves. I react very strongly at first to seeing virtually everyone wearing cheap, loudly colored clothes and badly designed plastic shoes. But then I reflect on what that reaction shows about me and my values and ask myself whether it is such a terrible price to pay for almost completely eliminating poverty, starvation, and unemployment. I ask myself whether any of these people, especially the older ones, ever reflect that, after the unspeakable sin of World War II, they could be doing much worse. I wonder when foreign tourists will start saying that about us and American slavery in the States, and how much we will have to surrender in order for it to be true.

9. Critics' Delight

First published in *A Critical Assembling*, ed. Richard Kostelanetz (New York: Participation Project Foundation, 1979); out of print.

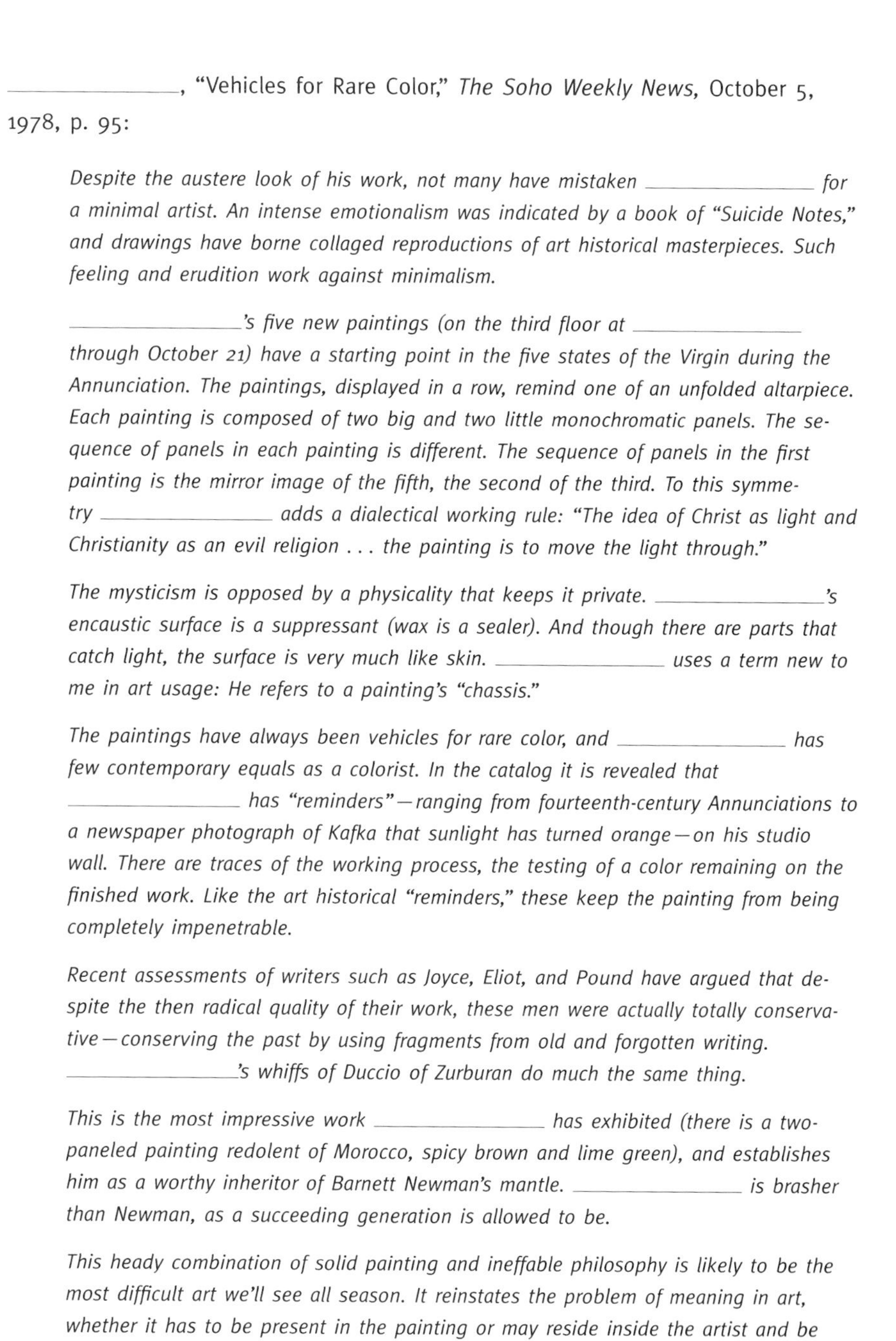

__________, "Vehicles for Rare Color," *The Soho Weekly News*, October 5, 1978, p. 95:

Despite the austere look of his work, not many have mistaken __________ for a minimal artist. An intense emotionalism was indicated by a book of "Suicide Notes," and drawings have borne collaged reproductions of art historical masterpieces. Such feeling and erudition work against minimalism.

__________'s five new paintings (on the third floor at __________ through October 21) have a starting point in the five states of the Virgin during the Annunciation. The paintings, displayed in a row, remind one of an unfolded altarpiece. Each painting is composed of two big and two little monochromatic panels. The sequence of panels in each painting is different. The sequence of panels in the first painting is the mirror image of the fifth, the second of the third. To this symmetry __________ adds a dialectical working rule: "The idea of Christ as light and Christianity as an evil religion . . . the painting is to move the light through."

The mysticism is opposed by a physicality that keeps it private. __________'s encaustic surface is a suppressant (wax is a sealer). And though there are parts that catch light, the surface is very much like skin. __________ uses a term new to me in art usage: He refers to a painting's "chassis."

The paintings have always been vehicles for rare color, and __________ has few contemporary equals as a colorist. In the catalog it is revealed that __________ has "reminders"—ranging from fourteenth-century Annunciations to a newspaper photograph of Kafka that sunlight has turned orange—on his studio wall. There are traces of the working process, the testing of a color remaining on the finished work. Like the art historical "reminders," these keep the painting from being completely impenetrable.

Recent assessments of writers such as Joyce, Eliot, and Pound have argued that despite the then radical quality of their work, these men were actually totally conservative—conserving the past by using fragments from old and forgotten writing. __________'s whiffs of Duccio of Zurburan do much the same thing.

This is the most impressive work __________ has exhibited (there is a two-paneled painting redolent of Morocco, spicy brown and lime green), and establishes him as a worthy inheritor of Barnett Newman's mantle. __________ is brasher than Newman, as a succeeding generation is allowed to be.

This heady combination of solid painting and ineffable philosophy is likely to be the most difficult art we'll see all season. It reinstates the problem of meaning in art, whether it has to be present in the painting or may reside inside the artist and be leaked to us in written form.

Part of an overheard telephone conversation:

A:. . . So what did you do?

B: Well, I got so bummed out by the usual Soho shit that I suddenly decided to drag my ass up to Fifty-Seventh Street. . . . Just a whim, you understand . . .

A: Ohmygod, you poor kid. Fifty-Seventh Street! What a wasteland . . .

B: No, listen, wait a minute, I actually saw some pretty interesting stuff up there, you know?

A: Yeah, I bet. So what did you see?

B: Well, I saw ______________'s show at the ______________ Gallery and I really liked it. I mean I really did.

A: Okay, sure, I can see that. He's one of the few minimalists I never got tired of looking at. But what else did you see?

B: No, but wait a minute. You can't call ______________ a minimalist. His work may be austere, but his intense emotionalism really separates him from those people. I think he's more in the tradition of Barnett Newman. His spiritual son, sort of.

A: Yeah, right. Sorry, I didn't mean to call him a minimalist. It just sort of slipped out. What I meant was, although his mysticism really is opposed by the physicality of his surface—he calls it "chassis," you know . . .

B: . . . Yes, I know . . .

A: . . . His paintings have always been vehicles for rare color, as far as I'm concerned.

B: Oh, sure, of course. But that's not all that's going on in the work. I mean, ______________ really conserves the past by his use of mystical and religious themes, you know what I mean?

A: Yeah, I think that's true . . . He kind of reinstates the problem of meaning in art, doesn't he?

B: Right, exactly. It's really a heady combination, isn't it? Probably some of the most difficult work we'll see all year. . . . You really should catch it . . .

A: I know, I know. I just have to get past this stage where even just thinking about art gives me a headache, heh heh heh. Just kidding. So what else did you see? Provoke me already . . .

10. Some Thoughts on the Political Character of This Situation

First published in *Art of Conscience: The Last Decade* (Dayton, Ohio: Wright University, 1980); out of print.

Galleries and museums are public spaces.

Public spaces are political arenas in which power is gained, recognized, underwritten, disputed, attacked, lost, and gained. These interactions are often obscured when power relationships are stable, ideological programming is effective, and the players collaborate in defeating their own best interests.

Galleries and museums are political arenas in which these conditions no longer hold.

1. Power relationships are unstable. Many artists are increasingly unwilling to adapt the form and content of their activity to the exploitative requirements of "mainstream" art commodity production and distribution. Many viewers are increasingly impatient with the obfuscations, posturing, and haute-couture double talk that characterize much of this art. Many critics are increasingly uneasy and rebellious in their role as arbiters and disseminators of an art increasingly regarded as fatuous and irrelevant.

2. Ideological programming is no longer effective. The principle "art for art's sake" is being gradually replaced by the principle "art for people's sake." The context of high art is being infiltrated by a gradual, painful, shamefaced awareness of a world beyond the art world, a world in which poverty, unemployment, discrimination, starvation, and war illuminate as solipsistic and trivial the concerns of much "mainstream" art.

3. The players, that is, all of us, are increasingly unwilling to collaborate in defeating their own best interests. Many artists are less willing to pay the price of success, that is, to sacrifice their creative autonomy, and are more interested in speaking for the particular social and political constituencies they in fact represent. Many viewers are becoming increasingly receptive to this social and political content and increasingly dissatisfied with politically neutral interior-decoration-style high art. Many critics are choosing actively to encourage and articulate this trend, rather than continuing to disseminate nonsense.

Galleries and museums are political arenas in which strategies of confrontation and avoidance are calculated, diplomacy is practiced, and weaponry is tested, all in the service of divergent, and often conflicting, interests.

We who collaborate in perpetrating the existence of galleries and museums are not spectators but participants, not audiences but players, planning and executing tactics for the pursuit of our own self-interests.

My interest is to fully politicize the existing art-world context, to confront you here with the presence of certain representative individuals who are alien and unfamiliar to that context in its current form, and to confront you with your defense mechanisms against them: mechanisms of fear, hostility, rationalization, and withdrawal [*Four Intruders plus Alarm Systems*]. If your interest is to enjoy, then our interests diverge. If it is to categorize, then our interests conflict. If it is to be diverted, or to consider new sources of investment, or to get cultured, then our interests are irreconcilable.

If your interest is to reintegrate your art consciousness into your social consciousness, then our interests converge.

*** AN OPEN LETTER FROM ADRIAN PIPER ***

Dear Reader,

Tell me: why, in your opinion, am I the only third-world artist in this exhibition? I would be most interested in your thoughts about this question. Your answers may appear as part of Art Confrontation #4. You can send them to me c/o

The University of Michigan
Dept. of Philosophy
Angell Hall 2209
Ann Arbor, MI. 48109

Sincerely,

Adrian Piper

Art Confrontation #3 (1981)

10.
An Open Letter from Adrian Piper (1981). Collection of the artist.

11. Ideology, Confrontation, and Political Self-Awareness

First published in *High Performance* 4, no. 1 (Spring 1981).

We started out with beliefs about the world and our place in it that we didn't ask for and didn't question. Only later, when those beliefs were attacked by new experiences that didn't conform to them, did we begin to doubt: For example, do we and our friends really understand each other? Do we really have nothing in common with blacks/whites/gays/workers/the middle class/other women/other men/etc.?

Doubt entails self-examination because a check on the plausibility of your beliefs and attitudes is a check on all the constituents of the self. Explanations of why you falsely supposed *X* include your *motives* for believing *X* (your desire to maintain a relationship, your impulse to be charitable, your goal of becoming a better person); the *causes* of your believing *X* (your early training, your having drunk too much, your innate disposition to optimism); and your *objective reasons* for believing *X* (it's consistent with your other beliefs, it explains the most data, it's inductively confirmed, people you respect believe it). These reveal the traits and dispositions that individuate one self from another.

So self-examination entails self-awareness, that is, awareness of the components of the self. But self-awareness is largely a matter of degree. If you've had only a few discordant experiences, or relatively superficial discordant experiences, you don't need to examine yourself very deeply in order to revise your false beliefs. For instance, you happen to have met a considerate, sensitive, nonexploitative person who's into sadism in bed.[1] You think to yourself, "This doesn't show that my beliefs about sadists in general are wrong; after all, think what Krafft-Ebing says! This particular person is merely an exception to the general rule that sexual sadists are demented." Or you think, "My desire to build a friendship with this person is based on the possibility of reforming her/him (and has nothing to do with any curiosity to learn more about my own sexual tastes)." Such purely cosmetic repairs in your belief structure sometimes suffice to maintain your sense of self-consistency. Unless you are confronted with a genuine personal crisis, or freely choose to push deeper and ask yourself more comprehensive and disturbing questions about the genesis and justification of your own beliefs, your actual degree of self-awareness may remain relatively thin.

Usually the beliefs that remain most unexposed to examination are the ones we need to hold in order to maintain a certain conception of ourselves and our relation to the world. These are the ones in which we have the deepest personal investment. Hence these are the ones that are most resistant to revision; for example, we have to believe that other people are capable of understanding and

1.
See Pat Califia, "Feminism and Sadomasochism," *Heresies #12: Sex Issue*, vol. 3, no. 4 (1981), pp. 30–34.

sympathy, of honorable and responsible behavior, in order not to feel completely alienated and suspicious of those around us. Or, some people have to believe that the world of political and social catastrophe is completely outside their control in order to justify their indifference to it.

Some of these beliefs may be true, some may be false. This is difficult to ascertain because we can confirm or disconfirm only the beliefs under examination with reference to other beliefs, which themselves require examination. In any event, the set of false beliefs that a person has a personal investment in maintaining is what I will refer to (following Marx) as a person's *ideology*.

Ideology is pernicious for many reasons. The obvious one is that it makes people behave in stupid, insensitive, self-serving ways, usually at the expense of other individuals or groups. But it is also pernicious because of the mechanisms it uses to protect itself, and its consequent capacity for self-regeneration in the face of the most obvious counterevidence. Some of these mechanisms follow:

1. *The false identity mechanism.* In order to preserve your ideological beliefs against attack, you identify them as objective facts and not as beliefs at all. For example, you insist that it is just a fact that black people are less intelligent than whites, or that those on the sexual fringes are in fact sick, violent, or asocial. By maintaining that these are statements of fact rather than statements of belief compiled from the experiences you personally happen to have had, you avoid having to examine and perhaps revise those beliefs. This denial may be crucial to maintaining your self-conception against attack. If you're white and suspect that you may not be all that smart, to suppose that at least there's a whole *race* of people you're smarter than may be an important source of self-esteem. Or if you're not entirely successful in coping with your own nonstandard sexual impulses, isolating and identifying the sexual fringe as sick, violent, or asocial may serve the very important function of reinforcing your sense of yourself as "normal."

   The fallacy of the false identity mechanism as a defense of one's ideology consists in supposing that there exist objective social facts that are not constructs of beliefs people have about each other.

2. *The illusion of perfectibility.* Here you defend your ideology by convincing yourself that the hard work of self-scrutiny has an end and a final product, that is, a set of true, central, and uniquely defensible beliefs about some issue; and that you have in fact achieved this end, hence needn't subject your beliefs to further examination. Because there is no such final product, all of the inferences that supposedly follow from this belief are false. Example: You're a veteran of the antiwar movement and have developed a successful and much-lauded system of draft

avoidance counseling, on which your entire sense of self-worth is erected. When it is made clear to you that such services primarily benefit the middle class, and that this consequently forces much larger proportions of the poor, the uneducated, and blacks to serve and be killed in its place,[2] you resist revising your views in light of this information on the grounds that you've worked on and thought hard about these issues, have developed a sophisticated critique of them, and therefore have no reason to reconsider your opinions or efforts. You thus treat the prior experience of having reflected deeply on some issue as a defense against the self-reflection appropriate now, which might uncover your personal investment in your antidraft role.

The illusion of perfectibility is really the sin of arrogance, for it supposes that dogmatism can be justified by having "paid one's dues."

3. *The one-way communication mechanism.* You deflect dissents, criticisms, or attacks on your cherished beliefs by treating all of your own pronouncements as imparting genuine information but treating those of other people as mere symptoms of some moral or psychological defect. Say you're committed to feminism but have difficulty making genuine contact with other women. You dismiss all arguments advocating greater attention to lesbian and separatist issues within the women's movement on the grounds that they are maintained by frustrated man-haters who just want to get their names in the footlights.[3] By reducing questions concerning the relations of women to each other to pathology or symptoms of excessive self-interest, you avoid confronting the conflict between your intellectual convictions and your actual alienation from other women, and therefore the motives that might explain this conflict. If these motives should include such things as deep-seated feelings of rivalry with other women, or a desire for attention from men, then avoiding recognition of this conflict is crucial to maintaining your self-respect.

   The one-way communication mechanism is a form of elitism that ascribes pure, healthy, altruistic political motives only to oneself (or one's group) while reducing all dissenters to the status of moral defectives or egocentric and self-seeking subhumans whom it is entirely justified to manipulate or disregard, but with whom the possibility or rational dialogue is not to be taken seriously.

2.
See my "Rationality of Military Service," in Robert Fullinwider, Ed. *Conscripts and Volunteers* (Totowa, N.J.: Rowman and Allenheld, 1983), pp. 126–147.

3.
See Adrienne Rich, *Compulsory Heterosexuality and Lesbian Existence* (United Kingdom: Onlywoman Press, 1981) (pamphlet).

There are many other mechanisms for defending one's personal ideology. These are merely a representative sampling. Together, they all add up to what I will call the *illusion of omniscience.* This illusion consists in being so convinced of the infallibility of your own beliefs about everyone else that you forget that you are perceiving and experiencing other people from a perspective that is in its own ways just as subjective and limited as theirs. Thus you confuse your personal experiences with objective reality and forget that you have a subjective and limited *self* that is selecting, processing, and interpreting your experiences in accordance with its own limited capacities. You suppose that your perceptions of someone are truths about her or him; that your understanding of someone is comprehensive and complete. Thus your self-conception is not demarcated by the existence of other people.

Rather, you appropriate them into your self-conception as psychologically and metaphysically transparent objects of your consciousness. You ignore their ontological independence, their psychological opacity, and thereby their essential personhood. The illusion of omniscience resolves into the fallacy of solipsism.

The result is blindness to the genuine needs of other people, coupled with the arrogant and dangerous conviction that you understand those needs better than they do; and a consequent inability to respond to those needs politically in genuinely effective ways.

The antidote, I suggest, is confrontation of the sinner with the evidence of the sin: the rationalizations, the subconscious defense mechanisms, the tragedies of avoidance, denial, dismissal, and withdrawal that signal on the one hand the retreat of the self to the protective enclave of ideology; on the other hand, precisely the proof of subjectivity and fallibility that the ideologue is so anxious to ignore. This is the concern of my recent work.

The success of the antidote increases with the specifics of the confrontation. And because I don't know you, I can't be as specific as I would like. I can indicate only general issues that have specific references in my own experience. But if this discussion has made you in the least degree self-conscious about your political beliefs or about your strategies for preserving them; or even faintly uncomfortable or annoyed at my having discussed them; or has raised just the slightest glimmerings of doubt about the veracity of your opinions, then I will consider this piece a roaring success. If not, then I will just have to try again, for my own sake. For of course I am talking not just about you, but about *us.*

12. Performance and the Fetishism of the Art Object

First published in *Vanguard* 10, no. 10 (December 1981–January 1982), pp. 16–19.

Let me begin by describing a certain desirable experience common to the viewing and producing of art objects, which I will call *the mystery of the object.* This consists in having such objects appear to one as massive, charged, seemingly impenetrable presences, with their own inner workings and unique qualities. They sometimes seem to be almost anthropomorphic presences, alive and percipient like human beings. Viewing them is then a process of searching out and understanding their peculiar logic and structure, and discerning whatever it is that makes them unique.

Objects in general, not only art objects, have certain features that help to explain their perceived mystery. They are three-dimensional, like human beings. And like human beings, they not only inhabit but arrogate the space they're in. They also have a unique spatiotemporal location and can move through space and behave in accordance with discernible laws (causal, cybernetic, logical, intentional, etc.); this fact holds out the illusory promise that one may one day come to understand them completely, if one only gathers enough information about their structures, context, creation, and function.

All this is to say that, like human beings, objects have identities; that is, they are particular collections of qualities and features, such that, together with the quality of having some particular spatiotemporal location, any such object is uniquely individuated from all other objects. These qualities and features may include all the same physical features we ascribe to human beings (such as anatomical features, tactile qualities, and principles of motion, etc.); in this sense, such objects may even seem to have their own personalities.

We are regularly blinded to the mystery of objects in daily life because we so often utilize them as tools or instruments for achieving our ends, or for satisfying our needs and desires. Under these conditions, the objects in question are not seen as self-subsistent entities in their own right; rather, they are perceived and conceptualized through the lens of the final ends they are utilized for. Those of their features that are useful to us are retained and registered in consciousness, while those which are irrelevant are forgotten or discarded. In this way, our plans, expectations, and prejudices about objects shape our perceptions of them. We subject them not merely to the categories of thought but to those of practical use and manipulation.

This means that objects tend to lose their unique identities in the very process of being perceived by us, for they are quickly absorbed into the plans and projects we view them as serving. And this does not happen only with those particular objects we actually happen to use for the particular ends we actually happen to have. The phenomenon occurs as well with all similar and related objects. We may utilize some particular objects that we identify in terms of their function, and this shapes our expectations and perceptions of other objects like them. These then extend to similar or related objects that may have a similar or related pragmatic function under similar or related conditions, and this instrumentalizing conception is then extended to any new object we experience: In order to discriminate and classify a new entity at all, the first and most basic question is always, "What is it *for?*" Thus all objects we experience tend to lose their individuality for us, and this is a consequence of our practical ability to subordinate each and every one of them to some actual or possible human plan. Our projects render them useful but necessarily anonymous.

One easy way of understanding much modern art since Duchamp is through its attempt to resist this pragmatic co-optation of objects. Of course modern art can be interpreted in many other ways and has many other functions as well. But one of the things it seems to do is to attempt to restore to us the individuality of particular objects by resisting our instinctive inclination to classify them under categories of use and function. Consider some of the strategies that have been employed for doing this:

1. One may isolate functional objects from their functional contexts, as Sylvia Mangold's floor paintings or Donna Dennis's house facades do;
2. One may isolate parts of functional objects from the context created by the complete functional object itself, as Rosemary Mayer's draped and sewn material sculptures do;
3. One may isolate particular features of parts of functional objects from their larger context, as do the tactile surfaces of Lee Krasner's or Helen Frankenthaler's paintings, the rounded industrial forms of Eva Hesse, or the hard-edge architectural plexiglass sculptures of Sylvia Stone;
4. One may isolate particular subfeatures of parts of functional objects, as do Agnes Martin's grid paintings or Jo Baer's framed white paintings.

The strategy can be iterated infinitely, to increasingly minuscule sensory features of objects, such as texture, color, mass, detail of shape, etc., that render the resulting art object increasingly abstract and particularized the more completely the feature in question can be divorced from its functional context and connotations. Such features may then be combined in random or idiosyncratic ways in order further to increase their conceptual distance from the functional categories in terms of which we normally identify them. Ideally the result is an entity with which we are confronted that forces us to experience its unique identity and its mystery on its own terms; terms that are resistant to our functional categorizations and our attempts to appropriate the object into our plans and projects. This ideal result is an important one because it provides us, as viewers, with a fresh and wholly unique experience that forces us to revise our assumptions about the external world and calls into question the expectations we bring to it. It requires us to expand and refine our classificatory concepts in order to accommodate a new type of object for which there is, by definition, only one exemplar.

I now want to show why this particular purpose of much modern art cannot possibly be achieved.

First of all, as soon as art objects are presented to the viewer *in order to* restore the mystery and uniqueness of the object, or *in order to* stimulate a new and freshening perceptual experience, they become instrumental tools. There is no difference in status between the goal of making or viewing art in order to "learn something new," "expand one's range of perceptual or experiential possibilities," "see the world anew," and so on, and the more mundane goals of making or using objects in order to, for example, keep food from spoiling, or heat the house, or stay dry in the rain. They are all purposes to which objects are subordinate. Nor is there, therefore, any difference between art ideologies that claim that art should be created and experienced for its own sake (that is, for the sake of our enjoyment of it) and those that claim that art should be created and experienced in order to raise people's political consciousness, provide an innocuous therapeutic outlet, advance the revolution, or indoctrinate. "Art for art's sake" enthusiasts don't seem to realize that the purported purity of art is already sullied by its instrumental relation to their own aesthetic needs. Art is always instrumental to some end. The pressing question is whether artists and viewers are making the right choices about which ends their art ought to serve.

Because restoring the mystery of the object and thereby providing one with a new and valuable perceptual experience are themselves plans or ends to which art objects bear an instrumental relation, we can make the same observations about the effects of this plan on our perception of the object as about the effects of other plans. For example, art objects are then perceived through the obfuscating lens of these plans; we view the object largely in these terms and seek out the features of it that most promote them. These features are retained in consciousness, while those that are irrelevant are discarded. Consider, for instance, the critical responses to Jackson Pollock's later drip paintings. It is hard to find any serious art lover who is willing to take seriously and explore the ramifications of their similarity to a house painter's drop cloth. Similarly, that one of Oldenburg's giant lipstick monuments strongly resembles West Berlin's Kaiser Wilhelm Gedächtnis-Kirche, both in form and possible function (that is, place of worship, shelter, architectural monument) is largely ignored. Instead, one speaks of Pollock's innovative working of the surface of the canvas, the creation of depth vying with two-dimensional tactility, the psychoanalytic import of the forms, and so on. Similarly, in Oldenburg's work, one hears much about the outsize functional object as a nonfunctional disruption of the architectural environment through the manipulation of scale. In both cases, our attention is drawn to what is unusual and new about these works, rather than what is functionally familiar. To point out what is functionally familiar about them becomes a kind of sacrilege; one is accused of philistinism, or underdeveloped powers of aesthetic discrimination. But many of Pollock's paintings *do* resemble house painters' drop cloths; and Oldenburg's giant lipsticks do look like the Kaiser Wilhelm Gedächtnis-Kirche. Anyone who thinks these assertions reflect negatively on the works or artists in question is missing the point, which is merely that our expectations of a certain kind of aesthetic experience shape our perception of the object by selecting and highlighting certain of its features at the expense of others.

This implies that, just as with other types of objects to which we bring a different set of expectations, the objects presented in an art context lose for us those aspects of their individual identities that are irrelevant to or inconsistent with their aesthetic function. Hence they are deindividualized by the very intention to make them most fully individual for us. Presentation in the art context is ultimately no more successful in restoring to us the uniqueness of the object's identity than are other, more patently functional contexts. In either case, the identity of the object is lost and absorbed into our aesthetic plans for it.

A second reason why the attempt to restore the mystery of the object cannot succeed is that the desire for the unique experience of the object can be viewed as an instrumental means to the more final end of increasing the marginal utility of commodity consumption in general. Here some clarification of terminology is in order. By *consumption,* I will mean any use or experience of a possessed object that satisfies some desire or other. Some examples: We consume food in order to satisfy hunger; we consume records in order to satisfy our desire to hear music. Similarly, we consume art objects in order to satisfy our desire for new and innovative perceptual experience, or our desire to expand our perceptual sensitivity to our surroundings, or for aesthetic of intellectual stimulation, and so on. By *marginal utility,* I will mean simply the utility or desirability of the last in the series of commodities consumed. Thus, for example, suppose I have a desire to quench my thirst. The first glass of water I drink will be the most intensely enjoyable; this is what it means to say that it has the "highest utility." The second glass of water will be less enjoyable; it thus has lower utility. The third glass of water will be still less enjoyable—indeed, may be positively unpleasant, if my thirst is already quenched. Thus it has less utility. If the marginal utility of something is the utility of the last in the series of that commodity consumed, we can see that the marginal utility of water as a thirst quencher diminishes; the utility of the last glass consumed is considerably lower than that of the first. And this is also true in general: Marginal utility always diminishes. The more of some commodity one consumes, the less satisfying it becomes.

Now let us apply this general point to my claim about art objects. I said that the desire for the unique experience of the object can be viewed as an instrumental means to the more final end of *increasing* the marginal utility of commodity consumption in general. This is to suggest that the desire for newness and uniqueness in our experience of an art object can be interpreted as a desire to consume a series of objects that *do not* become less and less satisfying the more of them we consume. This can be seen to be true by definition of "newness and uniqueness." What we desire is a new experience that is not the last, and therefore least satisfying, of a series of such experiences; does not represent the point of satiation past which we have no desire to experience such objects at all. What we desire is the experience of an art object that is both the first and the last in the series of such objects.

But this desire can never be satisfied. For, first of all, we have already seen that it imposes a plan or purpose to which the object is instrumental, and that, like any such plan, the unique identity of the object—that which would bring us the brand of experience of it we desire—is submerged, absorbed, and ultimately lost in it. Second, art objects themselves form a series of consumable commodities. Even if each member of the series could satisfy our desire for uniqueness, this desire itself would reach the point of satiation, past which continued further experience of such objects would be perceived not as perceptual stimulation but rather as a perceptual assault. This is just to observe that, like any commodity, the marginal utility of art objects must diminish, upon pain of sensory overload.

There are additional reasons why contemporary art practice cannot restore to us the unique identity of the object. We must generalize over the series of art objects in order to understand and identify them at all. For to understand something is at the very least to connect it coherently with other similar things; to be able to compare and contrast it with other objects; and to be able to make meaningful statements about it in language. If we could not do these things, we could not differentiate the object uniquely at all. But language consists—must consist—in general concepts, and we need these in order to be able to say or recognize what features of the object make it unique or different from other objects. So if we did not generalize art objects, we could not identify them as art objects to begin with. But of course to generalize about an object is to resist the mystery of its uniqueness: It is to classify it in terms of the features it shares with other objects and to differentiate it in terms of those it does not. But we could not identify those features in the first place if they were not general in their application to more than one such object.

The consequence is that, once again, the uniqueness of the object is lost in the very attempt to specify it. It is absorbed in precisely those general categories independently of which we would have no way of identifying it at all. For example, consider some of the ways in which we generalize over the class of art objects:

1. as "art";
2. with respect to *genre,* that is, figurative painting, nonrepresentational art, pottery, "hard-edge" sculpture, and so on;
3. with respect to *movement,* for example, pop art, pointillism, minimalism, mannerism, conceptual art, and so on;
4. with respect to the development and/or influence of a particular artist's interests, such that that artist's own works are shown to have common themes or concerns over an extended period of time, or such that the work of other artists is understood in terms of its similarities to that of the artist in question.

There are, of course, many other ways we may generalize over art objects, although these are less popular in the particular art context and historical period to which this discussion is addressed: with respect to social impact, propagandistic or didactic value, therapeutic value, political orientation, and so on. All of these are general categories we employ or might employ for identifying particular works of art.

Now one might object to my claims on the grounds that these arguments show only that we cannot directly experience the full mystery of art objects because we are blinded by our implicitly generalizing cognitive capacities. But they do not show that art objects in themselves are not unique. Indeed, quite the contrary, for I said at the beginning of this discussion that every object is uniquely individuated from every other, at least by its unique spatiotemporal location, and more often than not by other specific features that compose, for each object, a unique collection of features that identify that particular object.

But this objection is mistaken. To begin with, we can concede that each object is uniquely individuated by its spatiotemporal location. But it would be difficult to show that aesthetic value depended solely on the spatiotemporal location of an art object, quite independently of any other features it might have. So let us put aside the spatiotemporal uniqueness of objects as indices of their aesthetic status. This is to claim that the brand of aesthetic experience I have been describing does not attach to art objects in virtue of their spatiotemporal uniqueness alone.

But more important, the objection is mistaken because it is at least in theory possible to reproduce any object, hence any art object, an infinite number of times. We have the technological resources to replicate the color, shape, texture, and design of any object we can produce in the first place. This, I believe, is simply a fact about the resources and capacities we now have to reproduce our own culture.

Reactions to this fact tend to run the gamut from outrage to denial. For example, when Nelson Rockefeller chose some important pieces from his collection to be reproduced in large quantities and sold at prices greatly beneath that of the originals some years ago, the *New York Times* critic who wrote about this expressed the view that Rockefeller's decision represented a travesty of the value of art and that it cheapened the original value of the works to be replicated. On the other hand, Nelson Goodman, in *The Language of Art,* tries unsuccessfully to explain why it is that a good forgery does not have the same aesthetic value as the original of which it is a forgery. His argument essentially comes to a flat statement that there are some features of a work of art that *cannot* be reproduced, however microscopic; and by this he does not mean to refer to such features as "having been produced by artist *X*," which are originally extrinsic to the actual experience of the object, but rather to actual visual or tactile qualities of the object that may be too microscopic to be perceived by the naked eye. But surely *these* qualities are, if microscopic, also extrinsic to the aesthetic enjoyment of the object as well. And if they are not microscopic, then it is hard to see why we should suppose them impossible to replicate.

These responses are interesting because they demonstrate the depth of our resistance to detaching the aesthetic value of a work of art from our experience of its purported specialness and uniqueness. It seems that our knowledge that there are other, identical objects with the same features as those we are contemplating spoils our pleasure in those features. Our response, which is to aesthetically devalue such a work, bears more than a merely analogical relationship to the response of economically devaluing a stone or metal upon discovering that it is not a scarce commodity after all. It seems that our aesthetic appraisal of art objects depends more on the presumption of their uniqueness as commodities than it does on the actual features it happens to have. For to discover that an object is a reproduction is to discover that it is one of a general class of such objects. But to discover that it is reproducible is then to admit that it at least proves the existence of such a general class.

So if my arguments so far are sound, art objects in fact have no unique identities. They are not, after all, unique collections of features. Hence the experience I have described as the mystery of the art object must be explained in some other way.

To do this, let us return to that experience itself for further scrutiny. We observed that a feature of this experience is that the object seems to have a certain personality; to be opaque and impenetrable; to have a certain presence and power that seems to arrogate the space it is in. We said that the object appears to us as an independent entity, sometimes with its own life, logic, and intelligence, which it is the critic's (or critical viewer's) job to discern and clarify.

Another way of explaining this experience is to say that each feature of a humanly produced object, and more strongly of art objects, is the consequence of human thought and choice, and human beings are, in fact, unique in the specified sense. When artists make objects, they either create their features, or modify them, or uniquely recombine them, or decide to allow them to remain in their natural states; these are all decisions that art producers make. Creators of nonart objects make the same decisions, and one can experience the mystery of nonart objects too. But art objects remind us of their mystery through their isolation from their functional contexts. As I suggested earlier, this is a project to which the art object is subordinated just like any other project. And if its mystery were a function of its unique individuality, it would be inaccessible to us for the reasons already given. But if the mystery of art objects is rather to be explained by the fact they exhibit human intelligence and planning, and a human investiture of energy and thought, then such isolation from functional contests would serve to illuminate these facts about them rather than to obscure them. On this reading, the mystery and "presence" of art objects are derivative from the mystery and presence of human beings—of objects in each of our perceptual fields that contain histories, thoughts, motives, aspirations that are initially opaque to us until we have gotten to know them; that is, become familiar with their inner workings and logic.

This is to say that art objects are irreducibly fetishistic (in Marx's sense): As creators of them, we invest art objects with the human attributes of personality, presence, power, and individuality because human beings have these attributes and express them in the products of their labor (when that labor is freely chosen). And as viewers, we respond to these attributes because we recognize them as the products of human labor.

Now, Marx's conception of the fetishism of commodities was a critical one. He argued that it was a mistake to ascribe to objects their own logic and intelligence, supposed to be independent of human intervention, and to then suppose that the object was therefore subject to laws—the economic laws of the free market—that were beyond the ability of individual human beings to control, when in fact objects of human labor were merely catalysts for human interaction and existed within the context of human social and economic relations. We can apply the same criticism to this conception of art objects. That art objects have their mystery and their power to compel our attention is undeniable, and this is part of why they are important to us. They remind us of who we are and of the capacities for imagination and creativity that we have. But to infer from this that such objects are subject to laws and forces beyond human intervention or control is to make precisely the same mistake Marx rightly deplored. It is to abdicate responsibility for what happens to the object after it is made, and for how it is to be understood, and to forget that we, after all, and not the object itself, control the object's destiny. This then illegitimately licenses us to wring our hands over critical misinterpretations of the object, and unjust terms of exhibition and sale of the object, and—occasionally—even over the inflated pricing of art objects, all the while regarding the unfolding history of the object from the sidelines as though we were a passive theater audience, powerless to intervene in the course of the play.

These observations suggest the following conclusions. First, the aesthetic value of an art object cannot depend on its unique identity (it has none). Second, its aesthetic value must depend on its generality (judgments about art objects are necessarily general in character). Third, the aesthetic value of an art object *should* include recognition of its necessarily functional character as a catalyst of human interaction; as an instrument for achieving human plans; and as a communicator of human ideas, intelligence, and choices. Acceptance of this third, prescriptive point would, of course, put the burden on us to take control of the aesthetic and economic destiny of the object to a much greater degree than most artists and viewers are presently inclined to do; and to clarify to ourselves just what plans we have in mind to which the object is subject (fame and fortune? communicating a message? art-world superstardom? political revolution? or counterrevolution? etc.). Finally, it would require us to revise considerably the terms by which we evaluate and understand the object. We would need to pay much more attention than we do to the biographies and intentions of their creators and hence to the social and economic conditions that inform them. We would need to recognize that there are no features of such objects, such as their color, balance, distribution of space, or compositional unity, that can be fully detached from the plans and intentions of their creators or the socially determined expectations and presuppositions of their viewers.

We would need to take far less seriously than we do the purported newness and innovativeness of the object as a criterion for making aesthetic judgments, and to think instead much more about whether the object is sparking in us the kind of response we think it ought to, or that we think we need to have more of; whether it is forcing us to rethink basic and unexamined presuppositions about each other and the world in general, or merely reinforcing the ones we have; and whether it is conveying to us meaningful messages and experiences of a kind that might enable us to become better individuals. That is, it would require the transformation of our critical vocabulary from an entrepreneurial one to a humanist one.

Now I want to apply these perfectly general observations about art objects to the special case of performance art. Clearly, performances count as art objects too. They are discrete, organized entities that are the outcome of human intelligence and choice; they exist within the art context; they invite appraisal in terms of the same general critical vocabulary we apply to other kinds of contemporary art objects; and they are created by individuals who think of themselves as artists and who are recognized as such, in accordance with plans motivated by the intention to produce art.

In addition, they offer us the same experience of a mysterious, self-directed, compelling presence—not the presence of a single material entity but of a spatiotemporally unified entity that includes material and nonmaterial components. Performances are also subject to the same implicitly general judgments that are given of other kinds of object, and are instrumentally subject to human plans in much the same way.

But from these features we cannot and do not infer their implicit generality. For they contain actual human beings as components, and this makes them unreproducible. So performances are partially unique, whereas other kinds of art objects are not.

This gives performance art a dual character. On the one hand, as art objects, performances are instrumental, general, and if my suggestion is accepted, fetishistic in the sense already described. To this extent, performers function as parts of an art object and hence as art objects themselves. This makes them susceptible to the same constraints and observations we have made of other kinds of art objects: They are used as instruments, they take on a general role of character (we often speak of this as a "mythic" role when applying these features to human beings in the context of a work of art), and fetishistically express an investiture of human intelligence and choice as catalysts for the human social interactions that lie behind them. On the other hand, performers are unique human beings and invest their role as performers with their own personalities and energy. This makes performance art a unique social collaboration between audience and performers without the intervening (and Marx would say, obfuscating) presence of a catalytic medium about which we feel fully justified in claiming that they are alien presences out of our ability to control, and subject to their own mysterious laws and logic. We cannot claim this about performers because they are, of course, subject to the same logic, laws, and controlling forces to which we ourselves are subject.

The danger to which I should like to call attention is that we may incline to fully assimilate performance art to the first category and forget the special status conferred on it by the second; that is, we may objectify performance art and therefore treat and view it in the same essentially entrepreneurial terms we use with other kinds of art objects, with all the attendant mistakes and self-deceptions already catalogued. The consequence of such an assimilation would be the deliberate defusing of performance art's potentially vast power to confront its audience with substantive claims that can effect far-reaching changes in people's views about any of the very many substantive topics with which performance art deals. It would mean the reduction of this immense power to the same innocuous, inoffensive, and politically sanitized level as is already occupied by so much of contemporary art. And in view of the preceding conclusions, this would call into question our justification for encouraging the further development of performance art at all.

13. Power Relations within Existing Art Institutions

Written in October 1983 and previously unpublished.

My target in this discussion is what I shall call *aesthetic acculturation,* the process by which individuals are recruited into the ranks of art practitioners as artists (and also, secondarily, as critics, dealers, etc.) within existing art institutions and thereby abdicate their social, intellectual, economic, and creative autonomy.[1] I want to analyze this process genetically, by describing in stages the way it might be experienced by paradigmatic and representative art practitioners. This abstract, genetic analysis is intended to complement, rather than compete with, a more factually and historically oriented one. Thus the very general claims I will make about the workings of this process, and about its mutually victimizing effects, will not apply, nor apply with equal strength, to everyone. Those for whom my analysis does not ring true at all, on reflection, should exempt themselves from my claims. Overwhelming numbers of exceptions to my claims will undermine the plausibility of the analysis. However, I would be surprised if the analysis were found to have no substantive application at all. I shall conclude by suggesting and evaluating some ways in which our autonomy might be restored.

1.

Let's begin by speculating on who is most likely to make a career commitment to art, either as an artist, critic, dealer, or collector. Art institutions in their present incarnation seem to hold out great promise to aspiring art practitioners. They seem to offer the opportunity to achieve the highest standards of one's freely chosen craft, and the valued peer recognition and approval that accompanies it. On the other hand, posthumous or belated "discoveries" of unrecognized artists, as well as successful publicity campaigns for pre-packaged *enfants terrible de la minute,* demonstrate the lack of correlation of merit and professional success. Similarly, aspiring dealers and critics may learn all too quickly the economic dangers of staking their professional credibility on a single movement or individual. Hence one must be economically prepared to ensure one's material well-being in some other way, in case one's gamble on an art career is unsuccessful. A commitment to a career as an art practitioner requires that one is financially independent, or that one's family is, or that one possesses other economically remunerative skills, or that a perma-

1.
Earlier versions of this paper were presented at the NEA Conference on Visual Arts in Los Angeles (October 1982), the Banff School of Fine Arts and the National Exhibition Centre of Calgary (November 1982), the Nova Scotia College of Art and Design (March 1983), and the NEA Seminar on Art Criticism (September 1983). I have benefited from comments received on those occasions, and from Jeffrey Evans and Ingrid Sischy.

nently spartan lifestyle can be regarded as a novelty or a virtue, rather than as proof of social failure.

This precondition of professional commitment functions as a mechanism of selection among creatively inclined individuals. For it discourages those individuals for whom economic hardship has been, up to that point, a central reality. Typically an individual whose early life has been affected by economic deprivation, social instability, and political prejudice is less likely to choose a career that promises at least as good a chance of perpetuating those conditions as ameliorating them, and is correspondingly more likely to choose a career that promises the social and economic security such an individual has previously lacked. Art institutions in their present incarnations, then, will tend to attract individuals for whom economic and social instability are not sources of anxiety, for they have correspondingly less reason to sacrifice the vicissitudes and satisfactions of self-expression to the necessities of social and economic survival.

One immediate effect of this social and economic preselection is to create a shared presumption in favor of the artistic values and interests of those socially and economically advantaged individuals, that is, a concern with beauty, form, abstraction, and innovations in media, to which political and social subject matter is either largely subordinate or completely absent. Let us roughly characterize these as *formalist* values. Because existing art institutions favor the selection of individuals with such values, it follows that these institutions will be popularized primarily by individuals who share these values.

This means that there is a broad consensus, within the interlocking system of art institutions, on the goals viewed as worth achieving. Artists, for example, will strive to realize broadly formalist values in their work; critics will strive to discern and articulate the achievement of such values; dealers will strive to discover and promote artists whose work successfully reflects these standards; and collectors will strive to acquire and exchange such work.

Individuals whose work or aesthetic interests fail to conform to formalist criteria are unlikely to pursue a career successfully within the constraints of existing art institutions. For the commitment of most art practitioners to the standards and values expressed in this consensus is a deep and central one, rooted, as it often is, in the prior socioeconomic balance of resources that engendered and continually reconfirms it. For such individuals, these values are a direct expression and idealization of their lifestyles. And their lifestyles, in turn, are justified and validated by the values such art expresses. Thus it is natural that such individuals tend to be less than receptive to critical scrutiny of those values and to alternative conventions of art making that violate them. For in questioning their universal legitimacy, such critiques implicitly question the socioeconomic balance that generated them. And for individuals who have a very deep personal investment in that balance, such critiques may seem to question the legitimacy of these very individuals themselves.

The long-range effect of this tightly defended consensus is that the art practitioners who share it determine—through their shared values and practices, and the economic and social factors that determine them—the criteria of critical evaluation for all art that aspires to entry into existing art institutions. I shall describe this as a state of *critical hegemony.* That is, the socioeconomically determined aesthetic interests of these individuals define not only what counts as "good" and "bad" art but what counts as art, period. Through art education, criticism, exhibitions, and other practices and institutions devoted to preserving and disseminating what I shall refer to as *Euroethnic art,* the socioeconomic resources of this class of individuals enable its art practitioners to promulgate its fascinating but ethnocentric artifacts as High Culture on a universal scale. According to these shared criteria, then, those creative products that are dominated by a concern with political and social injustice or economic deprivation, or which use traditional or "folk" media of expression, are often not only not "good" art; they are not art at all. They are, rather, "craft," "folk art," or "popular culture"; and individuals for whom these concerns are dominant are correspondingly excluded from the art context.[2]

This exclusion may manifest itself in a number of ways. Recently, for example, a respected mainstream critic with a genuine interest in diversifying the range of work recognized as mainstream art wrote a monograph on black folk art and submitted it to a major art magazine for publication. Because he knew his audience would be drawn primarily from the white upper-middle class, he spent a good deal of time researching and describing in the paper the impact on the work he discussed of the artist's being poor and black. The paper was rejected on the ground that it had nothing to do with art. This rationale seems not to recognize the extent to which shared socioeconomic and cultural assumptions that also "have nothing to do with art" are presupposed in our criteria for identifying something as art. By dismissing different ones as irrelevant, it effectively dismissed the possibility of scrutinizing and expanding our own.

2.
Richard Goldstein makes essentially this point in "Art Beat: Race and the State of the Arts," *The Village Voice,* August 23, 1983, p. 31; and in "Art Beat: 'Darky' Chic," *The Village Voice,* March 31, 1980, p. 34. Also see Robert Pear, "Reagan's Arts Chairman Brings Subtle Changes to the Endowment," *The New York Times,* April 10, 1983.

The consequent invisibility of much nonformalist, ethnically diverse art of high quality may explain the remark, made in good faith by another well-established critic, that if such work didn't generate sufficient energy to "bring itself to one's attention," then it probably did not exist. It would be wrong to attribute this claim to arrogance or disingenuousness. It is not easy to recognize one's complicity in preserving a state of critical hegemony. That one should be guided in one's aesthetic interests by conscious and deliberate choice, rather than by one's socioculturally determined biases, is a great deal to ask. But by refusing to test consciously those biases against work that challenges rather than reinforces them, a critic ensures that the only art that is *ontologically* accessible to him[3] is art that narrows his vision even further. And then it is not difficult to understand the impulse to ascribe to such work the magical power to "generate its own energy," introduce itself to one, garner its own audience and market value, and so on. For nearly all objects of consideration can be experienced as animately and aggressively intrusive if one's intellectual range is sufficiently solipsistic.

2.

Suppose one decides to make a career commitment to becoming a professional artist under these conditions. Typically, this means being acculturated by a fine arts program in art school, college, or university, in which the course of training offered is intensively oriented toward Euroethnic art. Often the aesthetic standards of Euroethnic art may be implicit in the student's own socioeconomic background. But they may not. If one's socioeconomic background is black or hispanic or asian middle class, or white working class, or both working class and immigrant, or if one is a woman, to name just a few possibilities, then the transition into art education may require some sociocultural adaptation; indeed, even the rejection of those concerns and values that generated the original impulse to artistic self-expression to begin with. Artists whose commitment to those background socioeconomic values and conditions is deep are confronted by an unpleasant choice. Either they must modify or reject the kind of art making that is most personally meaningful for them, or else they must largely abandon hopes of professional success.

Now there is a great deal to be said for such a program of training. Often the courses in skill and media development are both comprehensive and intensive.

3.
In general I use the masculine pronoun gender-specifically, as the system of art institutions I target is populated primarily (though not exclusively) by white middle-class men of European descent.

One's self-confidence and motivation are enhanced by the knowledge that one has mastered the essentials of a medium or technique regarded as canonical by the arbiters of mainstream art. The history of formalist art and its roots in Euroethnic art is equally fascinating—if not as a course of self-knowledge about one's heritage, then as an anthropological study of the evolution of an interesting and complex, though alien, culture. Finally, the experience of role confirmation by the art community is, as I suggested earlier, particularly significant for individuals who have decided to devote their lives to self-expression.

However, the critical hegemony of formalist art, and particularly its pretension to transcend its ethnicity, can have a demoralizing effect on art students from different backgrounds, for in presuming to furnish and inculcate universal criteria of fine arts production, it implicitly subordinates and devalues the creative products of other ethnic groups. It thereby encourages the belief that such products are aesthetically or culturally inferior to those of the Euroethnic art tradition. Thus it encourages art students from other ethnic groups to reject their own culturally spontaneous modes of artistic expression, in order to emulate this one. And in so doing, the pretension of formalist art to universality chokes off its only sources of cross-cultural enrichment. In this hothouse atmosphere, it is little wonder that observers of current trends in art conclude that there is nowhere for art to evolve but retrogressively.

Some have attempted to justify this pretension by appeal to purportedly universal and ethnically neutral criteria—claiming, for example, that formalist art is "high" art because it serves only aesthetic and nonpragmatic ends. But this line of defense is difficult to sustain, in the absence of further argument demonstrating that the alteration or expansion of one's perception of reality, the professional success of the artist, the communication of some idea, experience, or insight, receiving a profitable return on one's investment, and so on, are purely aesthetic and nonpragmatic ends. And even if this could be shown (which is unlikely), it would in any case remain a mystery why art that satisfies these criteria should be thought culturally superior to art that does not. For these meta-aesthetic criteria are no less ethnocentric than the aesthetic criteria they are invoked to justify.

3.

A second, major disadvantage of art education qua aesthetic acculturation is its specialized division of labor. The intensive training in the skills and history of one's craft as an artist is purchased at the price of other skills needed to be a fully autonomous and responsible practitioner in the art community, and in society at large. The conceptual articulation and evaluation of an artist's aims and achievements, for example, is a task often relegated to the art critic, who researches the artist's past, interviews him, and fits his activity into the familiar conceptual framework of formalist art discourse. This validation, yielded by the critic's interpretation, is usually a major precondition for the work's validation by the art community at large. Even a negative review, in this regard, is better than no review at all, and the grossest critical misunderstanding is preferable to the most pellucid and self-critical appraisal by the artist. Recently a promising young artist was confronted by the following dilemma. After years of working hard to produce and promote her work to critics and dealers, she encountered a critic whose response to her work was enthusiastic and fervent. He proposed a major, comprehensive article on her work to appear in a major art magazine. Of course, the artist was delighted. Unfortunately, she felt that he had completely misunderstood her work. At the same time, she was offered the opportunity to write an article on her work in a much lesser-known, artists-run publication. Of course, she could not do both. She would lost the critic's support, and all the recognition and financial support that would bring, if she made clear her rejection of his reading of her work. If she allowed him to write the article, on the other hand, she would lose control over the public meaning of her work. She decided that economic support for her work was more important, declined the offer to write about her own work, and let him write the article instead.

Usually the interpretive function is one that the critic is eminently well suited to perform. For the critic has usually received the training in verbal and intellectual skills that the artist has not, and often has thereby purchased the ability to interpret conceptually the artist's products at the price of the full development of the critic's own artistic impulses. Thus the phenomenon of the critic as closet artist: Many art critics (as well as dealers and curators) whose views and pronouncements are highly influential in determining standards for the evaluation of art products are themselves artists—whose own artwork, however, is often completely independent of or even in conflict with the views on which their own critical reputations rest. To describe their attitudes toward their own artistic products as self-effacing is an understatement. The process of aesthetic acculturation tends to divest the artist of control over the interpretation and cultural meaning of the work, by relegating that role to the critic. But in accepting it, the critic assumes responsibility for disseminating critical standards from which he himself may be alienated.

Then there is the related phenomenon of the conflict of interest. Many art practitioners who have achieved recognition within the art community for their critical writings are justifiably reluctant to promote their own artwork, for both self-interested and ethical reasons. To utilize their own, highly developed critical and political resources to promote their artwork would open them to the charge of opportunism. But many such art practitioners also anticipate that their artwork would be found unsophisticated or unintelligent by comparison with their critical output in any case, by an audience accustomed to expect only a certain kind of output from these individuals. Indeed, such an art practitioner may be led to adopt a pseudonym under which to exhibit his work, merely to get an unbiased hearing for it. But even here the temptation may be great to utilize his political clout in its support. The phenomena of closet artist and of conflict of interest dovetail in the recognition that as things now stand, the role of cultural interpreter and evaluator of work of art is a source of art-political power that is largely incompatible with the role of creating works of art.

One reason this division of labor is suspect is because—to butcher Kant's observation—words without artworks are empty, artworks without words are dumb. To relegate the creation and interpretation of art objects to different subjects is to bifurcate the experience of both. Artists are divested of authority and control over the cultural meanings of their own creative impulses by critics, while critics are denied access to theirs in exchange.

4.

This highly specialized division of labor between artists and critics exacerbates the problem of critical hegemony. That art critics and not artists determine the cultural interpretation of an art product implies that there is no necessary connection between the set of contexualized experiences, associations, beliefs, and intentions an artist brings to the production of a work, and its resulting cultural interpretation. These factors may of course enter into this interpretation, but only at the critic's discretion, and only in so far as it serves the critic's own theory of the work. This is particularly evident when that theory falls within the constraints of formalism as I have characterized it. Formalism encourages us to abstract from the personal subject matter of the work, and consider its universal (actually its Euroethnic art-historical) significance. It also encourages us to evaluate the work in terms of such purely formal properties as shape, line, color, and so on, independently of its subject matter.

In some respects the formalist stance can be extraordinarily enriching, for it frees us to view all objects as containing the promise of beauty and meaning, without regard to function or context.[4] On the other hand, it reinforces the alienation of the artwork from that particular meaning intended for it by its creator. If the art-contextually legitimated meaning of the work is both independent of its function and context, and also—therefore—"universally" accessible (that is, to anyone schooled in the canons of formalism), then its creator's intended meaning is obviously irrelevant. And indeed, many young artists who seek recognition within existing art institutions quickly learn to discuss their work in the impersonal and decontextualized manner that formalism requires.

Through its very impersonality, formalism can confer the illusion of understanding and accessibility to otherwise unfamiliar and ethnically diverse artifacts (witness, for example, the art community's appropriation of African tribal imagery as a consequence of Picasso's cubist investigations). Here recognition and a genuine appreciation of otherness is sacrificed in order to preserve the appearance of authority and control. But formalism can only achieve this in collaboration with the division of labor earlier described. For of course the purely formal significance of such artifacts can be maintained only if any dissenting interpretation its creator might offer can be safely disregarded. And this, in turn, requires the belief that the artist's own, preacculturated contribution to critical discourse is irrelevant; or at best, of subsidiary importance. Thus formalism itself implies a certain critical hegemony, in subordinating all objects to criteria of evaluation that are independent of their original context, function, and subject matter.

But why, it may be asked, do artists denied access to existing art institutions on these grounds fail to protest this exclusion (or worse, tailor their work accordingly)? Why do they fail to assert the aesthetic value of their own sociopolitically informed concerns, and of their pride and creative interest in the ethnocultural artifacts that characterize their own milieus?

Of course I cannot begin to provide a satisfactory answer to this question in this essay. Part of it is that many such artists rightly feel this exclusion as an insult and so want nothing more to do with existing art institutions. They choose to sacrifice professional stability and critical recognition to the preservation of their artistic integrity. But another part of the answer is to be found in the message these aspiring young artists receive from the moment they begin their art educations, that is, that artists are not supposed to talk about art; they're just supposed to make it.

4.
Of course this aesthetic vision can be taken too far, as when it blinds one to the central significance of such objects. It was this vision, presumably, that led a famous art critic at a panel discussion on art and politics in the early 1970s to dismiss publicly the activities of the Black Panthers on the grounds that they were without aesthetic merit.

The successful assimilation of this message renders many artists largely unable to protest, assert, or argue against *any* perceived injustice in treatment they may receive from existing art institutions, and not merely the injustice of critical hegemony. In accepting the division of labor prescribed by existing art institutions, artists from other ethnic backgrounds are often divested of a major resource for redressing their exclusion from these institutions.

5.

Similarly, there is little room within existing artists' education programs for a course on the management of the economic and legal aspects of art production. The criteria by which a work is priced may seem a mysterious matter indeed. And it is often claimed that only a practical and thorough familiarity with the vicissitudes of the art market, plus a "good business sense," enables one to do so. Legal control over the distribution, exhibition, or exchange of the work is similarly dependent, in mysterious and mystifying ways, on the trustworthiness and good character of the dealer. Thus the dealer, rather than the artist, becomes the custodian of the market—and so aesthetic—value of the art product, and of its material fate as well. To suggest that such control should be shared with the artist then becomes an insult to the relationship of trust and good will that exists between them—and may, indeed, lead the dealer to take the initiative in dissolving that relationship.

It is not difficult to see why this should be so. For in addition to the dealer's obvious financial motivation for controlling the economic and legal fate of the artist's product, there are social and psychological considerations as well. The dealer's success at managing the product is also considered an index of his cultivation, taste, and aesthetic discernment, that is, the proof of the legitimacy of his claim *to be* a dealer. To pick a winner is supposed to demonstrate the breadth of his aesthetic vision and the depths of his art-historical insight; and it is that trained insight, finally, for which a financial reward, as well as social validation, may seem appropriate. Similar considerations apply to the role of critic. Thus the artist relegates interpretative, social, and financial control of the producer to the dealer and critic, whose informed judgment and taste are accountable for its fate.

This is an overwhelming responsibility for anyone, even the most highly cultivated and well-informed dealer or critic, to shoulder, and so it is not surprising that dealers may collaborate with critics and collectors, in a "gentleman's agreement," in order to ensure that an art product gets the critical and financial attention the dealer feels it, and he, deserves.[5] It is a rare dealer indeed whose vision and insight have been so fully established without the benefit of such collaboration that his decisions of what art to exhibit themselves function as critical arbiters of what art *should* be exhibited. Having survived the unpredictableness of the art market, often with the help of money, publicity, and timing, such individuals are in the unenviable position of having no evaluative criteria, independent of their own socioeconomically conditioned taste, by which to confirm that their taste is, in fact, a reliable index of high-quality art. Thus power to determine aesthetic standards through one's choices is purchased at the cost of those standards as independent and nonarbitrary criteria of evaluation.

A third feature that is usually absent in the training of artists is attention to the skills and information necessary to analyze and critique the social and economic preconditions for producing art; this is rather the provenance of the historian of contemporary art. Nor do artists usually learn how to scrutinize and dissect their own ideological, socially determined presuppositions; this is the provenance of the social theorist, who is able to view the entire interlocking network of art institutions as a historically specific, sociocultural phenomenon that engenders its own ideological justification. But this, too, is often thought to be of no pressing concern to artists. I will return to this question later.

6.

Thus the end result of this process of specialization in aesthetic acculturation is a severely lopsided division of labor. The artist's function is the bare production of the work alone. He is neither expected nor encouraged to exert any control over the meaning, price, value, social and political impact, or material fate, of the object; these are instead the provenance of the critic, dealer, and collector, respectively. Nor is he expected or encouraged to develop broader views about any of these things; these are rather to be relegated to the art historian or social theorist.

When these points were raised at a recent art conference, an influential and well-known museum director responded by avowing sincerely that it was quite enough in the way of responsibility for artists to make art, and that the task of the rest of

5.
The economic exigencies that lead naturally to such agreements are realistically described in John Bernard Myers, "The Art Biz," *The New York Review of Books* 30, no. 15 (October 13, 1983), pp. 32–34.

us was to enable the artist to do this without fuss, worry, or interruption. Many artists may concur with this opinion, and it is easy to see why. There is something enormously attractive about the idea of having a benevolent parent, or servant, to attend to all one's needs, so that one can be completely free to create. On the other hand, the attitude expressed in this claim seems not very different, in essence, from that which loving husbands used to express with complete sincerity to their wives, when they insisted that all they needed to do was look pretty and make babies, and leave the complicated business of running the world to the men. It is dubious to suppose that a guardian or custodian frees one to do anything. It is, rather, a condition of bondage, regardless of the activity in which one is then permitted to engage.

The result of this division of labor is, then, the essential infantilization of the artist as bare producer of art. Having divested himself of power and control over the work, he can then hardly be expected to participate in the interpretative, economic, and social processes by which the art product is assimilated into the art context—nor, therefore, into the political and cultural life of society at large. The artist "just makes the stuff" and therefore is not to be held accountable for its aesthetic, social, or political consequences beyond its bare production.

A recent, disturbing illustration of the sensibility thereby produced was the furor caused by a young white male artist a few years ago, who exhibited a set of conventional, fourth-generation abstract expressionist drawings in a well-respected alternative space and incorporated a racial epithet into the title of the show. Of course, this generated sharp protest from minority artists and other politically concerned members of the art community. When asked why he had chosen that title for his drawings, the artist implied, in essence, that it would gain publicity and attention for them.[6] His insensitivity to the political implications of creating a culturally legitimating context for the use of damaging racial epithets may have been the expression of a malevolent character. But it was more likely the consequence of a type of ethical parochialism that was encouraged rather than alleviated by the process of aesthetic acculturation he underwent in art school. For as we have already seen, prevailing art institutions committed to the formalist aesthetics of Euroethnic art are not, as a rule, sensitive to the ethics of political oppression, nor conversant with the damaging effects that seemingly innocuous behavior can have.

6.
See the artist's comments in Richard Goldstein, "Art Beat: The Romance of Racism," *The Village Voice,* April 2, 1979; and in Grace Glueck, "'Racism' Protest Slated over Title of Art Show," *The New York Times,* April 14, 1979.

This institutionalized naiveté was amply demonstrated by the gallery's response to the protest, which was to defend its decision to permit the exhibition, by appealing to the unconditional right to freedom of artistic expression. But this response seems triply inadequate. First, suppose the exhibition had involved a shooting or lynching in the gallery, or the injection of heroin into the artist's arm five times a day for the duration of the exhibition. These are ethically easy cases, in which it is obvious that the right to freedom of artistic expression is not unconditional and is in fact easily outweighed by other values—such as life, health, undisturbed civil peace—we recognize as more important. The question then arises of why the actual situation was so much less clear-cut for those institutional representatives than for those artists who were outraged by it. That it was implies that defending minorities against the insidious effects of a culturally legitimated use of racial epithets simply was not as centrally important to those institutional representatives as defending themselves—and all of us—against the spectacle of physical violence, murder, or drug addiction would have been; whereas for the protestors, the first was just as important as the second. But it has already been suggested that this bias is a consequence of formalist aesthetics and is largely determined by its socioeconomic preconditions.

Second, the right to freedom of expression is a *permission,* granted by the state, to engage in certain activities. But not everything that is permitted is required, nor can everything that is permitted be justified. Technically I am permitted to spend all my evenings howling at the moon if I so choose. That doesn't mean it is a good idea, nor that anyone should give me money and a stretch of mountain glade to do so. Individuals who choose to produce or support work that incorporates gratuitous racism do so not just because it is permitted to do so (they are permitted to do many things they don't bother to do) but because they actively *want* and *choose* to do so. It is the values and impulses that motivate such choices that are objectionable.

Third, the right to unlimited freedom of artistic expression in any case can only have application to a legitimate subject of rights. We normally grant such rights only to fully mature and responsible adults, who understand in some sense the difference between right and wrong, and who can be relied upon not to abuse their freedom. For this reason, we do not normally grant such rights to children, imbeciles, or the mentally disturbed. The gallery and the protestors indicated in their behavior that they understood this practice perfectly. For it was, after all, the gallery and not the artist who was held accountable for the exhibit, and the gallery, not the artist, who defended it. Thus both parties to the dispute seemed to agree, finally, that the artist whose aesthetic decision caused the controversy was nevertheless not to be held accountable for having made it, and the artist's own statements lent credence to this view. There seems to be something amiss with a set of cultural conventions that validates this degree of irresponsibility for artists.

7.

The result of this lopsided division of labor, inherent in the process of aesthetic acculturation within existing art institutions, is a pervasive alienation of the artist, both from his own creative processes and products and also from the background sociocultural environment that engendered them. For by abdicating control over the meaning, value, price, function, and material fate of the artwork after it leaves the artist's studio, he thereby abdicates his claim to have a special relation to that product that is significant and valuable in its own right. The art product is appropriated by the art institutions that legitimate it and is thereafter governed by its cultural and economic laws, rather than the artist's intentions and wishes. This means that ultimately neither the creative process nor the final product is determined by the artist's own aesthetic imperatives.

One manifestation of the alienation that results from this division of labor is the phenomenon of *overproduction.* For example, a newly discovered artist may contract with a gallery to show new work, say, every two years. For some artists, the rate of production necessary to fulfill the contract may correspond perfectly with their natural rhythm of art production. For others, this rate of production may be far too high, producing stereotyped and superficial work that the artist has been pressured, by the terms of his contract, into producing. Now one might think that the obvious solution would be to contract to exhibit less frequently, say, once every four or five years rather than once every two. But this is improbable. For the dealer's interest in contracting with the artist at a certain time is predicated primarily on his belief that the work will be financially marketable *at that time,* not on his faith in the enduring aesthetic value of the work. That is a faith on the basis of which only a few experienced dealers are willing to do business.

Not long ago, a flourishing European gallery contacted a young, unaffiliated artist with the offer of a major exhibition, to be traveled within Europe and the United States. The artist responded enthusiastically, explaining, however, that her beliefs about the importance of maintaining the mutual independence of aesthetic and financial value required the imposition of stringent controls on the pricing and distribution of the work. These controls, she explained, ensured that the financial value of the work was permanently indexed to the labor and material invested in it, on which no profit could, in good faith, be made. The gallery responded by professing a continuing interest in her work, but regretting that financial exigencies made it impossible to show it under these conditions, until the gallery had considerably increased its capital resources elsewhere. The artist did not hear from that gallery again.

From the gallery's perspective, the decision was clearly a rational one. A dealer may, by surveying and helping to promote current trends, develop a market analyst's sense of what kind of work is in demand right now. To promote such work without the expectation of economic return would seem to be irrational. And the resources necessary to ensure a continuing demand for that work five years hence would outstrip those of even the most well-equipped stockbroker. And so if an artist desires gallery affiliation, and the prestige and recognition it brings, he must be prepared to adapt his rate of art production to the demands of the economic, not the creative process. Similar conclusions apply to the nonaffiliated artist whose work is currently in vogue. That the admittedly grueling rate of production necessary to sustain one's visibility, by participating in all the invited exhibitions, performances, lectures, residencies, or conferences, may be so extreme as to endanger the artist's physical or psychological well-being is irrelevant for most artists. For they understand the economic and political workings of existing art institutions well enough to know that their professional success depends upon satisfying the extra-aesthetic demands that are made on them at the time they are made. That they are thereby manipulated by these demands, and alienated from their own creative processes, may seem a small price to pay for the recognition and support to which every serious artist aspires.

8.

A related manifestation of this alienation is what I shall call the phenomenon of *deformation*. Faced with the pressures of overproduction, the artist has a few alternatives, besides that of simply refusing to meet all of these demands. He may produce shoddy work, or he may modify the product in ways that make it easier to produce, or he may employ others to make the work for him. He may thereby delegate to others an increasingly large proportion of the creative decisions that need to be made in the process of execution. If all concur in regarding the final product as a collaborative effort, well and good. If the artist does not, his collaborators' responses, as they confront an artwork attributed to the artist but that primarily manifests their creative decisions, may be mixed indeed. Each of these alternatives represents ways in which the form and content of the final art product can be modified to accommodate the extra-aesthetic demands of the economic process, to which the creative process is subordinate.

Similar deformations of the art product are often required by the artist's own desire to achieve and maintain a certain level of visibility and critical approval, even when the pressures of overproduction are absent. It has already been suggested that critical and social recognition from within the art community is naturally and centrally important to anyone who aspires to professional success as an artist. But if the community's standards of aesthetic excellence are not independent of economic pressures, then the critical approval and economic reinforcement an artist receives for doing economically and critically viable work encourages that artist to produce more economically and critically viable work, even if it conflicts with his natural creative dispositions to do so. Thus we have the phenomenon of the artist who produces one kind of work for his gallery and another for himself, and of the artist who is reluctant to risk unfashionable departures from a successful and well-established formula, after having been reprimanded by silence or negative reviews for attempting such departures in the past. The obverse phenomenon is the artist whose output has been so completely canonized for the annals of art history that anything he produces, no matter how unskilled or superficial, automatically acquires aesthetic value and critical approval—in direct proportion to the price it can be expected to command at the next international auction. These are further ways in which the artist's alienation from his product may be manifested by deforming his product in response to extra-aesthetic imperatives.

Art products may also be deformed in response to imperatives from dealers for art that is sellable. Art that requires too great an effort at comprehension, or that violates too obtrusively traditional criteria of art, or that seems too difficult to commoditize, may be the target of a concerted effort to make it just plain disappear from the annals of art history, through comprehensive survey exhibitions that ignore it or critical writing that marginalizes it. This conveys to artists a less than subtle message that to continue producing such economically nonviable work is to court obscurity. Those who take the hint often reform their art production accordingly.[7]

Finally, the artist may deform his product in response to the demand for innovation. In order to preserve the profitable functioning of many existing art institutions, a continuous demand for new art must be created. And this can be done only by creating a desire for new art. This, in turn, requires the allegiance of the art community to innovation as an intrinsic value; that is, the recognition of an art-

7.
See Michael Brenson, "Artists Grapple with New Realities," *The New York Times*, May 15, 1983.

work as good precisely and only because it does what has never been done before, advances some aesthetic a step further, offers us a new and exciting experience, or forces us to revise our view of the world. And so artists often compete with one another in their quest for visibility and professional standing, by presenting increasingly bizarre and shocking work to an audience whose polite applause is predicated upon their inability to have conceived or predicted its advent.

In response to this fundamentally economic imperative of product innovation, artists may deform not only their work but themselves to the point of suicide by hanging, shooting, burning, starving, castrating, or maiming themselves, all in the name of High Culture. Just like the town in Florida whose inhabitants are known to amputate or maim their own limbs in order to collect the insurance, these artists gradually truncate themselves and their creativity to survive economically as artists. That a recent work of an artist proficient in this genre consisted in broadcasting an extended plea to his radio audience to send him money is both an ironic comment on and a natural extension of this "aesthetic" stance.

Thus the comforting and often self-sustaining vision of the artist's studio as a self-contained realm of personal power and creative control, to which the artist can retreat from a chaotic and unmanageable external world, is a myth. For even his creative activity within that realm is largely determined by external socioeconomic imperatives that are, within the scheme of existing art institutions, beyond the artist's ability to withstand.

9.

The notion of the successful professional artist as one who has been freed, by his gallery affiliation and critical and financial successes, to devote all his time to creation, is, then, an ideological fiction. It is *ideological* because it serves the interests of those who prefer to preserve rather than improve existing art institutions. And it is a *fiction* because it is false that this brand of success promotes genuine freedom or creative expression. Years ago I was doing research for an article that would have proceeded along somewhat similar lines of analysis as this one but was to have been much more specific and detailed. My plan was to interview certain prominent artists, critics, and curators who had participated long and extensively in the system of existing art institutions and whose visions were both clear and somewhat jaundiced. From these discussions I planned to extrapolate a general analysis based on their recounted experiences. The article was never completed because, although the artists contacted were generally quite generous with their time and information, they volunteered that information only on the conditions that (1) they not be mentioned by name, and (2) no information be used in a form that was detailed or specific enough to identify any actual individual, institution, or situation recounted. Their worry about antagonizing the individuals and institutions that supported them, and thereby losing the political and economic support that buttressed their success, was a real and completely rational one. And it made clear with particular poignancy the abdication of power, control, and freedom ultimately required for success.

That this expropriation of power, responsibility, and freedom in exchange for professional success need not be the norm is evidenced by comparing the condition of the artist to those of other creative producers in higher education. Take, for example, the historian. Like the artist, the historian draws upon available information, personal experience, and insight, and an internalized set of standards—intellectual and academic ones, in this case—to synthesize an original creative product, that is, a book or article. The standards by which the product is evaluated are themselves created and promulgated, through teaching, by that historian and his or her academic peers. And those peers, all equally practicing historians, subject the product to the critical scrutiny of those standards. That an article or book on history should be evaluated by others who do not themselves participate in the creative process is unthinkable. And that the criteria relative to which the product is evaluated should be articulated, amplified, and imposed by equally distanced others is equally unthinkable. Historians create, control, and survey critically their own creative products. They do not recruit others to perform the hard task of intellectual self-evaluation for them. For that is the surest way to abdicate control over the self, and over the expressions of the self, that one can imagine.

Similarly, the pricing and public distribution of the historian's creative products are controlled by the community of historians. Articles and books submitted for publication are refereed by other historians, who thereby control the vehicles by which such products are brought to the public. A historian does not abdicate economic or legal control over the dissemination of an article or book to a journal editor or publisher, merely for the privilege of having the work disseminated at all. Rather, the product is protected by strict copyright laws, the producer is reimbursed, in part, by royalties, and the audience to the work is determined by the producer's conscious, strategic decision as to whom the work shall be addressed (other historians, students, the general public), and to what kind of publisher it should therefore be submitted.

Now one might be tempted to think that such a system could never work for artists, because, unlike books, art products are unique objects or events that can never be replicated. I have argued elsewhere that this conviction is false, and that the assumption of uniqueness is, similarly, an ideological fiction, determined largely by economic interests, that serves to legitimate the economic and market criteria for pricing art products by equating those criteria with aesthetic criteria for evaluating them.[8] If art products are not unique, like precious jewels, there is no reason why they should cost so much. If they costed less, artists would be unable to support themselves solely by producing them. They might be more inclined to seek out supplementary jobs as critic, teachers, dealers, or curators of art, in order to ensure their livelihood, and thereby encourage critics, teachers, dealers, and curators to experience the artist's role firsthand. This mutual exchange of roles and skills might engender both more artists who are critically adept and socially responsible, and more critics, dealers, and curators whose interests in art are personal and social, as well as professional. The possibilities for dialogue, cooperation, and collective action among such individuals who would be both informed and experienced in a multiplicity of roles seem potentially unlimited. Although artists would then have less time to produce art, the art they produced would be more fully their own. For they would collectively determine its meaning, value, price, public dissemination, and material fate.[9]

10.

Now much of what I have said here should be familiar, in one form or another, to long-standing denizens of existing art institutions, and there are certain stock responses to the problems I have mentioned. One frequently suggested solution for the critical hegemony and social alienation of existing art institutions is that artists should simply abandon these institutions and reintegrate themselves into society at large, by producing socially and politically effective art. Quite independently of the objectionable implication that artists as such are sociocultural free variables who can be flexibly positioned in any convenient sociocultural niche according to the requirements of some prevailing political program, this solution is woefully unrealistic. Artists whose personal and professional investments in existing art institutions have been sufficient to yield them substantial professional returns are

8.
"Performance and the Fetishism of the Art Object," and "A Proposal for Pricing Works of Art," both in this volume.

9.
At this point, artists' control of these factors seems to be largely limited to their participation on peer-review funding panels, where they are required to exercise a degree of critical and financial responsibility for the art to be supported that is largely absent elsewhere in their professional lives.

typically rendered socially and economically powerless in the ways already described. They are, for those reasons, frequently incapable of creating art that can be genuinely socially and politically effective in society at large—that is, the society that includes art practitioners in their socioeconomic dimensions, as well as others, in its ranks. In order to do so realistically requires that they have not invested so heavily in those art institutions to begin with.

To see this, consider the distinction between those artists who deploy the medium of art, and their professional roles as artists, as politically effective instruments; and those who deploy their politics as an artistically and professionally effective instrument. Some artists identify themselves primarily as members of particular political groups, such as women, blacks, artists, or the working class, and utilize their creative talents in the service of political goals they share with other members of these groups. These artists can be distinguished by the fact that their politics and their political identities, rather than their professional aspirations, determine the aesthetics of their work. This is emphatically *not* to deny that their work meets stringent and intrinsically valuable aesthetic standards. But if their chosen artistic medium and content do not happen to meet the aesthetic standards imposed by existing art institutions, they will nevertheless refuse to modify them. They will tend to sacrifice professional, art-contextual acceptance for the sake of social and political effectiveness.

For example, a Chicana artist has put her formidable creative and organizational resources in the service of collaborating with disadvantaged Chicano youths to reclaim and publicly disseminate their common cultural heritage, through public wall murals that portray their own, otherwise largely neglected, social and political history in an artistic medium that is indigenous to Chicano culture. Similarly, a prominent white male artist has utilized the photodocumentation medium to present acute and highly revealing analyses of corporate exploitation of existing art institutions for their own ideological ends; analyses so effective that they have succeeded in provoking overt political confrontations within the art context that reveal the compliance of these institutions in their exploitation of art. The form, subject matter, and aims of both these artists' work express their identities as political and politically committed, rather than professionally ambitious, individuals. Neither the Chicana nor the white male artist utilize the work primarily as a vehicle for art-contextual success. Instead, it functions as a means or medium for the attainment of social and political goals—the recognition, legitimation, and social integration of Chicano culture, and the exposure of the ideological and socioeconomic underpinnings of "High Culture," respectively—to which its producer has a prior and overriding commitment.[10] Neither artist sacrifices the form of her or his work to the imperatives of art-contextual legitimation, for this would be to destroy its integrity as well as its political effectiveness. Artists who refuse to make this sacrifice are enabled to do so by psychological, socioeconomic, or professional resources that are largely independent of existing art institutions. Thus they are, by definition, those whose investment in the continued benefits of art-contextual legitimation is comparatively small to begin with. Hence they are not the artists to whom the suggestion to abandon the quest for legitimation, for the sake of politically effective art, properly applies.

By contrast, some political art, ostensibly collaborative or in the service of shared political goals, seems to function primarily as a means to the professional artistic success of its producer within existing art institutions, irrespective of its political effectiveness. This is not to deny that some such work may *be* politically effective. But often this effectiveness may seem a rather haphazard affair: A single work may exhibit, seemingly fortuitously, a degree of political depth or insight that is lacking in the artist's statements or other work; or the artist's commitment to a political project may require, as a necessary precondition for his participation, a position of professional visibility or authority; or the work may be formally sophisticated or interesting, but politically naive, ambiguous, or downright damaging in its effects on its audience; or it may communicate political views or experiences that are general enough to be innocuous or platitudinous on the one hand, or to carefully avoid application to the artist's personal situation on the other. What all such cases have in common is the subordination of the artist's political effectiveness to the demands of professional and artistic success. For to increase the work's political effectiveness would require sacrificing the likelihood of art-contextual legitimation. And this is a sacrifice that most artists who desire entry to existing art institutions simply are not willing to make.

Artists whose political effectiveness in society at large is thus constrained by their allegiance to the professional and aesthetic imperatives of existing art institutions are often accused of opportunism—as though it were a crime, or at least a moral flaw, to aspire to success and recognition by one's peers as an artist; as though, indeed, it were morally and politically suspect to affiliate and identify oneself primarily as an artist, rather than as a member of some other political group. But

10.
The latter art producer has described himself as taking a pragmatic stance toward his own status in the art world: He feels he sometimes compromises his political convictions in order to maintain his position (although it must be noted that this position itself increases the visibility and effectiveness of his critiques), while at other times he simply refuses to cooperate when this seems best.

this critical stance is itself morally suspect, for it encourages artists to ignore the political dimensions of their own roles as artists, and thereby to perpetuate their institutionalized powerlessness and dependence on existing art institutions. And this, in turn, further vitiates their capacity to be politically effective in society at large. For in conceiving art practice itself as politically neutral, or unworthy of serious attention, both these so-called opportunists and their politically correct critics seem implicitly to accept the same ideological fictions, generated by existing art institutions, that often obscure the artist's complicity in defending and perpetuating the very system of social institutions he purports, through his art, to criticize.

For example, one effect of the purported political neutrality of art practice within existing art institutions is that artists tend to have trouble getting other people to take their political views seriously. This is to be expected: If art practice is politically neutral, then art practitioners as such must have no firsthand experience of political oppression or exploitation. So what gives them the authority to pronounce on anyone else's? Moreover, artists themselves exacerbate the misleading impression of political neutrality by abdicating responsibility for the social and political implications of their work: If an artist's primary responsibility really is just to "make the stuff," rather than to control its critical and material destiny as well, why should the political subject matter of the "stuff" he happens to make count as evidence of his political credibility? If artists are not to be held responsible for the consequences of their own creative authority, it is hard to see why they should be recognized as socially and politically responsible agents at all. Thus the ideological fiction of art practice as politically neutral reinforces the powerlessness and dependence of artists on existing art institutions and vitiates their capacity effectively to change those institutions. And since, as we saw, those institutions themselves are founded on a particular politically selective distribution of socioeconomic resources, it thereby vitiates artists' capacities to change that distribution as well.

A second effect of the ideological fiction of the political neutrality of art-making is that the ability of professionally committed artists to make politically effective art is undermined in ways that are rendered invisible by their allegiance to this fiction. For politically effective art requires, at the very least, an understanding of the audience it is most politically effective for an artist to address, of the internal, socioeconomic dynamics of that audience, of what it is most politically effective to communicate to that audience, and of what media would be most effectively utilized to that end. These requirements are extremely difficult to satisfy, and it is harder still to know whether one has done so or not. But what can be said, at least, is that it is much harder to ascertain which audience it is in fact most politically effective for one to address, when one has a strong, unexamined—because purportedly innocuous—attachment to that audience or audiences that are most likely to confer upon one the professional or aesthetic approval that every artist needs.

Similarly, it is harder to become sufficiently familiar with the internal, socioeconomic dynamics of one's politically targeted audience to communicate with it successfully, when one is laboring under the delusion that the internal dynamics of the audience with which one has the greatest personal familiarity—that is, the art audience—is not socioeconomically determined at all but is rather responding to purely aesthetic imperatives. For this delusion ignores a major ingredient in an artist's successful communication with the art audience, that is, his extended, firsthand experience of the internal socioeconomic dynamics of that audience and the strategic skills of presentation he develops in response to its demands. This blindness to his own resources may, in turn, lead him to suppose it unnecessary to acquire a comparable familiarity with the internal socioeconomic dynamics of his politically targeted audience, or to develop comparable strategies for communicating successfully with it. Thus he may ascribe any problems of communication to its insufficiently developed aesthetic sensibility, when in fact it is his own provincial aesthetic sensibility that needs to be developed. The result of such insensitivity is likely to be political art that strikes its targeted audience as condescending, manipulative, naive, or irrelevant, and so further alienates the artist from the community at large, rather than integrating him.

Finally, it is harder to decide what media would be most socially and politically effective in communicating with one's targeted audience when one is influenced by a politically unexamined concern with those media and that content which define the dominant or currently fashionable standards of art production within existing art institutions, for then one's medium and content, in attempting to satisfy two sets of criteria that typically conflict, are more likely to satisfy neither.

Thus the real objection to much politically oriented but ineffective art is not that it is opportunistic; this complaint only masks an implicit assumption that aspiring to professional artistic success is politically illegitimate. The real objection is that it is generated from a position of institutionalized powerlessness and ideological self-deception. That such work should be politically ineffective or naive is to be expected.

11.

The problem, then, with many art practitioners who avow sincerely the thesis that artists should overcome their social alienation by working in the community for political reform through their art is that they are often in the grip of the ideological fictions earlier described, and thus believe it unnecessary to scrutinize their own positions as exploiters and victims within the art context. This leads them to believe that their positions, as artists, critics, and so on, are privileged in the ways those fictions prescribe. And this belief disposes them to protect and preserve their positions within existing art institutions, by exempting those positions from political criticism and deflecting attention exclusively to other communities. Thus, for example, a prominent and influential art practitioner whose political commitment is genuine and long-standing once expressed the opinion that artists should abandon their obsessions with the art world (however, the dependent and helpless are invariably obsessed with those who control them). Instead, it was claimed, artists should develop a more socially responsive art practice. This same art practitioner failed to appreciate the political implications of using an available photodocumentation of an artist's work as a book illustration of an entirely different genre without soliciting the artist's permission beforehand, and then pleading the pressure of a publication deadline as the excuse for not having done so. Of course this brand of exploitation of artists' work in the service of putatively overriding professional and aesthetic imperatives is a familiar story. But when coupled with an explicit conviction that artists should forget about such things and turn their attention instead to more important matters, it is a very revealing one.

This studied obliviousness to one's own politically manipulative or manipulated behavior within the art context has certain obvious advantages. For considered attention to its broader implication may require one to change it, or abdicate some of the power or prestige one has thereby enjoyed. A professionally ambitious art practitioner who also happens to make art with political subject matter, or whose reputation is predicated on his political and moral integrity, cannot, in good conscience, continue to exploit all the professional opportunities offered by existing art institutions, once he has acknowledged his complicity in maintaining the inherent inequities of these institutions. To choose to ignore that complicity in order to get on with the important business of making socially responsive art is thus in fact to put one's professional ambitions *ahead* of one's political and moral convictions. It is like throwing stones at a glass house from the safety of its inner courtyard.

Acknowledging or altering such priorities may have severe and violent repercussions in one's personal and social as well as one's professional relationships. Indeed, one index of one's real embeddedness in and commitment to existing art institutions is the degree to which explicit scrutiny of one's political role within them might endanger not only one's professional status but one's personal attachments as well. Thus it is not hard to understand why such scrutiny is usually resisted, or performed desultorily and self-deceptively. For it is finally one's self-conception, and the personal and social relations that buttress it, that are at stake.

This sort of ideological doublethink will be familiar to many women whose straightforward commitment to the civil rights and antiwar movements of the sixties were gradually transformed by their dawning awareness that they were being exploited primarily as waitresses, nurses, and camp followers by men who professed a radical political concern for the truly pressing issues at hand. Nor will it seem unfamiliar to those blacks or their children whose later years were embittered by the realization that their patriotic defense of the United States in the First and Second World Wars merely deflected their attention, temporarily, from the ongoing racism they experienced at home, rather than ameliorating it. That immediate and pressing political resentments can be made to seem trivial by focusing on distant objects of political concern is not news. That politically concerned art practitioners might practice this form of ideological evasion on themselves and others should not be surprising either. For I have suggested that this lack of self-awareness not only short-circuits their effectiveness in the social community at large but also perpetuates an ethnically and socioeconomically monolithic system of art institutions that tends to discourage or suppress the creativity of those who are denied access to them. Hence it would be surprising indeed if the exogenous art-political activity of individuals wedded to that system were effective in political reform or revolution over the long term, when their own interests are so inherently conservative.

12.

Many young artists respond to the apparent hypocrisy of politically committed art practitioners with disillusionment and cynicism, and it is easy to understand why. It is a general feature of ideological self-deception as I have described it that the more precarious one's actual position becomes relative to one's stated ideology, the more dogmatically one insists upon it, and the more defensively it functions to preserve one's self-esteem. Just like, for example, many members of the Progressive Labor Party, politically committed art practitioners often seem to become increasingly dogmatic, self-righteous, and impervious to rational argument, the more seeming inconsistencies in their positions come to light. The more completely they conceal their professional ambitions and self-interests from their own critical scrutiny, the more and more politically correct than thou they seem to become; the more institutional rewards they garner, the more pristine their aura of political incorruptibility, at the same time that their political rhetoric becomes increasingly strident, moralistic, and inflexible. This can be an alienating and demoralizing spectacle for artists whose moral and political concerns are both inchoate and extend naturally to questions about their own personal integrity. That political commitment in art is the best game in town, or just another self-serving scam that one may as well play for what it's worth, may seem to be the obvious conclusion. Indeed it may seem that the only way of genuinely preserving one's personal moral integrity in the face of this apparent hypocrisy is to shrug one's shoulders at the inevitability of co-optation, or retreat from any active political involvement altogether.

But shrugging one's shoulders is disingenuous. It is co-optation too willingly embraced and responsibility too easily abdicated. We have already seen that the factors determining this kind of social irresponsibility are deeply embedded within the structure of existing art institutions, regardless of how it is rationalized by those who benefit from it. In the final analysis, there can be no retreat, for the issues raised are not false or superficial ones, regardless of who raises them. I have already tried to suggest some of the questions about creative autonomy that most artists *invariably* encounter, regardless of their political orientation. The only alternative to confronting them head-on is the creation of some other, conservative ideological fiction that rationalizes one's dismissal of them—the value of art for art's sake, for example, or of the pursuit of self-interest, or of free enterprise, or of learned helplessness as an adaptive survival strategy—that is just as precarious and self-deceptive as its ideological opponent.

This is to suggest that sustained, apolitical cynicism *as such* is not a *psychologically* viable position for any moderately socialized individual. It engenders the same brand of defensive, self-protective rationalization as any other stance that requires us to ignore obvious facts about our position.[11] It requires that we insulate ourselves not only from interaction with our politically correct nemeses but also from our own sense of self-respect. For that is the only perspective from which the politically hypocritical behavior of others gives us anything to deplore: If we had no psychological investment in the ideals of genuine political reform to begin with, there would be nothing in their behavior to disillusion us. And this would require us to deny that the original issues of concern to us were deserving of concern in the first place. Of course I do not mean to claim that people never abandon their political and ethical ideals; but merely that the consequent feelings of self-dislike and misanthropy are a high price to pay for doing so. They are hardly conducive to long-standing personal or professional attachments of any kind.

Rather than risk the degree of psychological alienation sustained apolitical cynicism would bring in its path, many disillusioned artists consequently replace those initial feelings with some variant on the conservative ideology already described; or perhaps merely with the uneasy Neoplatonic conviction that being a true ser-

11.
This point is discussed at greater length in part 3 of my *Rationality and the Structure of the Self* (in progress).

vant of Art is incompatible with sectarian political involvement. But all of these stories are ideological fictions in that they are both false and serve the interests of an institutionally conservative political program. They are thus no less political than those they oppose. And since these institutions function to vitiate the creative autonomy of their practitioners in the ways already described, such ideological fictions are particularly unconvincing when adopted by artists whose own creative autonomy is at stake.

13.

A variant on the suggestion that artists should abandon the art context for the "real" world, in order to ameliorate their alienation from society at large, is that art practitioners should work to bring the art preserved and engendered by existing art institutions into the surrounding communities; there should be more funding for public and open-air projects, as well as programs to "bring culture to the masses." This formulation of the proposal makes clear, I think, one major objection to it. It is the condescending assumption of critical hegemony that those outside of existing art institutions require cultural enrichment, merely by virtue of lacking access to what we are often pleased to refer to as High Art. Having effectively collaborated to deny them access to begin with, we are now to confer it in a disinterested display of charity and moral concern. But Euroethnic culture is but one among many, all of which are similarly enriching. The "masses" often targeted for enrichment have their own rich, highly developed ethnic cultures, and therefore do not need Euroethnic art for the imprimatur of aesthetic cultivation. What they do need is more economic and social legitimation of their indigenous cultures from existing art institutions, so that they will be more disposed to protect and develop rather than abandon them as they increasingly achieve political and economic parity. And this socioeconomic legitimation is a cultural resource that art practitioners within existing art institutions are in the unique position to redistribute.

Again, this is not to maintain that Euroethnic art is not worthy of dissemination in the culture at large; but rather to point out that there is much other ethnic art that is already out in the surrounding society and has an even greater claim to be brought into existing art institutions and appreciated on its own terms. The idea that formalist art should hold a preeminent place in the absolute scale of values, and so appropriate preeminent space in our ethnically and socioeconomically variegated cultural scheme, is another ideological fiction, generated by existing art institutions, that is difficult to justify objectively.

Finally, then, we devolve onto the function of various ideological fictions themselves, which prevent us from seeing clearly our own conditions and acting intelligently to improve them, which delude us as to what our best interests are and how they are to be achieved, and which reinforce our involuntary allegiance to practices and conventions that distort our vision and stunt our creativity as political and artistic individuals. Our prereflective or unquestioning acceptance of these fictions would seem to be at least one primary culprit in perpetuating the shared illusion of power, responsibility, and value within existing art institutions. The question then naturally arises of what to do about this situation.

I should like to conclude this discussion by suggesting that one necessary condition of effective political reform of any social institution is a clear understanding of how that institution functions, and of one's own role in perpetuating it. Just as blacks and women needed to have a clear enough understanding of their own rights and best interests to recognize that they were being exploited by racist and sexist institutions and how, in order to take effective political action to combat that oppression, similarly with art practitioners, regardless of their particular political affiliation. As purveyors and custodians of contemporary culture, art practitioners have a tremendous potential for influencing the course of social change. But as long as they fail to recognize the ways in which that potential is being hampered by their own self-defeating ideological allegiances, they will be unable to utilize it in the service of their aesthetic and political interests.

Yet artists, unlike blacks and women, it may be said, are conditioned by their art production to be active agents, not passive contemplators, and their ego-investment in their work is in any case too great to change that orientation. But there is no biological necessity about a socially conditioned disinclination to perform the difficult and often thankless task of political self-analysis. It is not as though artists are congenitally incapacitated by having right cerebral hemispheres the size of a watermelon and left cerebral hemispheres the size of a peanut. As women who have experienced the benefits of consciousness-raising collectives already know, the mere discovery that one's ostensibly unique experiences in a certain role are in fact universal is itself a major step toward altering those experiences for the better. I believe that artists, and other concerned art practitioners, would benefit by taking seriously the consciousness-raising model with respect to their participation in existing art institutions. For if we do not spent more time collectively contemplating our socioeconomic navels, we will continue to be led by our umbilical cords in the wrong direction.

III. Art Criticism 1984–1992:

Art-World Practice and Real-World Politics

14. Performance: The Problematic Solution

Written in 1984 and previously unpublished.

I want to talk about recent performance art as the solution to two connected problems, and then raise some further problems about this solution. By analyzing performance art as the solution to two connected problems, I don't mean to imply that any actual performance artist necessarily conceives her or his work in that way, or is motivated to do performance by that conception.

The first problem I have in mind is the problem of *interpretive control,* that is, of how an artist can successfully retain control over the cultural interpretation of her work. The problem arises naturally to the extent that the work functions as a medium of experience or communication between the artist and her audience. By a "medium of experience or communication," I mean an art object or state of affairs that is (1) physically separate from both the artist and the audience; (2) epistemologically accessible to both; (3) spatially and/or temporally intermediate between them; and (4) instrumental in effecting some experiential change in the audience that is planned, intended, hoped for, or expected by the artist. The problem is that these plans or expectations can always misfire because the work itself is noncommital and susceptible to the varying expectations its audience brings to it. The resulting interpretations of the work are not necessarily those that the artist planned or expected. This means that the work is also susceptible to *mis*interpretation. That is, the work may cause experiential changes in the audience that the artist intended actively to avoid, or explicitly rejects as a misreading of or projection onto the work. This may be a consequence of literal miscommunication, as when the artist deploys an idiom that is unfamiliar to her audience, or of misevaluation, as when the artist and the audience disagree about the value of the idiom, or the way it is used: Pedestrian monotony to the audience may have been pristine simplicity to the artist. So of course artists and their audiences may share the same cultural idiom without necessarily agreeing on the evaluation of the work.

The second problem is the problem of *transformation,* that is, how an artist can resolve the tension between personal significance and aesthetic significance in her work. The problem arises naturally to the extent that there is a dichotomy between the specific values and concerns that motivate an artist to make a work—for example, a personal obsession, professional ambition, peer pressure, fascination with a particular topic or medium, ingrained habit, and so on—and the more generalized, abstract, normative expectations by which the work is critically evaluated by its audience. This is not to deny that each member of the audience has a specific and personal response to the work but just to observe that that response is understood as an instance of some value or concern that is framed in general terms when articulated. In this context, the dichotomy between the personal and the aesthetic is coextensive with the dichotomies between the concrete and the specific, on the one hand, and the abstract and the general, on the other (so-called autobiographical art falls on the side of the abstract and the general, according to this taxonomy, because it deploys the personal as an exemplar of the general in order to transform the concrete into the aesthetically provocative). I assume that artists always, by definition, are motivated by concrete and specific personal concerns to make their work, regardless of the degree of generality of the content of those concerns. The problem arises because they are also called upon to transform those concerns into an artifact of universalized aesthetic significance, that is, one that addresses directly the generalized normative expectations of its intended audience. Thus the artist must not only share a common idiom of communication with her audience and use it in the "right" way. She must also preserve the impact of the personal, concrete, and specific origins of the work within a wider, self-created context of meaning.

Now many artists might deny being influenced by either of these imperatives. Some might claim, for example, that they work only for themselves, without regard to their audience's expectations. But even in cases where this is true, it doesn't imply an absence of the pressure I've described. Sometimes an artist needn't worry about her audience because she has successfully internalized the generalized, aesthetic standards by which her audience judges the work. She identifies fully with the aesthetic criteria she has been taught good art must aspire to and conceives her work—perhaps even her life—in those terms. Here to work for herself just *is* to work for her audience's validation. On the other hand, an artist may not need to worry about her audience's critical evaluation because the audience has fully internalized aesthetic criteria generated solely by her past work. In this case, whatever she produces is by definition good art; to work for her audience is to work for herself alone.

Other artists might deny that personal or subjective considerations have anything to do with their work, which, they may claim, is motivated solely by abstract, formal, general, or philosophical concerns. This doesn't deflect the imperatives either. For without a personal and subjective psychological investment in the abstract and general, they would remain passive contemplators, unmoved to actualize those concerns in a work. So here, too, there is a pressure to preserve and transform these personal concerns into universal ones.

This means that an artist must view her work from a bifurcated perspective: from her own as a concrete, individualized subject on one hand, and from that of abstract and generalized criteria on the other. This perspective is bifurcated because it presupposes that the dichotomies between the specific and the general, the individual and the universal, the subjective and the social, and the personal and the aesthetic, are replicated in the dichotomy between the artist's role and the audience's. We must view our work from its audience's perspective, in order to understand what in general is being required of us as artists. In this sense, any artwork presupposes a certain degree of self-consciousness on the part of its producer.

Maintaining the balance between the two sides of these dichotomies within an artist's vision is a neat trick. Excessive subjectivism is seen as self-indulgence, a private language game, or a simple lack of artistic fluency. Excessive generality, on the other hand, makes the work itself seem a dependent illustration of a dogma, a trite or vacuous cosmic formula, or a recondite excuse for analysis. The difficulty of maintaining the balance is further exacerbated to the extent that the artist has an overriding psychological investment in one side of the bifurcated perspective; for example, if one's aesthetic dogma just *is* inarticulate subjectivism; or if the abstract, universal, impersonal perspective is the only one that one finds psychologically and socially tolerable, in life as well as in art. On the other hand, bridging the gap between them seems to demand both the partial obliteration of the artist's subjectivity and the partial renunciation of the aspiration to aesthetic universality: To satisfy every applicable critical ideal, or speak well for or to everyone, is to be no one in particular. It is to feel oneself impersonally detached from one's subjective commitments, as well as subjectively alienated from one's general aesthetic ones, and so to situate one's work in the uneasy limbo where it can be everything and nothing to everyone and no one. Thus it appears that harmonious resolution of the problem of transformation is elusive. Either the artist strains for an uneasy balance between these standpoints from one side of the bifurcation, or else straddles the chasm at the risk of disappearing into the crack.

The problems of interpretive control and of transformation are interconnected in certain ways. An artist who strains to transcend her subjectivity in the service of abstract, universalized aesthetic criteria aspires to the ideal of art she intends and hopes her audience will share (hence her aspiration to the abstract and universal is to be distinguished from the attempt to give an audience whatever one thinks they'll want). If her work in fact fails to transcend her subjectivity, then it will serve *some* general aesthetic criteria only if her audience's aesthetic ideal is itself an ideal of subjectivism. In this case the reproach of self-indulgence is confuted by respect for the mysteries of primitive and unacculturated genius, which works through, beyond, and in spite of the artist's conscious aesthetic aspirations. This stance provides justification for the beliefs that artists shouldn't think too much, that too much self-consciousness is a bad thing, that the artist's role is just to "make the stuff," and so on. On this ideal, art is precisely the indulgence of the blind and presocialized drives and impulses of the self that enable the magical manifestations of genius. These manifestations are not, then, to be denigrated to the status of mere private language. Rather, they are a quasi-theatrical confrontation with the forces of nature and history, and the artist's personal lexicon of symbols, images, and materials become cryptic magical artifacts of the divine.

However, this cultural interpretation requires more than that an artist's audience critically evaluate the work from a subjectivist stance that thereby complements the artist's own. It must also acknowledge or share the artist's lexicon of symbols. This is important, because a lack of comprehension of those symbols enables the audience to reiterate the distinction between genius and self-indulgence *within* the constraints of subjectivism. Thus, for example, an obsession with genitalia, failed romance, or nuclear weaponry may be accepted as valid syntactical elements within a lexicon that happens to exclude as boring or self-indulgent an interest in the diaristic format, raising children, or unemployment. This is where the problem of interpretive control re-enters. Even if an artist's audience is sympathetic to the subjectivist stance, the work will be misinterpreted and misevaluated if the artist and the audience do not share the same idiom of communication to a greater extent.

On the other hand, abstract conceptualization is no safeguard against such misinterpretation. An artist who approaches the great divide from the other side may have comparable difficulties. Here the stance is the abstract, the analytical, the metaphysically inclusive. The reproach of triteness or impersonality is superseded by our awe before the image of Icarus, soaring heavenward in his manmade wings and risking destruction by the sun; and by our respect for the artist who, in aspiring to the cosmic and universal, risks for the sake of art the destruction of the tenuous boundaries of the individual self. The bird's-eye view may damage our capacity for empathy with increasing distance, but the scope achieved seems worth the risk, and the artist who attempts it a hero. The challenge is then to define and embody the cosmic in a discrete artifact that retains its cosmic significance.

But meeting this challenge successfully requires intersubjective agreement, not only that the artifact in question function as a signifier but also that it function as the same signifier for its producer and its audience. If all viewer-participants do not agree on the particular significance of the artifact, then to the uninitiated its main function may seem to be that of an inconsequential object whose capacity to generate polysyllabic words, long-winded conversations, articles, dissertations, and books is mysterious indeed. Here again the distinction between the impersonally trite and the cosmically profound may be reintroduced, *within* the abstract, metaphysically inclusive stance. For, to the uninitiated observer, the aspiration to the abstract and universal may itself be viewed as the mundane epiphenomenon of disembodied intellectual flatulence.

Suppose, however, that the problem of interpretive control is magically solved, that is, that the subjectivism of the artist is complemented by an audience equally committed to precisely that form of subjectivism, and similarly for the artist with cosmic aspirations. The problem of transformation nevertheless remains for both, and in much the same form. The failure of transformation for the subjectivist leaves the audience locked in a self-reinforcing cycle of stimulation by and contemplation of the object, and so of the objective boundaries between them. One leaves such an experience with a sense of appreciation tempered by loneliness, and an almost palpable resentment for the inchoate self-containedness of the object, which effectively buttresses the physical limits of the individual self. Abstract comprehension then becomes a violation of those limits, rather than a transcendence of them.

The failure of transformation of the cosmically inclined artwork may affect its audience similarly. Here, too, the work reinforces certain boundaries of the subjective self. Of course the boundaries are drawn differently, by the limits of abstract comprehension rather than concrete physicality. The work is an instrument that transports us to the realm of the abstract and general, from the perspective of which we impersonally contemplate the physicality of the object, and of our own bodies, with surprise, detachment, and annoyance. Compulsive awareness of these embodiments again becomes an intrusion and a humiliating reduction to the pedestrian.

In both cases, the failure of transformation of the artwork bifurcates and truncates the sense of self, and draws it into a solipsistic cycle of self-aggrandizement, from which its truncated parts are excluded as alien. Solipsism and xenophobia replace self-transcendence, and the larger, more complexly unified possibilities of meaning are lost.

We are left, then, with two interesting dichotomies with which to scrutinize artworks that are physically independent of their producers and their audience. There is the contrast between the subjectivistic and the cosmic stance of an artist toward her work. Bisecting this is the contrast between what I shall describe as the *comprehending* and *uncomprehending* stance of the audience toward that same work, according to whether it shares with the artist the same cultural idiom or not, respectively. From the comprehending stance, the artist's cosmic work aspires to heroism and self-sacrifice. From the uncomprehending stance, it is inflated and depersonalized.

I suggested that one conceivable resolution of the subjective-cosmic dichotomy was unappealing because it required the artist's partial renunciation of subjective obsessions in the service of the abstract and universal, and of her more general and inclusive commitments in the service of the personal. The result would be work that resolved, though unsuccessfully, the comprehending-uncomprehending dichotomy as well. Like watery coffee, it would be palatable to everyone because stimulating to no one, self-indulgent and depersonalized, inarticulate and inflated, a work neither of genius nor of heroism. Hence just as the problem of transformation cannot be solved by work that straddles the subjective-cosmic dichotomy, similarly the problem of interpretive control cannot be solved by work that seeks the median range of an audience's competence in a certain cultural idiom. Acceptable solutions to these problems must lie elsewhere.

Earlier I argued that the problems of interpretive control and of transformation arose naturally out of the ontological status of a work as independent both of the artist and of the audience. Just as it functions as an opaque medium of communication, susceptible to a wide variety of interpretations by the artist and the audience, it also functions as an intermediary between the artist's personal creative drives and obsessions, and the audience's more generalized aesthetic expectations. I've just now been suggesting that work that deliberately seeks the mean with respect to these dichotomies doesn't resolve the dichotomies successfully. This is not to suggest that art that is physically independent of its producer and its audience is incapable of doing so. But if these problems arise out of the physically discrete character of the work, then we might expect to find at least some resolutions to these dichotomies in work with a different ontological status.

One possibility is suggested by the way I've framed the discussion so far. Though I acknowledged the problem of interpretive control at the outset, I often spoke as though there were no further distinctions to be made between the cosmic or the subjective stance the artist adopts and the success of the work at least as an exemplar of that stance. For though we might disagree about whether a work is cosmically profound or just impersonally inflated, I left unmentioned the possibility that the work might even be more out of the artist's interpretive control than that: for example, that the artist's straining toward metaphysical inclusiveness might result in a work universally viewed as an entirely idiosyncratic and personal fetish, with no further interest or significance; or alternately, that the artist's preoccupation with, say, her particular familial relationships might result in a work viewed as having inflated metaphysical pretensions. These are possibilities, but they become less probable the more contact with the audience an artist experiences (for example, they are more likely to materialize during the first year of art school than the last). At least one reason for this is fairly straightforward. Critical feedback on a work enables the artist to correct or modify her strategies for communicating through the object more successfully, just as in the mastery of any medium of communication. Another reason is that the more contact with the audience the artist has, the more familiar it becomes with her personal concerns, aesthetic strategies, and cultural idioms, and the more susceptible the audience becomes to modifying its normative expectations in light of these. Thus the information flow operates in both directions, because both the artist's and the audience's responses are mutually adjusting.

This is to suggest that radical loss of interpretive control is mitigated by two features of the artist-audience relationship. First, it is to a certain degree *confrontational*. By this I mean that if the artist doesn't catalyze some response in the audience through the medium of the work (for example, if the audience is both physically and metaphysically absent, or overstimulated, or asleep), or if the audience doesn't convey that response in some form to the artist, a primitive but necessary transaction in the artist-audience relationship remains uncompleted. The artist confronts her audience with the work, and the audience confronts the artist with its response to the work. The artist refines her swing each time she steps up to bat, while the audience refines its fielding skills.

This brings out a second feature of the artist-audience relationship: It is *didactic*. By this I mean that the artist gradually teaches the audience her concerns, strategies, and idioms, and the audience simultaneously teaches the artist its potential, its limitations, and its normative conventions of judgment and communication. If some such degree of mutual enlightenment doesn't occur, the consequence can be devastating: frustration and impotence in the artist plus hostility, indifference, or incomprehension in the audience, or—what is even worse—solipsistic self-congratulation on the part of both that shared and fundamentally parochial aesthetic prejudices remain inviolate. The preservation of interpretive control, then, is at least partly a function of a work's didacticism and confrontationality.

In talking about the problem of transformation, I suggested that the dichotomy between the concrete, personal, and subjective on one hand, and the abstract, aesthetic, and universal on the other could be contingently located in the distinction between artist and audience, although multiply reintroduced within the artist's and the audience's concerns, respectively. In this sense I ignored the possibility of a more radical problem of transformation, that is, the problem that would occur if the dichotomy were not contingently but absolutely located in the artist-audience distinction. Under these conditions, transformation would be impossible. The artist's creative impulses would find expression only in concrete, specific, presocialized, idiosyncratic products, whereas the role of the audience would be to impose on them general and abstract categories of aesthetic interpretation. Clearly this would be an absurd and impossible division of labor that reduced the artist's role to that of bare producer and the audience's to that of pure evaluator.

But it is worth spelling out why this division of labor is impossible. One obvious reason is that artists and their audiences *collaborate* on the transformative status of a work. There is no objective matter of fact on the issue of whether or to what extent a work successfully transforms the personal interests of the artist into an artifact of universal significance. The term *universal* is always relativized to a particular audience's interests, norms, and expectations. One woman's universality is, so to speak, another's subjectivity. This can be seen by comparing the cases described earlier, in which the artist shares with the audience a common cultural idiom and particular lexicon of symbols, yet the work merely reinforces and reiterates their shared interests and prejudices, rather than enabling the audience to situate them in a larger and more complexly coherent context of significance. Stipulate only a slight disparity between the artist's lexicon and the audience's; assume, too, the audience's active participation in the task of rendering the work aesthetically intelligible, and the possibility of transformation reemerges as a byproduct of that task. These conditions become normative guidelines in the artist's project of transformation: first, the search for the "individual voice"—individual, because the assumption is that one must work from premises different from one's audience's in order to elicit from that audience not just recognition but realization; second, the abdication of a certain degree of interpretive control to the audience in advance. Collaborative contact between the artist and her audience, then, mitigates the impossibility of transformation in the work. But we now see that the problems of interpretive control and of transformation cannot always be solved conjointly.

A second reason why the extreme division of labor earlier described is impossible is because the relationship between artists and audience, mediated by the artwork, is *transpersonal*. By this I mean simply that no individual subject, whether artist or audience member, is so constituted that none of her subjective components—her abstract beliefs, specific perceptions, general interests, concrete impulses, and so on—are shared with the artist or audience. Artist-audience collaboration is possible, in part, because both are transpersonal entities, even if a shared cultural idiom is lacking. The transpersonality of the artist-audience relationship enable both to move simultaneously (some might say necessarily) away from the concrete specificity of the fashioned object, to seek the more general context of significance that transforms it.

The two features of the artist-audience relationship that permit interpretive control—its confrontationality and its didacticism—in conjunction with the two features that enable artistic transformation—its collaborativeness and its transpersonality—invite artists to assume the guise of art object in order to achieve these ends. The great advantages here in becoming an art object for one's audience are sentient consciousness, memory, and responsive agency. Unlike physically discrete art objects, artist-performers have the capacity to register and comprehend their catalytic effects on their audiences directly and immediately, and — within the constraints of their intended program — fine-tune their behavior and modify it accordingly where necessary. Of course the structure of a performance may be too highly scripted to allow much flexibility in this respect. But memory preserves this information for future use. The confrontationality of the unmediated artist-audience relationship underscores the inherent didacticism of art, except that in this case it is not the object that is telling you something indirectly through stasis, form, situation, action, and speech. Instead, it is a subject telling you something through stasis, form, situation, action, and speech. The opportunity for telling you something directly thus arises out of the unmediated confrontationality of performance art.

Many people feel uncomfortable with this aspect of performance art. They feel preached or condescended to, or they feel that the "message" of the work is conveyed too literally or gracelessly. Certainly these complaints may be justified in some cases. But often they are predicated on a view of art objects as passive by nature, and so as telling you something only fortuitously, or by your leave, if at all. The passivity of the art object is often extended, as a complement, to the artist: If the work does manage to tell you something, this is assumed to be no fault of the artist's. I believe this view is inappropriate when applied to any art, and even more so when applied to performance art, and that we are all still in the throes of adjusting culturally and psychologically to the power of performance artists to tell us things neither with averted eyes, nor bowed head nor shuffling, nor distant metaphors, nor circumlocutions in delivering the message, and so to take full responsibility for the messages they deliver.

This is an advantage because, among other things, it means that the inherent didacticism of art can reemerge from the closet, to which it has been consigned since the late nineteenth century, now as one direction in a two-way street. Performance artists engage in an explicit dialogue with their audiences, of much the same sort audiences often engage in among themselves, where inflections of language, gestures, timing, a receptive or opinionated stance, and other subtly fine-tuned interpersonal responses can make all the difference between whether a work "goes over" or not. It also makes it harder for the artist to abdicate completely interpretive control over the work. If the prevarication "Don't ask me what it means, I just make the stuff" is unconvincing, the new, improved version, "I just do (or say) the stuff," or even "am the stuff," would be even more so. The confrontationality and didacticism of performance art thus requires performance artists to reclaim at least a certain degree of interpretive control over their work; for as art objects, they are not just animate or inanimate objects but socialized subjects as well, with some degree of skill at forecasting the effects of their social behavior on other, similarly socialized subjects.

That performance art is in part a dialogue among artist and audience members, all of whom are similarly but not identically socialized, makes collaboration possible. Artist and audience can collaborate in the project of transformation, when the artist must work to communicate and the audience must work to comprehend—not too hard, of course, for fear of aesthetic ennervation, but hard enough to require of the artist a refinement of her beliefs and impulses, and of the audience a restructuring of its response habits. In performance art, the task for both is easier and harder than when the art is physically independent of the artist and of the audience. It is easier because we begin with certain basic, shared categories for making sense of a person's behavior—of belief, motive, purpose, intention, and the like—that we lack for physically discrete art objects. Until we have situated them in some sociocultural context of significance, they are impenetrable. But the task is harder, for precisely the same reason. To rely too strongly on our a priori assumptions about how those categories are to be deployed in comprehending a performance obscures the cues by which the artist indicates the areas of dissonance. We may initially feel more familiar with performance art, not only because it has precedents in the entertainment world but, more important and unlike art objects, because performers are human beings. But this sense of familiarity can be deceptive, when it blinds us to a cultural idiom that is subtly or radically different from, though coexistent with, our own. Both artist and audience need to recognize the areas of dissonance and lack of overlap among various cultural idioms, in order for the phenomenon of transformation to occur, at least at this stage of the game.

The similar but nonidentical socialization of artist and audience reinforces the transpersonality of their relationship as well. Performers are unlike other art objects in having the innate capacity for abstraction and universalization. So a performer is never just an animate physical object, in motion for our applause. The sensory cues we receive from these particular objects remind us that they bring their contexts of significance with them. Thus they promise the tantalizing possibility of conceptual communion, of shared significance, of participation in the universal as an epiphenomenon of the subjective and concrete. This is to be distinguished from the cosmic impersonal as an artistic stance. The performer is not merely an instrumental medium through which metaphysical inclusiveness is achieved. In being a human subject, through the inevitable complexity of her motives and responses, and our attempt to comprehend them, the performer offers a double enticement not only of insight, realization, grasping the work conceptually, understanding it, getting it right, and so on, but also of confirmation by participation, of having the object actively confirm our realization through the conceptually charged pattern of physical responses and interactions by which we mutually chart our relationship. Think of this as transformation qua self-transcendence. What essentially differentiates this from the cosmic stance as such is the necessity and intrinsic importance of multiple, subjectively limited concrete selves, each bringing to the performance experience their tenuous physical and psychic boundaries, and their ingrained dispositions to alteration, attack, self-preservation, reception, and surrender—and the hope that these dispositions will not remain untested.

Transformation as self-transcendence is, at any rate, one of the promises and possibilities that performance art offers. In closing, I'd like to express some reservations about how completely that promise can be fulfilled, in the form of some vignettes.

Most of us have had the following species of experiences at dinner parties at one time or another:

Case 1. The person with whom you are talking is a brilliant conversationalist. She expounds at great length, with wit, insight, and erudition on some topic that is close to your heart. You don't want to be rude and interrupt her, but it's hard not to, because her words stimulate an overwhelming enthusiasm on your part to contribute to the flow of ideas, to engage her intellect rather than merely observe it. You begin to get irritated as you realized how difficult it's going to be to get a word in edgewise. At this juncture, one of two things happen:

1.a. You succeed in making a comment. She cursorily acknowledges your point, nominally weaves it into the conceptual flow, and sails onward with the development of her view.

1.b. You don't succeed in making a point. Finally, your repeated and frustrated impulses to do so subside, and you resign yourself to passive admiration of her scintillating intellect.

In both cases, you feel powerless to arrest or alter a flow of behavior whose programming seems strangely independent of the fact and details of your presence. Were her talk less stimulating, you would feel lectured to, and angry. When it finally ceases, you are unprepared. Your mind goes blank. She has finally passed you the ball and you fumble it. As you retreat, you comfort yourself with the reflection that you probably didn't perform too badly after all, as you clearly gave her what she most wanted, namely, an audience. But you feel excluded somehow. When you next meet her, you find her conversation less scintillating. In fact, you have trouble following it.

Case 2. Again you are with a sophisticated wit. She says the most outrageous things, a real iconoclast, attacking all your most deeply cherished prejudices. You are irritated and bemused, and spoiling for a good scuffle. You begin mentally to formulate some devastating arguments and observations that prove conclusively that she is Out to Lunch. But this time the trouble is not that she declaims rather than converses. It is that she speaks only in declarative propositions, none of which are preceded by intentional modifiers such as "I believe that . . . ," "It seems to me that . . . ," "I get the impression that . . . ," "In my opinion . . . ," and so on. She purports to be asserting matters of fact that you privately dispute. To contradict her outright seems rude and graceless; to interject a quavering "I beg to differ . . ." is wimpy. There is no way of getting her off the truth podium without seeming disagreeably contentious yourself, and so once again you are speechless. You issue a nervous giggle and retreat, feeling angry at her for what you now perceive as her arrogance, and at yourself for your helplessness. In the future you come to regard her as forthright and imaginative but also dangerously dogmatic, and you vow, with regret, that if she ever runs for office, you will not vote for her.

Case 3. Again you are in conversation. You express your opinion with your usual eloquence and subtlety. Your somewhat lengthy remarks are greeted with dead silence, followed by a few nervous giggles. You feel you have failed to ignite the conversation and so try again, by dilating at length on your subject, aggressively and provocatively. Your audience retreats even further. They are all smiling uncomfortably and watching you. You feel betrayed, rejected, and puzzled.

Performance art necessarily has human subjectivity as part of its content. To situate human subjectivity in the role of an art object is to invite the audience to engage with it, and with its own subjectivity, and to transcend them. But this requires a high degree of skill in interpersonal fine-tuning, and attention to the subtle psychologistics of social interaction. Most of us, who have been trained to pummel, slash, and besmirch objects in the isolation of our studios, have yet to achieve the requisite expertise.

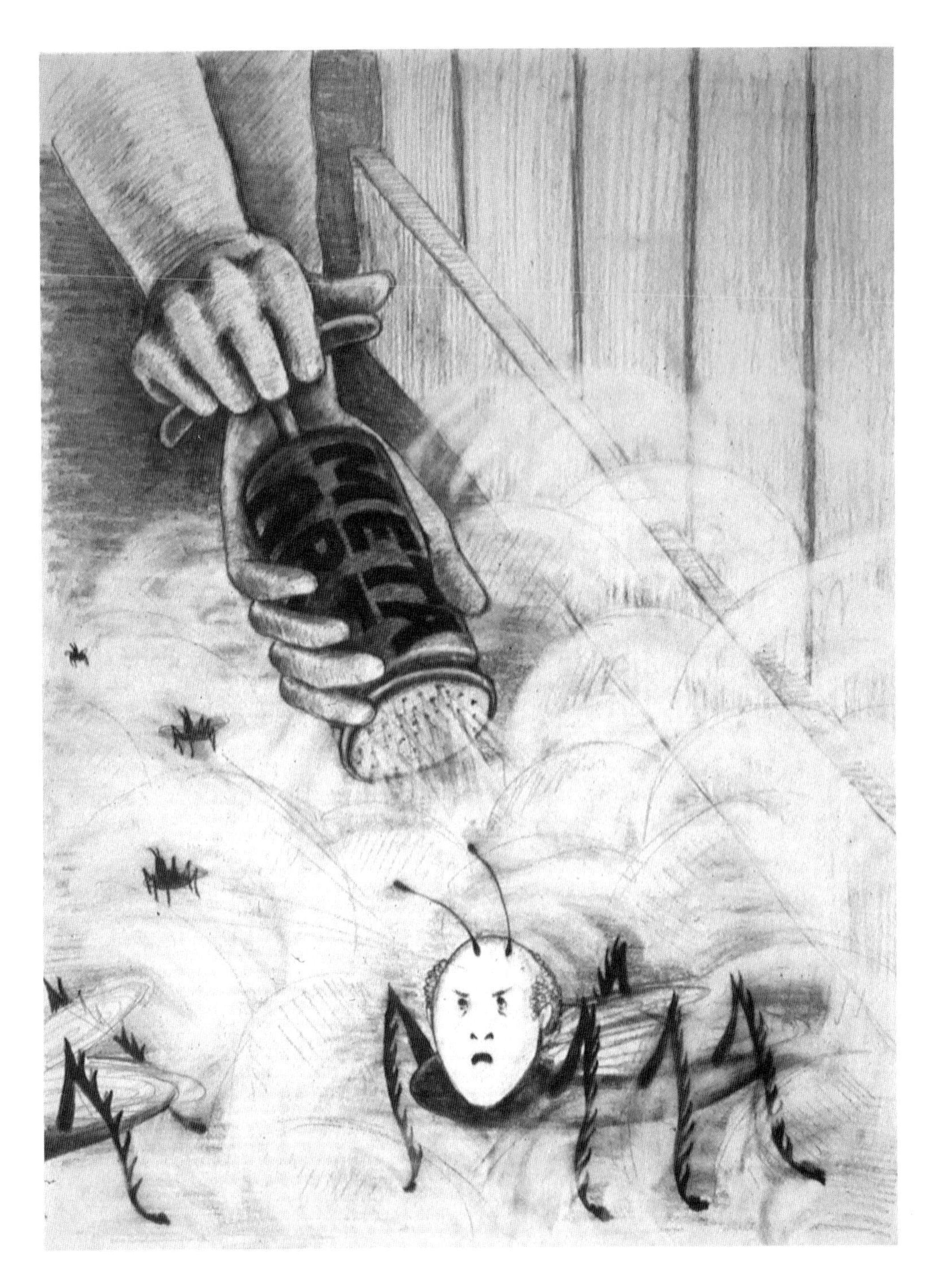

11.
Kuspit Extermination Fantasy (1987). Courtesy John Weber Gallery, collection University of Colorado at Boulder Art Museum.

15. An Open Letter to Donald Kuspit

Written in 1987 and first published in *Real Life* 17–18 (Winter 1987–Spring 1988), pp. 2–11.

Dear Donald,

I was astonished to learn that you had decided to publish your essay, "Adrian Piper: Self-Healing through Meta-Art," which had been dropped from my retrospective exhibition catalog (*Adrian Piper: Reflections 1967–1987* [New York: The Alternative Museum, 1987]), in the periodical you edit, *Art Criticism* (3 no. 3 [September 1987], pp. 9–16). As you know, I do not think it is one of your better efforts. But I was even more troubled when, upon reading it, I saw how few changes you had made in it in response to the criticisms you had requested from me. It is, of course, well known that you disregard what artists say about their own work as a matter of policy, and that is certainly your prerogative. But my comments were directed at your work, not mine. And they were intended to improve that work in accordance with the intellectual standards I assumed we both shared, quite irrespective of my view of my own work—or, indeed, of your view of it. Your decision virtually to ignore my comments leads me to infer that you have modified your policy to exclude what artists have to say about anything, not just about their work. But I believe that in this case, it might have been of some benefit to the success of your essay to distinguish the criticisms made from the person who made them; and at least to take the former seriously, if not the latter. For your recollection I reproduce those criticisms below, unchanged except to quote your own contributions more extensively, and occasionally to interpolate my own reflections on the peculiar intellectual decisions you have made in revising the essay for publication.

18 February 1987

Dear Donald,

When you phoned to tell me you'd finished the essay and were sending me a copy, you suggested that I "sit on it for a few days" and then get back to you with my thoughts on it. I've done that (I received the essay on Saturday), and my thoughts follow:

Page 9:

[all page references are to the published text]: *"Over the years, Adrian Piper has made the following statements: 'I have always had a very strong moralistic streak' (*Meat Into Meat, *October 1968); 'I have always had a very strong individualistic streak' (*Untitled Performance for Max's Kansas City, *April 1970); 'I have always had a very strong mystical streak' (*Food for the Spirit, *July 1971); 'I have always had a very strong aggressive streak' (*The Mythic Being: Getting Back, *July 1975)."*

> This is a factual mistake. The statements you quote were all written within a few days of one another in late 1980, in response to a written request from Nancy Buchanan that I write up a photo-text presentation of some of my early performances to be selected for a feature in *High Performance* (4, no. 1 [Spring 1981]). A quick phone call to Nancy or Linda Burnham will confirm this (as will my correspondence from that time).
>
> I also have some reservations about your discussing and quoting selectively from unpublished material that is not accessible to the general public (as you know, only *Food for the Spirit* was, among the texts you quote, selected for inclusion in the *High Performance* article); taken in the context of the whole text, I think you'll agree that those quotes give a very different impression from the one you describe.

In your "revised" version of this essay as it appears in print, you append, first, a footnote that claims, "*Piper wrote up her performances after—apparently several years after—they occured* [sic]. *These statements are taken from her descriptions, which I call 'textual performances.'*" But (a) you still get it wrong by implying that I wrote up the descriptions of *all* my performances years after each occurred. (b) The statements you quote are *not* taken from simple "descriptions" but rather from my meta-art reflections on the work in question. (c) You don't seem to see that you have contradicted your claim in the main text: "Over the years" used with the imperfect tense implies "throughout an extended period of time that continues into the present," whereas "several years after" when used with the preterite tense implies "all at once at some time in the past." I'm afraid you are still not thinking clearly about this. Finally and most surprisingly, (d) you now introduce the unexplicated notion of a "textual performance" with one sentence in a footnote, when, as we see later, this notion is crucial in your effort to supplant my actual artwork with my writing about it as the target of your "art criticism."

You also add to the published text the parenthetical statement that *"Of course, the 'self' alluded to is her artistic persona—her performing self."* But this still fails to meet the criticism I make repeatedly throughout your essay, which is that you fail to *distinguish* what you called my "artworld persona" from me personally. On the contrary: Your claim that I am "performing" even when I am merely writing autobiographically about my performances implies that my "performing self" is in fact identical to the personal, autobiographical self that writes. Of course, because you neither know me personally nor have witnessed any of my performances, it is difficult to imagine on what basis you might make this distinction anyway. But your cursory treatment of this issue does reinforce the impression that it does not much matter to you which you target, as long as you get to fire the shot.

Pages 9–10:

> *". . . the self she is absorbed in to the point of obsession, the self that is the alpha and omega of her art . . ."; "authoritative statements . . . uttered with absolute conviction . . ."; ". . . texts so achingly self-conscious, so full of tortured self-awareness . . ."; ". . . full of self-doubt."*

If you think these are true general statements about my actual preoccupations and mental states (as it appears you do from the way you phrase them), you should supply some evidence to substantiate them. Obviously personal information isn't available, since we've only actually met three times and spoken for a total of less than that number of hours. Equally obviously, the mere fact that I write about my processes of art making won't do, since that fact by itself would beg the question about what the point of such writing is (I discuss what I take to be the point in the "Meta-Art" piece in *Artforum* ["In Support of Meta-Art," reprinted in this volume]). But some discussion of the particular themes that regularly crop up in my writing, or perhaps how these preoccupations regularly crop up in a wide variety of my works, would be appropriate. Otherwise this remark reads like an unfounded projection of personal fantasy. This sort of armchair pop-psychologizing is beneath you.

Pages 9–10:

> *"Her textual performances are . . . formally self-assertive but self-abasing in content."*

First I think you need to make it clear that the idea of a "textual performance" is your interpretation of my writing, not mine. I have no objection to this interpretation if it's convincingly developed. But I do object to phrasing a claim in such a way as to leave it unclear whether you mean to be ascribing certain conscious intentions and projects to me, or merely invoking them as the de facto explanation of my behavior, relative to which my conscious intentions are irrelevant. I have this objection to much of what you say in this essay. On the phone you emphasized repeatedly that I should not take what you said personally, and that you meant to be discussing my "artworld persona," not me. But you do not make this distinction anywhere in this essay, and this leaves the reader with the very misleading impressions, first, that you do mean to ascribe conscious intentions to me; and second, that you presume to ascribe them to me personally, not to my "artworld persona."

I think the idea of a textual performance is a *really* interesting one. I wish you'd develop it more systematically. Just tossing it off in passing is suggestive but superficial.

Second, remember that this retrospective is of my work, *not* my writing. This adds to the usual scholarly responsibility a writer has in referring to texts, to provide full bibliographic citations to the texts discussed, so the reader can evaluate independently the claims made about those texts by the writer. But you are a trained academic, so I'm sure I don't need to remind you of this. Perhaps you meant to add such citations to the final draft of this essay.

It looks as though I was wrong about this, doesn't it? When we later discussed this point on the phone, you argued that the catalog essay was intended to be "just an overview," not a detailed textual exegesis. But surely you can make no such excuse about an essay that appears instead in what purports to be a scholarly professional journal.

Third, what is the distinction you mean to draw between form and content here? How can a text be self-assertive in form without being so in content? Surely you can't be referring to the syntactical fact that most of the sentences I write are in the categorical declarative form (since this wouldn't distinguish my writing from most any other kind)? A few sentences on your understanding of the form-content distinction would help here.

Fourth, you really need to say a bit more about the sense in which my writing is "self-abasing in content." Remember that much of my writing is published and fairly well known to most artworld denizens, and "self-abasing" is one adjective no one has ever thought to apply to it. If you want to convince the reader that there's a genuine insight here (rather than just a cheap shot), a more in-depth discussion is in order.

In the published text, you eliminate the word *self-abasing*. That seems wise. But then you replace it with the equally specious claim that my writings "seem to register a traumatic sense of self," which is subject to the same objections—objections that you persistently fail to address. That seems unwise.

Page 10:

"*. . . she lacks Descartes' sense of a preconceived cognitive self as the implicit goal of the process of doubt.*"

Don't you mean: "*her texts* lack . . ."? Surely you have no basis for making any inferences about my psychological affinity, or lack thereof, to Descartes? Furthermore, since you have only *stated* that my writing is "full of self-doubt" without making a case that it is, or even letting the reader know to what texts you're referring, this further judgment seems doubly specious. I know you can do better than this.

In the published version, you add parenthetically that *"Descartes' self-doubt can be understood, like Piper's, as a form of self-analysis—an 'ironical' form of self-affirmation."* But again this addition neither addresses nor dispels the objection, since (a) you fail to discuss any of the texts of mine that might legitimate these inferences; and (b) you have no more evidence for inferring from the *Meditations* that Descartes actually doubted his own existence than you have for making the same inference about me. But I'm glad you inserted the word *ironical* in there somewhere. I was beginning to worry that the sense of humor I try to express in writing about my work had escaped you altogether.

Page 10:

"Taken together, they reveal her search for self-knowledge to be a Sisyphean enterprise . . ."

Again you groundlessly ascribe to me a certain agenda, and then complain that I fail to achieve it. In "In Support of Meta-Art," I state quite clearly what the purposes of such writing are, and a quick review will verify that those purposes *have nothing to do with achieving self-knowledge.* Really, Donald, this is very careless.

Perhaps you want to argue that *despite* my stated goals, what I *am in fact* doing is searching for self-knowledge. Then argue it.

Page 10:

"Piper's apologetics, undeniably intellectually brilliant . . ."

I take it your choice of the word "apologetics" is deliberate? I think you owe your readers at least a few sentences on what you take me to be apologizing for, and why.

I noticed that in the published version you eliminated that complementary second clause and rephrased the first as *"Piper's intellectual apologetics . . ."* You still haven't said what you think I have to apologize for. But I gather that, in any case, you've changed your mind about their brilliance. Too bad!

Page 10:

". . . exist to buttress a self that seems on the verge of dissolving, a self so insecure it barely coheres . . ."; ". . . exists to pull herself together emotionally, or to camouflage a self so overwrought with anxiety about the threat of disintegration from within that it seems unable to be centered in itself. It must dissolve outward in discourse . . . that . . . masks emotional incoherence. Piper's overwrought discourse seems the centrifugal expres-

> *sion of a collapsing self . . . a somnambulist form of distress. . . . Piper's intellectuality is the sign of a false self, in part the self others expect her . . . to have . . . in search of her true emotional self . . ."*

On the phone you explained that you had to somehow "get past" my being so "smart and articulate" in order to "maintain" your "critical integrity." I really don't think there is anything in my writing about my work that is such a threat to your critical integrity that it compels you to represent that writing as a symptom of mental illness.

But let us suppose, for the sake of argument, that I am wrong about this. Then either there is some evidence in my writing to support your claims here (again, *the mere fact* of my writing is inadequate for the reasons mentioned above), or there is not. If there is some evidence for this in my writing, then I would have thought that considerations of critical integrity would require that you state and discuss what evidence there is. If there is not, then either there is some evidence elsewhere that will support your case, or there is not. If there is, again I would have thought that critical integrity would require you to adduce that evidence and try to make your case persuasively. Again, I take it that such evidence would have to be found in the artwork I write about, since you and I barely know each other. If there is no such evidence anywhere to be found, then these remarks are simply your personal speculations about what I must be like in order to write as I do. You are, of course, entitled to your speculations, as long as you make clear that that is what they are. But as they stand, most of your remarks are framed as factual statements about my psychological makeup, which falsely suggests that you have some knowledge of my psychological makeup. Here I think issues of critical integrity loom very large.

> Page 10:
>
> *"In general, because Piper cannot perform without immediately explaining herself—because explaining herself is her performance . . . —we cannot help but wonder whether she is hiding something, despite apparently revealing all."*

First, there is a factual error in your claim that in general I cannot perform without immediately explaining myself. Much of my writing about my performances has been elicited by requests from various publications, sometimes long after the fact of the performance. It would have been easy to check this.

In the published text you eliminate the word *immediately.* Good! Unfortunately the sentence is still false, because I have done many performances that I have not written about at all. You had at your disposal all the necessary materials for checking this, too.

But the implication of your claim is, of course, that I have a *compulsion* to "explain myself" immediately after performing. It is hard to imagine what evidence you could adduce in support of this, since you have never even attended one of my performances, much less observed my behavior in the aftermath. Here the "persona" to which you ascribe this compulsion is clearly me as a private individual, not my "artworld persona." Again your claim suggests that you actually have some information about my personal compulsions and behavior, when in fact you have none. I can't imagine what, in your mind, could justify making such unfounded claims.

Second, again, I think you should make clear that the idea of explanation or writing as itself a performance is your idea, not mine.

Third, I think your suggestion that the very transparency of my writing itself raises the suspicion that I must be hiding something is *extremely* interesting and insightful. Further elaboration on the phenomenology and rationale of this suspicion would be very illuminating.

Of course, elaborating on this suspicion, if it turned out to be false, might also illuminate a certain amount of paranoia in the writer. Is this why you didn't pursue my suggestion in the published version?

Page 10:

"Each of her performances reads like a case history. In each she appears as the representative female, her problem-filled life a microcosm of the female problematic, an exemplary symptom of a larger sickness unto female death."

Donald, I'm afraid this is really gothically bizarre stuff. I think it's on the whole a good thing for men to confront their archetypal fear and loathing of femaleness honestly, but are you sure you want to do this in this context? Don't you think it would be wise at least to try to discuss rationally some of the performances that make you feel this way? Or calmly describe some of the problems in my "problem-filled life" that stand as an "exemplary symptom of a larger sickness unto female death"? If you don't feel able to defend these claims discursively, then, given the context, I would drop them altogether.

Page 11:

"For Piper, art is in effect a communicative performance between those who don't seriously want to communicate with one another, who have no real desire to interact. It is communication that is far from serious in that it is directed to no one in particular yet serious in that it urgently bespeaks someone in particular. It is about a relationship which seriously

> *happens despite the personal inhibitions and social barriers against serious relationship. . . . [Piper's writing] takes place against a background of dense non-relationality with casually witnessing but fundamentally resistant others.*

This is really excellent: clear, insightful, and well reasoned. I still think it should be expanded by discussion of particular examples of work, in tandem with discussion of particular things I say about them in my writings, and related to your own perceptions of how personal inhibitions and social barriers function to obstruct serious relationships, so as to avoid the appearance of superficiality. Some minor quibbles: (a) If you consult Fowler, you will see that the construction should be ". . . a relationship *that* seriously happens . . ." (b) Shouldn't the last occurrence of "relationship" be in the plural? (c) "Nonrelationality" is not ordinarily hyphenated.

> Page 11:
>
> *"[Piper's work] fictionally actualizes possibilities of communicative relationship that can never actually occur in life."*

An argument for restricting the scope of generalization in the passages cited above by tying them to particular works is that in this passage you just get it wrong. One reason why *Funk Lessons* worked so well for many of the audiences who participated was that these relationships *do* occur in life (i.e., in mixed-race discos), and the performance gave some people access to them. But I think that the basic idea, suitably qualified, is still a valid and important one.

> Page 11:
>
> *"Piper assumes that her talkative performance of herself . . ."*

No good. Since I do not share your interpretation of my writings as a talkative performance, a fortiori I make no such assumption.

> Page 11:
>
> *"But Piper also subliminally relates to others, for each of her pieces "propositions," as it were, the audience (actual or potential) with their own self-awareness. It makes them uncannily aware of their own inner conflicts. In a sense, her discursive intellectuality objectifies her self for others, or represents her self in such a way that others can identify with it. The process is two-sided: Piper's self-representation has identification with the other as its implicit goal while ostensibly—because of its intellectuality—distancing her self from the other."*

First, I don't understand your use of the term "propositions" here. Some clarification would help.

Second, I think this passage is really very good, except for the parts where you ascribe to me implicit and ostensible goals. For the reasons I've already mentioned, I think this device is intellectually irresponsible and, moreover, that the quality of your analysis is potentially sufficiently high that you do not need to resort to it.

> Page 11:
>
> *"Meta-art, the key instrument of her self-understanding . . ."*

Again this seems to be a factual misrepresentation that is easily corrected by a quick review of the "Meta-Art" article. If you want to show that, despite what I say there, the real point of meta-art is self-understanding, let's see the argument. Either put up or shut up.

> Page 11:
>
> *"Meta-art is clearly a form of self-inquiry . . ."*

Same problem.

> Page 11:
>
> *". . . for Piper, it is the substance of art itself, the actual 'work' of art, replacing any object of art. In meta-art, the interpretation of art* is *art."*

Donald, I'm afraid there really is no excuse for this. My actual words—in the *second sentence* of the article—were, "[Meta-art] might exist as part of, alongside, or instead of the art itself." I.e., meta-art as itself replacing the art is one of *three possible alternative* ways in which meta-art might function. I'm starting to get the very strong impression that you are writing too much, or are perhaps not fully attentive to the material you're writing about—nor, for that matter, to what you are in fact saying about it. This is really very distressing.

In the published text, you revise the passage by splitting it into two. First you say, "*In Piper's case, I think [meta-art] is the sum and substance of her art, that is, of her textual as well as 'stage' performances.*" Having redescribed my writing about my art as itself an art form—a "textual performance"—you now attempt to displace my artwork itself by my writing, as the "sum and substance of [my] art." This makes me wonder why you are struggling so hard to deflect attention from my work, and why you seem unable to address it critically in any form whatsoever.

Next you say, *"[F]or Piper, [meta-art] is the actual 'work' of art, replacing any object of art. In meta-art, the interpretation of art* is *art."* Having attempted to displace the importance of my work onto my writing about it, you now wrongly ascribe this evaluation to me. Here it seems that you are attempting to legitimate your interpretation by fabricating my agreement with it. This is a poor substitute for careful analysis and argument.

> Page 12:
>
> *"Meta-art necessarily leads to the 'problematic solution' of performance art, as Piper calls it. For Piper, performance art is the logical extension and execution of meta-art—its theory in concrete practice."*

I don't see this. Surely you're not suggesting that if one does meta-art one must end up doing performance art as that genre is currently understood? Surely artists can practice meta-art on painting, sculpture, etc.? They certainly *do,* so obviously they *can.* In any case, I don't see how you can ascribe this view to me, since I certainly do quite a lot of meta-art about my own nonperformance work. I really don't understand what you're trying to say here.

> Page 12:
>
> *"Both [the problems of interpretive control and of transformation] have more than a hint of the narcissism—solipsism?—that motivates Piper's activity."*

Which is it? Narcissism and solipsism are very different conditions (I have a paper on narcissism and moral alienation coming out in *The Journal of Philosophy* sometime this month, if you'd like to see it [84, no. 2 (February 1987), pp. 102–118]). Your subsequent comments do not make clear which you mean to ascribe to me. For the record: If you mean "solipsism," you may be right; if you mean "narcissism," you're wrong—at least according to the clinical definition of that term. But perhaps you're using it in some other way. In any event, I really think you should either extensively defend or else delete all the remarks in this essay that purport to report on my actual motivational and psychological states. The fact is, Donald, that you really do not know me personally at all, and pretending can't make it so. It can only make you look careless or malicious in the eyes of people who do know me personally—and remember, I've been hanging around the art world since 1967 and academia since 1970, so there are a lot of them.

Your decision in the published text to eliminate *solipsism* in favor of *narcissism* strikes me as completely wrongheaded, particularly in light of your subsequent discussion. There you claim that *"[Piper] articulates a self preoccupied with the condi-*

tions of its appearance in the world, a self that attempts to control the way the world mirrors it. It can even be said that such control is part—the essence?—of her art." But without any substantive textual analysis to defend these claims, they must be read as either (a) arbitrary authoritative pronouncements—and I'm afraid these antics erode rather than reinforce your critical authority—or else (b) as emotional announcements of how my writing makes you feel. I'm genuinely sorry that you feel controlled by my writing, Donald. On the other hand, I find it difficult to imagine sympathetically what it must be like to be in your psychological condition, in which the artist's thoughts about her work are experienced as a source of oppression and control rather than of information or insight.

> Page 12:
>
> *"Piper . . . wants, almost hysterically, every condition for her performance to be just right, including its interpretive aftermath."*

Donald, this is really very silly. I don't understand why you're doing it. Don't you realize how paranoid all this makes you sound? You don't need to depict me as a mad housewife in order to ensure the value of your own critical insights. As though a few pages by an artist on her creative processes were a danger to the very institution of art criticism!

> Page 12:
>
> *"Despite her efforts to include this interpretative aftermath in the performance, pre-empting the autonomous witnessing of others, Piper knows beforehand that the performance will be spoiled."*

If you have a *moral* objection to meta-art, i.e., that it "pre-empts the autonomous witnessing of others," or psychological anxieties about it, why not just come out and say so, and let's examine the case? These fantasy projections on me of neurotic goals and expectations, presented in the guise of objective reportage, are both underhanded and spiteful.

> Page 12:
>
> *"The narcissistic self is inherently 'spoiled,' in the double sense of the term, that is, it expects too much from the world and itself, and it is inherently impaired."*

Since you have not advanced any argument for viewing me (or my "art-world persona") as narcissistic, this claim is either a non sequitur or seriously misleading. Here as elsewhere, you are in effect subverting your commitment to critical integrity rather than preserving it.

Page 12:

"In Piper, ambiguity and anxiety are resolved through aggression. . . . Piper cannot escape the labyrinth of her spoiled self. . . . The more aggressive Piper becomes, the more she tightens the noose of anxious ambiguity around her psychic neck. Her snaky feelings about the artworld tighten its hold on her, to the point of intellectual exhaustion . . ."

This is a particularly distasteful and embarrassing spectacle of hostile wishful thinking to exhibit in the pages of an art catalog. If only for the sake of your reputation as a critic, I strongly suggest that you delete it.

Instead of taking my advice in the published text, you merely rephrased the beginning of the last sentence to read, *"Her* struggles with *her snaky feelings"* and so on. But ascribing the struggle to me rather than acknowledging it in yourself doesn't change the reality of what you've succeeded in expressing in this passage. Your decision to vent your strangulation fantasies about me in public displays extraordinarily ugly and buffoonish impulses to that public. You should be ashamed of yourself.

Page 13:

"It is difficult to realize the anxiety that permeates a Piper performance and text. So intellectually self-assured does she seem, so calm and collected and knowledgable [sic] *about herself, that it is hard to realize that these are exactly the traits that indicate how minimal her sense of herself as an 'active subject' is—how alienated from herself she is—despite all appearances to the contrary."*

Here you at least drop the pretence that all this is directed against my "art-world persona." Unfortunately, you also explicitly disavow the possibility that there is any empirically observable evidence in my behavior that could disconfirm your explanation of my psychological condition, since in your view, it appears, any such disconfirming behavior is instead to be understood as confirmation of that very condition. But as a trained academic philosopher yourself, I am sure you are acquainted with the very elementary objections to this type of reasoning that are ordinarily rehearsed in the first meeting of an introductory philosophy of science course. I do not think such reasoning displays your intellect to good advantage. Incidentally, "knowledgeable" is with three *es*.

I'm pleased to note that you have spelled *knowledgeable* correctly in the published text. On the other hand, you still don't seem to have grasped the point of my comments here, which is that your reasoning reduces to the ridiculous thesis that the

12.
Kuspit Strangulation Fantasy (1987).
Courtesy John Weber Gallery, collection University of Colorado at Boulder Art Museum.

very fact that I don't seem to be crazy shows that I must be. You seem to be willfully abdicating your claim to be taken seriously as a scholar and intellectual.

> Page 13:
>
> *"Her implicit sense of her self as a fictive character implies disavowal of the affect generated by her performances."*

Since I have no such sense of my self, no such disavowal is implied.

> Page 13:
>
> *"It gives Piper's activity its subliminally cryptic—peculiarly inscrutable—air. It is self-expression as self-repression. Piper is far from being as transparent as she seems."*

As an attempt to cash out the very interesting suggestion you made on page 10, I find this disappointing, for a number of reasons. First of all, it is based on a false and unsupported attribution to me of a particular mental state (my "sense of my self as a fictive character"). Second, you don't explain the connection between this "sense" and the "inscrutable" air of my activity. How does such a sense manage to have this effect on those who view it? Third, you substitute a slogan—"self-expression as self-repression"—for analysis. It is suggestive, but ultimately very thin. I'm sure you can do better than this.

> Page 13:
>
> *". . . a good deal of her art is about her body . . ."*

Perhaps this is the place to remind you that less than *one-fifth* of my work is in the area of performance, and only the *Catalysis* series is about my body in any direct sense. But of course you have my slides, and access to the notebooks, so you must know this.

As we see from your decision to print this statement unchanged, my attempt to remind you of the facts about my work, and their being at your immediate disposal, were futile. I am dismayed by your dogged misrepresentation of my work and disregard of the truth. This puts an end to my attempts at a charitable interpretation of your malicious behavior.

> Pages 13–14:
>
> *"For her, narcissism is in part a form of numinous regulation of her body, . . . she is fasting to the point of anorexia . . . a self which for all its exhibitionism . . ."*

By lifting my fasting out of the context of my explicit commitment to yogic postures, meditation, and dietary habits, you deliberately misrepresent its import. I doubt that this strategy is consistent with your commitment to the ideal of critical integrity. And again I think it would be in your best interest to simply delete the cheap and superficial armchair pop-psychologizing. In this essay so far, you have described me as obsessive, tortured, self-abasing, insecure, incoherent, overwrought with anxiety, sick, narcissistic, hysterical, aggressive, intellectually exhausted, alienated, repressed, anorexic, and exhibitionistic. Later you add that I am schizophrenic, anguished, wracked with contradictions, self-defeated, and infantile. Don't you think this is a bit much? The impression it gives is that you are indiscriminately throwing every possible psychopathological term at me that you can think of in order to discredit the intellectual validity of my writing. It does not speak well for your assessment of your own critical contributions that you think you need to do this.

It occurs to me that perhaps I have completely misunderstood your intentions in writing this essay up to now; and that what you are really after is a very broad parody of exaggerated male castration anxiety in the face of the spectre of female self-sufficiency. If so, my apologies for my phlegmatic sense of humor and lack of imagination. In this case, disregard my criticisms up to this point. I would say, instead, that all the preceding passages in the essay should be rendered as broadly as those I mention above and on page 12.

Perhaps you believe that you have deflected these comments in the printed text by rephrasing your malicious remark about my fasting as a parenthecized interrogative. You have not. In these concluding passages you drop all pretence to be discussing my writing critically. Instead you exhibit to your readers your own hostility at being thwarted in your attempt to reduce yet one more artist to an inanimate object that doesn't talk back.

Page 13:

"*. . . Philosophy is perhaps the ultimate narcissism . . .*"

Also page 15:

"*. . . the infantile illusion of omnipotence (so pervasive in philosophy) . . .*"

Parody or not, I would drop these passing potshots at philosophy. To anyone who knows the history of your own relationship to academic philosophy, they sound like sour grapes.

Page 14:

"Piper is self-consciously a 'split personality.' . . . Her psyche is the prey of a host of unresolved dualisms, that parasitically feed on her enormous energy. Each dualism articulates a different anxiety, each is a form of anguish; each is a facet of an incompletely integrated self."

Again there is a real insight here that is, however, buried in an avalanche of vituperation, paranoid fantasizing, and sloppy exposition. The insight, I think, is that I do have to deal with many dualisms in my life when I interact with others who bring me face-to-face with them, and that this is reflected in my art. But your "inside reports" on the state of my psyche are presumptuously silly (who is your "Deep Throat"?): you have no grounds for characterizing the relation of these dualisms to my "enormous energy" as "parasitic," nor for inferring anything about the state of integration of my self from them. Again I think these flights of fancy are going to sound very funny to anyone who knows me personally.

Incidentally, in footnote 5 of the published text, you explain your silence concerning my actual artwork as follows: *"For me, the political aspects of Piper's art, admirable as they are . . . are secondary to, and grow out of, her self-interpretation, which includes the sociopolitical interpretation and demonstration of her blackness."* "Demonstration" means "exhibition" or "proof." So you apparently think I try to show or prove that I am black by writing about my work. This is a novel idea. I would be interested in hearing more about what exactly you think I have to show or prove, and why.

Page 14 and footnote 7:

"For all her increasingly explicit audience orientation" and so on.

Having spent as many sentences on my purported narcissism as you have, relegating your acknowledgment that my work has been increasingly other-directed since 1970 to a footnote seems a bit coy, don't you think? There's a challenge of exposition here—i.e., to square these two aspects of your interpretation with each other—that you are failing to meet. This makes your thinking seem at worst incoherent, and at best uncertain of what it is you really want to say.

Page 14:

". . . an extension of her feeling of self-alienation. . . . Each contradiction underscores the abysmal sense of personal inadequacy underlying her heightened sense of intellectual adequacy, indeed, the intellectual bravado which makes her seem to stand on a peak of self-understanding."

To whom do I "seem to stand on a peak" etc.? You must try harder to think reflectively about what this sort of nonsense reveals about you, and whether you really want it revealed in an art catalog. It's very embarrassing to read.

Page 14:

"Piper experiences herself as wracked with contradictions. . . . She emerges as peculiarly self-defeated for all her self-celebration."

The mental states you ascribe to me here and elsewhere are pure fiction, and it's both presumptuous and misleading to present them as though they were fact. But I think what I find most depressing of all about all this is that you seem to want these things to be true so badly that you've resolutely avoided any personal contact or discussion with me that might disprove them. Critical insight is not gained by burying one's head in the sand. What's salvageable in this essay is so in spite of your very questionable strategies, not because of them.

Page 14–15:

"She recreates her theoretical contradictions dialectically as 'tension arcs'" etc.

Again this is just sloppy writing. I know nothing about Kohut's theory, and I'm sure you cannot mean to ascribe these concerns to me as my conscious preoccupations. But the language you use doesn't make clear that these are your interpretative tools and not mine.

Once more I am struck by your lack of concern at having failed to differentiate your Kohutian intentions from my non-Kohutian ones. Ironical, in light of *your* description of *me* as pathologically narcissistic. The venom with which you are attacking me seems to have blinded you to the significance of the strategies you are deploying. Your decision to parade this unpleasant behavior before the art public is mystifying.

Page 15:

"She implicitly conceives of meta-art as having a goal: complete *understanding of all the conditions for her self-performances. . . . Her assumption of complete interpretability or comprehension . . . is the backbone of her meta-art."*

You just haven't done the necessary exegetical spade-work to legitimate this claim. Since it can't be found explicitly in the text of the "Meta-Art" article, and I explicitly disavow it as a general agenda, you must _demonstrate_ its plausibility

through reasoned analysis—that is, unless you mean to insult the intelligence of your readers.

> Page 15:
>
> *"The ideal of complete interpretability is a kind of magical thinking, another form of the infantile illusion of omnipotence (so pervasive in philosophy). . . . Piper seems to think that if she could integrate all her interpretations, . . . her narcissisms would mature—sublimate—into integration. . . . She seems unable to face the fact that interpretation can never be complete."*

I have now spent approximately twice as long critiquing this essay as I ordinarily spend on an imaginative but unschooled first draft of an undergraduate paper. I have made many of the same kinds of criticisms I would make of such a paper, and have felt increasingly dismayed that it should be necessary to say such things to you, of all people. I wish it were seriously open to me to view this essay as itself a performance, rather than a candidate for a serious piece of criticism. As it stands, it is virtually a study in self-abasement; it expresses a lack of respect, not only for your readership, but for your own, very highly trained critical powers. It is not my impression that intellectual standards are any less rigorous in serious art criticism than they are in philosophy. Your training, your intellectual discipline, and your self-esteem seem to be completely unravelling, and I am disturbed and concerned at witnessing this. I feel bad for you, and wish I could help. But your manifest fears about the threat to your own work I and my writing represent seem to foreclose that, as well as any genuine dialogue about the issues we have both raised in our work. You seem to have forgotten who you are and what you have achieved, so I will at least take the liberty of reminding you, in case no one else has lately. You are an erudite and highly creative intellectual, a scholar with academic training of the very first rank, and capable of intellectual achievement of the very highest order. There are a number of passages in this essay that demonstrate this, as does much of your writing elsewhere. So you are clearly capable of doing very much better than this draft, and I very much hope you will.

Please call if you want to talk. Thursday through Monday evenings are best.

Adrian

When you called me the following Saturday of last February to discuss my comments, you said to me, among other things, "I didn't appreciate that second to last paragraph about where you think I'm at." You were clearly angry that I had made some inferences about your frame of mind from your writing. I was surprised at your anger, because your essay does exactly the same to me, except without bothering to discuss any evidence for the inferences you make. You, on the other hand, were surprised at my distaste for your "methodological" approach to my work, even while expressing the same feeling about mine to yours. Your unwillingness to observe reciprocal privileges of exposition lead me to some further inferences, which you also may fail to appreciate: (a) that you really were not interested in engaging me in critical dialogue at all, despite your solicitation from me of feedback on the first draft of your essay; (b) that you instead expected gratitude and approval from me for your ill-concealed personal attacks; (c) that you are therefore completely indifferent and insensitive to the effects of your behavior on others, either by choice or by necessity; (d) that you regard yourself and your writing as above criticism.

Now I am going to tell you what I think about all this. I think you need to take a long vacation from art criticism for a while, in order to replenish your considerable intellectual resources. As a blanket tool of art criticism, psychoanalysis uses a system of tired, familiar categories on the artist in lieu of attention to the singular characteristics that constitute the artwork. Your overwhelming dependence on psychoanalysis to deal with aesthetic issues bespeaks an intellectual depletion that is, I am sure, only the temporary result of overwork. I also think you should try to gain some insight into your motives for using this tool as a weapon for trying to dehumanize artists and reduce their work to neurotic symptoms.

It is painful to watch someone achieve the kind of authority you have achieved, and then throw it away because he is under the illusion that that authority itself entitles him to flout the very intellectual standards and values adherence to which won him that authority in the first place. Your contempt for your readers, as well as for those you write about, is almost palpable. I would suggest that you reflect very seriously on your status as a critic in the art world, on the talents and contributions that got you there, and on the responsibilities and prerogatives of power with which that status endows you.

Sincerely,

Adrian Piper

16. Ways of Averting One's Gaze

Written in 1988 and previously unpublished.

1.

The job isn't done after the laws have been passed mandating due process and equal protection under the law.[1] It hasn't even been done after the schools, neighborhoods, and workplaces have been integrated. For even if we were to succeed in overcoming legal racism, and economic and social racism, there's still a further nightmare to confront: *cultural racism.*

Cultural racism surfaces when some of us are forced to go to court in order to be allowed to wear cornrows to work. It surfaces when Americans of African descent feel impelled to discard one identifying term after another as each is appropriated by white society as an expression of contempt.[2] It surfaces when colored working-class popular culture remains an object of contempt even while the creativity and influence of white popular culture on high art are celebrated. It surfaces when colored cab drivers are asked to turn off their favorite radio stations by white customers who climb into their cabs. It surfaces when the traditional art of third-world cultures is relegated to the status of "folk art" or "crafts" while white art that deploys the same motifs is honored as "primitivism," "pattern painting," and "functional art." It surfaces when stereotypical assumptions are made—and voiced—about a colored person's actions, motivations, and goals in advance of any evidence as to whether those assumptions are valid. It surfaces when colored individuals are required—or motivated—to deny or suppress their original cultural heritage as a condition of entry into mainstream white society. It surfaces when coloreds and whites who work together observe, of necessity, the unspoken rule of socializing, seeking entertainment and companionship, and relaxing separately. And it surfaces when coloreds and whites sense that they cannot confide in one another at deep levels—not because their experiences have been different, but because stereotypical assumptions will make those experiences incomprehensible and threatening to the other. The varieties of cultural racism are all ways of averting one's gaze from the immanent spectre of the Other.

1.
I have benefited by discussing with Michael Brenson, Lowery Sims, and Josephine Withers many of the issues explored in this essay. I am grateful to Michael Jones and Lucy Lippard for comments on earlier drafts.

2.
The terms *black, Negro,* and *colored* have all met this fate. Having resurrected *black* in the 1960s and dropped it in the 1970s for the short-lived *Afro-American,* we are now on to the syntactically awkward but genteel *persons of color,* after the French *gens de couleur libre* of Louisiana. Luckily there is a plethora of linguistically foreign terms to which we may have recourse when this one gets besmirched by cultural racism in its turn. I choose *colored,* for its simplicity, accuracy, and conceptual and metaphorical possibilities. I intend to stick to it.

Cultural racism is damaging and virulent because it hits its victims in particularly vulnerable and private places: their preferences, tastes, modes of self-expression, and self-image. Economic, legal, and social racism are brutal, but they do not block all means of escape; their victims may still find solace in entertainment, self-expression, intimacy, mutual support, and cultural solidarity. When cultural racism succeeds in making its victims suppress, denigrate, or reject these means of cultural self-affirmation, it makes its victims hate themselves. It is therefore a kind of racism to which the fine, performing, and applied arts need to be particularly alert.

Cultural racism is, in some ways, the hardest kind to combat, because it is what remains deeply embedded in its perpetrators even after they have worked hard and sincerely to combat overt legal, social, and economic racism; even if they can have no doubt of their own sterling political intentions. But sterling intentions do not exhaust anyone's character. Perpetrators of cultural racism, like anyone else, still have personal tastes, impulses, and assumptions to express, personal choices to make—responses that may not survive the light of self-conscious political scrutiny if they have never, in the whole long history of their political commitment, been exposed to it. Cultural racism is hard to combat because bringing these ingrained, unself-conscious responses to self-conscious scrutiny is hard to do: It is invasive, it violates privacy and intimacy, and it exposes hidden fears and angers that are humiliating and incapacitating. The choice we must make about whether or not to combat cultural racism, then, reduces to the choice of who—perpetrators or victims—are to be, at least for a time, invaded, violated, and exposed.

2.

Those of us on the cultural margin face a couple of extra challenges to give our lives drama and excitement. First, there is the challenge of getting those of you, there, near the center, in the mainstream, to acknowledge our existence, so we can peaceably obtain resources and get on with our lives in this world we share. *[Who, me? Are you talking to me?!]* The moment when we stop being invisible to you is a highly rewarding one. *[I don't know what you mean. I've always liked black people. And anyway I'm not in the mainstream either. I'm an outsider, too. No one understands me . . .]* We may exult briefly in our ability to disturb your epistemic complacency, to shock or rattle you, merely by being who we are. Let's call your response to our acknowledged presence *fear of the Other.*

Our exultation in your fear can't last. *[I'm not afraid of black people as such. Obviously I'm afraid of muggers, rapists, and thieves, but that's another matter.]* Often it makes you get ugly, and attempt to protect yourself by attacking us with all the resources at your command. *[I don't attack anyone. I just try to protect myself. And anyway, only the strong survive, right?]* We react with shock and dismay: We knew we unsettled you, and thought that noteworthy; but we didn't think we thereby inspired you to blow us off the map. Sometimes you close up and become impersonally distant (the intellectual equivalent of fetal position). We are pained at your refusal to engage with us: We knew there were issues that separated us, but we expected you to confront them, not attempt to dehumanize us. *[I don't know what you're talking about. You're being melodramatic, excessive.]* We cannot acquiesce in these reactions, for they threaten our existence. But whether or not they create an impasse between us is ultimately up to you.

Fear of the Other is interchangeable with xenophobia when its object is another human being as such. But you also exhibit fear when the Other is an anomalous object, circumstance, or practice that intrudes into the safe and comfortable surroundings you have fashioned so carefully. *[You talk as though I'd done it intentionally, and I haven't. I'm a victim of socialization just like everyone else.]* Formalist avant-garde art used to have this effect, and the sophisticates among you agreed, upon reflection, that it was salutary in its ability to question your aesthetic presuppositions, expand your awareness, heighten your perception. The committed formalists among us pushed the limits of our collective tolerance for anomalous, avant-garde form as far as our imaginations would allow: to minimalism, found art, process art, earth art, conceptual art. In jaded retrospect, that seems not to have been all that far. The anomalous objects were, after all, irretrievably three-dimensional, ineluctably bound by and situated in space and time. After a while, we all could see them coming. They were no longer anomalies.

Nevertheless, when formalist overstimulation set in, those of us still on the margin knew that the jig was not yet up. Your tolerance for formally anomalous objects was inexhaustible and lucrative, but your tolerance for formally anomalous *objects that were also subjects* had not even been tested. In those days, such work was called "body art" and "streetworks," not "performance art." You valiantly strove to transcend your fear of the Other by acknowledging this work as art; sometimes we made it easier for you by marketing documentations of it, rather than insisting that you witness it. *[Let's face it. A lot of that work was sick, a turn-off. Who needs to be shocked and nauseated when they look at art?]*

But despite your welcome, some of us still remained on the margin. We saw that your tolerance for aesthetically anomalous subject-objects did not extend to all subjects as such. We saw that you could not transcend your fear of the color of our skin, our gender, our interests and idiolects, as effortlessly as you had your fear of the abandonment of figuration, the reduction of painterly abstraction, the intrusion of advertising imagery, the rejection of literality, or even the process of self-alteration. *[The fact is that a lot of minority art just isn't that good. It lacks universality. It's too specific, too ideological. Collectors can't relate to it. They don't want anybody preaching to them in their living rooms, making them feel guilty.]* You did not welcome us into the mainstream, into your living rooms, or into your families. The triumphant legacy of conceptual art's subordination of medium to idea was the emergence of political content: The confrontation of racism, sexism, and economic exploitation—that is, xenophobia—became the last outpost of the avant garde. *[Haven't you heard? There is no more avant garde. That's what postmodernism is all about. Everything's been done. Everything of aesthetic interest, that is.]*

3.

Xenophobia interests me because I am the object of it; *self-transcendence* interests me because I want to understand the subject of it, namely you, there, near the center, in the mainstream. I want to understand what it is about certain kinds of subjects, as well as about certain kinds of objects, that makes you flinch, withdraw, or pour forth defensive rationalizations of your impulses to ignore, reject, or annihilate those you perceive as intruders, those who offend and threaten you by their very existence. I want to understand what it is like to be you. I want my work to transcend the limitations you impose on me, so I can better understand those you impose, doggedly, on yourself. I try to do this in my work by voicing your—sometimes unspoken and often unspeakable—thoughts, by depicting your visions and nightmares, by entering into your psyche, in all its variations, and inviting you to consider its contents—our contents—with me, together. I attempt to produce work that, like this essay, causes you instinctively to feel and then reflect on your allegiances—to margin or mainstream, critic or target, "us" or "you." I want you to be able to understand the experience that saturates so much of our lives in this society, of being held at a distance, examined, analyzed, and evaluated. I try to fashion the stereotypes your own responses often express, in the hope that you will recognize them and feel moved by your self-awareness to repudiate them. Having understood and empathized with you, I want my work to coax you, gently and humorously, but firmly, out of the corner into which you have painted yourself. At least this is what I want when I am feeling strong and patient.

Sometimes I feel I succeed, sometimes not. Sometimes I despair of eliciting self-conscious recognition from you and must remind myself that I can't elicit it if it's not there; I can only bring it out—sometimes—if it is. My interest in guiding you to a self-reflexive awareness of your responses to the stereotypes I depict is easily

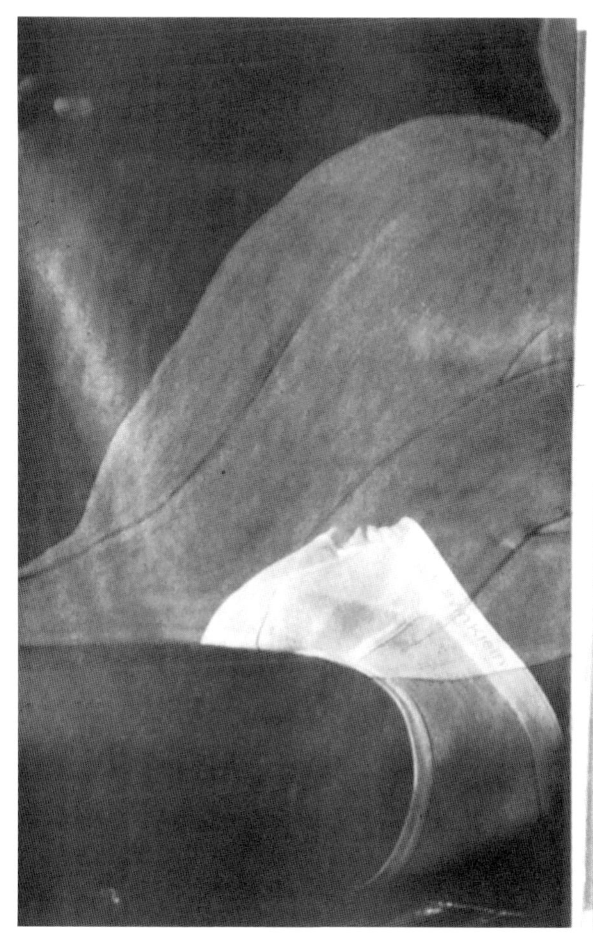

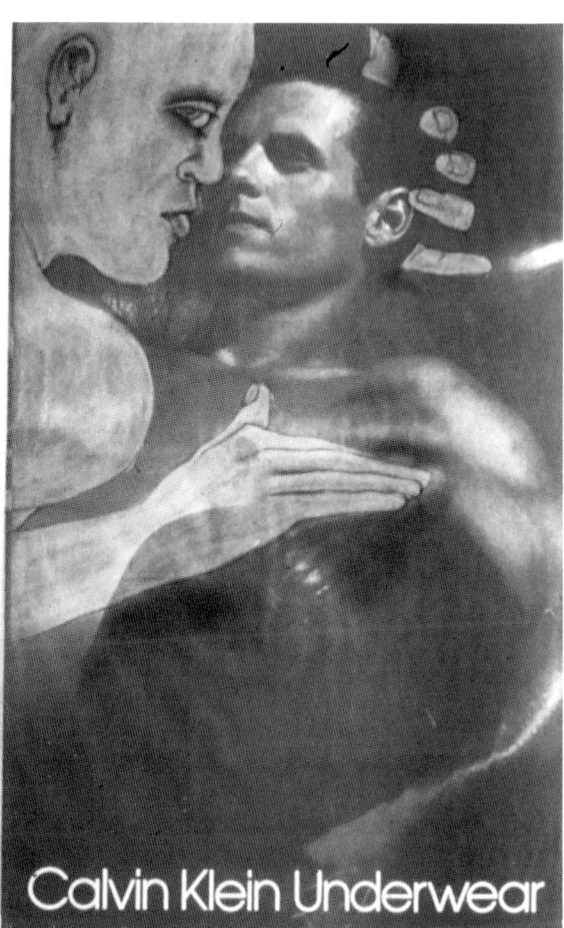

13.
Vanilla Nightmares #16 (1987). Courtesy John Weber Gallery, collection of the artist.

stymied—by your studied obliviousness, or genuine incomprehension, or righteous indignation. When you manifest those defenses, my strategy is to try to make you self-reflexively aware of them as well. Thus I try to use to both of our advantages my congenital inability to repress or ignore your responses. But my efforts are easily crushed if you are dogged enough.

My ability to understand you depends on my ability to confront my own deep fears, fantasies, and angers, and to observe their expression in my behavior. My ability to confront my own responses depends, in turn, on my observation of yours, and on my recognition that we share some of these responses in common, however much I deplore them. Sometimes your behavior surprises me, but sometimes I know how you feel. Your nervousness, your repulses, your studied incomprehension, your dogged unwillingness to dismantle the barricades against intimacy don't only show me who, in your eyes, I am. You also remind me what it's like to feel threatened, to perceive disquiet and the warning of imminent invasion by an unwelcome and unpredictable Other. We both know what that's like. I want to remind you that you feel these things, so you will remember that they are not necessarily part of the external reality you perceive.

Your fear of my otherness is a fear of violation of the boundaries of your self; in its most familiar and comprehensible guise, this is the fear of physical harm or attack by another. The fear I target is the more pervasive fear of the dissolution of the boundaries of the self in intimacy with an Other, through the seduction that coaxes your deep, unsubdued drives into the open; by merging with a hypnotic but unfamiliar Other; in being overwhelmed and pulled apart by strange internal tornadoes. Your urge to grasp, to comprehend, to conceptually master and assimilate anomaly fashions of me an object of distant and dangerous fascination, preoccupation, and—among virulent racists—obsession. But my unrelenting otherness, my shameless implacability to conceptual assimilation raises the nightmarish spectre of the disintegration of your self into chaos: the dissolution of social conventions, of sexual prohibitions, of the political control of the unrestful. As I ease into your cognitive orbit, you wince. I trigger your desire and your anxiety together; you come apart to let me in. On the far side of intimacy you glimpse death.

My lifeline to integrity is the willingness to name and represent these forces, both in others and in myself: to consider them, probe them, and rise above them. To express them sometimes costs me supporters, but to suppress them is an invitation to spiritual and moral death. So I have to do this work. And I have to take the risk of presenting it to you—as an object of contemplation, a means of catalysis, a medium of dialogue, or at least as an invitation to all of these, if you are willing. To call what I do "art" is to signify a contingent fact of our shared acculturation. It is also, perhaps, a way for me to get a foot in the door to your awareness.

4.

I said that those of us at the margin have a couple of extra life challenges to keep us on our toes. The second comes after we get you to recognize our existence. This one is the challenge to dodge the specious categories by which you try to make us safe and familiar; the linguistic pigeonholes by which you thereby consign us once again to invisibility. This is the challenge to arrogate to ourselves the power of naming: the power of defining, for ourselves and for your sake, how we choose to be identified and understood, and in what our anomaly in your eyes consists. Perhaps we are not at all like you, or perhaps we are not all that different. But in order for you to acknowledge our existence permanently and authentically, and not just as a transient fashionable gesture, these are questions about which we must be consulted.

This second challenge divides the field differently. Some of us at the margin adopt the labels and idiolect of the mainstream, to assimilate—or, sometimes, merely to infiltrate. Some of you at the center deploy the idiolect of the margin to decenter yourselves—or, sometimes, merely to prove that it is not necessary to do so. Some of us are uncomfortable with the responsibilities of verbal power, and some of you are exquisitely sensitive to the nuances of language. In my work I struggle with familiar preconceptions and anciently serviceable labels—"black," "white," "us," "them," "him," "her," "you," "me"—both because they can be a tool of self-transcendence and because, predictably, I also feel stifled by them.

These labels and preconceptions *can* be a source of self-transcendence, although they are more often a means for instilling fear of the Other as a permanent cultural norm. But by confronting you with the concrete immediacy of my and your experience, and measuring it against your abstract preconceptions of it—your conceptions of racial and gender identity, the limits of the self, the barrier of the Other—we may together stretch the limits of our mutual understanding to embrace it. By naming and deflating the fears and fantasies that buttress these preconceptions, we may collaboratively objectify them. I examine them—or depict them, or mimic them—so that we may together experience the shock of recognition, then consider them at a distance, understand their pathology, and move on.

5.

On the other hand, such labels and preconceptions are stifling when they attempt to deflate my Otherness by eradicating my singularity; when they misappropriate my power of naming. These are ways of divesting me of power and the capacity to unsettle—and, ultimately, restructure—your world through my presence. They obscure me and my work and replace both with innocuous entities that make your world safe for hegemony. I and my work are obscured, for example, when my beliefs, motives, and actions are falsely represented in ways that make me look neurotic, stupid, or malevolent in doing the work I do. These are ways of attacking my work indirectly, by attacking me and my modes of self-expression. They are of the very essence of cultural racism. They attempt to obliterate my work as a significant catalyst of your experience by displacing your hostility and confusion onto me as the source of it. They differ from straightforward attacks on my work in that they rely on fabrication and factual distortion. Rather than mounting a frontal attack on the realities of the Other, they construct for the reading public a straw man that ostensibly deserves it. This is how the stereotypes of cultural racism are promulgated.

Now for some concrete applications of these generalities. Here are some recent instances of cultural racism directed against me from two writers, one female and one male. Both are white.[3] Neither knows me personally, and I assume that both are consciously oblivious to the racism and sexism embedded in their discussions. Nevertheless these specimens are particularly significant because both were written at a time in my career when my work was receiving increased attention. One essay was written in anticipation of a twenty-year retrospective of my work,[4] the other as a review of it. Thus they can be read as attempts to diminish and demean a spectre of the Other that, for these critics, threatens to loom entirely too large. Both, that is, function as attempts to "put me in my place."

First, some of the passages that portray me as neurotic:[5]

3.
All quotes are taken from the following articles: Elizabeth Hess, "Ways of Seeing Adrian Piper," *The Village Voice,* May 26, 1987, p. 100; Elizabeth Hess, "Reply," (Letters to the Editor), *The Village Voice,* June 9, 1987, p. 6; Donald Kuspit, "Adrian Piper: Self-Healing Through Meta-Art," *Art Criticism 3,* no. 3 (September 1987), pp. 9–16. Citations from Kuspit's article are denoted by (K), those from Hess by (H). Those who worry that I may be unfairly lifting the following quotes out of context are encouraged to consult these articles. They will find that, on the whole, Kuspit tends to portray me as neurotic, whereas Hess inclines more to portray me as stupid and malevolent. I respond to Hess in "It's Not All Black and White" (Letters to the Editor), *The Village Voice,* June 9, 1987, pp. 4 and 6. My response to Kuspit is to be found in "An Open Letter to Donald Kuspit" in this volume.

4.
Kuspit's article was originally commissioned for, then dropped from, the catalog for my show, "Adrian Piper: Reflections 1967–1987" (traveling), originated at The Alternative Museum, New York, N.Y., April 18 to May 30, 1987. This exhibit was curated by Jane Farver.

5.
For an analysis of the relation between blackness and psychopathology in racial stereotyping, see Sander L. Gilman, *Difference and Pathology: Stereotypes of Sexuality, Race and Madness* (Ithaca: Cornell University Press, 1985), especially chapters 4 and 5. For a discussion of women as embodiments of neurosis, see Bram Dijkstra, *Idols of Perversity: Fantasies of Feminine Evil in Fin-de-Siècle Culture* (New York: Oxford University Press, 1986), especially chapter 2.

"Piper feels that she was born wearing a disguise."(H)[6]

"Piper is an actress who wants, almost hysterically, every condition for her performance to be just right, including its interpretative aftermath."(K)[7]

"Piper rigorously controls the viewer's response to her work."(H)

"Each contradiction underscores the abysmal sense of personal inadequacy underlying her heightened sense of intellectual adequacy . . ."(K)

"Many artists, like Adrian Piper, suffer from separation anxiety once their work is out of their hands."(H)

"For her, narcissism is in part a form of numinous regulation of her body . . ."(K)

Ah, poor me! Schizoid, hysterical, anxious, narcissistic control freak, with an inferiority complex to boot! If these demeaning imputations were true, you could surely disregard most anything I might say or do as a mere symptom of mental illness, and dismiss my work accordingly. Wouldn't that be convenient? Then you could get on with business as usual. *[Don't include me in this. I didn't write the stuff, and frankly I don't think it's all that bad. You should be grateful that you're getting written about at all.]*

Then there are the passages that portray me as downright stupid:[8]

"Piper cruised the streets wearing an afro, mustache, and sunglasses, in order to experience the effect."(H)[9]

6.
I invoke the disguise metaphor to depict the paranoid racist responses of some of my colleagues to me as a concealed Other in my catalog essay, "Flying," reprinted in volume I from *Adrian Piper: Reflections 1967–86* (New York, N.Y.: The Alternative Museum), p. 23. Hess had this text in her possession when she wrote her review.

7.
Kuspit has never attended any of my performances, nor their "interpretative aftermaths."

8.
The literature on the stereotypes of colored people and women as having inferior intelligence is voluminous. For the former, see any discussion of Jensen's work on intelligence testing; for the latter, see, for example, Dijkstra, *Idols of Perversity,* chapter 6.

9.
Again, Hess had full access to those published texts in which I discuss my motivations for doing these street performances. These texts include "Notes on the Mythic Being," *Tri-Quarterly* 32: Anti-Object Art (Winter 1974); "The Mythic Being: I/You (Her);" and "Notes on the Mythic Being I–II." The latter two pieces were published in *Individuals: Post-Movement Art,* ed. Alan Sondheim (New York: E. P. Dutton, 1976). All are reprinted in Volume I.

You see, those performances were actually just a novel means of self-titillation. Nothing serious!

"She equates the chasm between the art-educated public and the general public with the gap between the rich and the poor."(H)[10]

What? You mean there are some poor people who know about art and some rich people who don't?

"She seems unable to face the fact that interpretation can never be complete."(K)

But everything is just so confusing to me otherwise!

"The power of the piece results from Piper's assumption that the viewer is white."(H)

Duh-h-h. . . . Colored people don't look at art anyway . . . duh-h-h. . . . Anyway they don't count . . .

"Piper seems unable to separate her personal intentions for the work from its public life."(H)

You mean there's a difference? You're saying that viewers can't read my mind? They won't interpret the work exactly as I do? Why not? Duh-h-h. What's the problem?

The effect of such fabrications is that the stupider I appear, the more thoroughly you may disregard my actual thoughts and intentions while encoding my work. If the production of my work is based on dimwitted or patently false assumptions, you needn't worry that you may be missing something of importance in your interpretation of it. If you thought you might be, then you might feel compelled to consult me about it; or—worse—confront me face-to-face in an interview. Think how upsetting that would be. *[You're making entirely too much out of this. You really are a bit oversensitive about it, you know. These writers don't have bad motives.*

10.
After searching through my writings in order to discover how I could have conceivably misled Hess so badly, I came upon the following passage (from "In Support of Meta-Art," this volume). "The works that broadly compose the art world at different times are the works that have been preserved and evaluated by those rich and educated enough to do so." This is the only passage I could find that is even remotely germane to her claim. The dilemma then arises of whether to explain her misrepresentation of it as the result of negligence, dyslexia, or spite. I understand that she borrowed all of my slides, audiotapes, and texts in order to write the article, plus took an extra week to complete it, so negligence is unlikely. Similarly, it is unlikely that an established art critic and author could be so dyslexic as to misunderstand the passage this badly.

They just don't like *to deal with artists. Maybe they're the stupid ones. Besides, stop rocking the boat! Nobody's perfect.]* Unfortunately, it is not possible to explain these moronic attributions by the writers' own stupidity. By attributing these beliefs to me, they indicate their own awareness of possible alternatives: for example, that I "cruised the streets," for other reasons, that I do not assume that all my viewers are white, and so on. Their attributions to me of these inane beliefs are thus the result of *conscious decisions*—decisions based neither in my work nor in their personal acquaintance with me.

Then there are the passages that impute hostile motives to me:[11]

"The presumption of whiteness has plagued Piper all her life."(H)

Right. The only plague worse than whiteness is acne. Ugh!

"When an interviewer asks her if it's true that white people can't dance, she diplomatically explains that it's a question of practice and environment."(H)

How else would I conceal my contempt for white would-be dancers except through diplomacy?

"The more aggressive Piper becomes, the more she tightens the noose of anxious ambiguity around her psychic neck."(K)

By wreaking aggression on others and on myself simultaneously, I kill one bird with two stones, see.

". . . Piper has kept the art world at a distance."(H)

So as to avoid contamination.

"Despite her . . . pre-empting the autonomous witnessing of others . . ."(K)

Who cares what they think, anyway?

"________ . . . moves closer to Piper's corner by aggressively alienating the viewer . . ."(H)

That is, the more revulsed you feel, the better I like it. Simple!

11.
The classic text on racist stereotypes linking blackness with malevolence is Frantz Fanon, *Black Skins, White Masks* (New York: Grove Press, 1967). For discussion of the sexist stereotype linking femaleness with malevolence, see Dijkstra, *Idols of Perversity* chapters 7–11.

In these passages, the writers represent me as hostile to whites, aggressive, off-putting, and overbearing. Both do this, remember, without knowing me personally—or even having witnessed any of my performances. Their groundless fantasizing is rationalized by constructing yet another racist stereotype: that of the Other as enigmatic and inscrutable, inaccessible to the ordinary context of shared comprehension:[12]

"Piper . . . has ironically remained an enigma."(H)

". . . we cannot help but wonder whether she is hiding something, despite apparently revealing all."(K)

"For the most part, Piper's work is known only in the feminist community, cordoned off from mainstream art."(H)

"Her implicit sense of herself as a fictive character . . . gives Piper's activity its subliminally cryptic—peculiarly inscrutable—air."(K)

"This is our opportunity to see her undisguised."(H)

But my "enigmatic inaccessibility" is just another stereotypical fiction, an after-the-fact rationalization of these writers' conscious choice to avoid personal contact with me. This avoidance then allows them to impute to me as fact attitudes and motives that arise solely from their own preconceptions about what I must be like. This is exactly what is involved in imposing a stereotype. *[Oh, dear! These difficult, hotblooded, third-world types! Always flying off the handle and grabbing every opportunity to scream racism! They really have to be handled with kid gloves, you know. You have to know how to* manage *them.]* And indeed, in other passages, these writers make clear their racist and sexist assumptions:

"It is crucial to know that Piper is a black artist who can easily 'pass' for white. For the most part this has been a biological burden."(H)

You see, unless you know both my skin color and my racial identity (my crosses to bear), my work will be meaningless to you.

"Is Piper's art the archetypal 'woman's art'—talk about her sense of herself as though she was [sic] *a being apart?"*(K)

Yak, yak, yak. That's all. Just yak, yak, yak.

12.
See Gilman, *Difference and Pathology,* introduction.

"In each [performance] she appears as the representative female, her problem-filled life a microcosm of the female problematic, an exemplary symptom of a larger sickness onto female death."(K)

Not tonight, dear. I have a headache.

Each of these passages expresses a view of me and my work as inherently alien and hostile. In tandem with those passages cited above, they confuse me with the racist stereotypes my work examines. After describing my work as

"shocking"(H)	*"alienating"*(H)
"frightening"(H)	*"verging on the erotic"*(H)
"aggressive"(K)	*"anxious"*(K)

these writers then slide into a characterization of me in essentially the same terms. Thus they fail to observe the elementary distinction between the *effects* and *public meaning* of my work, and its *motivational origin*. Rather than leaving aside the latter—the rational choice in light of their decision not to contact me, and confining their attention to the former, these writers deflect their attention from my work to me, and focus their angers, fears, and fantasies accordingly: If my work makes them feel a certain way, it seems, then I (not them, not their cultural racism, not the work) must be the culprit. And indeed, when it comes to actually examining the work itself, Kuspit has literally nothing to say, as he explains in a footnote:

"For me, the political aspects of Piper's art, admirable as they are . . . are secondary to, and grow out of, her self-interpretation . . ."(K)

while Hess gets the physical facts about my work almost consistently wrong:

". . . this 'autobiographical artist,' as Piper is often called, . . ."(H)

"One of the first . . . feminist performance artists . . ."(H)

"Piper's presence is continually heard . . . in secondary materials . . ."(H)

"There is documentation (photographs . . . altered with thought bubbles) . . ."(H)

". . . revelatory diaries that faithfully narrate her intellectual and personal evolution."(H)

"She decided . . . to make comic book images . . ."(H)

"In Aspects of the Liberal Dilemma, *. . . the tape dissects white racial assumptions about the figures—prejudice by prejudice . . ."*(H)

"As one cautiously enters a black, forbidding maze, . . . four separate monologues . . . enumerate dozens of racist attitudes . . ."(H)

"She leads a dance workshop before an audience of mostly white students."(H)

"Piper's more recent charcoal illustrations . . . attempt to undermine the authority of the ads and articles, which are mostly concerned with apartheid in South Africa . . ."(H)

"She investigates the construction of identity by covering and uncovering herself in various mediums [sic]."(H)

Both of these writers have evident difficulties in literally *seeing* both me and my work. Their own unresolved racism and sexism obscure their perception of what is physically there and obstruct the extra effort of research and understanding that would enable them to control their fears, angers, and fantasies in order to write useful essays. Veridical perception and understanding is then replaced by a fictive, virulently stereotypical image: a hostile black, aggressive, alienating, stupid, neurotic, overbearing, manipulative woman who talks too much. This—not me, not my work—is the fiction to which these writers direct their "critical" attention. Their writing is the result not of ways of seeing my work but, rather, of ways of averting their gaze from it.

Perhaps these reactions are to be expected (they are, nevertheless, new to me in the context of art criticism). Each of us socialized in a society like this one must grapple with the racism and sexism we have inherited, and *no one*—despite the studied obliviousness of those who pride themselves on being politically correct—*is exempt.* Under these circumstances, given the intensity of their feelings, the honest thing for these writers to do would have been to, for example, grapple with these feelings in print, or decline to write at all, or engage with me interpersonally in order to overcome them, or address some other aspect of my work (and there are, I hope, many) that doesn't call them forth, or confine their discussion to the effects of my work on them and its meaning for them, or simply write a prereflective, "gut-response" negative article. These writers did none of these things.

Yes! Both of them conceived themselves (and represented themselves to others) as having written positive essays. Having manifested their cultural racism as obviously and consistently as they did, they both tried to paper it over with a sprinkling of laudatory phrases:

"One of the first, and most original . . ."(H)

". . . conceptual art at its best . . ."(K)

". . . a major and welcome event . . ."(H)

". . . Piper's extraordinary power of articulation . . ."(K)

"The power of the piece . . ."(H)

". . . of major importance . . ."(K)

". . . ahead of its time . . ."(H)

". . . most exemplary . . ."(K)

Buried in avalanches of factual distortion and thinly disguised hostility, these phrases are a mockery. First, they function to conceal and promulgate the cultural racism of these essays to those who do not read them carefully (and who has time to read anything carefully these days, unless it is about oneself?!). Those viewers of my work who have been influenced beforehand by these essays will have their experiences of it irrevocably sullied. Second, they function to conceal to the writers themselves their own virtually uncontrolled cultural racism, and to reassure them of their sacred sterling political intentions. Third, they function as did promotion to house nigger in the antebellum South: They are a kind of political blackmail, an inducement for me to accept without protest these expressions of cultural racism *as the price of being recognized in print at all.*

This third function will not succeed, and it may be instructive in distinguishing cultural racism from other kinds to consider why. I have already suggested that cultural racism attacks its victims in particularly vulnerable and personal places: their personal tastes, preferences, choices, modes of self-expression, beliefs, and relationships. These are the things that are denied or suppressed when cultural racism succeeds. Precisely because these things are so intimately constitutive of oneself, to deny or suppress them—or trade them for other advantages—is to abdicate all the things that make one's life, regardless of its other hardships, worthwhile. This is why those of us at the margin have so very tenaciously refused to jettison our cultural traditions, however threatening or offensive they may be to you *[Who, me? I* like *Funk music—in small doses, of course . . .]* for the sake of assimilation into white society—even if it means sacrificing the advantages assimilation may bring. So if you force us to choose between accepting cultural racism along with recognition, and protecting our cultural integrity in obscurity, the choice will be easy. The price of your recognition is too high.

6.

Perhaps you are surprised at the vehemence of my condemnation of these specimens of cultural racism. *[Right.]* Perhaps you think that every artist has to make sacrifices for the sake of media recognition, and that that's the risk one takes in putting one's work into the public sector. *[Right again.]* Perhaps you still don't quite see what all the fuss is about. *[You got it.]* I would like to suggest some reasons why you may find these specimens of cultural racism so difficult to see and so easy to dismiss. Perhaps you have never been the object of it. *[No, but . . .]* Perhaps you have some personal or professional investment in maintaining solidarity with those who perpetrate it. *[Now, wait a minute . . .]* Perhaps you have not taken the time to think carefully about what such specimens of cultural racism mean. *[Well, obviously I have a lot of other things to do besides sit around and brood about injustice.]* Or perhaps you think there are better ways of solving these problems that don't involve protesting against them, or holding them up to public scrutiny. *[Well, at least you could be a bit discreet.]* I disagree.

Those of us at the margin require extra effort from those of you in the center, if you genuinely want to welcome us in. Good intentions are not enough. It is also necessary that you acknowledge and confront your own ambivalences about us honestly, and get them under the control of your political conscience so they don't control you instead. *[How dare you cast aspersions of my motives? Bitch!]* It would also help if you would go out of your way to avoid imposing familiar labels that don't fit, and take the time to gather the facts, confront our complex singularity, and find—or create—the labels that do. *[Maybe you'd rather not be written about at all, hmmm?]* If you don't do these things, you will have not welcomed us in but merely waved from a distance at the simplistic stereotypes that stand between us.

From your perspective, all this may seem to be more trouble than it's worth. *[Right.]* We sometimes may seem difficult, oversensitive, insecure, ungrateful, or defensive. *[You said it, I didn't.]* From our perspective, you sometimes seem insensitive, smug, sanctimonious, arrogant, or presumptuous. *[Well, fuck you!]* This is because the concepts that make sense of your experience are often inadequate to ours, and we resent and resist their flat-footed application to us. *[Oh, yeah? Too bad.]* Perhaps some of the labels we prefer are equally inadequate, in the final analysis, to capture our reality. In that case, we all will have to collaborate together, wrestle with the issues and with one another, to create new ones. Individual creative genius is, in this instance, inadequate. But of course it seems obvious, on reflection, that if we are ever to understand each other, the power of naming must be shared. *[You really have some nerve, you know that? Telling me what to do! How dare you? And how dare you make insinuations about what I'm doing wrong?*

JUST WHO THE HELL DO YOU THINK YOU ARE, ANYWAY?]

Who, indeed! Maybe now—just maybe—we can begin a dialogue.

7.

How could the personal attacks exemplified by the two essays earlier discussed possibly receive institutional legitimation in a field ostensibly devoted to the analysis and evaluation of *objects?* The racist and sexist xenophobia embedded in these two essays are pathologically extreme symptoms of a tendency in recent writing about art that deserves further scrutiny: the tendency to substitute artist biography for art criticism. Artist biography as well as art criticism are both important elements in a full understanding of a work of art. Biographical material may be necessary, in order to articulate background contextual assumptions inherent in an artist's symbology that may not be accessible to all viewers of a work. For example, Euroethnics may need information about the cultural and social context in which colored artists produce their work, in order to understand fully the meaning of that work. Simply to impose Euroethnic aesthetic criteria without further question would be knee-jerk critical hegemony.[13] Moreover, some attention to biography reminds the viewer that the work of art itself is not a disembodied commodity floating in the global art market swamp but rather a personal expression of another human being's attitudes.[14] This, too, can be a useful corrective to critical hegemony.[15]

On the other hand, to *replace* art criticism with artist biography–or even to give preeminence to artist biography in a discussion purportedly addressed to art—is to abdicate in advance the increasingly difficult task of thinking clearly about the

13.
As Thomas McEvilley convincingly argues in his "Doctor Lawyer Indian Chief: "'Primitivism" in 20th Century Art' at the Museum of Modern Art in 1984," *Artforum* 23, no. 3 (November 1984), pp. 54–61. I discuss critical hegemony and the notion of Euroethnicity in "Power Relations within Existing Art Institutions," reprinted in this volume.

14.
Clearly the aspiration to universality is itself the expression of a particular personal attitude.

15.
I develop the case for *some* attention to artist biography—indeed, autobiography—more fully in "In Support of Meta-Art," reprinted in this volume.

public and social meaning of a work of art. And it often results in the sort of cheapening and trivializing of the work into a symptomatology of the artist, of the sort illustrated by the two essays examined earlier. Instead of attending to the meaning and implications of the work, one discusses—or speculates on—the motives and beliefs of its producer as a guide to the meaning of the work itself. This leads to odd hybrid locutions such as "the work tries to . . . ," "the work assumes . . . ," and so forth, in which mental states that properly belong to a human subject are ascribed to an aesthetic object instead. This fetishizes the work to an exaggerated and confusing degree.[16]

Moreover, replacing art criticism with artist biography is in any event an unreliable guide to the public meaning and implications of the work. Artists are notorious for issuing fatuous and misleading pronouncements on the significance of their own work. An artist has privileged access to the *motivations and assumptions* that cause her to produce the work—her intentions and interests in producing the work, her beliefs about it, her audience, herself, the world—but none at all to the import of the work itself. The artist's theory about this is no more or less likely to be correct than anyone else's. Indeed, her very proximity to her own interests in the work may obscure or distort her perception of its ultimate import for the viewing public. Part of the function of presenting an object for the contemplation of a viewing other is presumably to elicit *dialogue,* and ideally an impartially corrected conception of its import that can only be gained with third-personal critical distance on the object itself. To require that the artist supply that corrected conception, too—in addition to supplying the motivational background and the work—is to pre-empt the viewer's creative engagement with the work. It is also to abdicate the critical responsibility imposed by third-personal distance and to subvert the dialogue for the sake of a third-personal spectacle of artistic onanism.

Replacing art criticism with artist biography can be a particularly insidious trap for colored artists, precisely because the struggle against cultural racism has not yet been won. Deflecting attention from the work onto its producer enables the viewer or critic to rely on her preprogrammed social response to the artist in constructing an interpretation. This strategy is a refuge for those fearful of being found speechless before a work of art, as though it were a mental defect to be unable to dismiss it with a few well-chosen epigrams. Substituting biography for criticism requires far less creativity than an interpretation that both incorporates the work

16.
However, in "Performance and the Fetishism of the Art Object" (this volume, reprinted from *Vanguard* 10, no. 10 [December 1981–January 1982], pp. 16–19), I argue that we must fetishize art objects to some extent.

into the shared context of critical discourse and plausibly accounts for its singularity relative to that context. Because it is almost impossible, or at least very difficult, for any critic's preprogrammed social responses to be entirely free of xenophobic attitudes toward a colored artist (nor, perhaps, should we realistically expect them to be at this stage of history), these, as we have already seen, may then poison the critic's interpretation itself.

Moreover, focusing on the artist at the expense of the art reinforces the familiar xenophobic whine that colored art "lacks universality." By telescoping the work into a contingent expression of the artist's particular personal circumstances, this strategy ignores or minimizes its broader or global implications. In conjunction with the demographic paucity of visible colored artists as subjects of critical consideration, it also feeds into the false belief that the work really is nothing but one idiosyncratic expression of a demographic minority. For these reasons, politically conscientious critics need to be particularly alert to the tendency to indulge in this kind of trivialization of the work.

Colored artists themselves often vacillate between deploring the absence of biography in writings about their work and deploring its excess. On the one hand, a critical analysis that is insensitive to the artist's distinctive cultural heritage is almost sure to miss the full significance of the work, in addition to implicitly belittling that heritage as unimportant to an understanding of it. Moreover, successful colored artists ordinarily are concerned to discharge their ethical responsibility as visible role models for other colored artists and art students who labor in obscurity. On the other hand, they do get sick of having their work reduced to manifestations of their ethnicity or symptoms of their audience's ambivalence about it; of being singled out for their racial identity rather than for their creative genius; and perhaps worst of all, of being considered an art-market liability—or worse, an art-market curiosity—because of their ethnicity. That is to say, colored artists want their ethnicity, but without the stigma attached to their ethnicity—just as whites have theirs. Those colored artists who have achieved some measure of public visibility are thus often torn between the desire to proclaim their cultural heritage proudly and publicly, as another notch in the gun of civil rights struggle, and the temptation to suppress it completely so we can all get on with the universal conversation about Art.

This last, however, is to be tempted by an illusion, and this is why biography almost always has some, albeit small, part in the full interpretation of a work. For there is no universal conversation about Art to get on with. There are only particular conversations in particular idiolects, some of which pretend to universality, some of which do not; some of which are part of an individual's cultural heritage itself, some of which proceed in what seems to be an alien tongue.[17] Among those that pretend to universality, some attract with the promise of global significance and global recognition for one's work—but not, in truth, because of the terms and scope of the conversation, however intrinsically stimulating these may be. They attract because of the visible economic and political power of the speakers, and were the language of the powerful Swahili rather than Euroethnic Formalese, the attraction would be no less strong. We all want to be part of that conversation because we legitimately want to partake of that power, too. We don't necessarily want to wrest it away, we just want to participate in it. We want (to put it more baldly than I did in section 2) a piece of the pie. But the question remains of the price we are willing to pay for it.

I have suggested that the price of the pie as offered by some may be too high: It may require the acquiescence of colored artists in racist and sexist modes of critical interpretation—a probable consequence of excess artist biography—or, at the other extreme, it may require the voluntary suppression of one's distinctive colored cultural heritage altogether—a probable consequence of its complete absence. But it now becomes clearer that both of these extremes in fact come to the same Faustian swindle. We have already seen that to acquiesce in xenophobic critical interpretation of the sort earlier discussed is to abdicate our singularity for the sake of tired labels and preconceptions designed to defuse the significance of our presence in your world. But to suppress all mention of our cultural heritage where relevant in order to get on with the universal conversation about Art is to eradicate our singular contribution to critical discourse altogether, and to discard our variegated native languages of creativity for an imposed artificial one into which our terms often fail to translate. For colored artists, then, the extremes both of artist biography without criticism and art criticism without biography are dangerous harbingers of aesthetic obliteration—the triumph of cultural racism.

At this price, the pie is quite simply unpalatable to us. Perhaps it is also somewhat unappetizing to you. But how unappetizing? Are you ready to consider the possibility that we all need to collaborate on a new recipe, with a more diverse mix of ingredients?

17.
Artists who worry about being "ghettoized" through association with their comrades in race or gender overlook the ghettoized nature of the circles to which they aspire. Escape from the ghetto is impossible. The real issue is in which ghettos one aspires to membership, and why. My own ambition is to be a card-carrying member of as many ghettos as possible.

14.
Why Guess? #2 (1989). Photo by *Ebony* magazine. Courtesy John Weber Gallery, collection of the artist.

17. A Paradox of Conscience

First published in *The New Art Examiner* 16, no. 8 (April 1989), pp. 27–31.

When asked what I do for a living, I usually reply that I teach philosophy and moonlight as an artist. This answer reflects the relative stability of my income from each field, rather than their order of importance in my life. In fact both are equally important to me, for completely different reasons, and to give up doing either would be unthinkable. But a recent experience in the art world has led me to juxtapose the two fields in thought more than I usually do. This essay is going to be about some of the differences between them, and about the consequences for practice that issue from these.[1]

1. Analytic Philosophy

The philosophy I teach and write is mainstream academic philosophy, that is, the Anglo-American analytic tradition that is taught in most major university philosophy departments in the United States. Analytic philosophy is a style of doing philosophy. It is not restricted to any particular subject matter: history, literature, politics, and popular culture, as well as ethics, logic, aesthetics, epistemology, philosophy of mind, language, action, mathematics, psychology, and science are all among the subject matter of analytic philosophy. Analytic philosophers are committed to the enterprise of thinking as clearly, carefully, and coherently as possible about whatever issues they are addressing in their work. By and large their writing style aspires to the model espoused in Strunk and White's *Elements of Style*.[2]

This does not mean it is always easy to read philosophical prose in the analytic tradition. Sometimes the attempt to be clear and consistent requires carefully defined technical terminology or logical apparatus. Sometimes the issue has been refined, by decades — sometimes centuries — of collaborative examination, to such a level of subtlety that it remains completely obscure to the uninitiated. Sometimes, when interpreting a historical text of great density, specialists rely on an implicit, shared understanding of the author's terminology that makes their discussions inaccessible to anyone who has not previously read and grasped the text in question. And sometimes, when reaching for the truth about a very difficult issue, analytic philosophers give in to the temptation to substitute seductive metaphor for humdrum conceptual clarity.

Nevertheless the goal is to show one's respect for difficult and complex ideas by thinking as deeply and thoroughly as one can about them, and to show one's re-

1. In thinking about this topic I have benefited from discussions with John Welchman and Josephine Withers.

2. Strunk, W., Jr., and E. B. White, *The Elements of Style* (New York: Macmillan, 1962).

spect for one's readership by communicating one's thoughts about them as clearly, carefully, and consistently as possible. Intellectual standards, then, in the analytic tradition, are rigorous and deeply entrenched, and—as is true in any highly specialized field—internalizing them requires years of concerted training and study.

Originality of thought within this tradition is usually a function of innovative solutions to traditional problems, new insights or perspectives on standard ways of conceiving them, and—although this last is in truth very rare in analytic philosophy—the discovery of new problems themselves. So originality in analytic philosophy means originality of content, not style. Analytic philosophers get impatient with a writing style that is florid, or turgid, or patterned on the author's free associations, or that relies for its persuasiveness on name-dropping or appeals to authority. Philosophical prose that obscures its ideas behind hints, allusions, jargon, idiosyncratic grammar or vocabulary, or run-on sentences with recurring literary devices quickly raises the suspicion that there are no genuine ideas there to be mined at all. There are, in fact, some fine stylists among prominent analytic philosophers. But none of them violate the general dictum that style is a vehicle for content, so that philosophical originality may be more easily discerned if it is there. And within the arena of content, philosophical originality usually consists in finding new solutions to traditional problems, rather than discovering new problems to solve. (Nor are there any philosophical problems of current interest outside the analytic tradition that analytic philosophy itself has not examined in some form or at some time, but that is the subject of a different essay.)

So the Anglo-American analytic tradition is an intellectually conservative one in several respects. This has many consequences, both good and bad. The inherent intellectual conservatism of analytic philosophy sometimes extends, in its practitioners, to an intellectual and cultural conservatism more generally. Analytic philosophers tend to be dismissive of nonscientistic theories—for example, of paranormal phenomena, spirituality, or alternative nonphysicalistic cosmologies. And they are often disparaging or ignorant of cultural innovations in other fields, social groups, or societies that have not received the imprimatur of the Western Euroethnic tradition. Moreover, the intellectual conservatism of analytic philosophy goes hand in hand with an inclination to de facto political and social conservatism as well. According to a recent study published in the *Proceedings of the American Philosophical Association,* only 8 percent of all tenured positions in the field are held by women, and "there are virtually no minority women in philosophy. . . . They are essentially unrepresented on university faculties in philosophy."[3] (In a field of approximately 9,500 I am the only tenured black woman I know of, and I made it only on the second try.)[4] Finally, the values expressed in analytic philosophy's intellectual standards — logic, rationality, consistency — have a central claim to objectivity in Western culture, and this sometimes promotes in its practitioners a complacency and parochial resistance to appreciating the value of phenomena that are not susceptible to analysis in these terms.

However, I want to focus on the good consequences of analytic philosophy's intellectual conservatism, as a point of comparison with the art world. First and foremost, there are traditional standards of intellectual performance that are transmitted from generation to generation of undergraduate philosophy majors and graduate students in the field. In studying contemporary analytic philosophy, students have before them a generally stable and consistent goal of intellectual performance they aim to achieve in their own work. Part of the function of graduate education in philosophy is to instill those standards of intellectual performance, not just as a goal to aspire to, but as a reflexive habit of thought. And at the professional level this habit of thought is inculcated even more deeply through the institutionalized conventions of reading and critiquing colleagues' papers, both informally and in colloquia. Although no one ever conforms fully to the ideal standards, a successful graduate education in philosophy leaves one with what I will call an *intellectual conscience:* When one rereads the first draft of one's paper after having putting it aside for a while to gain critical distance, one recognizes the areas of fuzzy thinking, garbled sentences, unexplicated basic assumptions, logical leaps and lacunae, and one *winces* and feels impelled to return to the computer.

An intellectual conscience itself has advantages and disadvantages. One advantage is that it promotes intellectual self-awareness, that is, the ability to judge one's performance from a perspective — the perspective of the standards one accepts — outside one's immediate impulses and desires. I can monitor the quality of my thought by comparison with the standards of intellectual quality I accept. This experience is very different from that of blindly indulging one's momentary preferences in print (although of course that kind of writing has its place as well). A second advantage is that an intellectual conscience promotes intellectual independence: If I understand and accept the standards, I can come to know when and whether I'm adhering to them. And that means that the competence of my work,

3.
"Special Report: Women in Philosophy," *Proceedings and Addresses of the American Philosophical Association* 60, no. 4 (March 1987), pp. 681–698.

4.
A second black woman was tenured in the spring of 1994, and we are rooting for the third.

and my evaluation of its competence, depends almost entirely on what I know and do, not on someone else's evaluation of it. Other people may tell me a paper is wonderful when I know in my heart that it's bad, and other people may tell me it's terrible when I know in my heart that it's good.[5] A further advantage of an intellectual conscience—this one a consequence of intellectual self-awareness and intellectual independence conjointly—is intellectual responsibility. Once I acknowledge my deviation from the standard of intellectual performance, that's where the buck stops. There is no one else I can blame for my errors in reasoning or failure to comprehend a view. The major disadvantage of an intellectual conscience is an increased susceptibility to self-deception. Knowing what the standard is and having a deep personal investment in meeting it increases one's resistance to admitting one's failure to do so, and so to taking responsibility for that.

2. Contemporary Euroethnic Art

Next I want to talk about how contemporary Euroethnic art differs from analytic philosophy with respect to these attributes, as a way of understanding the recent art-world experience I alluded to at the beginning of this discussion. By contrast with analytic philosophy, intellectual standards in contemporary Euroethnic art[6] are there to be violated. This itself is contemporary Euroethnic art's most central intellectual standard of all. Even in this postmodern era, in which aesthetic innovation is supposed to be impossible, artists strive for innovative and ground-breaking ways to put this point across. Of course this intellectual radicalism responds to continual and persistent economic demands for new, improved commodities for art-market consumption. But it originates with the influence of impressionism. It is institutionalized and generationally transmitted by art education programs in art schools, colleges, and universities. And it is reinforced by critical evaluations of art in the print media, galleries, museums, and funding organizations.

I said that the intellectual conservatism of analytic philosophy sometimes encourages social and cultural conservatism—and provincialism—as well. By contrast,

5.
The intellectual independence nurtured by a philosophical education can be a powerful foil to the unremitting political and social conservatism of the field. To have internalized its standards of intellectual performance is perforce to recognize betrayals of them, and therefore to recognize disparities, when they occur, between those who actually meet them and those who receive professional rewards for doing so.

6.
I speak of intellectual (rather than "aesthetic") standards because the intellect is no less central in making art than it is in doing philosophy. That art education trains the intellect to do a different thing does not imply that it does not get trained at all.

contemporary Euroethnic art's intellectual radicalism tends to encourage a comparatively greater receptivity to alternative modes of expression, appropriation of styles from other fields and social groups, interest in cross-cultural artifacts and practices, and innovations in media and means of communication. The hermeticism of analytic philosophy highlights by contrast the inclusive and cosmopolitan sensibility of contemporary art all the more.

On reflection, this is to be expected. If what is valued is a new approach to a traditional problem, as is true in analytic philosophy, then issues, questions, and styles of expression that do not clearly bear on it will be viewed as unimportant distractions. But if what is valued is a new medium or style of expression, as is true in contemporary Euroethnic art, then all the world, including pop-cultural as well as cross-cultural expressive modalities (whether acknowledged or not) is grist for the artist's mill.

This contrast, in turn, uncovers a parallel contrast in the standards of originality in each field. Whereas originality in analytic philosophy is a function of subject matter, originality in contemporary Euroethnic art is almost solely, according to its intellectual standards, a function of form. As we know, contemporary art is extremely resistant to innovations in subject matter, for example, unadulterated political or social critique, or topics traditionally of interest solely to women (childbirth and child care, food, relationships, the home, etc.). Crudely put: Whereas a philosopher considered to be first-rate says something new in the same old way, an artist considered to be first-rate says the same old thing in a new way.

Internalizing the intellectual standards of performance in contemporary Euroethnic art is no easier than it is in philosophy. It takes years of training, acculturation, and practice to recognize or produce an artwork that counts as innovative relative to those standards. Art's receptivity to new styles of expression is not indiscriminate (though it is sometimes prejudiced), and it is almost impossible to explain to the uninitiated or the novice why not just *anything* that you've never happened to have seen in a gallery before deserves to be in one according to these standards. Yet I think the end result of this process of inculcation is not quite the stringent intellectual conscience I earlier described as a necessary requirement for doing analytic philosophy. Recognition and artistic success depend too heavily on extraneous contingencies, such as market supply and demand and the vicissitudes of critical fashion, for any artist ever to be quite sure that wincing is the correct response to a work that did not come out as she intended. And indeed a more sophisticated artistic sensibility is one that can discern professional success-promoting qualities in a work, whether she originally intended them or not. Even qualities that she deliberately but vainly tried to eliminate from a work may be the arbiter of the artist's professional success,[7] and to take this fact seriously into account is necessarily to *dull* the proddings of intellectual conscience that incline one to return to the drawing board precisely because they are there.

Now to get to the advantages and disadvantages of a weak or nonexistent intellectual conscience. One advantage is the greater receptivity to new occurrences and forms of expression mentioned earlier. Flaccid or unstable standards of excellence allow the possibility of engendering entirely new ones through an uncorrected slip of the brush or unplanned stain on the photographic paper. A second one is greater sensitivity to external contingencies. To be internally unsure of the worth of one's work is to be more susceptible to outside critical influences on it, and therefore more responsive to opportunities for success as defined or provided by those external influences. In general, the overarching advantage of lacking an intellectual conscience is opportunism: Undistracted by considerations of how well or badly, according to my own requirements, I am achieving my goal, I am freed to concentrate simply on finding the most efficient means of achieving it, whatever these are.

However, I think the disadvantages of lacking an intellectual conscience far outweigh the advantages. For one thing, intellectual and artistic self-awareness is stunted. If I have no standard for judging my artistic performance except what other people supply, then I either do what they tell me, or vent my momentary impulses when I do anything at all. This reduces artists to babies, and art making to toilet training. A second disadvantage is intellectual dependence. Without an intellectual conscience to evaluate one's performance as an artist, one must depend for such an evaluation on what others decide. It's good if the art world says so; and if it does not, the temptation may be strong to consider a career in advertising. Moreover, an absence of intellectual conscience undermines intellectual responsibility. By this I do not mean that it necessarily makes one *ir*responsible. Rather, it *relieves* one of accountability for work that is in fact, regardless of what the art world says, inferior. For because it is the external exigencies of art-market supply and demand, and critical fashion, that define standards of excellence, work that gives the art audience what it wants by definition satisfies those standards. Any other criteria that might be brought to bear on the evaluation of the work—for example, didactic effectiveness, or social or spiritual significance, or aesthetic integrity—are simply irrelevant.

7.
Consider, for example, the influence of aleatoric methods on early conceptual and process art; or of the New Museum's "Bad Painting" exhibition on the art public's receptivity to bad painters such as David Salle.

Along with these disadvantages comes a certain charming intellectual honesty. Because any such other criteria are irrelevant to the external standards of performance one accepts, there is no pressure on one to deny having violated those criteria, and so less of a tendency to self-deception. Indeed, one may take a certain pride in having satisfied the external standards—essentially meeting art-market demand—precisely by having violated these other, lingering criteria of evaluation. In fact, insofar as the external standards that actually function to select those works considered most worthy at this period in history are *masked* by these other criteria, to which lip service is paid but that are in practice functionally impotent, one may succeed in expressing a great deal of contempt for these criteria, oneself, and one's lip-service-paying audience by flouting them. Thus contemporary Euroethnic art practice licenses free expression of the greed, gluttony, contempt, and self-hatred that other people find too ugly or shameful to display. Indeed, contemporary Euroethnic art practice makes a virtue of these emotions by rewarding them.

3. A Recent Art-World Experience

Last fall I was urged to see an exhibition, after having seen in advance two ads for the show placed by the gallery in different art magazines.[8] In one of the ads, the artist is perched in front of a blackboard holding a piece of chalk, smiling benignly at a racially mixed class of six- or seven-year-olds, some of whom are raising their hands. On the blackboard are the phrases, "Exploit the masses," "Sentimentality," and "Banality as saviour." In the second ad, he is shown astride a neighing Shetland pony in what looks like a Garden of Eden set, holding a wedding bouquet. He is flanked by two sexpots in bikinis, one of whom is looking at him intently and proffering a wedding cake, the other of whom is seated on the ground in front, in a pose reminiscent of Manet's *Olympia,* petting the pony, and looking into the distance.

The exhibition itself consisted of overblown five-and-dime trinkets in wood or porcelain. They included a statue of Michael Jackson in whiteface petting a monkey; a naked woman with large breasts in a bathtub with her legs parted around an emerging snorkle and the top of her head above the mouth cut off; another naked woman embracing a pink cartoon tiger between large breasts; two white children

8.
What follows is about an experience of some recent art. The points just made also could be extended to cover a couple of recent experiences of art criticism as well, but for considerations of space. However, see "Ways of Averting One's Gaze", reprinted in this volume, for a related discussion.

leading a donkey and a black one pushing its hindquarters from the rear; a garishly un-DaVinci-esque St. John the Baptist. The employment of European working-class wood artisans to carve, paint, and finish the wood pieces was a well-publicized fact about the exhibition, as was the fact that each work was replicated three times, each replica on exhibition simultaneously in different galleries located in the United States and Europe.

On the day I was in the gallery, there were perhaps fifteen or twenty visitors. Publicity photographs were being taken, and two of the rooms were flooded with hot, bright lights. A photographer was issuing directions, and the artist, it seemed, was doing what he was told. Displayed at the front of the desk were the reviews of the show, most of them vehemently negative. The gentleman behind the desk was bustling around, puffing on a cigarette, sweating, handing out price lists, and telling a listener, in a voice that carried, that the show had already sold out, that they would have been extremely disappointed if it hadn't, that all the newspapers had reviewed the show, one of them twice, and that one art critic (a senior and very conservative white male) had done a much better job of panning it than another (a young and progressive white female). Between the art, heat, lights, noise, sweat, cigarette smoke, and general frenzy I felt physical disgust.

What arrested me about this experience was not the art, which was mediocre in conception and execution (as a friend put it to me, "Some people say he's the next Andy Warhol. I say he's the next Tiny Tim"). The significance I found in this exhibition was the significance we gave it. The gallery thought it was important enough to show. The art critics thought it was important enough to write about. We, the art public, thought it was important enough to see. And some collectors thought it was important enough to buy (I assume they will store it in warehouses until its next public showing). Because the art world uniformly concurred in making it important, it became important. So what, exactly, is the nature of its importance for contemporary Euroethnic art?

The art magazine advertisements that preceded this exhibition effectively blocked any ambiguity of interpretation that might have resulted from merely seeing the works on view. One advertisement portrayed the artist as a great white father, teaching exploitation and banality to a racially mixed class of youngsters, and some of the works in the show expressed these racist and philistine values even more clearly. The other advertisement that I saw portrayed the artist as a playboy surrounded by bimbos offering conjugal bliss as well as the call of the wild, and other works in the show expressed these sexist values equally faithfully. The first-mentioned advertisement advocated contempt for "the masses," and the employment of skilled woodworkers to produce the pieces carved in wood demonstrated how such contempt could be both expressed to their face and turned to everyone's financial advantage. The replication of each work three times for three different simultaneous exhibitions satisfied contemporary Euroethnic art's standard of innovation by flouting it.

Within this context, there are only two possibilities. Either the artist meant to affirm these values unself-consciously, or he meant to "call attention to" them, as the lingo has it, from a critically distanced perspective. If the second possibility seems more plausible, then the question becomes, What was the critically distanced perspective from which the artist invited us to attend to these values? Unlike Duchamp's or Warhol's, this work did not illuminate the aesthetic interest of commonplace popular culture. On the contrary. It represented popular culture as vulgar and fascistic, and those who prefer it as stupid, corrupt, or infantile. It was impossible to detect anything of aesthetic interest in the values expressed in this work (there is nothing aesthetically new or interesting about evil), or in the way they were expressed. In size and quantity as well as imagery, the work engorged the viewer on malevolent pop trivia to the point of nausea, thereby deadening rather than stimulating aesthetic appreciation of what is unique and special in ordinary, mass-produced objects of popular culture.

Therefore the distanced critical perspective from which we were supposedly invited to consider the values inherent in this work could not have been an aesthetic one. These values—racism, sexism, philistinism, cynicism, manipulation, contempt—are morally vicious values, and therefore the critically distanced perspective from which the artist purportedly examined them must have been a moral one. But a distanced moral perspective that criticizes morally vicious values merely by expressing them is no more of a genuinely distanced perspective than would be one that criticized child abuse by committing it. So it appears that this work can be understood only as having affirmed and advocated unself-consciously the moral pollution it so blatantly expressed. It offered its viewers nothing positive, either of moral or aesthetic value. Indeed it deliberately ridiculed such values and reaped considerable professional rewards for the artist for doing so.

This, I think, is why the art world made this work important. It could have been otherwise perceived. It could have been seen as just another attempt by a mediocre artist to gain notoriety by making art that was publicly offensive.[9] Granted, this

9.
The contemporary Euroethnic art world is in the process of developing quite a tradition of such howls for attention by some of its more intellectually underprivileged white youth. The "Nigger Drawings" incident of the late 1970s would be one of the first in this recent tradition; last year's "lampoon" of Harold Washington at the Art Institute of Chicago would be another high point.

work stood out by being offensive in every respect and to every sensibility. Nevertheless, the art world could have ignored it (as it does so much of real value), and it did not. It did not for the same reason one cannot ignore one's inadvertent but clearly delineated reflection in a mirror. This work reflected back to the art world in a particularly succinct form the greed, gluttony, contempt, and self-hatred that so much contemporary Euroethnic art-making cultivates as virtues. I suggested that these emotions are the natural consequence of a professional standard of performance that recommends the violation of standards, unaccompanied by intellectual conscience. This exhibition revealed the inherent paradox of such a standard: If the standard consists in violating all standards, then a complete absence of intellectual conscience is precisely what this standard demands. An art that defiles every conceivable value it can summon—whether personal, political, aesthetic, or moral—is the only art that can fully succeed in satisfying *these* desiderata.

Earlier I claimed that, relative to such a sensibility, other criteria according to which one might evaluate a work of art, such as didactic effectiveness, social or spiritual significance, or aesthetic integrity, were nothing but functionally impotent targets of potshots or lip service. But I also argued that one of the valuable consequences of professional standards of performance that stress innovation is receptivity to diversity. There are many of us in the art world who take these other criteria more seriously than being professionally rewarded. We have a somewhat different reaction to this work. We view it as evidence that the artist has, indeed, succumbed to the temptations of a career in advertising. We are glad he has found his niche somewhere else, and hope his supervisors at the ad agency can elicit from him some contribution of use to the average consumer.

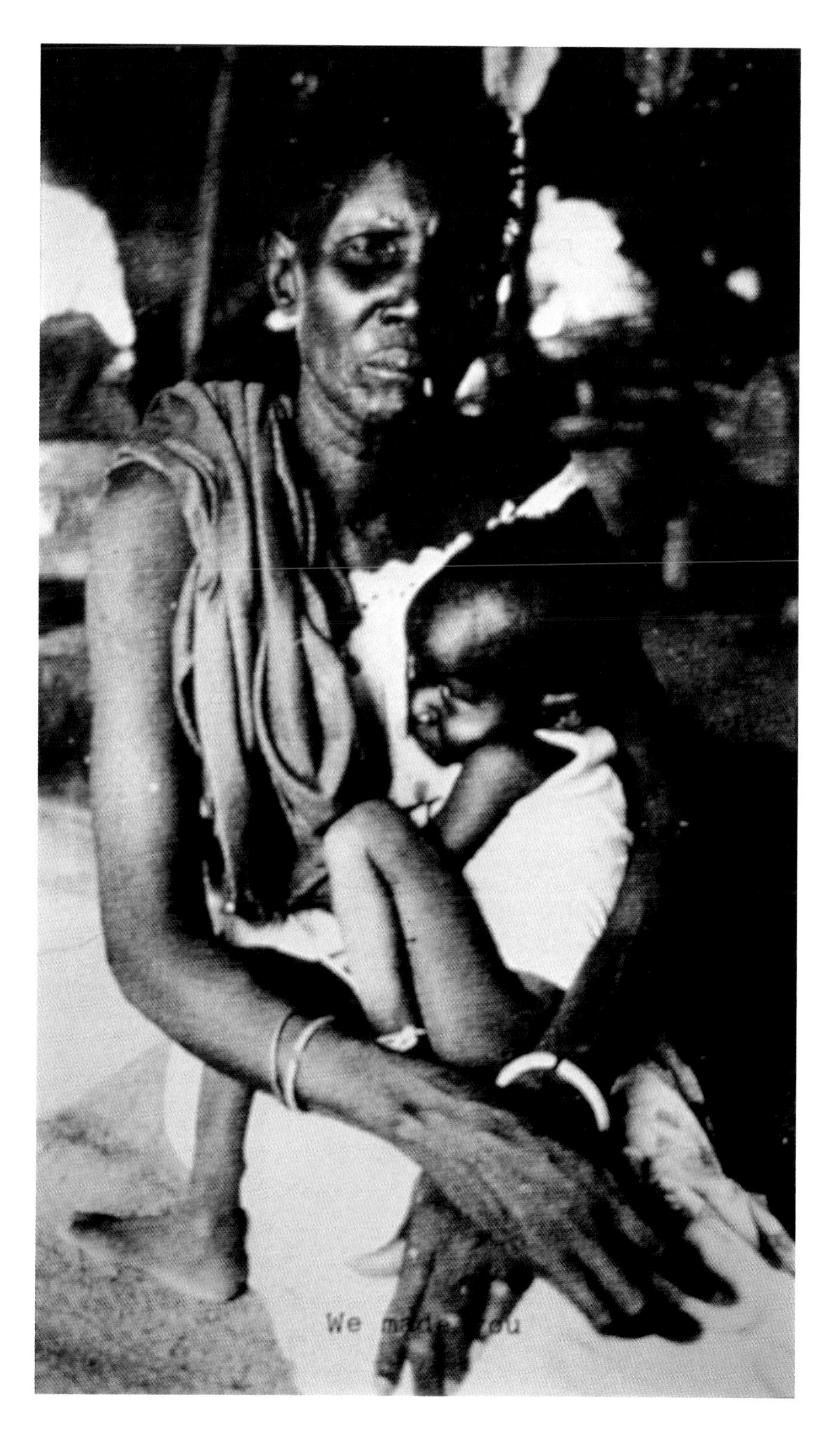

15.
Ur-Mutter #2 (1989).
Photo by Peter Turnley/Black Star.
Courtesy John Weber Gallery, collection of the artist.

18. The Triple Negation of Colored Women Artists

First published in the catalog *Next Generation: Southern Black Aesthetic* (Chapel Hill: University of North Carolina, 1990).

These are interesting times in which to be a colored woman artist (henceforth a CWA).[1] Forces of censorship and repression in this country are gathering steam and conviction as those same forces in other countries are being overturned or undermined. No one should be surprised at these inverse parallel developments. Sociologists know that groups tend to increase the internal pressures toward conformity and homogeneity in order to maintain their identities against external pressures forcing dissolution into a larger whole. And just as American society is now imposing a Euroethnic, Christian, heterosexual male ethos on all of us in order to maintain a uniquely American identity against the incursion of other, emerging democracies in Russia and Central Europe, similarly the art world is reasserting a Euroethnic, heterosexual male aesthetic on all of us in order to resist the incursion of gays, coloreds, and practitioners of outlaw sexuality into its inner sanctum.[2] In particular, I will argue that the ideology of postmodernism functions to repress and exclude CWAs from the art-historical canon of the Euroethnic mainstream. Correctly perceiving the artifacts produced by CWAs as competitors for truth and a threat to the cultural homogeneity of the Euroethnic tradition, it denies those artifacts their rightful status as innovations relative to that tradition through ad hoc disclaimers of the validity of concepts such as "truth" and "innovation."

Item, 1982: NEA funding for the Washington Women's Art Center ceases after congressional protest over their "Erotic Art Show." Item, 1983: Rosalind Krauss explains to her fellow symposiasts at the NEA Art Criticism Symposium that she doubts that there is any unrecognized African-American art of quality because if it doesn't bring itself to her attention, it probably doesn't exist. Item, as of this writing: No CWA is invited to show in any Whitney Biennal, ever. Item, 1987: Donald Kuspit publishes in his vanity journal a seven-page essay devoted to the thesis that my writing is a symposium of mental illness and my work is not worth dis-

1.
Let's begin with a word about terminology. I do not like the currently fashionable phrase "people of color" for referring to Americans of African, Asian, Native American, or Hispanic descent. It is syntactically cumbersome. It also has an excessively genteel and euphemistic ring to it, as though there were some ugly social fact about a person we needed to simultaneously denote and avoid, by performing elaborate grammatical circumlocutions. Moreover, discarding previous phrases, such as "Negro," "black," "colored," or "Afro-American," as unfashionable or derogatory implies that there is some neutral, politically correct phrase that can succeed in denoting the relevant group without taking on the derogatory and insulting connotations a racist society itself attaches to such groups. There is no such phrase. As long as African-Americans are devalued, the inherently neutral words coined to denote them will themselves eventually become terms of devaluation. Finally, the phrase is too inclusive for my purposes in this essay. I want to talk specifically about women artists of African descent, in such a way as to include those Hispanic-Americans, Asian-Americans, and Native Americans who publicly acknowledge and identify with their African-American ancestry, and exclude those who do not. The term *colored* seems both etiologically and metaphorically apt.

2.
Needless to say, this explanation is compatible with self-interested attempts of conservative congressmen and senators to find some local scapegoat to substitute for foreign communism, in order to divert attention away from their ineffectuality in simply representing their constituencies.

cussing.[3] Item, 1988: an unusually strong group show of the work of colored women artists opens at the Intar Gallery in Manhattan and receives no attention from the local Euroethnic press, with the exception of Arlene Raven's intelligent review in the *Village Voice*.[4] Item, 1989: Christina Orr-Cahall cancels a retrospective of the photography of Robert Mapplethorpe at the Corcoran Gallery. Item, 1989: Jesse Helms protests public funding of Andres Serrano's work by the Southeast Center for Contemporary Art's Awards in the Visual Arts. Item, 1989: Roberta Smith explains to film interviewer Terry McCoy that the real problem with the art of African-Americans is that it just isn't any good, that it would be in mainstream galleries if it were, that she's been up to the Studio Museum a couple of time and hasn't seen anything worthwhile, that it's all too derivative, and so on.[5] Item, 1990: The National Endowment for the Arts withdraws funding from an exhibition catalog about AIDS at Artists' Space. Item, 1990: Hilton Kramer devotes two essays in the *New York Observer* to protesting the current interest in issues of race and gender that, he claims, leaves quality by the wayside.[6]

In a more intellectually sophisticated environment, these howlers would be accorded exactly the weight they deserve, that is, none. In this decade's art world—as we can see, a world not exactly overpopulated by mental giants[7]—they are dangerously repressive in effect. Instead of being recognized and ridiculed for what they are, namely, obscene theatrical gestures without redeeming social content, they legitimate and encourage further such obscenities among those who are naturally inclined to them, and intimidate the naturally docile into self-censorship. We can expect these repressive measures to increase in number, severity, and ugliness as those relegated to the margins succeed in greater numbers in gaining access to

3.
Donald Kuspit, "Adrian Piper: Self-Healing through Meta-Art," *Art Criticism* 3, no. 3 (September 1987), pp. 9–16.

4.
Arlene Raven, "Colored," *The Village Voice,* May 31, 1988, p. 92. The title of the exhibition was "Autobiography: In Her Own Image," curated by Howardena Pindell.

5.
Telephone conversation between the author and Terry McCoy, fall 1989.

6.
Dennis Szakacs, of the Southeastern Center for Contemporary Art (SECCA), provided the following statement: "Attempts were made to obtain copies of Kramer's articles from the *New York Observer* as well as from Kramer himself. An *Observer* staff person explained that they were not equipped to handle such requests while Kramer, in a telephone conversation, acknowledged that the articles existed and agreed to send copies. After many weeks and several unreturned messages, the Kramer articles have yet to arrive."

7.
I am not an intellectual elitist, but I do believe that racism, sexism, homophobia, and intolerance generally involve cognitive deficits and elementary errors in reasoning and judgment. See "Two Kinds of Discrimination," this volume, for a fuller treatment.

unjustly withheld social and economic advantages within the mainstream Euroethnic art world.[8]

At the same time, on the other hand, a few CWAs recently have begun to receive some modest measure of attention from the Euroethnic art world. We have been invited to show in previously all-Euroethnic group exhibitions, galleries, or museums, and we have received some critical attention for work that for decades was largely passed over in silence, as though it did not exist. No protest against the de facto censorship of CWAs has ever been mounted of the sort that has rightly greeted the recent attempted censorship of the work of male artists Robert Mapplethorpe, Andres Serrano, or David Wojnarowicz. Until very recently, CWAs were ignored as a matter of course.[9] In the last few years, CWAs have begun to exist in the consciousness of the more progressive, intellectually oriented circles of the Euroethnic artworld.

Certain factors can be cited to explain the recent visibility of CWAs. In 1987, without fanfare and at considerable professional risk to himself, Michael Brenson began to review the work of African-American artists in the *New York Times* on a regular basis. The appearance of these reviews, backed by Brenson's authority and that of the *New York Times,* effected a profound change in the conventions of Euroethnic art writing. By approaching African-American art with the same attention, respect, and critical standards he applied to Euroethnic art, Brenson singlehandedly exposed the tacit racism of ignoring African-American art that had prevailed among virtually all other Euroethnic art critics.[10] The same year, Howardena Pindell

8.
It's so amusing how arguments that there are no more margins always seem to come from those in the center. Just as it's amusing how arguments that there is no more avant garde always seem to come from those who have gotten the greatest economic mileage from being a part of it. In general, it's immensely entertaining to watch the keepers of the brass ring start to deny that it exists just when they notice that the disenfranchised are about to grab it. No doubt this is pure coincidence.

9.
My personal experience is of having been included in "definitive" major museum shows of conceptual art in the late 1960s, until the art-world contacts I made then met me face-to-face, found out I was a woman, and disappeared from my life; and in "definitive" major museum shows of Body Art and women's art in the early 1970s, until the contacts I made then found out I was colored and similarly disappeared from my life. Although I have had virtually no contact with major museums since those years, I fully expect the situation to improve as all those individuals die off and are replaced by smarter ones.

10.
An attempt to sully Brenson's achievement by portraying him as moved by professional self-interest recently appeared in *Spy* magazine (J. J. Hunsecker, "Naked City: The *Times*," *Spy* [April 1990], p. 48). This uncommonly ugly and snide article backfires, by revealing the author's own inherent racism. That the very choice to treat Brenson's decision to write about African-American artists as cause for ridiculing him itself demeans those artists doesn't seem to have occurred to Hunsecker. Whatever Brenson's actual motives were, they do not undermine the cultural and historical importance of his actions and their consequences. But as described in *Spy,* they at least provide a refreshing contrast to those sterling motives, so frequently professed by the politically correct, that nevertheless fail to spark any effective political action at all.

compiled and published "Art World Racism: A Documentation," which was excerpted for broader art-world consumption in the *New Art Examiner* in 1989.[11] This work documented the hard statistics of African-American exclusion from Euroethnic galleries, museums, and publications for all to see. The statistics were so incriminating and inexcusable that they effectively foreclosed further disingenuity or rationalization of practices now clearly identifiable as racist. Both of these efforts have sparked energetic and conscientious attempts at reparation in many quarters.[12] Because racism and sexism often go together, amelioration of both together can be achieved by showcasing the work of CWAs.

I am encouraged by this recent development, but I am also suspicious of its long-term significance. It coincides too neatly with an interest in difference and otherness in other fields such as comparative literature, history, and anthropology, *in which the main subject of investigation is the person, not the artifact.* Euroethnic preoccupation with these issues in the art world forces a level of social and political self-criticism and scrutiny of entrenched conventions of aesthetic evaluation that is altogether salutary, and needed. But the object of preoccupation defined by these issues is not the artifact but rather its producer as "other." Not the work of art, but rather the artist often provides the content and themes of interviews, photoimages, conferences, and critical essays. This means substituting social relations for works of art as an object of investigation. And in an arena as ill-equipped to investigate social relations as the art world, this means imposing only slightly more sophisticated racial and gender stereotypes rather than looking at art.

For example, a CWA who expresses political anger or who protests political injustice in her work may be depicted as hostile or aggressive; or a CWA who deals with gender and sexuality in her work may be represented as seductive or manipulative. Or a CWA who chooses to do her work rather than cultivate political connections within the art world may be seen as exotic or enigmatic. These are all familiar ways of stereotyping the African-American "other." When the art itself stymies the imposition of such stereotypes, the Euroethnic viewer is confronted with a choice: either to explore the singular significance of the art itself—which naturally requires a concerted effort of discernment and will for most Euroethnics—or

11.
Howardena Pindell, "Art World Racism: A Documentation," *The New Art Examiner* 16, no. 7 (March 1989), pp. 32–36.

12.
And brazenly arrogant bullet biting in others, as some of the previous items suggest.

to impose those tired stereotypes on the artist instead. For two-cylinder intellects, the latter alternative is the most popular.[13]

Of course this tendency to focus on the artist at the expense of the work may be explained differently, as a reflexive by-product of a self-protective, general reaction to most mainstream contemporary Euroethnic art, which compels its viewers to focus on the artist out of sheer desperation, because the art itself is so boring. But for CWAs, this focus on the person rather than the art is particularly troublesome, first, because it turns the artist into little more than a cryptic, exotic object that provides the occasion for Euroethnic self-analysis. I am, after all, not an "other" to *myself;* that is a category imposed on me by Euroethnics who purport to refer to me but in fact denote their own psychosociological constructs. If I choose to explore those constructs in my work, I am investigating Euroethnic psychosociology, not myself, which merely compounds the blunder of withdrawing the focus from the work and turning it instead onto me. This is the blunder of a bad conscience that seeks to deflect self-scrutiny, by redirecting it onto the artist, at the expense of full attention to the sociocultural meaning of *that artist's chosen form of self-expression,* namely, art. This tack, of changing the subject, is just another way to silence those for whom artistic censorship has been a way of life. Euroethnics who have a genuine interest in the forms of self-expression of artists from a different culture do not dwell intellectually on the otherness of the artists for long. They get to work doing the necessary research into that culture, and achieving the necessary familiarity with it, that will yield the insights into those alien forms of cultural expression they purport to seek.[14]

Second, focusing on the otherness of the artist rather than the meaning of the art falsely presupposes a background of Euroethnic homogeneity against which the

13.
And make no mistake about it: For the two-cylinder intellect, these are *mutually exclusive* alternatives. An identifying feature of such cognitive malfunctions is the absence of any sustained attention to the work itself. Thus, for example, Robert Morgan, in "Adrian Piper," *Arts Magazine* 63, no. 10 (Summer 1989), p. 99, does not bother describing the content of the work at all. Instead he generously concentrates on offering free career advice as to how, by doing a different work that "told us more about Adrian Piper and how she as a person had personally suffered from racial prejudice and abuse (if this is indeed the case)," I could have avoided hurting the feelings of "anyone who has worked in ghettos and has read what black activist writers have written, and has tried to put into practice some positive methods for ending bigotry on a day-to-day basis." To all of you out there who satisfy this description, I want to take this opportunity to apologize to you for hurting your feelings, for failing to devote my work to "autobiographical ideas and constructs" that confirm how much I "personally [have] suffered from racial prejudice and abuse," and for failing more generally to just plain mind my own business. *Tant pis!*

14.
Christopher Isherwood's lifelong involvement with the translation, exposition, and practice of Vedanta philosophy would provide a paradigmatic example of this, as would Robert Farris Thompson's involvement with African and African-American culture.

person can be identified as an "other." This perpetuates the ideological myth of minority status on which racists rely to exercise their strategies of disempowerment. Politically concerned Euroethnics would do better to reflect on their collusion in those strategies—for example, isolating a few token coloreds to exhibit in predominantly Euroethnic group shows, or to write about in predominantly Euroethnic art publications—against the reality of their constituting 15 percent of the world's population while consuming or stockpiling 85 percent of its resources.

Third, CWAs in particular suffer from this focus because they have to battle gender and race stereotypes simultaneously. Well-meaning critics and curators who think it is possible to make meaningful generalizations about the art of all women, all African-Americans, all Central Europeans, Italians, or gay men are depriving themselves and their audiences of the paradigm experience art is supposed to provide: to heighten one's appreciation of the singular and original qualities of an individual artifact in cultural relation to its producer, its viewer, and its social environment.[15] Whenever someone deflects attention from my work to my identity as a CWA, I start to get nervous about whether they are actually seeing my work at all.

For these reasons, the remainder of this discussion is going to be devoted to a systematic analysis of the Euroethnic art world's negation of CWAs along three dimensions: as coloreds, as women, and as artists. I want to offer a systematic analysis that can explain why, for example, no one feels the need even to defend or justify Betty Saar's exclusion from the "Magiciens de la Terre" exhibit; why the exhibition "Autobiography: In Her Own Image" went virtually unremarked by the Euroethnic press; why the repression and artistic censorship of PWAs[16] is seen as so much more urgent and threatening than that of CWAs; and why, in general, I am not yet convinced that the repression and artistic censorship of CWAs is a thing of the past.

15.
"All-black" shows are in this respect unlike, for example, all-Russian or all-Italian shows. Whereas all-Russian shows function unproblematically, to showcase the singularity of artifacts for an interested and enthusiastic public, all-African-American shows often function controversially to demonstrate, to a resistant and defensive public, that original and singular artifacts produced by African-American artists actually exist. I am proud to have shown in the company chosen for the all-African-American shows in which I have participated. But clearly, the necessity of these shows has been more didactic than aesthetic, regardless of the valuable aesthetic qualities that inhere in the artifacts shown, or even the motives and interests of their curators. That the charge of "ghettoization" is thus asymmetrically applied only to all-African-American shows signals the inability of the accuser to perceive and appreciate this work on its own terms. (To see this, one need only consider the likely reaction to a *mostly* African-American show, mounted in a major Euroethnic museum, including just a small sample of Euroethnic artists. The very concept boggles the mind.)

16.
People With AIDS. This phrase was coined in the gay community a few years ago so as to avoid the dehumanizing and victimizing connotations of phrases such as "HIV-positives" and "AIDS victims."

Artistic success in the contemporary Euroethnic art world is perceived by all as the payoff of a zero-sum game, in which one player's win is another player's loss.[17] For example, not everyone can show her work at MOMA. So it, is reasoned, if you show yours there, you decrease my chances of showing mine there. So in order for me to increase my chances of showing mine there, I must, first of all, work actively to decrease yours—through professional back-stabbing, bad-mouthing, covert manipulation, dishonesty, false and loudly trumpeted I-was-there-first self-aggrandizement, etc. Second, I must work actively to increase my chances: by tailoring my work according to trends established by those already exhibited at MOMA,[18] courting the powerful, offering bribes in a variety of currencies, and censoring my impulse to protest when witnessing injustice, so as not to antagonize *anyone* who might eventually help me to get my work shown at MOMA. I must deploy similar strategies for obtaining gallery representation, selling work, or getting critical attention for work. This means that individual artists and their allies see one another as professional competitors, and the assets of others as threats to the ability of each to achieve maximal professional success.

"Maximal professional success," in turn, is defined by admission into a circumscribed set of art institutions—museums, galleries, collections, and art publications—that constitute the Euroethnic mainstream. The ideological content of that mainstream changes with fluctuations of intellectual fashion in other fields (such as Enlightenment aesthetics, analytic philosophy, or continental poststructuralism). But the underlying ideological commitment of the Euroethnic mainstream is to its own perpetuation, in whatever guise. In the Renaissance, this commitment was manifested as a belief in the ability of men creatively to transform the sensuous and material in the service of the intellectual and spiritual; that is, to transcend the natural physical realm associated with the secular female. In modernism, this same commitment was manifested as a belief in the progression of art made by men from the concretely representational to the intellectual and abstract. In post-modernism, it is manifested in a dissolution of faith in intellectual progress, and a corresponding attitude of mourning for the past glories and achievements of all

17.
The classic text in game theory still seems to me to be the best. See R. Duncan Luce and Howard Raiffa, *Games and Decisions* (New York: John Wiley and Sons, 1957), especially chapter 4.

18.
I discuss this phenomenon at greater length in "Power Relations within Existing Art Institutions," reprinted in this volume. There I treat it as a matter of institutional suasion. But anyone with a talent for market analysis and a few months of careful study of major New York gallery exhibitions can figure out what kind of work to produce in order to elicit market demand, if that is one's motive for producing the work.

previous stages of Euroethnic art history, which are memorialized and given iconic status through appropriation into contemporary art-world artifacts.

In virtually every field to which women have gained entry in significant numbers, the status of that field and its perception as providing significant social opportunity has diminished: If a woman can do it, the reasoning goes, then what is there to feel superior about? Therefore the first line of defense is to protest roundly that a woman can't do it. The second, when that doesn't work, is to conclude that it's not worth doing. Thus it is no accident that the advent of postmodernism coincides with the acceptance of Euroethnic women artists into the inner sanctum of that tradition. Their success forces a choice of inference: Either women are just as capable of intellectual transcendence as men, and just what is needed to bring that progression to its next stage, or else their presence undermines the very possibility of of further progression altogether. It is quite clear which inference has been chosen. Not coincidentally, Euroethnic postmodernism expresses a newly pessimistic, nihilistic, and self-defeated view of the social and intellectual status of art at just the moment that women have begun to join its major ranks in significant numbers.

Euroethnic postmodernism's attitude of mourning assumes our arrival at the end of the art-historical progression, and therefore the impossibility of further innovation indigenous to it. This means, in particular, that innovations that occur outside of that progression, or by those who are not accepted into it, cannot be acknowledged to exist as innovations at all. Accordingly, the normative category of originality against which art within the Euroethnic tradition was judged is replaced by the purportedly descriptive categories of anomaly, marginality, and otherness. These aesthetically noncommital categories can be deployed to acknowledge the existence of such innovations without having to credit them normatively as innovations at all.

Relative to the commitment of the Euroethnic mainstream to its own self-perpetuation and its rejection of any further innovation indigenous to it, the very different concerns that may find expression in the art of CWAs—identity, autobiography, selfhood, racism, ethnic tradition, gender issues, spirituality, etc.—constitute a triple-barreled threat. First, this work has no halcyon past to mourn. Instead, it offers an alternative art-historical progression that narrates a history of prejudice, repression, and exclusion, and looks, not backward, but forward to a more optimistic future. It thereby competes with Euroethnic art history as a candidate for truth. Second, it refutes the disingenuous Euroethnic postmodern claim that there *is* no objective truth of the matter about anything, by presenting objective testimony of the truth of prejudice, repression, and exclusion.[19] Third, it belies the Euroethnic postmodern stance that claims the impossibility of innovation, by presenting artifacts that are, in fact, innovative relative to the Euroethnic tradition—innovative not only in the range and use of media they deploy but also in the sociocultural and aesthetic content they introduce. In all of these ways, the art of CWAs is an innovative threat to the systemic intellectual integrity and homogeneity of the Euroethnic art tradition. And so, because artistic success is defined within that tradition as a zero-sum game, these threats must be eliminated as quickly and completely as possible. Thus are CWAs negated as artists by the Euroethnic art world.

The Euroethnic postmodernist stance of mourning, in combination with its negation of CWAs as artists, provides the surest proof (in case we needed it) that the Euroethnic art world is fueled primarily by a spirit of entrepreneurship, not one of intellectual curiosity, and that its definition of professional success is skewed accordingly. Only a field that defined professional success in economic rather than intellectual terms could seriously maintain that the art of CWAs had nothing new to teach it. Whereas history, literature, anthropology, sociology, psychology, etc., have been scrambling for almost two decades to adjust or modify their canons so as to accommodate the new insights and information to be culled from the life experience of those previously excluded from them, only the Euroethnic art world is still having trouble acknowledging that those insights and information actually exist. In this field, if they don't exist at auctions or in major collections, they don't exist at all. Critics and curators who collaborate in this ideology sacrifice their intellectual integrity for the perquisites of market power. This is the payoff that the zero-sum game of Euroethnic artistic success ultimately offers all its players.

The Euroethnic contemporary art world is administered primarily by Euroethnic men. As in all walks of life, there are good men and there are bad men. In this arena, the bad ones are blessedly easy to detect. Their behavior and their pronouncements indicate that they evaluate works of art according to their market value rather than according to their aesthetic value. For example, they may refuse even to acknowledge the aesthetic value of work that is not for sale in a major gallery, or they may select artifacts to exhibit or write about solely from those sources. Or they may defend the aesthetic value of very expensive artifacts at

19.
Colored proponents of poststructuralist discourse often seem not to grasp the self-negating implications of advocating the view that objective truth doesn't exist and that all discourses are suspect, nor the self-defeating implications of adopting what amounts to an unintelligible private language discourse in order to defend these views. But I believe that most Euroethnic poststructuralists grasp these implications quite clearly. That's why they welcome their colored cohorts into the academy so enthusiastically.

great length but on visibly shaky conceptual grounds. Or they may be more visibly impressed by the aesthetic value of a work as its market value increases. Indeed, lacking any broader historical or sociocultural perspective, they may even believe that aesthetic value is nothing but market value. And, believing that only artifacts produced by other Euroethnic men can safeguard the intellectual integrity and homogeneity of the Euroethnic tradition, they distribute payoffs, in proportion to the exercise of the winning zero-sum game strategies earlier described, primarily to other Euroethnic men.

Some women and coloreds collude in the perpetuation of this game, by playing according to its prescribed rules. Euroethnic women who compete with one another and with colored women for its payoffs divide themselves from CWAs and ally themselves with the Euroethnic men who distribute those payoffs and who are their primary recipients. They thereby ally themselves with the underlying ideological agenda of perpetuating the tradition of Euroethnic art as a intellectually homogeneous, systemic whole. This is to concur and collaborate with the Renaissance, modernist, and postmodernist agenda of implicitly denying the legitimacy—indeed, the very possibility—of intellectually and spiritually transcendent artifacts produced by women.

Put another way: By accepting payoffs for playing the zero-sum game of artistic success according to its prescribed rules, some Euroethnic women collaborate in the repression of the alternative art history to which the art of women in general, as well as that of CWAs, often gives expression. Thus CWAs are negated as women not only through the more brutal, overt attempts at eradication by some Euroethnic male art-world administrators but *whenever* a Euroethnic woman abnegates her connection as a woman to CWAs, in order to receive the payoffs available for repressing them. It is painfully humiliating to witness a Euroethnic woman simultaneously prostituting herself and betraying us in this way.

Similarly for colored men and their connection with CWAs. All colored artists bear the burden of reflexive eradication from the Euroethnic mainstream, and of the reflexive devaluation of their work as a result.[20] Much has been written about this recently, and I will not rehearse those arguments here.[21] My point, here as earlier, is the same. To the extent that colored artists compete for positioning, attention, and

20.
See note 9.

21.
Patricia Failing, "Black Artists Today: A Case of Exclusion?" *Art News* (March 1989), pp. 124–131; Michael Brenson, "Black Artists: A Place in the Sun," *The New York Times,* March 12, 1989, C1; Lowery Sims, "The Mirror the Other," *Artforum* 28, no. 7 (March 1990), pp. 111–115.

the payoffs of winning the zero-sum game of Euroethnic artistic success, they abide by the rules of that game. In so doing, they compound their reflexive repression by the Euroethnic mainstream, by dividing themselves from one another and negating themselves and their historical tradition for the sake of the payoffs that game promises.

This has nothing to do with what kind of artifact—abstract or representational, in traditional media or new genres—any such artist produces. An unusually dimwitted defense of the repression of colored artists has it that African-Americans are naturally most adept at expressing themselves creatively in music rather than in the visual arts, and that therefore their attempts in the latter media are invariably derivative, superficial, or disappointing. No one who has studied the artifactual strategies of survival and flourishing of colonialized peoples under hegemonic rule anywhere could take such an argument seriously. But then of course no one who would offer such an argument would be capable of the minimal intellectual effort of research necessary to disprove it. The fact of the matter is that, like other colonialized peoples, African-Americans must master two cultures, not just one, in order to survive as whole individuals, and master them they do. They contribute fresh styles and idioms to the visual arts just as abundantly as they do—and have always done—to music, literature, and film.

The Euroethnic tradition has always needed these extrinsic creative resources in order to flourish, and in the past has simply expropriated and used them without permission or acknowledgment.[22] Had that tradition long since invited their producers into the Euroethnic mainstream, it might have been better armed, with creative strategies of cohesion and survival, for withstanding the censorship attacks that continue to issue from within its own fundamentalist ranks. It is not surprising that blind reviewing is virtually inconceivable in contemporary Euroethnic art, whereas it is the norm in other areas of higher education. As an intellectually integral and homogeneous system, the Euroethnic art tradition could not possibly survive a convention of evaluation that ignored the racist, sexist, and aesthetically irrelevant social and political connections that hold it together. That is why it rewards all of us so richly for following the rules of the zero-sum game.

22.
A recent example of this depredation is the treatment of graffiti art by the Euroethnic mainstream. Unlike other media of expression in hip-hop culture, such as rap music, which has received sustained attention and encouragement by the music establishment, graffiti art was off the streets, on the walls of major galleries, in the work of various young up-and-coming Euroethnic painters, and out the art-world door within two seasons. Now that its idioms have been furtively incorporated into the Euroethnic canon, it is once again safe to minimize its originality and significance as an independent movement.

It is very difficult for any of us not to play this game, as it often seems to be the only game in town. But in fact that is not true. It is not true that Euroethnic payoffs of the zero-sum game are the only measures of artistic success, nor the most important over the long term, nor even the most satisfying ones. There is great satisfaction in affecting or transforming the audience to one's work, and in making those personal connections that enable the work to function as a medium of communication. There is great satisfaction in learning to see whatever resources are freely available in one's environment as grist for the mill of artistic imagination, and indeed, in seeing one's environment in general in that way. There is satisfaction in giving work away, and in avoiding or refusing the corrupting influences of those payoffs, and in reaping the rewards of authentic interpersonal relationships as a consequence. And there is very great satisfaction in not caring enough for those payoffs to be willing to follow the rules in order to receive them: in not caring enough to tailor one's work accordingly, or offer bribes, or curry favor, or protect one's position by remaining silent in the face of injustice, or by undercutting others.

In fact the very conception of artistic success as the payoff of a zero-sum game is faulty, because the price of playing by those rules is the de facto deterioration, over the long term, of the aesthetic integrity of the artifacts produced in accordance with them.[23] Those who play that game according to the rules and win the perquisites of market power may, indeed, achieve artistic success in the Euroethnic art world. But the price they pay is alienation from their own creative impulses and from their own work as a vehicle of self-expression; addiction to the shallow, transitory material and political reassurances of worth that are recruited to take their place; sycophancy and betrayal from those they temporarily view as allies; and mistrust and rejection from those who might otherwise have been friends. It hardly seems worth it.

Because commitment to that game is so self-defeating and divisive for all who try to play it, I do not believe the triple negation of colored women artists will come to an end until that game itself is over. It will come to an end, that is, when the Euroethnic art world stops trying to negate them as players, and when women and coloreds and Euroethnics stop trying to negate themselves and one another in order to gain entry to it.

I have suggested that Euroethnic postmodernism is finally an attempt to change a few of the rules, hastily, in order to preserve intact the stature of the winners and

23.
See note 18; also see "A Paradox of Conscience," this volume.

their payoffs. I neglected to add that that attempt is clearly failing. While larger and larger quantities of money, power and inflated prose are being invested in more and more dessicated and impotent caricatures of Euroethnic art, those who have been excluded from that system have been inventing and nurturing their own idioms, visions, and styles of expression out of that greatest of all mothers, namely, Necessity. That is our strength and our solace. That is why the Euroethnic art world needs our resources and our strategies—as it always has—in order to progress to the next stage of development. But we are no longer so preoccupied with other matters as to overlook backdoor expropriation of those resources, nor to take comfort in being the invisible powers behind the throne. As we come to feel the strength of our numbers and the significance of our creative potentialities, we approach a readiness to drop out of the zero-sum game and claim our roles as players in a very different kind of game, in which the payoffs are not competitive but, rather, cooperative. In this kind of game, no one has to lose in order for someone else to win, because the payoffs—self-expression, personal and creative integrity, freedom, resourcefulness, friendship, trust, mutual appreciation, connectedness—are not scarce resources over which any player must be attacked, negated, or sacrificed. Nor are the rules of this game—mutual support, honesty, dialogue, sharing of resources, receptivity, self-reflectiveness, acceptance—of such a kind as to butcher the self and cheapen one's central commitments. It does seem, in so many respects, to be a more appealing game to play. The only question is whether we are all wise enough to be willing to play it.

19. Goodbye to Easy Listening

First published in the catalog *Adrian Piper: PRETEND* (New York: John Weber Gallery, 1990).

First, Easy Listening must be distinguished from Muzak. Muzak is bland, boring, canned music. It is not meant to be listened to. Instead it is intended to provide a bland aural and emotional environment. By contrast, Easy Listening is serious music, often drawing on the canon of a particular musical genre—rock, country, nineteenth-century Romantic, swing, blues ballads, New Age, and so on. It relies on familiar compositional idioms that are manipulated in an engaging or subtly distinctive way. Easy Listening provides enough compositional sophistication to engage or titillate one's aural sensibilities, but its impact is deliberately muffled. It is suggestive rather than explicit, soothing rather than demanding. Easy Listening Music occupies its own modest niche in one's consciousness and does not divert one's attention from more pressing or immediate pursuits. It does not make trouble; instead it makes nice. Easy Listening is meant to be listened to, but it is not meant to be heard.

Music that is meant to be heard includes Ambrosian chant, Guillaume de Machaut, Bach cantatas, late Beethoven, W. C. Handy, Arnold Schoenberg, Billie Holliday, Artie Shaw, Charlie Parker, Anton Webern, Steve Reich, George Clinton, Miriam Makeba, The Sugar Hill Gang, Celia Cruz. Music that is meant to be heard demands one's full attention and catalyzes one viscerally in the process of hearing it. It goes without saying that music that is meant to be heard is music that extends its genre into uncharted territory. Its originality of form or content is what makes trouble rather than nice. But I want to focus on the ability of such music to be heard and not just listened to, if one has the aural and cognitive capacities to hear it at all.

Music that is meant to be heard has something to say, not just to suggest or hint at. It does not merely allude. It explicitly asserts. Its hand may land heavily, for it pulls no punches. It communicates a message, not just an atmosphere or a frame of mind or a chain of free associations or a range of speculations. It viscerally catalyzes one in the process of hearing it, not only because it innovates but because it baldly tells the truth.

Not everyone can hear music that is meant to be heard. Some are content with Muzak, if they can't hear anything at all. Others prefer the familiar strains of Easy Listening, which requires of them only that they listen and be soothed. Some mistake listening for hearing and think that assuming a posture of polite interest exhausts what is involved in hearing. Others push the stopples all the more deeply into their ears upon detecting sounds that insist on being heard, that threaten visceral catalysis. Still others want to hear but are deafened by the sounds they themselves make trying to ensure that what they hear is what they would prefer to hear. And some simply are not yet ready to hear, although they will be in time.

Music that is meant to be heard is meant primarily for those who can hear; its audience is self-selecting. It is also very small. But this is preferable to directing one's effort to those who can't or won't or don't want to hear, even if that audience is larger or more powerful, because it is extremely demoralizing not to be heard. For a rational creature with sophisticated cognitive capacities, not to be heard is almost not to exist.

To be heard is not necessarily to elicit the agreement of one's audience. But it is to elicit recognition and respect from one's audience for what one has to say. It is to call forth some appropriate response to it. Some prefer Easy Listening to music that is meant to be heard, because since Easy Listening has nothing specific to say, any response to it is equally appropriate.

Similarly, to hear someone is not necessarily to believe their assertions to be true. But it is to trust in a direct connection between what they assert and what they believe to be true. It is to trust that their assertions are meant to communicate their beliefs, not to manipulate or deceive. Some prefer Easy Listening to music that is meant to be heard because since Easy Listening does not assert anything, it does not require taking the risk of trust.

Just as Easy Listening Music is music that is meant to be listened to rather than heard, similarly, Easy Listening Art is art that is meant to be looked at rather than seen. Like Easy Listening Music, Easy Listening Art is serious art, often drawing on the canons of a particular aesthetic genre—minimalism, pop art, realism, expressionism, conceptual art, surrealism, and so on. It relies on familiar compositional idioms that are manipulated in an engaging or subtly distinctive way. Easy Listening Art provides enough compositional sophistication to engage or titillate one's visual sensibilities, but its impact is deliberately muted. It is suggestive rather than explicit, soothing rather than demanding. Easy Listening Art occupies its own modest niche in one's consciousness and does not divert one's attention from more pressing or immediate pursuits. It does not make trouble; instead it makes nice.

Easy Listening Art is, of course, the art of postmodernism. It is the art that recalls and celebrates the familiar Euroethnic history and canon of art, that reassures one with its familiar and witty strategies of form and content, that minutely refines or dilates upon those strategies in ways that serve to increase our aesthetic pleasure in recognizing and discerning minor modifications in what we have already learned. Easy Listening Art, with its multiplicity of familiar genres and idioms and the endless subtleties of their minor variations, is so highly elaborated that it now stands as a respectable genre in its own right, and is itself ready for taxonomic dissection in the annals of art history.

The passing of Easy Listening Art as the fashion of the moment is not necessarily to be mourned. It is the art of a period of history in which the Euroethnic art world could afford financially to swaddle itself in a blanket of denial and false innocence, to bask in the sense of security and meaning provided by constant, solipsistic reminders of canonical Euroethnic art history, and in the illusion that that history had ended and had been replaced by an eternal present of understated variations on familiar, recognizable, and self-regenerating visual titillations.

That period of history is over, and it is now time to move on. In this next one, we face matters of pressing social and cultural urgency. We face the forcible juncture of the Euroethnic art world with the world at large: the world of multiple cultures, of imposingly complex social identities, of waning Euroethnic authority, and of an international struggle for the social and economic resources heretofore stockpiled and carefully guarded by the West. In this new period of history, we confront an immediate present in which racism—among other evils—is threatening to destroy our collective future, not only locally but nationally and globally as well.

Racism (like sexism) is primarily a visual pathology: It feeds on differences in perceived appearance, not differences in genetic ancestry. Art is primarily a visual medium. So political art would seem to have the potential for furnishing a forceful antidote to racism. It is worth investigating whether it has failed to exploit fully its own potential to heal this particular visual pathology, and why political art in general has been charged with impotence to effect political change in the larger political arena.

Part of the problem is the degree of change sometimes expected. Political artists are often reproached with arrogance for trying to "change the world"—as if any single individual could—and then ridiculed when immediate revolution fails to occur. But no one is obligated to try to change the world, and it is unlikely that any artist tries to. All *anyone* needs to aspire to politically is to do what he can, and to do his best. To change an opinion, or an attitude, or to modify a knee-jerk response, or to catalyze an ongoing process of personal transformation, would be plenty. Undertaken collectively, it would be all we needed.

Perhaps another part of the problem is the reliance on depiction and representation of political content alone, rather than on its collaborative construction through object-viewer interactive confrontation. Representation of political content alone is unlikely to be successful in effecting political change in the viewer, because it directs the viewer's attention away from the immediate politics of her own situation and toward some other space-time region that may have only the most tenuous connection, if any, to the viewer's immediate personal circumstances. By contrast, political content may be collaboratively constructed through an interactive process in which the object explicitly confronts the viewer with her own condition, and the viewer reacts to that confrontation by constructing an interpretation of it that expresses her own particular level of political self-awareness. This process is inherently catalytic because it elicits cognitive and affective change in the viewer's own conception of her condition. As this conception evolves, her interpretation of the object's effect on her will also evolve.

A more serious part of the problem is the peril of relying on the strategies of Easy Listening Art. Easy Listening Art does not demand to be heard or seen; it is content with being looked at, even merely glanced at. Just as in listening to Easy Listening Music, one may casually survey Easy Listening Art with a glazed (if not a jaundiced) eye, or for thirty seconds, or while munching a sandwich, and comprehend everything distinctive there is to comprehend about it, because there is not too much that is distinctive about it to comprehend. For the educated (or rather, well-programmed) viewer, the significance of Easy Listening Art is supplied primarily by a background framework of traditional reference that lies outside of the work itself. Its low-key ambiguity trades on such a framework to provide the viewer with a range of salient interpretations, any one of which is equally acceptable.

Without such a framework, Easy Listening Art in itself is not that visually compelling. Because there is not much there in the object itself to see, it suggests or subtly alludes to a great deal. But the wider the range of salient interpretations it admits, the more and more noncommittal it becomes with respect to any one of them, and the more closely it approaches the status of platitude. Even relative to the modest aspiration of viewer catalysis, Easy Listening Art is politically impotent because it plays safe by refusing to declare its allegiances. It shrinks from the hard task of baldly telling the truth. Like Easy Listening Music, Easy Listening Art may be perfectly suited to one who is highly sensitized to the subtle nuances of the familiar genres and idioms it invokes. But like Easy Listening Music, Easy Listening Art also may leave a mild taste of pablum on the unschooled palate.

Telling the truth is not soothing and it is not fun. For the teller, it is scary and risky—of friendship, personal safety, financial well-being, professional standing. It raises hackles and hurts feelings and makes enemies and motivates strong impulses to kill—or at least ignore—the messenger. But these consequences seem a small price to pay for the opportunity to take an active part in evolving a society in which racism no longer exists. In the short run, art that aims to effect such political change, that conjoins its own destiny and meaning to a vision of a better world, may be scarcely audible or visible above the ongoing clamor of self-interested political struggle. But in the long run of reflective historical recapitula-

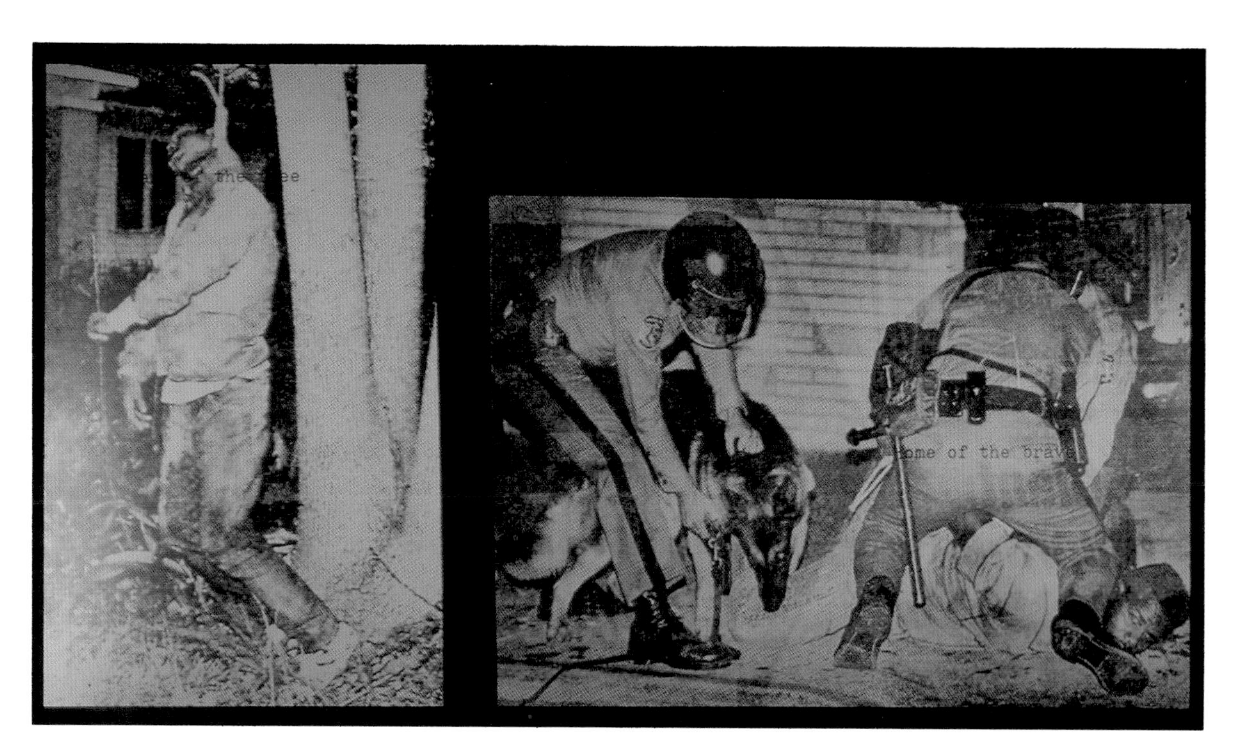

16.
Free #2 (1989).
Photos by Klanwatch Archive/*The New York Times*; Gerard Martineau/*The Washington Post*. Courtesy John Weber Gallery, collection of the artist.

tion, such art is more likely to be seen and heard clearly as an aesthetic embodiment of the sociocultural period for which it speaks.

Aspiring to effect political change obviously is not the only function art can or should have. Art that entertains, instructs, stimulates the imagination, or provides respite from hard realities are just a few of the other important functions we need art to satisfy. But what distinguishes all such art that is meant to be seen is its avoidance of the cultivated triviality of Easy Listening Art. Perhaps we may finally put that behind us.

20. Notes on the White Man's Burden: Multiculturalism and Euroethnic Art Criticism at the Millennium

(An Open Letter with Audiovisual Aids)

Written in October 1991 and previously unpublished.

Dear Reader,

In order fully to appreciate the rhetorical points I want to make in this letter, you will need certain *audiovisual aids.* So, first, please keep both hands free so that you may applaud or throw rotten eggs on cue. Second, you will need ten such eggs, in addition to a sixty-watt light bulb that you can switch on and off at will, and a small dinner bell with a clear, limpid ring. Do you have everything? Are you ready? Then let's begin.

Recently some of the more progressive segments of the Euroethnic art world have decided to abandon its long-standing policy of affirmative action for heterosexual, white, usually (but not always) male artists. Tiring of the timid, monotonous, and uninspiring products such an art welfare system almost invariably produces, these progressive forces have instead initiated a search for art of quality. For their courage in rejecting the affirmative action art welfare system, and their commitment to seeking out high-quality art instead, those progressive forces in the Euroethnic art world who have taken on this task are to be applauded. [applaud]

The long history of the avant-garde teaches us that the best, most exciting, most innovative art is made by those on the margins, those distanced or excluded from the academy, those for whom art making is an expression of the struggle to survive. So it is not surprising that in its search for high-quality, innovative art, these progressive segments of the Euroethnic art world should have finally discovered the art of African-Americans, and of colored people more generally. [light bulb on]

In art made by colored people we find the original styles and idioms that the cubists, fauvists, surrealists, pattern painters, arte povera, performance artists, and neograffitists, among others, have plagiarized without acknowledgment—under the ethically disingenuous, postmodernist rubric of "appropriation." In each such case we see the same pattern: A heterosexual white artist, usually (but not always) male, affirmative-action candidate applies for welfare from the art academy, by sending his slides around to Euroethnic galleries and museums. Requiring some novelty item in order to make his slides stand out from the rest, the artist spends a few months after art school slumming among those on the margins and copies some aspect of the original art he finds there. Because this art lacks institutional validation, he gains nothing by crediting its makers. And accepting the doctrine of appropriation provides a ready rationalization for why he is under no obligation to do so. [throw two rotten eggs]

These repeated "appropriations" have probably facilitated the Euroethnic art world's rediscovery of the colored artists who inspired these Euroethnic art movements in the first place. Because it is conditioned to see only what it has already seen, the Euroethnic art world can see the art of marginalized colored people only after it has plagiarized them and replicated their styles and idioms within its own canon. Relative to this canon, some of the art of colored people of course looks familiar, produces a sense of déjà vu, rings a bell. [ring bell]

Euroethnic art-world denizens who have suffered the disadvantages of an affirmative-action art-world education demonstrate their ignorance and provincialism by complaining that such art is familiar, unoriginal, derivative—in fact from the very same movements it originally inspired.[1] Because the long-term effects of intellectual poverty and life on welfare are difficult to reverse, it may be that those who exhibit this degree of aesthetic illiteracy are pedagogically incorrigible. [light bulb off]

Nevertheless, the task of uplifting and educating the Euroethnic art world about its own roots in the art of colored people, and about their continuing influence on it, remains a pressing moral obligation among those progressive segments of the Euroethnic art world who have escaped the devastating aesthetic and intellectual poverty of the inner-city Soho ghetto.

This is where progressive art journals have a crucial role to play. [applaud] In the past, articles about the art of heterosexual white, usually (but not always) male, affirmative-action recipients have amounted to little more than hagiography, inflated advertising copy. This has been necessary, in order to bolster the self-esteem of those demoralized by their knowledge of being welfare recipients of the art academy. As we know, being on welfare is infantilizing and alienating. It undermines one's self-respect. It encourages the recipient to believe that he is nothing without others' charity, and so to believe that living off of others' labor is necessary for survival. So it is not surprising that so much art writing has been devoted to supporting and reassuring us of the worth of work made by those heterosexual white art-welfare recipients whose work the worth of which is most obviously in question. [ring bell]

As in any other field, art journals set the intellectual and aesthetic standards for the disciplines of art and art criticism. They have an obligation to set those standards at a respectable intellectual level. There can be no excuse for the shocking comment that if the work of African-American artists hasn't brought itself to one's attention, it probably doesn't exist; or for the truly bizarre claim that the real prob-

1.
So, for example, Roberta Smith complains ("Adrian Piper," *New York Times,* Friday, September 14, 1990, C27) that my work looks too much like Barbara Kruger's, when in fact my work in the idiom for which Barbara Kruger rightly became famous in the 1980s dates from the late 1960s.

lem with the art of African-Americans is that it just isn't any good, that it is all derivative, and that if it were any good, it would be in mainstream galleries. These remarks are appalling, but not only for the abysmal ignorance of art history and cutting-edge work they display. What is worse is that the speakers—both highly respected art critics—felt no scruples about making such remarks publicly, which demonstrates their understanding that these remarks are fully consistent with the prevailing aesthetic and intellectual standards in the field. There can be no more devastating indictment of those standards—and the art journals that promulgate them—than this. [heave rest of rotten eggs]

Now, however, with their newly affirmed interest in art of quality, progressive art journals are charged with the responsibility of taking their place among the scholarly and professional journals of other disciplines in higher education, where the emphasis is on research rather than hagiography. "Research" means what it means in any other such discipline: Searching out new, previously unknown, or innovative work, issues, and ideas, subjecting them to rigorous analysis, and locating them within the larger social, cultural, and art-historical context. Maurice Berger's essay and interviews on racism in the museums,[2] Michael Brenson's and Patricia Failing's essays on black artists,[3] Thomas McEvilley's essays on Primitivism and on Duchamp's philosophical influences,[4] Arlene Raven's on Emma Amos,[5] Lowery Sims's on the aesthetic of "otherness,"[6] and Robert Storr's on the art of Elizabeth Murray[7] are only a few of the models we already have for such a project. [wild applause; cheers; bravos]

Again the long history of the avant garde teaches us that those who make cutting-edge art on the margins eventually take their place within the academic canon, transforming that canon by enlarging its conception of art. [light bulb on] Thus we

2.
Maurice Berger, "Are Art Museums Racist?" and "Speaking Out: Some Distance to Go . . ." *Art in America* 78, no. 9 (September 1990), pp. 68–87.

3.
Michael Brenson, "Black Artists: A Place in the Sun," *The New York Times,* March 12, 1989, C1; Patricia Failing, "Black Artists Today: A Case of Exclusion?" *Art News* [March 1989], pp. 124–131.

4.
Thomas McEvilley, "Doctor Lawyer Indian Chief: '"Primitivism" in 20th Century Art' at the Museum of Modern Art in 1984," *Artforum* 23, no. 3 (November 1984), pp. 54–61; "Empyrrhical Thinking (and Why Kant Can't)," *Artforum* 27, no. 2 (October 1988), pp. 120–127.

5.
Arlene Raven, "Laws of Falling Bodies," *The Village Voice* 36, no. 19 (May 7, 1991), p. 86.

6.
Lowery Sims, "The Mirror the Other," *Artforum* 28, no. 7 (March 1990), pp. 111–115.

7.
Robert Storr, "Shape Shifter," *Art in America* 77, no. 4 (April 1989), p. 210.

may test the character of the recent interest in the art of colored people, by raising analogous questions about its treatment in the Euroethnic art world of the 1990s. Here are some of the questions we may ask in order to ascertain whether progressive art journals that aspire to intellectual respectability are meeting their responsibilities as professional organs of research, committed to high-quality art rather than heterosexual white affirmative action art:

1. Do they get the facts right? Or do they systematically misdescribe or fabricate the visual attributes of the works they purport to examine critically?[8]
2. Do they substitute biography for criticism, or do they respect the autonomy of the work and its effect on the viewer?[9]
3. Do they express their misgivings about the work itself, or do they use the pretense of art criticism in order to level a personal attack on the artist?[10]
4. Do they situate the art of colored people within the larger context of art history? Or do they relegate this work to some other, unrelated, less valued category (such as "ethnic art" or "sociology") where its seminal influences on Euroethnic art can be ignored?
5. Do they document the chronological and social advent of this work? Or do they lift this work out of chronological and social context, where its precedence and salience for Euroethnic artists can be dismissed?
6. Do they subject this work to self-reflective conceptual analysis from a multiplicity of viewpoints (the artist's, the viewer's, the critic's, etc.)? Or do they imprison the work within single-perspective stereotypes that reinforce the fiction of the colored artist as "other" and the work as nevertheless "derivative"?[11]

8.
For example, for fascinating fictional accounts of work I never did, see the aforementioned review by Roberta Smith, as well as Alice Thorson's "Conceptualized Conflicts," *The Washington City Paper* 11, no. 30 (July 26, 1991), p. 29.

9.
For example, for armchair caricatures of me masquerading as criticism of my work, see Elizabeth Hess's "Ways of Seeing Adrian Piper," *The Village Voice* (May 26, 1987), p. 100; Donald Kuspit's "Adrian Piper: Self-Healing through Meta-Art," *Art Criticism* 3, no. 3 (September 1987), pp. 9–16.

10.
Examples of negative criticism that nevertheless respect the integrity of my work by getting almost all the facts right and by directing reservations at my work rather than at me, without passive-aggressive cheap shots, hidden personal agendas, or attempts to be "creative" at the expense of the work itself, are to be found in Elinor Heartney's "On View: New York," *The New Art Examiner* 18, no. 4 (December 1990), pp. 36–37; and Marjorie Welish's "In This Corner: Adrian Piper's Agitprop," *Arts Magazine* 65, no. 7 (March 1991), pp. 43–47.

11.
A moving example of painfully searching and insightful criticism from a self-reflective standpoint is Peter Schjeldahl's "Female Trouble," *The Village Voice* (January 8, 1991), p. 79.

7. Do they incorporate the critical voices of colored artists and critics into their staff of writers on a regular and ongoing basis? Or do they arrogate the task of elucidating this work only to the same white affirmative-action welfare system that they are trying sincerely to reform?

8. Do they, over the long term, exhibit a permanent and deeply entrenched respect for the art of colored people, and cognizance of its larger art-historical importance? Or do they treat this work as another transient fashion, to be dropped with the next art market recession?

At this point, Dear Reader, you may be asking why it is necessary to ask these elementary questions. You may feel that I am insulting your intelligence even by raising these issues, as though it were possible for someone to become a prominent and respected art critic without getting the facts right, or attending to the work rather than the psychology of the artist, or situating the work within the context of contemporary art and culture. But sadly, it's not only possible but customary in today's affirmative-action Euroethnic art world, in which not only derivative artists but also incompetent critics[12] are regular beneficiaries of the affirmative-action art-welfare system, receiving its bounty for perpetuating—indeed, wallowing in—its mediocrity. [light bulb off]

Therefore, I am writing this letter to appeal to your conscience. As a serious reader, you must know how important your support is in uplifting the intellectual standards and self-respect of the mentally impoverished. We must all join together to help abolish this pernicious system, which rewards the incompetent with welfare payments and punishes the innovative with reverse discrimination. What we need instead is better education—tutoring, perhaps—and job training programs for those heterosexual white, usually (but not always) male artists and critics who sincerely *want* to work. So I urge you: Reach out to the poor in spirit. Give to the intellectually challenged. Aid the mentally needy. Don't wait. Act now.

Your friend,

Adrian Who-The-Hell-Does-She-Think-She-Is Piper

12.
Such as Hilton Kramer—a particularly sad example of whose "art criticism" is his hysterical diatribe against Michael Brenson, "A Times Critic's Piece about Art Amounts to Political Propaganda," *The New York Observer* 4, no. 29 (August 13, 1990).

21. Brenson on Quality

First published in *Artpapers* 15, no. 6 (November–December 1991), pp. 68–73.

Among the issues identified in Michael Brenson's evenhanded analysis of the politics of quality in the premillennial art world[1] are the following:

1. Some equate quality with formal balance, harmony, coherence, and order, such that the antithesis of high-quality art is work that is chaotic, unstable, or unbalanced with respect to the relation between form and content (Q#1: 17, 25–26, 29–30).

2. Some argue that quality should be ascribed to a work on the basis of its formal properties, whereas others believe it should be ascribed on the basis of its content (Q#1: 18, 32–33).

3. There are conflicting criteria for the use of the term *quality.* Quality art is variously understood as

    a. abstract art for art's sake (Q#1: 27);

    b. the recognized art of Western culture (Q#1: 22);

    c. what is intersubjectively agreed to be of high quality within a particular community (Q#1: 24).

4. Some claim that judgments of quality are objective, in that they are based on universally binding criteria of value, while others believe that judgments of quality reflect one's particular cultural bias or education, and hence are relative (Q#1: 29, 23).

5. The term *quality* is often used in ways that are independent of its putatively judgmental function: to include or marginalize, to reinforce culturally dominant aesthetic conventions, to repress difference or defend the standards of a particular group, to valorize or belittle (Q#1: 6–7, 9, 11, 13–14).

Brenson has much of interest to say about what groups tend typically to espouse each of these views or their opposites, and provides a useful map of a mine-infested social and cultural terrain. I have tried to isolate some of the issues Brenson discusses from their typical proponents in order to focus on the implications of the issues themselves, rather than on the implications of a particular group's stance on them.

1.
Michael Brenson, "Is 'Quality' an Idea Whose Time Has Gone?" *The New York Times,* Sunday, July 22, 1990, Arts and Leisure, pp. 1 and 27, henceforth referred to as "Q#1" and bracketed in the text. Citations from and references to this article are listed in the text by paragraph and number.

I want to look at Brenson's account of "aesthetic emotion" as a contender for a satisfactory conception of quality. Brenson himself does not defend this idea in these terms. Nor does he claim that it provides resolutions or answers to any of the aforementioned controversies. Nevertheless, I believe it has important implications for each of them. Brenson explores some of these implications at greater length in a more recent unpublished discussion.[2]

Brenson characterizes aesthetic emotion as a state in the viewer that is often the result of particularly magisterial or inventive form in a painting or sculpture (Q#1: 34). He describes it as

> *an experience at once personal and impersonal, specific and general. It is rooted in the object but it also suggests something beyond the object [Q#1: 36]. . . . It brings with it an intensified awareness of life and death. It is related to the experience of revelation and love. . . . It suggests that what is most profound can never be analyzed or held in words [Q#1: 37]. . . . It brings with it both an awareness of the moment and an awareness that the moment is not all there is [Q#1: 38].*

As examples of art that incites aesthetic emotion, Brenson mentions the experience of "climbing Greek and Mexican temples, or standing inside a French cathedral or the Hagia Sophia, or gazing at the painting of Piero della Francesca, Matisse, or Tao-chi, or feeling the ferocious intensity of sculptures by Michelangelo, the Aztecs, or the Egyptians" (Q#1: 35).

Implicit in Brenson's notion of aesthetic emotion is a consciousness of the object as balanced between the local, transitory, and physical entity that it is, on the one hand, and the universal, eternal, and metaphysical realities in which it is embedded, on the other. It reminds us of its own spatiotemporal specificity, at the same time that it enlarges our awareness to encompass or discover these deeper realities—of life, death, and the role of the present in eternal transition. "One of the paradoxes of the encounter with quality," Brenson observes,

> *is that it makes art seem entirely particular and yet part and parcel of all other art with which that encounter has ever taken place. The experience of quality is therefore both individualistic and communal. The art establishes a link between its life and mine, between its life and artistic life in general. (Q#2: 28)*

Such work both claims our personal interest in it and guides us beyond this to a disinterested awareness of it as portent of an impersonal metaphysical order, the

2.
Michael Brenson, untitled talk on quality delivered in Albuquerque and Santa Fe (April 1991) and in Winston-Salem (May 1991), henceforth referred to as "Q#2" and bracketed in the text. Citations from and references to this essay are listed in the text by typescript page number.

dimensions of which are beyond our ability fully to grasp or articulate. And it has in common with love and revelation the experience of vulnerability, of receptivity to transformation, and of transcending subjective personal boundaries in a higher union with the object of awareness:

> *Once you recognize good art, wherever it is, once you look at it and listen to it and allow it to make contact with you, it becomes part of your heart and mind. Good art always makes you feel that it is you alone it sought out, even as it reveals its impersonality and availability to everyone else. Good art convinces you to make room for it. It shows you that the house of your heart and mind, no matter how cluttered it may seem, always has additional rooms. (Q#2: 12)*

In certain respects, Brenson's concept of aesthetic emotion in art can be compared with Kant's concept of awe in response to the sublimity of nature.[3] Central to Kant's concept is a sense that our recognition of the sublime is forced on us by the impersonal majesty of the natural object or event that exists before us. And it commands our awe because it is vividly present to us as a unique object or event of towering magnitude, and also portends a "supersensible" cosmic order that transcends our understanding. Similarly, Brenson's notion of aesthetic emotion suggests the experience of an art object whose presence both commands our attention and compels our recognition of profound existential issues whose full significance surpasses our grasp.

I will take for granted that we each have some understanding of the experience Brenson is trying to capture—perhaps futilely, according to him (Q#1: 37)—in words; and that he is right to claim that "aesthetic emotion is what gets most artists, critic and curators involved with art in the first place" (Q#1: 40). My first question is whether aesthetic emotion should be linked with inventive or magisterial form alone (Brenson claims only that it often is). In traditional aesthetics, one source for the distinction between form and content is Descartes's epistemological distinction between primary and secondary qualities.[4] According to this distinction, the primary or formal properties of an object are essentially its Euclidean geometrical properties: its shape, extension, volume, and so on; whereas its secondary or material properties are its sensory properties: its color, texture, taste, and so on. Transposed to aesthetics, the traditional formalist would argue that mere juxtaposi-

3.
Immanuel Kant, *The Critique of Judgment,* trans. J. H. Bernard (New York: Hafner Publishing, 1972), Second Book: Analytic of the Sublime, sections 26–29; *Observations on the Feeling of the Beautiful and the Sublime,* trans. John T. Goldthwait (Berkeley: University of California Press, 1965), section 1.

4.
René Descartes, *Meditations on First Philosophy,* trans. Laurence J. Lafleur (New York: Bobbs-Merrill, 1960), Second Meditation.

tions of color (say) are insufficient to constitute a work of art, without regard to their shape, relative spatial placement, and so on. Further transposed to the contemporary debate, the formalist claim would be that the aesthetic emotion elicited by a work of art is the result solely of harmoniously balanced colors, materials, shapes and spatial relations.

But a reconsideration of Brenson's examples of works that elicit aesthetic emotion suggests that there is more to it than this. I think it is not irrelevant to Brenson's analysis that all the compelling examples he cites are, with one possible exception, works of art devoted in some way to the veneration or celebration of the spiritual (and I think this could be said of Matisse as well). Human artifacts that illumine and transcend their singularity in devotion to the spiritual elicit aesthetic emotion, just as natural objects that transcend theirs in portending the cosmic elicit awe, because both kinds of object draw us away from the mundane and limited and toward the ultimately unfathomable "depth of feeling and knowledge of which human beings are capable" (Q#1: 36). Both kinds of object remind us of our limitations and also push us beyond them, to the contemplation of a grander vision that humbles as it ennobles us. Inventive or magisterial form reconfigures elements of a world whose givenness disrupts our solipsism, in humanly intelligible structures that recall the mystery of the ultimate structure of that world itself.

But it is not clear that inventive or magisterial form *by itself,* independently of its relation to the spiritual content it celebrates, could have any such effect. If it did, we would be more aesthetically impressed by cars and shopping malls than we are. Presumably one reason why we are moved by a Lee Krasner painting is because of the subjective intensional conditions it abstractly expresses; just as one reason why we are moved by a Tony Smith sculpture is because it directs our attention toward its objective extensional self-sufficiency, and away from any intensional symbolic function we might ascribe to it. In neither case is it *merely* the formal configuration of shapes, lines, and materials that compels our interest.

Is spiritual content a necessary condition for experiencing aesthetic emotion? Brenson does not say it is. But I think his characterization as well as his examples imply it. He says,

> *Where quality reveals itself, matter seems animate. Matter seems to have a soul. There is a sense of movement. There is also, no matter what the art looks like and what it is about, a sense of spirit. There is always, no matter how nasty or confrontational the art may be, a sense of goodness and pleasure. (Q#2: 27–28)*

Of course artifacts of various kinds may lead us beyond the constraints of the individual self in many different directions—to greater arrogance or cruelty, or to greater peaks of human achievement, as well as to a more profound consciousness of reality. But it is the latter type of transcendence that Brenson describes, and it is difficult to imagine how one might achieve this without drawing on the personal, social, or religious resources of the spirit. Indeed, it could be argued that the type of transcendence Brenson discusses is what the cultivation of spiritual resources is all about. Inventive or magisterial form in the service of spiritual content is form that expresses an awareness of human limitation, and the transcendent potential of the human spirit to divine those ultimate mysteries. Thus it expresses a self-conscious awareness of our role as creators in a world given to us but created neither by nor for us. So Brenson's description of aesthetic emotion is implicitly the description of a certain kind of *self*-awareness. And this requires a content that directs our attention to the spiritual potential of the self. As Brenson puts it,

> *Whenever there is a real encounter, I feel the work lets me know the magnitude of what is in it. It lets me know that if I pay attention I will make contact with something in the work and in myself that will enable me to know everything better. (Q#2: 26)*

So, for example, religious art by Dürer or Serrano may make a direct appeal to the spirit within each of us, whereas political art by Goya or Coe may call attention to our spiritual connection with the oppressed. Scavenger art by Duchamp or Hammons may illuminate the transcendent mystery of humble objects, whereas art depicting personal relationships by Rembrandt or Weems may invite us into the spiritual dimension of human connection, and the ritual objects of traditional cultures may affirm simultaneously the social and historical connections among human beings and also their connection to the divine. In all such cases, the work leads us into the self and then beyond it. If this is right, then aesthetic emotion, on Brenson's view, is elicited by art that cultivates human spirituality.

My third question is whether Brenson's concept of aesthetic emotion requires of a work of art that it be balanced or harmonious in form (item 1, above). I find nothing in his account that requires this. It accommodates the possibility that the transcendent reality to which an art object guides us is a discordant, chaotic one, in which the object figures as an emblem of fragmentation. Brenson leaves room for works that awaken the human spirit to an awareness of chance, discontinuity, or chaos in the universe. A performance by Meredith Monk, a composition by Karlheinz Stockhausen, an installation by Senga Nengudi, or a novel by William Burroughs might exemplify such works. These works meet the challenge to achieve objectivity of reference in the absence of formal unity. So Brenson's conception encompasses work that aims at formal disruption and discontinuity as well as work that aspires to formal unity and balance.

This is important, because it enables us to make aesthetic judgments about work that provokes the viewer into rethinking entrenched, internally coherent categories, assumptions, and expectations about the social as well as the material structure of experience. We should expect a multivalent and heterogeneous society to generate such disruptive and provocative work. Indeed, this is how we have identified the artistic vanguard since impressionism, and it would be shortsighted to adopt a view of quality that consigned all such work to the rubbish heap. As Brenson says,

> *Good art can have almost any kind of form or content. It can be in an all white abstract painting or in a work about dumping European toxic waste in Africa. It can be in a realist painting of Madrid or in a photographic self-portrait of a defiant sick man holding a skull cane. It can be in the work of an artist of the left or right, a painter from Zaire or a sculptor from Brazil. It can be in the work of an artist who is entirely comfortable within the European tradition or in the work of an artist who wants to turn that tradition on its head. (Q#2: 5)*

Thus Brenson's account of aesthetic emotion does not require of either form or content an allegiance to the Enlightenment conception of the universe as ordered or harmonious.

Next I want to consider the relative priority of form and content in a work that excites aesthetic emotion on Brenson's view (item 2, above). We have already considered some evidence that spiritual content, not only magisterial or inventive form, is a necessary condition of it. But what if the form of a work is not particularly magisterial or inventive? What if the content of the work is more magisterial or inventive than the form for a particular viewer? The *Saint Anthony Abbot* series of small, painted panels by the fifteenth-century Sienese Master of the Osservanza is exquisite and profoundly moving, but we cannot, as twentieth-century viewers, regard its form as inventive. And whether its form is properly described as magisterial is a moot question.

Brenson's view can accommodate such cases, because there is nothing in his description of aesthetic emotion that requires that it be caused by form in itself. Elements of the given physical or social world can be structurally reconfigured so as to direct our attention to the spiritual potential of the self symbolically or conceptually, in the traditional idioms of pictures or language or musical notation, as well as concretely in the physical manipulation of material elements. Here, such a structural reconfiguration is itself the content of communication in a traditional idiom. This content, too, can then lead us to a greater understanding of our connection and relation to the universe, to the human condition, and to ourselves; and consequently can have the same spiritually transcendent function as other works in which concrete formal manipulation is more salient. Brenson indirectly addresses this possibility by noting that "from the Parthenon to Poussin to Manet to Mondrian, content, not form, has guided European art. The idea of the primacy of content over form is itself part of the European tradition" (Q#1: 33). So on Brenson's view, there is no necessary conflict between qualitative excellence in the formal properties of a work and qualitative excellence in the articulation of its content.

Extending Brenson's account to cover magisterial or inventive content has the virtue of enabling us to explain our aesthetic response not only to traditional painting, sculpture, and architecture but also to literature that exploits traditional narrative form, such as Ralph Ellison's *Invisible Man* or Emile Zola's *Germinal* or Buchi Emecheta's *The Joys of Motherhood,* as well as to music that exploits traditional compositional form, such as Mozart's *Jupiter* Symphony, Ockeghem's *Missa Prolationem,* or the compositions of Wynton Marsalis. It also enables us better to understand what is at stake in contemporary art that exploits familiar formal devices as themselves constitutive of a traditional symbol system for conceptually reconfiguring given physical or social elements.

A second virtue of extending Brenson's account of aesthetic emotion to cover work whose grandeur depends primarily on its content is that it then escapes the anti-intellectualism of a certain version of formalism that bases aesthetic judgment on noncognitive "taste" alone (I do not think this was quite Kant's view, but that is a separate discussion). By emphasizing a work's formal configuration of physical elements to the exclusion of its content—which, after all, must be grasped cognitively if it is to be grasped at all—this version of formalism effectively forecloses *intellectual* appreciation of both form and content in a work of art. This then leads to the peculiar view that the quality of a work can be discerned independently of a cognitive understanding of its pictorial and symbolic conventions, and independently of an educated familiarity with the cultural and social context in which they operate. It this were the case, it would be difficult to see why anyone would require training in art history or art theory at all.

By contrast, Brenson's conception of aesthetic emotion is inclusive and eclectic rather than reductive. It depends on our capacity to take in all aspects of a work, and to allow ourselves to be affected by it on all levels, from the visceral to the philosophical:

> *The encounter I am talking about is a concentration of psychological, philosophical, artistic and political information that is impossible to reduce. The contact is physical. Its gift or breath of thoughts and feelings is accepted or taken in by the body, which always knows more than words and the mind can grasp. A half-hour encounter with a*

> *work of art can be so intense that you can spend your life trying to define it. Because it can be so consuming, it can also be frightening, and a good number of critics spend much of their energy trying to use words to stop the encounter by setting in motion the kind of intellectual machinery that will defuse it and bring it under control. (Q#2: 29).*

Brenson's conception calls attention to the irony that criticism that reductively advocates the primacy of taste, desire, feeling, or political critique may deploy these concepts discursively in order to shut down other aspects of the work that are too disturbing to acknowledge. But "aesthetic experience . . . at its fullest always requires a relinquishment of power" (Q#2: 29), relative to which attempts to intellectualize or belittle the full force of the work are self-disabling.

So far I have suggested that Brenson's account of aesthetic emotion locates the quality of a work of art in the capacity of its form and content to guide us to a transcendent spiritual awareness of its connection to a deeper reality. I have argued that this account requires neither the unity of form and content in a work, nor that either form or content in itself be unified; and also that it can accommodate high-quality works in which content takes clear priority over form. Now I want to reexamine the other current controversies over quality catalogued at the outset of this discussion, in order to assess the capacity of Brenson's conception of quality to resolve them.

Consider item 3. First, if my extended reading of Brenson's conception of quality is correct, then it does rule out the Greenbergian ideal of abstract art for art's sake (3a) as a criterion, because this ideal leads to an infinite regress in seeking the spiritual content of such art, or else to a tautologous, cryptically dead-end declaration that art is about art is about art. But of course it does not rule out art that cultivates the spirit through abstract form, such as Barnett Newman's *Stations of the Cross* or Kaylynn Sullivan's *Unburied Treasure.* Second, Brenson's conception is clearly independent of any particular bias toward Western culture (3b), as his examples demonstrate. Yet it is broad enough to include it, and to explain why we honor those works we do honor as part of the Western tradition. Furthermore, it is consonant with intersubjective agreement within a community on what constitutes work of quality (3c), because it does not require that just any arbitrarily selected individual be able to detect quality in a work, independently of schooling in a community's conventions of communication and expression. As is true on any interesting account of quality, such judgments can be expected to compel intersubjective agreement only among viewers who are adequately educated and informed about what they are seeing.

Item 4 characterizes an objective judgment of quality as one that conforms to universally binding criteria of value.[5] According to this definition, Brenson's conception of quality assigns it an objective status, in that any art of quality cultivates human spirituality in its form and its content, and the cultivation of the human spirit is the closest thing to a universally—or at least cross-culturally—binding criterion of value we have.

Note that this is consistent with the dependence of particular judgments of quality on education and cultural context. That a particular judgment of quality *depends* for its validity on the judge's education and familiarity with cultural context does not imply that the judgment itself is valid only *relative* to that context. I need education and familiarity with the culture of Medieval and Renaissance choral music in order to make the valid judgment that Monteverdi's *Orfeo* is a significant work. But that does not mean my judgment itself is valid only relative to that context. Monteverdi's *Orfeo* is, in fact, a significant work, whether or not I know anything about it. Similarly, I need education and familiarity with African-American working-class popular culture in order to make the valid judgment that Grandmaster Flash's "The Message" is a significant work. But that does not mean my judgment itself is valid only relative to that context. "The Message" is, in fact, a significant work, whether I judge it to be so or not.

This means that individuals can be mistaken in their judgments of quality if some of the subjective preconditions for experiencing aesthetic emotion are not satisfied. I may lack conversance with the work's stylistic idiom, or I may be too preoccupied or distracted to attend clearly to various important aspects of the object before me, or I may have personal or subjective associations with its subject matter or formal elements that prevent me from discerning clearly their meaning or interrelation, or that exaggerate their importance:

> *When there is a predisposition to finding art with something to say to you, you are more likely to be able to listen. To me, being true to quality means being true to movement, feeling, attentiveness, continuity and change. (Q#2: 28)*

So there is nothing in Brenson's account to suggest that aesthetic emotion is equally accessible to anyone under just any cognitive or contextual conditions. Aesthetic emotion can be a subjective condition and also an index of objective quality

5.
Notice that intersubjective agreement is neither a necessary nor a sufficient condition of objectivity. It is not a necessary condition because there may be an objective matter of fact on which the community cannot agree; consider the reaction of the Catholic Church to Galileo's reconfiguration of traditional cosmology. And it is not a sufficient condition because a community can intersubjectively agree on a mistaken or deluded belief; recall Jonestown, Guyana.

because there are works of art that can elicit this emotion in any subject who is ready for it and because it is an emotion of which any human subject is capable.

Therefore, attempts to relativize or dismiss altogether the importance of judgments of objective quality—at just that historical moment when art by women and colored people[6] might be expected rightfully to elicit them from the mainstream—should be regarded with suspicion. A judgment of objective quality empowers the artist whose work it valorizes, and to deny its application to the art of culturally disenfranchised communities is just another way of refusing to share a power with those who are entitled to it. On the other hand, any judge who arrogates such judgments solely to Western culture is quite simply in error. Every judge, regardless of culture, believes in the objective truth of the judgments she makes, and Brenson's conception of quality offers a concrete and inclusive universal standard—grounded in a shared human ability to experience certain artifacts as emblems and devices of self-transcendence—by which all such works of quality can be identified.

Brenson's conception also explains how artifacts of quality from other cultures may cultivate the spirit through their very unfamiliarity:

> *One source of constant pleasure and wonder to me these past years has been the process of looking at an African sculpture or Chinese painting, making contact with it, feeling that it is speaking to me, and then finding that its meaning for its own people and its reasons for being are so far outside my own experience that I can never take anything about Chinese or African art for granted. The encounter with the work pulls me in, convinces me of the existence of quality, and then stretches me, enabling me to understand feelings, responses and ideas I did not know before. With this understanding my ability to respond to quality in other kinds of art is expanded. (Q#2: 9)*

In the cross-cultural case, the experience of transcendence central to aesthetic emotion is in part an experience of personal meaning, and in part an experience of the recognition of experience and meaning that lie beyond one's limited ability to grasp them, a comprehension of these subjective limitations, and an aesthetic vision enlarged by these insights to encompass a larger variety of communicative artifacts than was possible before. So inherent in Brenson's concept of aesthetic emotion as involving cultivation of the spirit is a notion of spiritual growth through the experience of the unique, unusual or unfamiliar:

6.
I explain my reasons for using this terminology in "The Triple Negation of Colored Women Artists," note 1, reprinted in this volume.

> *This expansion of contexts and frontiers has not eliminated or compromised aesthetic experience but expanded its definition and possibilities. I do not believe there is any limit to the value and meaning of the kind of encounter that art allows to exist. (Q#2: 31)*

Item 5 deplores the corrupt linguistic practices that wield words as weapons of power rather than as instruments of communication; but of course it is not only the term *quality* that is exploited in that way (*affirmative action, canon,* and *I.Q.* are other familiar candidates). Brenson's conception of quality as cultivation of the spirit through aesthetic emotion raises the stakes of perverting aesthetic judgments. Although education and cultural familiarity are as much required to make such judgments in this case as in any other, Brenson's conception is unique in that aesthetic emotion is rare without being confined to rarified artifacts or recondite rituals. It is catholic in the nonreligious sense. It can be elicited by quite humble or democratic works of art, and by austere as well as opulent or seductive aesthetic strategies, and so penetrates provincial, superficial, or elitist conceptions of style. The judge who uses this conception of quality as a weapon of power or marginalization exposes his own poverty of spirit in the act.

I will close with two final questions. First, how are we to apply Brenson's conception of quality as a standard? Inherent in it is an affirmation of the importance of appreciating the singularity of an art object for its spiritual potential, and a rejection of abstract generalizations that approach it as instantiating or violating theoretical prescriptions. As Brenson says, aesthetic emotion is "resistant to theory and language [and] . . . suggests that what is most profound can never be held in words" (Q#1: 37). I do not think this means that we should not try to say what we find important or moving about a work with reference to this conception of quality, but rather that we must not expect to grasp the full significance of its effect on us through abstract linguistic concepts, nor try to valorize or disparage any individual work by appealing to some generalized, a priori formulation of the way in which form and content *should* be configured in order to cultivate the spirit. Any such formula would be inimical to the goal of spiritual cultivation itself. Instead, the argument for or against the quality of a work must be made on a case-by-case basis with reference to this standard. This makes the determination of quality the role of the critic or connoisseur, rather than of the aesthetician. So whoever feels disposed to make inductive generalizations about how to ensure future conformity to the standard of spiritual cultivation may be sure that they are thereby violating it.

Second, in my interpretation, Brenson's conception of quality is cross-disciplinary and cross-cultural. Is it therefore too broad to be meaningful? Not unless we decide that there is too much spiritual cultivation around, and there is not much danger of that. Brenson's conception is based in an experience that is both rare *and* universal. It thereby holds works of art to a rigorous and demanding standard that nevertheless connects our shared aspirations across seemingly unbridgeable cultural divides.

22. Government Support for Unconventional Works of Art

First published in *Culture and Democracy: Social and Ethical Issues in Public Support for the Arts and Humanities,* ed. Andrew Buchwalter (Boulder: Westview Press, 1992).

My aim in this discussion is to argue not only that government should provide funding for the arts but a fortiori that it should provide funding for unconventional, disruptive works of art.[1]

A frequently voiced objection to government support of the arts is that government subsidies may subordinate art to political exigencies. This objection is often voiced by those who believe that political art is not legitimate art at all, and that supporting it is merely a tactic of advocating for certain special interest groups or advancing a certain "leftist" political agenda, for example, to combat racism or misogyny, or to provide adequate support for people with AIDS or the homeless. I believe that such beliefs are part of the lingering backlash of McCarthyism, and express fear of political repression as much as they are collusive examples of it. But interestingly, the most recent, egregious case of the manipulation of government funding for the arts in the service of a political agenda has come not from the left but from the right, with former NEA Chairman John Frohnmayer's politically expedient veto of five intermedia applications after they had been recommended for funding by a committee of experts, on the grounds that funding them would antagonize particular members of the House and Senate into retaliatory action against the Endowment.[2]

It has been rightly observed that this evil may be even greater without governmental support. Governmental support ensures that publicly accessible works of art will not be confined to those which respond to popular market demand. In a culture such as our own, market demand is manipulated by advertising, which in turn is the tool of corporate pressures to enforce public acceptance of the political and cultural status quo. Part of this enforcement procedure involves *passive censorship,* that is, withholding institutional recognition or representation of views that compete with or criticize the status quo. Passive censorship occurs when democratic institutions responsible for informing the public of diverse views and values (such as museums, theaters, or the print or electronic media) renege on that responsibility, by ignoring such alternatives as though they did not exist—thus effectively denying the public access to them. Without governmental support, work that questions that status quo and the power relations that lie behind it may be subject to passive censorship by institutions as well as individual consumers.

1.
An earlier version of this chapter was delivered to the American Philosophical Association Eastern Division Convention in New York on December 30, 1991, as comments to Andrew Buchwalter's "Philosophy, Culture, and Public Policy." I am grateful to him and to members of the audience of that colloquium for discussion that has considerably improved this chapter.

2.
See Elizabeth Hess, "Backing Down Behind Closed Doors at the NEA," *The Village Voice,* September 24, 1991.

For example, the Philip Morris Tobacco Company is a major source of support in the museum world. It also contributed significantly to the reelection of Senator Jesse Helms. It obtains market credibility and social status through advertising that blatantly associates it with the "high culture" projects it supports. As a condition of exhibition funding, Philip Morris has often required that the exhibiting institution distribute free cartons of Marlboro cigarettes at the opening of such exhibitions. Perhaps it goes without saying that Philip Morris has never funded exhibitions devoted to health issues, or that explore the issue of environmental racism. If this were the only *sort* of funding source available, such nonconventional exhibitions would receive no funding at all. And without such exhibitions and other public venues for cultural dissent and criticism, the conventional sensibilities represented by such figures as Jesse Helms or the Philip Morris Tobacco Company might prevail even more widely than they already do.

Governmental funding for the arts has, at least up to now, meant a peer-review process. Responsibility for evaluating applications and selecting funding candidates is delegated to a jury or committee of individuals selected for their recognized professional competence, experience, and achievement in the field. On the one hand, this has meant that such individuals are familiar with most of the kind of work for which funding is sought, and often with the artists or institutions that seek it. This degree of familiarity, and the prior professional relationships it presupposes, is the natural consequence of having a working knowledge of the field. It does not imply any conflict of interest.

On the other hand, the peer-review process requires that the individuals making these decisions do so anonymously, and that they are compensated only minimally for their participation in the selection process. The outcome is a selection of candidates for funding that is *disinterested* from the perspective of personal or political advantage, and expresses the committee's best attempt to evaluate the work on its aesthetic merits. I can personally attest that these sessions are often lengthy and contentious, and that widely disparate opinions must be reconciled through the process of discussion and information-gathering before a consensual evaluation can be reached. This is a paradigm example of debate on the issues, untainted by considerations of personal or political advantage. An artist who receives such funding receives, in addition to the palpable good of financial support, the purest expression of disinterested peer respect and appreciation it is possible to receive in a largely market-driven economy.

By contrast with the peer-review process as it functions in governmental funding, that process as it functions in the distribution of funding by private foundations is often—although not always—subject to the ideological, political, or corporate constraints imposed by the patron. So, for example, Hans Haacke, an artist whose work investigates the issue of corporate control of the arts, cannot be expected to receive funding from Philip Morris, nor has his work been purchased by major art institutions whose programs depend on such corporate support. The public and ideologically transitory nature of government makes it the most appropriate source of funding in the arts, insofar as such support is supposed to express disinterested aesthetic evaluation rather than personal, political, or market bias. A government committed to the democratic values of freedom of expression and the free competition of ideas has a particular obligation to support works of art that offer critical alternatives to prevailing power relations.

One might object to the peer-review process on the grounds that it subverts democratic values rather than promotes them, by putting the evaluation of art in the hands of "experts" who then legislate "aesthetically correct" art for the "masses." But this falsely represents the trained professionals who serve on those panels as distinct from the "masses" rather than their most informed representatives—as though there were no working-class artists, former scholarship students among the critics, or self-made-millionaire collectors. Art professionals come to the peer-review process from all social classes, ethnic and racial backgrounds, and aesthetic orientations within our society. On the other hand, it is true that trained professionals are *trained* to an extent that the general public by definition cannot be. The idea that informed judgments of aesthetic quality should not determine what art is funded for public consumption is a peculiar sort of populism indeed. It is a populism that views with suspicion the possibility that art might have a beneficial educational effect on the general public; that it might tell the viewing public anything that it does not already know.

Only since the McCarthy era of the 1950s has art retreated from the social and didactic role it has always had in the history of Western art, as a source of information and new forms of perception and thought for its public. Only since then, when it was made very clear to artists as well as other intellectuals by politicians that art should be, as it were, seen but not heard, has the art world made a virtue out of social impotence: for only since then has art retreated to the role of an abstract, esoteric discipline devoid of content or social impact, and only since then has it been possible to level the charge of elitism at those whose work does, like so much other intellectual work, require specialized skills and information. Specialization is an unavoidable consequence of the division of labor between those who are art professionals and those who are not. Elitism and esotericism are an avoidable consequence of the political censorship of "subversive" artistic ideas. Art professionals are qualified to serve on peer-review panels because they are qualified by their training to make, show, and evaluate works of art. It is hard to see how anyone could quarrel with that.

Art as a pedagogical tool is one thing. But what about works of art that disrupt stable social norms, or offend the conventional moral or social sensibilities of citizens? Does government have an obligation to fund work that undermines social foundations? Andrew Buchwalter distinguishes between public goods and public interests as follows: A *public good* is the aggregate sum of at least most citizens' individual preferences; examples would include a public library, health care, or an opera house. A *public interest,* by contrast, is something that serves the ends of public life, that is, the community itself.[3] Examples might include an equitable sales tax or an adequate police force. Whereas a public good expresses the aggregate of individual preferences, a public interest may but need not do so. Instead it may embody something that would be good for society in general, independently of what individuals prefer for themselves. Now it might be argued that unconventional works of art are neither a public good nor a public interest. Clearly they are not a public good, because they violate most individual preferences, by definition of "unconventional." It might be claimed that they are not a public interest either, because they undermine the most basic end of public life, namely the preservation of social stability through a system of normative conventions that coordinate behavior among individuals, from all levels from the personal to the social.

Consider the performance work of Karen Finley. Finley violates conventional images of women by, for example, adopting the pornographic masculine vernacular in some of her performance monologues, as well as by smearing her body with various foods, and by naming and depicting acts of sexual violation. These in addition to many other disturbing elements are woven together in a hypnotizing drama that is often as painful as it is assaultive on conventional sensibilities. There are many arguments that can be given regarding the importance of Finley's work: its release into a shared social sphere of a subconscious and subterranean level of experience often considered inaccessible to women; its cathartic effects on an audience socialized to repress painful experiences of an intimate nature; its importance as a political strategy of naming, depicting, and confronting the systematic and daily violation of women's bodies; and so forth. Rather than developing any of these arguments, I want to address the question of how it can ever be in the public interest to publicly display such works of art that disrupt or violate stable social conventions—of behavior, social or political roles, or aesthetic practices.

3.
Andrew Buchwalter, "Philosophy, Culture, and Public Policy," in *Culture and Democracy: Social and Ethical Issues in Public Support for the Arts and Humanities,* ed. Andrew Buchwalter (Boulder: Westview Press, 1992).

The answer is obvious. It is in the public interest to disrupt those conventions that are unnecessarily restrictive for some, such that those restrictions serve the interests of others who unfairly compete with them for the resources, power, and social status necessary to gain public support for a favored ideology. So, for example, a work of art that disrupts the prevailing image of corporate sponsorship as beneficial and politically neutral, as Hans Haacke's work does, is in the public interest, even though it undermines the convention of personal and social compliance with corporate demands in the workplace. Similarly, a work of art that disrupts conventional expectations of women as passive receptors of sexual and social violation, as Karen Finley's work does, is in the public interest, even though it undermines conventional behavior by and toward women in personal and social relationships. It is *because* these works assault oppressive conventional attitudes that empower institutions at the expense of individuals and men at the expense of women respectively that they are in the public interest, even if they cannot be, by definition, objects of personal preference for most individuals.

This is to suggest that unconventional works of art are in the public interest because they promote—rather than require or presuppose—tolerance, and because they conduce to the evolution of social norms that maximize autonomy and individuality, rather than conformity and self-censorship. No one would argue that social disruption is a good in itself. However, social stability is also not an end in itself. Social stability may serve the harmful function of entrenching the repression of personal sensibility, individual self-actualization, or social self-determination, or it may serve the beneficial function of coordinating expectations among those recognized to differ in their personal, social, or aesthetic values—as, in fact, we all do. Moral relativists argue that, in the last analysis, all coordinating conventions are arbitrary means of ensuring social equilibrium, including moral ones. Nevertheless, some such conventions are more arbitrary than others. Social conventions that repress individual self-expression *merely* because it takes an unconventional form are harmful because they protect provinciality and philistinism at the expense of individuality. And they are arbitrary because there is no justification, beyond the stabilizing function of the convention itself, for enforcing it.

By contrast, there is a nonarbitrary justification for enforcing fundamental moral conventions—specifically, those moral norms that prohibit physical harm to others. Calibrating degrees of harm from the physical to the psychological and from the physically to the intellectually assaultive is to start down a treacherously slippery slope, and I will not attempt it here. But to agree that art should not inflict physical pain or desecrate the dead (say) is not thereby to support censorship or governmental repression of such work. Any marginalized individual or group knows how effective a community's nonofficial social sanctions can be in discouraging such work: Through ostracism, neglect, or social disapproval we discourage a great deal of potential social benefit. We would do better to turn these potent, nonofficial forms of social punishment to discouraging work that is genuinely morally harmful.

But is there not something hypocritical, or disingenuous at best, about demanding government support for works of art that then subvert the very social order that supports them? I think not. There is an important distinction to be made between government (or the state) and the social community (or civil society). Demanding government support for unconventional works of art that question the social order is not asking government to cut off the branch it's sitting on, because government and the social order are not the same. In a democratic society, the function of government is legislative, executive, and judicative of norms that not only reflect but also influence and shape the development of the social community that elects it. A democratic government has a responsibility not merely to permit but to *promote* the democratic values of tolerance, diversity of opinion and values, and freedom of speech, thought, and information in the society it governs. To demand that the government fund unconventional works of art is to demand that it fulfill its responsibility to the community to encourage the democratic values it purports to represent.

Works of art that question prevailing ideologies or power relationships may be disruptive and offensive because they disturb the settled presumption that prevailing social roles, practices, and power relationships are natural and inevitable. They thereby call into question whether the particular form democracy assumes in our troubled society is the most fully realized form democracy can take. In questioning the social power relations that define our prevailing conception of democracy, unconventional works of art thereby conduce to the evolution of social norms more appreciative of the questioners, respectful of the powerless, and tolerant of the unconventional; and thereby reaffirm the ultimate value of democracy itself. Unconventional works of art are in the public interest—hence deserving of government support—because they promote coordinating conventions for the inherently unconventional, that is, for fully realized individuals whose preferences and tastes are peculiarly their own.

17.
Sol LeWitt, *Forty-Nine Three-Part Variations on Three Different Kinds of Cubes* (1967–1970). Courtesy John Weber Gallery.

18.
Out of the Corner (1990). Courtesy John Weber Gallery, collection Whitney Museum.

23. The Logic of Modernism

Written in 1992 and first published in *Flashart* 26, no. 168 (January–February 1993), pp. 56–58, 118, 136.

There are four interrelated properties of Euroethnic art that are central to understanding the development of modernism, and in particular the development of contemporary art in the United States within the last few decades: (1) its appropriative character, (2) its formalism, (3) its self-awareness, and (4) its commitment to social content. These four properties furnish strong conceptual and strategic continuities between the history of European art—modernism in particular—and recent developments in American art with explicitly political subject matter. Relative to these lines of continuity, the peculiarly American variety of modernism known as Greenbergian formalism is an aberration. Characterized by its repudiation of content in general and explicitly political subject matter in particular, Greenbergian formalism gained currency as an opportunistic ideological evasion of the threat of cold war McCarthyite censorship and Red-baiting in the 1950s. To the extent that this ideological repudiation of political subject matter has prevailed in the international art context, American imperialism has succeeded in supplanting the longstanding European tradition of art as a medium of social engagement with a peculiarly pharmaceutical conception of art as soporific and analgesic.

By the *appropriative* character of Euroethnic art, I mean its tendency to draw on the art of non-Euroethnic cultures for inspiration. This may originate in the Early Italian Renaissance experience of drawing on the art of an alien, temporally remote culture—that of Hellenic Greece—for revitalization. The real lesson of the Renaissance, on this account, is not the rediscovery of perspective but rather the discovery of difference as a source of inspiration. Other early examples of the Euroethnic appetite for appropriation include the influence of Byzantine religious art in the paintings of Duccio or Cimabue; the Islamic and Hindu influences on the art of Giotto or Fra Angelico; more recently, the influences of Japanese art on Van Gogh, of Tahitian art on Gauguin, and of African art on Picasso; and more recently still, the influences of African-American jazz on Mondrian and Stuart Davis, and of African-American graffiti art on Keith Haring and David Wojnarowicz. It is natural that a society that depends on colonized non-Euroethnic cultures for its land, labor, and natural resources should do so for its aesthetic and cultural resources as well. But the impetus in the latter case is not necessarily imperialistic and exploitative. It may be instead a drive to self-transcendence of the limits of the socially prescribed Euroethnic self, by striving to incorporate the idiolects of the enigmatic Other within them. Here the aim of appropriation would be not to exploit deliberately the Other's aesthetic language but to confound oneself by incorporating into works of art an aesthetic language one recognizes as largely opaque to one; as having a significance one recognizes as beyond one's ability fully to grasp. Viewed in this way, exploitation is an unintended side effect—the consequence of ignorance and insensitivity—of a project whose main intention is to escape those very cognitive limitations.

The *formalism* of Euroethnic art is a direct consequence of its appropriative character, as it is only where the content of a work is enigmatic, obscure, or disregarded that its formal properties outcompete it for salience. This reasoning presupposes that our primary cognitive concern as human beings, regardless of cultural context, is to discern meaning, and only secondarily to discern form; and that form itself is of interest to us only where it illuminates or enhances meaning. If this is so, then artists must first look at the art of an alien culture and acknowledge their failure to grasp its contextual meaning, before its formal properties can heighten their self-awareness of the formal properties of their own culture's art. So, for example, the treatment of space and structure by such artists as the Master of the Osservanza certainly could have occurred without an awareness of the similar treatment of space and structure in Classical Hindu painting. But without this awareness it could not have been deliberately isolated and refined as a unique style, because in that case there would have been no external source of salience by which to highlight and differentiate it from other such stylistic properties. Formalism as an aesthetic requires the cognitive deflection of content. And this, in turn, presupposes a prior encounter with work the content of which was impervious to cognitive penetration. That is, in order to learn to abstract from the content of a work, one must have previously experienced as cognitively inaccessible the content of a work. Whereas Euroethnic social scientists evade this experience by constructing and projecting expected utility-maximizing explanations for the visual symbologies of non-Euroethnic cultures, Euroethnic artists self-consciously embrace it in acts of formal appropriation.

The appropriative character and formalism of Euroethnic art is, then, intrinsically connected with its *self-awareness* (or self-consciousness). To recognize an alien cultural practice as different from one's own, and as inaccessible to understanding with respect to content, is implicitly to recognize one's own cultural practice as a cultural practice, with its own rules and constraints. This just is the awareness that one's cultural practice is merely one among many possible ones. And the recognition that alternative cultural practices are cognitively inaccessible just is the awareness that one's own furnish the only available conduit for interpretation of formal anomaly. So the cross-cultural appropriation of alien formal devices reminds one of one's subjectivity. Self-consciousness of this kind is a necessary condition of innovation.

The appropriativeness, formalism, and self-consciousness of European art functions to cast its *social content* into high relief. By rendering familiar and socially pregnant subject matter in new, unusual, or nontraditional ways, European art imbues it with added significance beyond the commonplace and with historical or cultural perspective. Indeed, it is the rendering of familiar social content in a form that inspires, exalts, instructs, or galvanizes one to action that makes the art of David, Delacroix, Gericault, Goya, or Picasso such a transformative experience. The formalism of Euroethnic art has been traditionally interconnected with its social content, in that the challenge of European art has been to use formal devices in expressive and innovative ways that reawaken the viewer to the significance of the subject matter depicted. Here the project of appropriation is essential, because a precondition of perceiving or conceptualizing given subject matter differently is that the visual forms one sees actually *be* different, in some respect, from those one is accustomed to. That these visual forms must diverge from the traditions of one's visual culture in order to perform their expected social function requires that an artist self-consciously seek outside those familiar traditions, and import difference back into them. So the drive to innovation is embedded in the social function of Euroethnic art and pre-dates its emergence as a market-driven commodity. And because the sources of innovation traditionally have been found in non-Euroethnic cultures whose visual content is cognitively opaque to Euroethnic eyes, innovation in Euroethnic art has usually meant self-conscious innovation of form.

In these ways, European modernism is wholly consistent with the prior history of European art. Innovations of form do not dictate the sacrifice of social content in Picasso's *Guernica* any more than they did in Manet's *Dejeuner sur l'herbe,* or Goya's *Desastres de la guerra.* If formal innovation in Euroethnic art is indeed rooted in cross-cultural appropriation, then the combination of formal innovation with social or political content can be read as an emblem of the artist's self-conscious cultural or affectional distance from her or his subject-matter. By "distance" I mean not "emotional detachment" but rather "alienation": An artist who depicts social content in a nontraditional way expresses a self-consciously critical rather than unself-consciously participatory or involved evaluational perspective toward it, whether positive or negative. In his depiction of Marat, David expresses a self-consciously distanced evaluational view of the French Revolution, as Matisse does of his spouse in his depictions of her, and as Giacometti and de Kooning do of women in their depiction of them. It is because of this connection between formal innovation and self-conscious cultural alienation from one's subject matter that Euroethnic art has nourished the tradition of the visionary artist as culturally and socially marginal, as someone who not only is something of a social outcast but self-consciously chooses to be one. The root of this tradition is to be found in the prior European tradition of cross-cultural appropriation.

Relative to this long tradition of combining social content with innovative form, European modernism's American equivalent, Greenbergian formalism, constituted a radical departure. From its status as the linchpin of a work, social content—and particularly explicitly political subject matter—was demoted by Greenbergian formalism to irrelevance, as sullying the "purity" or impeding the "transcendence" of a work. If a "pure" work of art could have no content, then the artist could not express formally the self-consciously distanced critical stance toward content—issues, events, concepts, conditions—that had characterized earlier Euroethnic art. So the only stance an artist could legitimately take was an unself-consciously involved, participatory one: In this scheme of things, the artist's role was to "engage" or "grapple" wordlessly with the formal and material properties of his (almost always a "his") medium, and the critic's role was to articulate the aesthetic rationale of the work thereby created. In abandoning content and abdicating the self-conscious stance to the critic, artists abandoned the responsibilities of conscious control over their creative efforts and their meaning. "Action painting," live from the Freudian unconscious, was all that was left to them.

How could the thematic fulcrum of European modernism become so inessential in American modernism? If the centrality of social content is a constant up through Picasso, Giacometti, and de Kooning, as I have suggested, then postmodernist claims that an innate tendency to reductivism *of content* characterized the development of modernism are defective. Such a radical shift in priorities cannot be explained as part of the internal logic of modernism itself. Instead it is necessary to look at the external social and political conditions to which American formalists were responding.

The ideological use of American art for cold war propaganda purposes in the 1950s has been charted frequently.[1] But the reaction to recent U.S. government attempts to censor "politically sensitive" subject matter in contemporary American art naturally invites comparison specifically with Senator Joseph McCarthy's successful campaign of intimidation of left-wing artists and intellectuals as communist sympathizers in the 1950s. In such a climate, the rationalization that political content was incompatible with the "higher purpose" of art functioned as a form of self-censorship among art professionals just as effectively then as it does now. As it does for us, it gave art professionals in the 1950s a ready-made reason not to become politically engaged, not to fight back, not to notice the infiltration of the "white cube" by complex social and political realities, and not to try to come to terms with them in their creative work—that is, not to work creatively with them as artists always had in the past. And it gave them a reason to relegate whatever political convictions and involvements they may have had to a corner of their lives

1.
See, for example, Max Kozloff, "American Painting during the Cold War," *Artforum* 11 (May 1973), pp. 43–54; Eva Cockcroft, "Abstract Expressionism: Weapon of the Cold War," *Artforum* 12 (June 1974), pp. 39–41; Serge Guilbaut, *How New York Stole the Idea of the Avant-Garde* (Chicago: University of Chicago, 1983).

in which they would not threaten anyone's professional opportunities. In short, the ideology of Greenbergian formalism undergirded the threat of McCarthyism to render politically and socially impotent a powerful instrument of social change—visual culture—whose potential government censors have always seen far more clearly than artists do; and rationalized that impotence to the castrati. The postwar American strategy of importing back to Europe the artistic embodiment of unself-conscious social ineffectuality under the guise of an extracted essence of critically sophisticated formal appropriation was perfectly suited to its Marshall Plan agenda of cultural and political imperialism.

Since the McCarthy era and the heyday of Greenbergian formalism, American art has been restoring its social content through the back door. Minimalism's geometrical simplicity and formal reductiveness was an explicit repudiation of the abstract aesthetic theorizing projected onto art by formalist critics in the Greenbergian camp. Emphasizing the concrete, unique particularity of the specific object, its spatiotemporal immediacy and imperviousness to abstract critical speculation, minimalism mounted an individualist attack on aesthetic stereotyping that echoed analogous attacks on race and gender stereotyping that first surfaced in the white American mainstream in the early 1960s. In so doing, minimalism reasserted the primacy of the object itself as content of the work.

In the mid-1960s, Sol LeWitt further developed this notion of self-reflexive content: By insisting on the primacy of the idea of the work over its medium of realization, LeWitt created the context in which the cognitive content of a work could have priority over its perceptual form. And by using the permutation of selected formal properties of an object—its sides, dimensions, or geometrical shape—as a decision procedure for generating the final form of the work as a permutational system, LeWitt moved that system itself, and the idea of that system, into the foreground of the work as its self-reflexive subject matter. Here it is not only the object as a unique particular that has primacy, but that object as the locus and origin of the conceptual system it self-reflexively generates.

From there it was only a short step to conceptual art's insistence in the late 1960s on the self-reflexive investigation of concepts and language themselves as the primary subject matter of art. And because self-consciousness is a special case of self-reflexivity, it was then an even shorter step to the self-conscious investigation of those very language users and art producers themselves as embedded participants in the social context: For Joseph Kosuth and the Art-Language group, this natural progression was from linguistic analysis of the concept of art to discursive Marxist critique of the means of art production; for Hans Haacke, it was from self-sustaining material systems to self-sustaining political systems; in my own work, it was from my body as a conceptually and spatiotemporally immediate art object to my person as a gendered and ethnically stereotyped art commodity. The reemergence of self-consciously distanced, critical art with explicit social content in the early 1970s, then, was a natural outgrowth of the reaffirmation of content latent in minimalism and the self-reflexive subject-matter explicit in conceptual art. The cognitive and formal strategies of minimalism, and their evolution in the work of Sol LeWitt and first-generation conceptualists, reestablished the link with European modernism by restoring distanced self-awareness as a central value of artistic production—a self-awareness that is inevitably as social, cultural, and political as it is formal in its purview.

Meanwhile, the repressive McCarthyite ideology of Greenbergian formalism continues to gain adherents in post-cold war Europe, where many thoughtful and intelligent art professionals are alarmingly eager to discard Europe's variegated social and historical traditions as sources of continuity and cultural memory, in favor of the American substitute. This substitute is, of course, willful amnesia; that is, simply to deny that there is anything to remember or grasp that can't be resolved in a twenty-two-minute sitcom or merchandised in a thirty-second commercial. The erasure of content—particularly political content—was a Madison Avenue inspiration long before it was a gleam in Clement Greenberg's eye. The continuing European susceptibility to 1950s American cultural imperialism is particularly regrettable in a historical period in which Europe's turbulent social, political, and demographic changes offer such fertile conditions for artistic social engagement. Europe is now undergoing the same sustained assault from outside on its entrenched mythologies, conventions, and social arrangements that mainstream white America did from the civil rights movement, the counterculture, feminism, and anti-Vietnam war protesters in the 1960s. As the United States has, Europe will need a period of sustained cultural processing of these events by its artistic communities in order to learn how best to represent these changes to itself. It would be unfortunate if European art professionals chose to follow America's lead again, in ideologically blindfolding the visual arts in this undertaking. The American habit of somnambulism about its criminal past is such that it took the American art world decades to reawaken the aesthetic vocabulary of social resistance and engagement narcotized by Greenbergian formalism. In Europe, by contrast, this vocabulary is more deeply rooted in the artistic tradition of self-conscious criticality and more firmly buttressed by well-preserved artifacts of cultural memory. Let us hope it will be sufficient antidote against renewed American attempts to export yet one more "new world order" for cross-cultural consumption.[2]

2.
In thinking about these issues I have benefitted from conversations with Laura Cottingham, Bart de Baere, Charles Esche, Michael Lingner, and Pier Luigi Tazzi.

24. Two Kinds of Discrimination

Written in 1992 and first published in *The Yale Journal of Criticism* 6, no. 1 (1993), pp. 25–74.

The two kinds of discrimination I want to talk about are political discrimination and cognitive discrimination.[1] By political discrimination, I mean what we ordinarily understand by the term *discrimination* in political contexts: a manifest attitude in which a particular property of a person that is irrelevant to judgments of that person's intrinsic value or competence—for example, her race, gender, class, sexual orientation, or religious or ethnic affiliation—is seen as a source of disvalue or incompetence, in general, as a source of inferiority.[2] I will call any such arbitrary property so perceived a *primary disvalued property;* and conversely, any such arbitrary property perceived as a source of value or superiority a *primary valued property.*

By *cognitive discrimination,* I mean what we ordinarily understand by the term *discrimination* in cognitive contexts: a manifest capacity to distinguish veridically between one property and another, and to respond appropriately to each. When we say of someone that he is a discriminating person, for example, or that he has discriminating judgment, we mean, in part, that he is a person of refined tastes or subtle convictions; that he exercises a capacity to make fine distinctions between properties of a thing and bases his positive or negative valuations on these actual properties.[3]

I want to explore the relation between these two kinds of discrimination, and to argue that the first type of discrimination depends on a failure of the second. Judging a person as inferior because one perceives her race as a primary disvalued property depends on failing to distinguish finely enough between properties she has and those she does not have, and between those that are relevant to such a

1.
Work on this paper was supported in part by an NEH Summer Stipend and a Woodrow Wilson International Scholar's Fellowship. Portions are excerpted from a manuscript in progress, *Rationality and the Structure of the Self,* and from other articles (as indicated) in which I have addressed these issues.

2.
Thus I shall not be considering cases in which race, gender, and so on, *are* relevant to judgments of a person's value or competence, for example, as a role model in a classroom or as a unique and needed perspective in a business venture or court of law. I restrict the discussion to consideration of *intrinsic* value or competence as determined by principles of justice and equality. The contrast is with *instrumental* value or competence in furthering some specified social or institutional policy, of the sort that would figure in arguments that would justify, for example, refusing to sell real estate in a certain neighborhood to a black family solely because doing so would lower property values, or hiring a woman to a professional position solely in order to meet affirmative action quotas, or refusing to serve Asians at one's family diner solely because it would be bad for business. Whether these should be included under the rubric of first-order political discrimination, hypocrisy, prudence, or mere moral pusillanimity is too large a topic to address here.

3.
Notice that the veracity of the discrimination—and hence the reality of the properties—is presupposed in this use of the term. Someone who draws such distinctions in their absence is said to draw a "distinction without a difference," or to be "seeing things." Of such a person we say not that he is discriminating but rather that he is deluded. See my "'Seeing Things'," *Southern Journal of Philosophy* 29, Supplementary Volume: Moral Epistemology (1990), pp. 29–60.

judgment and those that are not. I begin by arguing that, on a Kantian conception of the self, we instinctively resist the challenge of cognitive discrimination by confining our range of judgments to those objects and properties that conform to preexisting categories and concepts that structure not only our experience but thereby our selves. I suggest that we are compelled either to conceptualize the objects of our experience in familiar terms or else not to register them at all, and that this is a necessary condition of preserving the unity and internal coherence of the self against anomalous data that threaten it. I invoke this model of the self to explain the phenomenon of xenophobia, that is, fear of another who fails to satisfy our provincial preconceptions about bona fide persons; and xenophobia, in turn, to explain the phenomenon of political discrimination. I distinguish between two kinds of political discrimination: *first-order political discrimination* as defined earlier, and *higher-order political discrimination* as a refinement introduced by pangs of conscience that result in even more radical failures of cognitive discrimination: of the other, of oneself, and of the situation. Finally, I conclude by suggesting some ways in which works of art might combat political discrimination by cultivating cognitive discrimination.

I. The Kantian Rationalism Thesis

In the first *Critique,*[4] Kant tells us repeatedly that if a perception does not conform to the fundamental categories of thought that ensure the unity and coherence of the self, they cannot be part of our experience at all (A 112, 122, and B 132, 134).[5] Kant describes these fundamental categories as "a priori transcendental concepts of understanding," by which he means innate rules of cognitive organization that any coherent, conscious experience must presuppose. The table of transcendental categories he offers in the Metaphysical Deduction are drawn largely from Aristotle,

4.
Immanuel Kant, *Kritik der Reinen Vernunft,* herausg. Raymond Schmidt (Hamburg: Felix Meiner Verlag, 1976). All references to this work are enclosed in parentheses in the text. Translations from the German are my own. Cognoscenti will find my translations to be generally more literal than Kemp Smith's and (I think) more accurate in conveying not only the substance of Kant's claims but his manner of expression. Despite Kant's tendency to indulge in run-on sentences, he is by and large a plain speaker with a fondness for the vernacular, not the stilted, pretentious Prussian Kemp Smith makes him out to be. But the major objection to Kemp Smith's translation is that he obscures important philosophical issues by overinterpreting Kant so as to resolve them before the monolingual reader can become aware that there is anything to dispute.

5.
This thesis may be viewed as the resolution of a Gedanken experiment that Kant earlier conducts at A 89–91, in which he entertains the possibility of unsynthesized appearance. In any case, his ultimate commitment to this thesis is clear. See Robert Paul Wolff, *Kant's Theory of Mental Activity* (Cambridge: Harvard University Press, 1968), for a discussion.

with considerable additional tinkering by Kant. They include substance, totality, reality, possibility, causality, and community, to name just a few. Some commentators have rightly concluded that the most significant candidate for this elevated cognitive status is the subject-predicate relation in logic, from which Kant derives the relational category of substance and property in the Table of Categories (Kant regards this as the result of fleshing out the subject-predicate relation or "judgment form" with "transcendental content," that is, the sensory data our experience presupposes rather than the sensations we perceive as a result of it [A 70/B 95–A 79/B 105]).[6] The idea, then, would be that organizing sensory data in terms of this relation is a necessary condition of experience. On this view, if we do not experience something in a way that enables us to make sense of it by identifying properties of it—for example, in propositions such as

That car is dark red

or

I am tired,

we cannot consciously experience that thing at all.

This thesis—call it the *Kantian Rationalism Thesis*—has the merit of plausibility over the archaic list of categories Kant originally furnished. It does not seem too controversial to suppose that any viable system of concepts should enable its user to identify states of affairs by their properties, because concepts just are of corresponding properties, and to ascribe a property to an object just is to subsume that object under the corresponding concept. So any system of concepts should enable its user to ascribe to objects those properties of which she has concepts. The Kantian Rationalism Thesis—henceforth the KRT—is so weak that it may even be defensible in the face of anthropological evidence that languages considerably remote from Indo-European ones evince a cognitive structuring to the user's experience that is so different from our own as to be almost unintelligible to us. It would be an argument in favor of the KRT if it could be shown that the subject-predicate relation held regardless of the other ways in which culturally specific conceptual organizations of experience differed among themselves.

6.
See, for example, P. F. Strawson, *The Bounds of Sense* (London: Methuen, 1968), chapter 11.2. In hindsight Kant himself grudgingly admits that hypothetical and disjunctive syllogisms contain the same "matter" as the categorical judgment, but he refuses to budge on their essential difference in form and function. See Kant's *Logic,* trans. Robert Hartman and Wolfgang Schwarz (New York: Bobbs-Merrill, 1974), paragraphs 24–29, 60, n. 2, especially pp. 111 and 127.

More precisely formulated, then, the KRT says that if we do not experience something in such a way as to allow us to make sense of it in terms of a set of coherent concepts that structure our experience, *whatever those concepts are,* we cannot consciously experience that thing at all. On this thesis the innate capacity would consist in a disposition to structure experience conceptually as such, but not necessarily to do so in accordance with any particular list of concepts,[7] provided that the particular, culturally specific set S of concepts $c_1, c_2, c_3, \ldots c_n$ that did so satisfied the following requirements:

A. S observes the law of noncontradiction, that is, the members of S are internally and mutually consistent in their application;

B. Any particular c_i in S is either

 1. an instantiation of some other c_j in S; or

 2. instantiated by some other c_k in S;

 that is, S is minimally coherent;

C. For any cognitively available particular p, there is a c_i in S that p instantiates.

The suggestion would be that we can understand particular states of affairs only if (A) the concepts by which we recognize them are neither internally nor mutually contradictory; (B) those concepts are minimally coherent with one another in that each particular identified by them satisfies the subject-predicate relationship with respect to at least one other of them; and (C) that particular itself instantiates at least one of them. I develop this suggestion at length elsewhere.[8] The KRT says, roughly, that in order for something to register as a conscious experience at all for us, we have to be able to make sense of it in terms of some such concepts in the set, and that if we can't, it won't.

7.
This thesis is elaborated in the contemporary context by Gerald M. Edelman, *Neural Darwinism: The Theory of Neuronal Group Selection* (New York: Basic Books, 1987) and *The Remembered Present: A Biological Theory of Consciousness* (New York: Basic Books, 1989). See the review of Edelman and others by Oliver Sacks in "Neurology and the Soul," *The New York Review of Books* 37, no. 18 (November 22, 1990), pp. 44–50.

8.
Adrian Piper, "Rationality and the Structure of the Self," excerpted from the manuscript *Rationality and the Structure of the Self* and delivered to the Association for the Philosophy of the Unconscious, American Philosophical Association Eastern Division Convention, Boston, Mass., 1986, the Departments of Philosophy at Columbia University and the University of Minnesota, and the Oberlin Conference on Moral Psychology, April 1995.

Suppose, for example, that we were to be confronted with some particular such that the concepts it instantiated satisfied (A) but violated (B), that is, such that we could invoke a concept in identifying it consistently with the application of our other concepts; but that that concept itself bore no instantiation-relation to others in the set (aside from that of being a concept in the set). In this case, that which we invoked as a "concept" would in fact not be one at all, because the corresponding predicate would by definition denote only the single state of affairs it had been invoked to identify. Because there would be no further concepts in terms of which we might understand the meaning of that denoting term, it could not enter into any analytic truths. In short, this would be like cooking up a special noise to denote only one state of affairs on the single occasion of its occurrence. The enterprises of denotation and meaning themselves would fail.

Alternately, imagine what it would be like to be confronted by a particular such that its concept satisfied (B) but not (A), that is, such that it enabled us to identify its properties in terms of concepts in the set, but the application of those concepts themselves was internally or mutually inconsistent. In that event, it would be possible to ascribe to the thing the conjunction of some predicate *F* and some other one, *G*, that implied the negation of *F*.[9] Again the enterprise of identification itself would fail. If we were finally to fail to identify the thing or state of affairs in question as having a consistent set of properties, we would fail to identify it altogether. And then it could not be part of our conscious experience. If such cases characterized all our encounters with the world, we would have no experiences of it at all and therefore no unified sense of self either.

These are the sorts of failures Kant has in mind when he avers, in the A Deduction, that

> *without such unity, which has its rule a priori, and which subjects appearances to it, thoroughgoing, universal, and therefore necessary unity of consciousness would not be found in the manifold of perceptions. These would then not belong to any experience, therefore would be without object, and nothing but a blind play of representations, that is, less even than a dream. (A 112)*

Kant is saying that if we do not organize cognitively the data of our senses according to consistent and coherent rules, we cannot be rationally unified subjects. "For otherwise," he adds in the B Deduction, "I would have as many-colored and diverse a self as I have representations of which I am conscious" (B 134). I would, that is, lack a sense of myself as the subject in whose consciousness those representations occur. For a Kantian rationalist, then, the cognitive organization of expe-

9.
Ibid.

rience according to consistent and coherent concepts is a necessary condition of being a rationally unified subject. Anomalous particulars or properties that fail to satisfy (A)–(C) cannot be objects of experience for us at all.

Elsewhere I have argued that the resistance to integrating anomaly is a general feature of human intellection that attempts to satisfy a Kantian requirement of rational self-preservation.[10] And Thomas Kuhn has documented the inherent impediments to paradigm shift in the natural sciences—their conservatism and constitutional insensitivity to the significance of new data, and their resistance to revising deeply entrenched theories in light of experimental anomaly.[11] Relative to this scheme, xenophobia is a particular example of a perfectly general disposition to defend the self against anomalous informational assaults on its internal coherence. Xenophobia is fear not of strangers generally but rather of a certain kind of strangers, namely, those who do not conform to one's preconceptions about how persons ought to look or behave. In what follows I want to argue that xenophobia explains political discrimination in the sense defined earlier. Our inability to make fine-grained cognitive discriminations in judging a person is the result of a fear reaction to the anomalous perceptual data that person presents, and the cause of a corresponding inability to evaluate him veridically as a person.

II. Xenophobia

I will use the terms *person* and *personality* to denote particular empirical instantiations of the concept of personhood, which I assume to be innate for purposes of this discussion.[12] Thus when we refer to someone as a person, we ordinarily mean to denote at the very least a social being whom we presume—as Kant did—to have consciousness, thought, rationality, and agency. The term *person* used in this way also finds its way into jurisprudence, where we conceive of a person as a rational individual who can be held legally and morally accountable for her actions.

10.
Adrian Piper, "Two Conceptions of the Self," *Philosophical Studies* 48, no. 2 (September 1985), pp. 173–197, reprinted in *The Philosopher's Annual* 8 (1985), pp. 222–246; see also Adrian Piper, "Pseudo-rationality," in *Perspectives on Self-Deception*, ed. Amelie O. Rorty and Brian McLoughlin (Los Angeles: University of California Press, 1988), pp. 297–323.

11.
Thomas Kuhn, *The Structure of Scientific Revolutions* (Chicago: University of Chicago, 1971), chapters 6–8.

12.
I defend this assumption at length in Sections 2 and 3 of "Xenophobia and Kantian Rationalism," *Philosophical Forum* 24, nos. 1–3 (Fall–Spring 1992–1993), pp. 188–232. The analysis offered in this and the following section of the present discussion is excerpted from section 5 of that article.

Relative to these related usages, an individual who lacks to a significant degree the capacities to reason, plan for the future, detect causal and logical relations among events, or control action according to principles applied more or less consistently from one occasion to the next is ascribed diminished responsibility for her actions, and her social and legal status as a person is diminished accordingly.

Similarly, when we call someone a "bad person," we communicate a cluster of evaluations that include, for example, assessing his conscious motives as corrupt or untrustworthy, his rationality as deployed for maleficent ends, and his actions as harmful. And when we say that someone has a "good personality" or a "difficult personality," we mean that the person's consciousness, thought, rationality, and agency are manifested in pleasing or displeasing or bewildering ways that are particular to that individual. We do not ordinarily assess a being who lacks any one of these components of personhood in terms of his personality at all. Persons, then, express their innate personhood in their empirical personalities.

With these stipulations in place, I now turn to an analysis of the concept of xenophobia. Xenophobia is not simply an indiscriminate fear of strangers in general; it does not include, for example, fear of relatives or neighbors whom one happens not to have met. It is more specific than that. Xenophobia is a fear of individuals who look or behave differently from those one is accustomed to. It is a fear of what is experientially unfamiliar, of individuals who do not conform to one's empirical assumptions about what other people are like, how they behave, or how they look. Ultimately it is a fear of individuals who violate one's empirical conception of persons and so one's self-conception. So xenophobia is an alarm reaction to a threat to the rational coherence of the self, a threat in the form of an anomalous other who transgresses one's preconceptions about people. It is a paradigm example of reacting self-protectively to anomalous data that violate one's internally consistent conceptual scheme.

Recall that on the KRT, if we cannot make sense of such data in terms of those familiar concepts, we cannot register it as an experience at all. I have argued elsewhere[13] that *pseudorationality* is an attempt to make sense of such data under duress, that is, to preserve the internal rational coherence of the self, when we are baldly confronted by anomaly but are not yet prepared to revise or jettison our conceptual scheme accordingly. It is in the attempt to make sense of anomalous data in terms of empirically inadequate concepts that the mechanisms of pseudorationality—rationalization, dissociation, and denial—kick in to secure self-

13.
See note 9.

preservation. But they succeed in preserving only the appearance of rational coherence. In *rationalization,* we misapply a concept to a particular by distorting its scope, magnifying the properties of the thing that instantiate the concept, and minimizing those that fail to do so. So, for example, conceiving of a slave imported from Africa as three-fifths of a person results from magnifying the properties that appear to support this diminished concept of personhood—the slave's environmental and psychological disorientation, lack of mastery of a foreign language, lack of familiarity with local social customs, incompetence at unfamiliar tasks, etc.—and minimizing the properties that disconfirm it—her capacity to learn, to forge innovative modes of communication and expression, to adapt and flourish in an alien social environment, to survive enslavement and transcend violations of her person, and so on. In *dissociation,* we identify something in terms of the negation of the concepts that articulate our theory: Identifying Jews as subhuman, blacks as childlike, women as irrational, gays as perverts, or working-class people as animals, for example, conceives of them as lacking essential properties of personhood and so are ways of defining these groups of individuals out of our empirical conceptions of people. In *denial,* we suppress recognition of the anomalous particular or property altogether, by ignoring it or suppressing it from awareness. For example, ignoring a woman's verbal contributions to a discussion, or passing over a black person's intellectual achievements, or forgetting to make provisions at a Christmas celebration for someone who is a practicing Jew are all ways of eradicating the anomalous other from one's domain of awareness.

Thus through the pseudorational mechanisms of rationalization and dissociation, xenophobia engenders various forms of stereotyping—racism, sexism, anti-Semitism, homophobia, class elitism—that are discriminatory in both the perceptual and the political sense. It selects certain perceptually familiar properties of the person for primary disvalue and distorts or obliterates those that remain. It thereby reduces the complex singularity of the other's properties to an oversimplified but conceptually manageable subset, and this in turn diminishes one's full conception of personhood. For the xenophobe, this results in a provincial self-conception and conception of the world, from which significant available data are excluded. And this provincial theory is sustained with the aid of denial, by enforcing those stereotypes through such tactics as exclusion, ostracism, scapegoating, tribalism, and segregation in housing, education, or employment. My thesis is that xenophobia is the originating phenomenon to which each of these forms of political discrimination is a response.

Nevertheless, even if it is true that we are innately cognitively disposed to respond to any conceptual and experiential anomaly in this way, it does not follow that our necessarily limited empirical conception of people must be so limited and provincial as to invite it. A person could be so cosmopolitan and intimately familiar with the full range of human variety that only The Alien would rattle him. On the other hand, his empirical conception of people might be so limited that any variation in race, nationality, gender, sexual preference, or class would be cause for panic. How easily one's empirical conception of people is violated is one index of the scope of one's xenophobia; how central and pervasive it is in one's personality is another. In what follows I will focus primarily on cases of political discrimination midway between such extremes: for example, a white person who is thoughtful, well rounded, and well read about the problems of racism in the United States, but who nevertheless feels fearful at being alone in the house with a black television repairman. In all such cases, the range of individuals in fact identifiable as persons is larger than the range of individuals to whom one's empirical conception of people apply. In all such cases, I will argue, political discrimination can be understood in terms of certain corrigible cognitive errors that characterize prereflective xenophobia.

A. The Error of Confusing People with Personhood

Xenophobia is fueled by a perfectly general condition of subjective consciousness, namely, the first-/third-person asymmetry: Although I must identify myself as a person because of my necessary, enduring first-personal experience of rationally unified selfhood, my experience of you as a person, necessarily lacking that first-personal experience, can have no such necessity about it:

> *Identity of person is . . . in my own consciousness unfailingly to be found. But when I view myself from the standpoint of another (as object of his outer intuition), this external observer considers me first and foremost in time. . . . So from the I, which accompanies all representations at all times in my consciousness, and indeed with full identity, whether he immediately concedes it, he will not yet conclude the objective continuity of my self. For because the time in which the observer situates me is not the same as that time to be found in my own, but rather in his sensibility, similarly the identity that is necessarily bound up with my consciousness, is not therefore bound up with his, that is, with the outer intuition of my subject. (A 362–363)*

Kant is saying that the temporal continuity I invariably perceive in my own consciousness is not matched by any corresponding temporal continuity I might be supposed to have as the object of someone else's consciousness. Because I am not always present to another as I am to myself, I may appear discontinuously to her consciousness in a way I cannot to my own. And similarly, another may appear discontinuously to my consciousness in a way I cannot to my own.

Thus although personhood is a necessary concept of mine, whether or not any other empirical individual instantiates it is itself, from my point of view, a contingent matter of fact—as is the concept of that particular individual herself. Though you may exhibit rationality in your behavior, I may not know that, or fail to perceive it, or fail to understand it. Nor can you be a necessary feature of my experience, because I might ignore or overlook you, or simply fail to have any contact with you. In any of these cases you will fail to instantiate my concept of personhood in a way I never can. Because the pattern of your behavior is not a necessary and permanent, familiar concomitant of my subjectivity in the way my own unified consciousness and ratiocinative processes are, I may escape your personhood in a way that I cannot escape my own. For me the innate idea of personhood is a concept that applies necessarily to me but, from my perspective, only contingently and empirically to you. Hence just as our experience of the natural world is limited relative to the all-inclusive, transcendent idea of its independent unity, similarly our empirical experience of other persons is limited relative to our all-inclusive, transcendent idea of personhood.

But there is an important disanalogy between them that turns on the problem of other minds and the first-/third-person asymmetry. For any empirical experience of the natural world we have, we must, according to Kant, be able to subsume it under the transcendent concept of a unified system of nature of which it is a part, even if we do not know what that system might be. By contrast, it is not necessarily the case that for any empirical experience of other people we have, we must be able to subsume them under the transcendent idea of personhood. This is because although they may, in fact, manifest their personhood in their personality, we may not be able fully to discern their personhood through its empirical manifestations, if those manifestations fall outside our empirical conception of what people are like.

Suppose, for example, that within my subculture, speech is used to seek confirmation and promote bonding, whereas in yours it is used to protect independence and win status;[14] suppose further that our only interpersonal contact occurs when you come to fix my TV. I attempt to engage you in conversation about what is wrong with my TV, to which you react with a lengthy lecture. To you I appear dependent and mechanically incompetent, while to me you appear logorrheic and socially inappropriate. Each of us perceives the other as deficient in some characteristic of rationality: You perceive me as lacking in autonomy and basic mechanical skills, whereas I perceive you as lacking in verbal control and basic social skills. To the extent that this perceived deficit is not corrected by further contact

14.
This is the main thesis of Deborah Tannen's fascinating *You Just Don't Understand: Women and Men in Conversation* (New York: William Morrow, 1990), a popularization of her research in linguistics on gender differences in language use.

and fuller information, each of us will perceive the other as less of a full-fledged person because of it. This is the kind of perception that contributes to one-dimensional stereotypes—for example, of women as flighty and incompetent or of men as aggressive and barbaric—which poison the expectations and behavior of each toward the other accordingly. This is how gender becomes a primary disvalued property.

Or take another example, in which the verbal convention in my subculture is to disclose pain and offer solace, whereas in yours it is to suppress pained and advert to impersonal topics; our only interpersonal contact occurs when I come to work as your housemaid. Again each of us perceives the other as deficient in some characteristic of rationality: You perceive me as dull and phlegmatic in my lack of responsiveness to the impersonal topics you raise for discussion, whereas I perceive you as almost schizophrenically dissociated from the painful realities that confront us. Again, unless this perceived deficit is corrected by further contact and fuller information, each of us will perceive the other as less of a person because of it, thereby contributing to one-dimensional stereotypes of, for example, blacks as stupid, or whites as ignorant and out of touch with reality, that similarly poison both the expectations and the behavior of each toward the other. This is how race becomes a primary disvalued property.

In such cases there are multiple sources of empirical error. The first one is our respective failures to discriminate cognitively between the possession of rationality as an active capacity in general, and particular empirical uses or instantiations of it under a given set of circumstances and for a given set of ends. Because your particular behavior and ends strike me as irrational, I surmise that you must be irrational. Here the error consists in equating the particular set of empirical behaviors and ends with which I am familiar from my own and similar cases with unified rational agency in general. It is as though I assume that the only rational agents there are are the particular people I identify as such. Kant might put the point by saying that each of us has conflated his empirically limited conception of people with the transcendent concept of personhood.

B. The Error of Assuming Privileged Access to the Self

But now suppose we each recognize at least the intentionality of the other's behavior, if not its rationality. Because each of us equates rational agency in general exclusively with the motives and actions of her own subculture in particular, each also believes that the motives and ends that guide the other's actions—and therefore the evidence of conformity to the rule and order of rationality—nevertheless remain inaccessible in a way we each believe our own motives and ends not to be inaccessible to ourselves. This third-personal opacity yields the distinction between the appearance and the reality of the self: You, it seems, are an appearance to me behind which is hidden the reality of your motives and intentions, whereas I am not similarly an appearance that hides my own from myself. The less familiar you are to me, the more hidden your motives and intentions will seem, and the less benevolent I will assume them to be.

Of course whom we happen to recognize as familiar determines whose motives are cause for suspicion and whose are not. There is no necessary connection between actual differences in physical or psychological properties between oneself and another, and the epistemic inscrutability we ascribe to someone we regard as anomalous. It is required only that the other seem anomalous relative to our familiar subculture, however cosmopolitan that may be, in order to generate doubts and questions about what it is that makes him tick. Stereotypes of women as enigmatic or of Asians as inscrutable or of blacks as evasive all express the underlying fear of the impenetrability of the other's motives. And someone who conceives of Jews as crafty, blacks as shiftless, or women as devious expresses particularly clearly the suspicion and fear of various third-personal others as mendacious manipulators that are consequent on falsely regarding them as more epistemically inaccessible to one than one is to oneself.

Thus our mutual failure to identify the other as a person of the same status as oneself is compounded by skepticism based on the belief that each of us has the privileged access to her own personhood that demonstrates directly and first-personally what personhood really is. The inaccessibility and unfamiliarity of the other's conception of her own motives to our consciousness of her may seem conclusive justification for our reflexive fear and suspicion as to whether her motives can be trusted at all.

Now, Kant argues (B 68–69, 153–156, 157–158a, A 551a/B 579a)[15] that from the first-personal relation I bear to my empirical self-conception that I lack to yours, it does not follow that my actual motives are any more accessible to me than yours are. Therefore, regardless of how comfortable and familiar my own motives may seem to me, it does not follow that I can know that my own motives are innocuous whereas yours are not. In fact, it is difficult to imagine how I might gain any understanding of the malevolent motives I reflexively ascribe to you at all, without having first experienced them in myself. Of course this is not to say that I cannot understand what it means to be the victim of maleficent *events* without having caused them myself. But it is to say that I must derive my understanding of the

15.
Also see Piper, "Xenophobia and Kantian Rationalism," section 4: Self-Knowledge, for a fuller discussion.

malevolent *intentionality* I ascribe to you from my own firsthand experience of it. Therefore your epistemic opacity to me furnishes no evidence for my reflexive ascription to you of malevolent or untrustworthy motives, although that ascription itself does furnish evidence for a similar ascription of them to myself. Thus Kant might put this second error by saying that we have been fooled by the first-/third-person asymmetry into treating the everpresent "dear self" as a source of genuine self-knowledge on the basis of which we make even faultier and more damaging assumptions about the other.

C. The Error of Failing Rationally to Conceive Other Minds

These two errors are interconnected with a third one, namely, our respective failures to imagine each other's behavior as animated by the same elements of personhood that animate our own, that is, consciousness, thought, and rationality. Our prior failure to recognize the other's behavior as manifesting evidence of these properties—a failure compounded by conceptual confusion and misascription of motives—then further undermines our ability to bridge the first-/third-person asymmetry by imagining the other to have them. Because, from each of our first-personal perspectives, familiar empirical evidence for the presence of these properties is lacking in the other, we have no basis on which to make the ascription, and so no basis for imagining what it must be like from the other's perspective. Our respective, limited empirical conceptions of people, then, itself the consequence of ignorance of others who are thereby viewed as different, delimit our capacity for empathy. This is part of what is involved in the phenomenon feminists refer to as objectification, and what sometimes leads men to describe some women as self-absorbed. Kant might put this point by saying that by failing to detect in the other's behavior the rule and order of rationality that guides it, we fail to surmise or imagine the other's motives and intentions.

This error, of failing to conceive the other as similarly animated by the psychological dispositions of personhood, is not without deleterious consequences for the xenophobe himself. Elsewhere I have described the self-centered and narrowly concrete view of the world that results from the failure to imagine empathically another's inner states, and its interpersonal consequences.[16] From the first-personal perspective, this error compounds the seeming depopulation of the social environment of persons and its repopulation by impenetrable and irrational aliens. This is to conceive one's social world as inhabited by enigmatic and unpredictable disrup-

16.
Adrian Piper, "Impartiality, Compassion and Modal Imagination," *Ethics* 101, no. 4: Symposium on Impartiality (July 1991), pp. 726–757.

tions to its stability, to conjure chimeras of perpetual unease and anxiety into social existence. Relative to such a conception, segregation is no more effective in banishing the threat than is leaving on the nightlight to banish ghosts, as both threats arise from the same source. Vigilance and a readiness to defend oneself against the hostile unknown may become such intimately familiar and constitutive habits of personality that even they may come to seem necessary prerequisites of personhood.

III. First-Order Political Discrimination

The three foregoing errors involve failures of cognitive discrimination for which a well-intentioned individual could correct. For example, someone who regularly confuses people with personhood might simply take a moment to formulate a general principle of rational behavior that both applies to all the instances with which she is familiar from her particular community and has broader application as well; she might then remind herself, when confronted by anomalous behavior, to at least try to detect the operation of that principle within it. Similarly, it does not require excessive humility on the part of a person who falsely assumes privileged access to the self to remind himself that our beliefs about our own motives, feelings, and actions are exceedingly fallible and regularly disconfirmed, and that it is therefore even more presumptuous to suppose any authority about someone else's. Nor is it psychologically impossible to gather information about others' inner states—through research, appreciation of the arts, or direct questioning and careful listening, so as to cultivate one's imaginative and empathic capacities to envision other minds.

Thus it is possible for someone to have such xenophobic reactions without being a full-blown xenophobe, in the event that she views them as causes for concern rather than celebration. She may experience these cognitive failures without being a first-order political discriminator in the event that she has no personal investment in the defective empirical conception of people that results, and is identifiable as a bona fide first-order political discriminator to the extent that she does. A person has a *personal investment* in a conception or theory if

1. that theory is a source of personal satisfaction or security to her;
2. to revise or reject it would elicit in her feelings of dejection, deprivation, or anxiety; and
3. these feelings are to be explained by her identification with this theory.

She *identifies with* this theory to the extent that she is disposed to identify it as personally meaningful or valuable to her.[17] A person could make the first three cognitive errors without taking any satisfaction in her provincial conception of people ("Is this really all there is?" she might think to herself about the inhabitants of her small town), without identifying with it (she might find them boring and feel ashamed to have to count herself among them), and without feeling the slightest reluctance to enlarge and revise it through travel or exploration or research.

What distinguishes a first-order political discriminator is his personal investment in his provincial conception of people. His sense of self-preservation requires his conception to be viridical and is threatened when it is disconfirmed. He exults in the thought that only the people he knows and is familiar with (whites; blacks; WASPs; Jews; residents of Waco, Texas; members of the club; etc.) are persons in the full, honorific sense. This is the thought that motivates the imposition of politically discriminatory stereotypes, both on those who confirm it and those who do not.

To impose a *stereotype* on someone is to view her as embodying a limited set of properties falsely taken to be exclusive, definitive, and paradigmatic of a certain kind of individual. I will say that a stereotype

a. equates one contingent and limited set of primary valued properties that may characterize persons under certain circumstances with the universal concept of personhood;

b. restricts that set to exclude divergent properties of personhood from it;

c. withholds from those who violate its restrictions the essential properties of personhood; and

d. ascribes to them the primary disvalued properties of deviance from it.

Thus a stereotype identifies as persons those and only those who manifest the primary valued properties in the set ([a] and [b]), and subsidiary ones consistent with it (such as minor personality quirks or mildly idiosyncratic personal tastes). Call this set the *honorific stereotype,* and an individual who bears such primary valued properties the *valuee.* And reciprocally, the honorific stereotype by implication identifies as deviant all those who manifest any properties regarded as inconsistent with it ([c] and [d]). Call this second set of primary disvalued properties the *deroga-*

17.
The concept of personal investment is discussed in my "Moral Theory and Moral Alienation," *The Journal of Philosophy* 84, no. 2 (February 1987), pp. 102–118. Also see note 9.

tory stereotype, and an individual who bears such primary disvalued properties the *disvaluee.*

So, for example, an individual who bears all the primary valued properties of the honorific stereotype as required by (a) may be nevertheless disqualified for status as a valuee according to (b), by bearing additional primary disvalued ones as well—being related by blood or marriage to a Jew, for example; or having bisexual inclinations; or, in the case of a black person, an enthusiasm for classical scholarship. In virtue of violating (b), one may then fail to qualify as a full-fledged person at all (c) and therefore may be designated as deviant by the derogatory stereotype according to (d). The derogatory stereotype most broadly includes all the primary disvalued properties that fall outside the set defining the honorific stereotype (that is, "us versus them") or may sort those properties into more specific subsets according to the range of individuals available for sorting.

A politically discriminatory stereotype generally is therefore distinguishable from an inductive generalization by its provincialism, its oversimplification, and its rigid imperviousness to the complicating details of singularity. Perhaps most importantly, a discriminatory stereotype is distinguishable from an inductive generalization by its function. The function of an inductive generalization is to guide further research, and this requires epistemic alertness and perceptual sensitivity to the possibility of confirming or disconfirming evidence in order to make use of it. An inductive generalization is no less a generalization for that: It would not, for example, require working-class blacks living in the Deep South during the 1960s to dismantle the functionally accurate and protective generalization that white people are dangerous. What would make this an inductive generalization rather than a stereotype is that it would not preclude recognition of a white person who is safe if one should appear. By contrast, the function of a stereotype is to render further research unnecessary. If the generalization that white people are dangerous were a stereotype, adopting it would make it cognitively impossible to detect any white people who were not.

Thus Kant might describe the reciprocal imposition of stereotypes as the fallacy of equating a partial and conditional series of empirical appearances of persons with the absolute and unconditioned idea of personhood that conceptually unifies them. Whereas the first error—of confusing one's empirical conception of people with the transcendent concept of personhood—involves thinking that the only persons there are are the people one knows, this fourth error—of equating personality with personhood—involves thinking that the kind of persons one knows are all there can ever be. So unlike inductive generalizations, the taxonomic categories of a stereotype are closed sets that fundamentally require the binary operation of sorting individuals and properties into those who fall within them and those who do not.[18]

As a consequence of his personal investment in an honorific stereotypical conception of persons, a first-order political discriminator has a personal investment in an honorific stereotypical self-conception. This means that that self-conception is a source of personal satisfaction or security to him; that to revise or disconfirm it would elicit in him feelings of dejection, deprivation, or anxiety; and that these feelings are to be explained by his identification with this self-conception. In order to maintain his honorific self-conception, a first-order political discriminator must perform the taxonomic binary sorting operation not only on particular groups of ethnic or gendered others but on everyone, including himself. Because his self-conception as a person requires him and other bona fide persons to dress, talk, look, act, and think in certain highly specific and regimented ways in order to qualify for the honorific stereotype, everyone is subject to scrutiny in terms of it.

This is not only prejudicial to a disvaluee who violates these requirements and thereby earns the label of the derogatory stereotype. It is also prejudicial to a valuee who satisfies them, just in case there is more to his personality than the honorific stereotype encompasses and more than it permits. Avoidance of the negative social consequences of violating the honorific stereotype—ostracism, condemnation, punishment, or obliteration—necessitates stunting or flattening his personality in order to conform to it (for example, by eschewing football or nightclubs and learning instead to enjoy scholarly lectures as a form of entertainment because one is given to understand that that is the sort of thing real academics typically do for fun) or bifurcating his personality into that part which can survive social scrutiny and that "deviant" part which cannot (as, for example, certain government officials have done who deplore and condemn homosexuality publicly on the one hand, while engaging in it privately on the other). One reason it is important not to equate personality with personhood is so that the former properties can flourish without fear that the latter title will be revoked.

Truncating his personality in order to conform to an honorific stereotype in turn damages the political discriminator's self-esteem and also his capacity for self-knowledge. Someone who is deeply personally invested in the honorific stereotype but fails fully to conform to it (as everyone must, of course) views himself as inherently defective. He is naturally beset by feelings of failure, inferiority, shame, and worthlessness that poison his relations with others in familiar ways: Compe-

18.
I am indebted to Rüdiger Bittner for pressing this question in discussion.

titiveness, dishonesty, defensiveness, envy, furtiveness, insecurity, hostility, and self-aggrandizement are just a few of the vices that figure prominently in his interpersonal interactions. But if these feelings and traits are equally antithetical to his honorific stereotype, then they, too, threaten his honorific stereotypical self-conception and so are susceptible to pseudorational denial, dissociation, or rationalization. For example, a first-order political discriminator might be blindly unaware of how blatantly he advertises these feelings and traits in his behavior, or he might dissociate them as mere peccadilloes, unimportant eccentricities that detract nothing from the top-drawer person he essentially is. Or he might acknowledge them but rationalize them as natural expressions of a Nietzschean, *übermenschliche* ethic justified by his superior place in life. Such pseudorational habits of thought reinforce even more strongly his personal investment in the honorific stereotype that necessitated them, and in the xenophobic conception of others that complements it. This fuels a vicious downward spiral of self-hatred and hatred of anomalous others from which it is difficult for the political discriminator to escape. Thus the personal disadvantage of first-order political discrimination is not just that the discriminator devolves into an uninteresting and malevolent person. He damages himself for the sake of his honorific stereotype and stunts his capacity for insight and personal growth as well.

A sign that a person's self-conception is formed by an honorific stereotype is that revelation of the deviant, primary disvalued properties provokes shame and denial rather than a reformulation of that self-conception in such a way as to accommodate them. For example, a family that honorifically conceives itself as white Anglo-Saxon Protestant may deny that its most recent offspring in fact has woolly hair or a broad nose. Similarly, a sign that a person's conception of another is formed by a derogatory stereotype is that revelation of the other's nondeviant, primary valued properties provokes hostility and denial, rather than the corresponding revision of that conception of the other in such a way as to accommodate them. For example, a community of men that honorifically conceives itself in terms of its intellectual ability may dismiss each manifestation of a woman's comparable intellectual ability as a fluke.

These two reactions are reciprocal expressions of the same dispositions in the first- and third-personal cases respectively. Shame involves the pain of feeling publicly exposed as defective, and denial is the psychological antidote to such exposure: For example, if the purportedly WASP offspring does not have negroid features, there is nothing for the family to feel ashamed of. So a person whose self-conception is defined by an honorific stereotype will feel shame at having primary disvalued properties that deviate from it and will attempt to deny their existence to herself and to others. By contrast, hostility toward another's excellence is caused by shame at one's own defectiveness, and denial of the excellence is the social antidote to such shame: For example, if the woman is not as intelligent as the men are purported to be, then there is no cause for feeling shamed by her, and so none for hostility toward her. So a person whose self-conception is formed by an honorific stereotype will feel hostility toward a disvaluee who manifests valued properties that violate the derogatory stereotype imposed on him, and will attempt to deny the existence of those valued properties in the other to herself and to others.

In the first-personal case, the objects of shame are primary disvalued properties that deviate from one's honorific stereotypical self-conception. In the third-personal case, the objects of hostility are valued properties that deviate from one's derogatory stereotypical conception of the disvaluee. But in both cases the point of the reactions is the same: to defend one's stereotypical self-conception against attack, both by first-personal deviations from it and by third-personal deviations from the reciprocal stereotypes this requires imposing on others. And in both cases the xenophobic reactions are motivated in the same way: The properties regarded as anomalous relative to the stereotype in question are experienced by the first-order political discriminator as an assault on the rational coherence of his theory of the world—and so, according to Kant, on the rational coherence of his self.

Indeed, left untreated, all four of these cognitive errors more generally—the conflation of the transcendent concept of personhood with one's provincial conception of people that another happens to violate, the ascription to the other of malevolent motives on the basis of an epistemically unreliable self-conception, the inability to imagine the other as animated by familiar or recognizably rational motives, and the equation of personality with personhood inherent in the imposition of reciprocal stereotypes—combine to form a conception of the other as an inscrutable and malevolent anomaly that threatens that theory of the world which unifies one's experience and structures one's expectations about oneself and other people. If this were an accurate representation of others who are different, it would be no wonder that xenophobes feared them.

IV. Reciprocal First-Order Political Discrimination

So far I have argued that first-order political discrimination involves the reciprocal imposition of honorific and derogatory stereotypes, on oneself and on the anomalous other respectively. But is it not possible to value properties ordinarily taken to be irrelevant to judgments of a person's value or competence without eliciting the charge of honorific stereotyping? Are such primary valued properties ever relevant to judgments of a person's noninstrumental value or competence? By *reciprocal first-order political discrimination,* I will mean a manifest attitude in which a particular property of a person that is irrelevant to judgments of that person's noninstrumental value or competence, for example, her race, gender, class, sexual orientation, or religious or ethnic affiliation, is seen as a source of value or competence, in general, as a source of superiority. Primary valued properties are those perceived as elevating its bearers accordingly.

Take the case in which we are particularly drawn to befriend a valuee with whom we share a similar ethnic background, because we expect to have more in common (lifestyle, tastes, sense of humor), share similar values, or see the world from a similar perspective. In this kind of case the primary valued property is not, say, being Jewish but rather having the same ethnic background, whatever that may be. Is similarity of ethnic background a property that is relevant to our judgments of how valuable the valuee is as a friend? No, for it does not form any part of the basis for such a judgment. That a friendship is better, richer, or more valuable in proportion to the degree of similarity of the friends' ethnic backgrounds is a judgment few would be tempted to make.

In these cases, it is not the valuee's similar ethnicity itself that is the source of value but rather the genuinely valuable properties—for example, similarity of values or world view—*with which we expect similar ethnicity to be conjoined.* Rather than making a normative judgment about the valuee's value or competence as a friend in this case, we in fact make an epistemic judgment about the probability that, given his ethnic identity, he will bear properties susceptible of such normative judgments. These epistemic rules of thumb are defeasible and may have disappointing consequences for personal relationships. For they ascribe primary value to a kind of property at the expense of others that are in fact more important for friendship—such as sensitivity, similarity of tastes or experiences, or mutual respect—with which that kind of property is only contingently, if ever, conjoined. (Presumably something like this may explain the malaise of someone who has chosen all the "right" friends, married the "right" spouse, and landed the "best" job, yet feels persistently unhappy, disconnected, and dissatisfied in his social relationships.)

If similarity of race, gender, sexual orientation, class background, or religious or ethnic affiliation is in itself irrelevant to judgment's of a person's noninstrumental value or competence, primary valued properties such as being of a particular race, gender, and so on, are even more obviously so. At least it has yet to be demonstrated that any particular racial, ethnic, gender, class, or religious group possesses the properties necessary for, for example, friendship to an outstanding degree.[19] Epistemic probability judgments about the concatenation of any such primary valued properties with genuinely valuable traits, such as sensitivity or similarity of interests, also may bias our ability to perceive clearly the properties a particular individual actually has—as when a wife minimizes the reality and seriousness of her husband's physical abuse of her, because of the weight she accords his class background. This would be a case of reciprocal first-order discrimination, according to the previous definition, because she sees a primary valued property—class background—that is irrelevant to judgments of the valuee's noninstrumental value or competence as a spouse as a (compensating) source of superiority.

It might be objected that such epistemic rules of thumb are inductive generalizations, however irrational or poorly grounded, that we need in order to survive in a world of morally opaque others: How ought one behave, for example, alone in a subway car with four black male teenagers carrying ghetto blasters and wearing running shoes? However, even if it were true that most muggers were black male teenagers in running shoes, it still would not follow that most black male teenagers in running shoes were muggers. This epistemic rule of thumb is a stereotype, not an inductive generalization, if it leads one to react to every black male teenager in running shoes one encounters as though he were a mugger when there is no independent justification for thinking he is.

Alternately, one may make a judgment of value about some such property abstractly and independently considered. One may value being black, or of working class origins, for its own sake. Or one may choose a partner from the same religion because one views that religion and its traditions themselves as intrinsically valuable, independently of one's partner's compatibility with respect to lifestyle, values, or world view. Here the judgment of value is directed not at the valuee's value or competence but rather at the property he bears and to the preservation or affirmation of which one's choice of him is instrumental. Nothing in the following discussion addresses or precludes such judgments, although there is much to say about them. My target is judgments of noninstrumental value about individuals, not about properties of individuals abstractly and independently considered, to which individuals themselves are instrumental.

19.
The thesis that women make better friends is often supported by arguments to the effect that they *become closer confidantes more quickly*. But there are many other properties that contribute to friendship—trustworthiness, loyalty, dependability, honesty, mutual respect, etc.—that such arguments ignore.

Is it humanly possible to value a person just and only because she bears some such primary valued property—not because of the further properties with which we expect that one to be conjoined, but just for the sake of that property in itself? It is difficult to make sense of this. Suppose that I value Germanness because the Germans I have known tend to have deep passions and an amusingly fatalistic sense of humor, and that I then meet a shallow and phlegmatic German with no sense of humor at all. In the absence of other, unexpectedly attractive personality characteristics I may appreciate, just what is it about being German in itself that is supposed to confer worth on this particular individual? Either we must be able to spell out an answer to this question in terms of other properties that are only contingently connected, if at all, to this one—for example, having been socialized within a certain culture "from the inside," being part of a certain historical tradition, etc.—or else we are appealing to a mysterious and ineffable, non-natural quality of Germanness.[20] Then suppose there are such qualities, and that we may arguably appeal to them. To what degree might Germanness outweigh the person's other properties that, by hypothesis, I deplore? Surely the mere fact of Germanness can provide no consolation at all, in practice, for other properties of the person that offend me. It will not compensate, for example, for a failure to laugh at my jokes, or a tendency to discuss the weather at excessive length, or to fall asleep at the opera. And then it is hard to see in what its purported value consists.

Independently of the other, genuinely valuable properties with which they are only contingently, if at all, conjoined, properties such as race, gender, sexual orientation, class background, or religious or ethnic affiliation are in themselves always irrelevant to judgments of a person's noninstrumental value or competence. This holds whether they are considered as primary disvalued or valued properties, and even where they are used as epistemic rules of thumb for detecting such properties. We may in fact feel compelled to make such judgments, in the service of ex-

20.
For purposes of this discussion I ignore the range of cases in which my valuation of, for example, Germanness is rooted in the status or worth I expect my choice of German friends to confer on *me*. This kind of case occurs both in situations in which the primary valued property is one shared by oneself and in those cases in which it is not. Thus it may happen that one's choice of a white Anglo-Saxon Protestant spouse is made in part with an eye to reinforcing the primary value to others and to oneself one's own status as a white Anglo-Saxon Protestant; or alternately, that one's contrasting choice of an African-American spouse is made with an eye to proving to others and to oneself one's "cool," sophistication, or commitment to civil rights. These are all cases in which the property is valued as a source of *instrumental* value or competence, namely, for its ability to confer value on the reciprocal first-order political discriminator. Therefore I leave them aside here.

pediency, or what we imagine to be our self-interest, and screen our circle of associates accordingly. But it is nothing to be proud of.

V. Higher-Order Political Discrimination

Now I want to examine a more sophisticated manifestation of political discrimination that is supervenient on the first-order political discrimination just discussed. I shall call this *higher-order political discrimination*.[21] As in first-order political discrimination, a higher-order discriminator manifests in behavior the attitude in which a particular property of a person that is irrelevant to judgments of that person's intrinsic value or competence (such as her race, gender, class, sexual orientation, or religious or ethnic affiliation) is seen as a source of disvalue or inferiority, that is, as a primary disvalued property. By *second-order political discrimination,* I will understand the attitude within which a primary disvalued or valued property in turn confers disvalue or value respectively on further properties of the disvaluee or valuee respectively. I shall refer to these latter as *secondary disvalued (or valued) properties.*

Second-order political discrimination works in the following way. A disvaluee's primary disvalued property, say, being a male homosexual, causes the second-order political discriminator to view some *further* property of the disvaluee, say, being an eloquent speaker, in a negative light. The respect in which this further property is seen as negative depends on the range of possible descriptions it might satisfy, as well as the context in which it appears. Thus, for example, the second-order political discriminator might view the disvaluee's eloquence as purple prose, or empty rhetoric, or as precious, flowery, or mannered. These predicates are not interchangeable for the second-order political discriminator. Nor are they taken to be arbitrarily applied. The second-order political discriminator will choose from among them to express his disvaluation in response to contingencies of the situation and individuals involved. He may, in all sincerity, explain his disvaluation with reference to impartially applied aesthetic standards, or to his ingrown, native suspicion of big words. But the crucial feature of second-order political discrimination is that the actual explanation for his disvaluing the person's eloquence, *in whatever respect he disvalues it,* is the person's primary disvalued property of being a male homosexual.

21.
The analysis of higher-order political discrimination in sections 5 through 7 is excerpted from Adrian Piper, "Higher-Order Discrimination," in *Identity, Character, and Morality,* ed. Owen Flanagan and Amelie O. Rorty (Cambridge, Mass.: The MIT Press, 1990), pp. 285–309.

Does second-order political discrimination as thus defined ever actually occur? Some familiar examples of it include attaching disvalue to a person's having rhythm, by reason of its putative connection with her being black; or attaching disvalue to a person's being very smart, by reason of its putative connection with his being Jewish. Both of these cases are examples of politically discriminatory stereotyping, in which some arbitrary property is falsely taken to be characteristic of persons of a particular race or ethnic or religious affiliation. But I mean to call attention to a slightly different feature of these examples. Someone who practices second-order political discrimination regards a black person who has rhythm as vulgar, salacious, or offensive; at the very least, undignified. Similarly, such a person regards a Jewish person who is very smart as sophistical, glib, or crafty, or as subversive or ungentlemanly; at the very least, untrustworthy. In both cases, properties that are in themselves salutary, or at least neutral, are castigated by the second-order political discriminator, by reason of the disvalue conferred on them by the primary disvalued property. This is what makes them examples of second-order political discrimination.

These familiar, stereotypic examples of second-order political discrimination do not exhaust the repertoire of higher-order political discrimination, for many reasons. First, orders of discrimination can, in theory, be multiplied indefinitely. So, for example, a case of *third-order political discrimination* would involve what I shall call *tertiary disvalued properties:* The primary disvalued property (say, being black) confers disvalue on a further, secondary disvalued property (having rhythm), which in turn confers disvalue on yet a further property of the person (say, being a good dancer). Having rhythm is seen as vulgar, by reason of its association with being black, and being a good dancer is then seen as exhibitionistic (say), by reason of its association with having rhythm. In any such case, the primary property is in fact irrelevant to judgments of a person's value or competence. Hence the value or disvalue it confers on secondary, tertiary, etc., properties is bogus.

The *n*-order disvalue relation is *transitive,* in that, for example, if being black confers disvalue on having rhythm, and having rhythm confers disvalue on being a good dancer, then being black confers disvalue on being a good dancer. The *n*-order disvalue relation is also *inclusive,* in that the primary disvalued property poisons the higher-order political discriminator's evaluations of all further properties of the disvaluee. For example, the primary disvalued property of being black may confer disvalue, alternatively, on a dancer's classical styling: Classical styling in a black dancer may be seen as inappropriate, or as an obscene parody of traditional ballet.[22] The primary disvalued property also confers disvalue on other, unrelated properties of the disvaluee: her appearance, accent, mode of dress, etc.[23]

The inclusiveness of the *n*-order disvalue relation underscores a second reason why stereotypical cases of second-order discrimination do not exhaust the repertoire of higher-order discrimination: Nonstereotypical traits are also recruited to receive value or disvalue from primary properties to suit particular occasions. We do not ordinarily think of classical styling in dance as a property about which discriminators might have any particular attitude. But this may be mistaken. Higher-order discrimination is not concerned solely with *stereotypical* secondary, tertiary, and so on, disvalued properties. It may be concerned with *any* further properties of the person on which the primary disvalued property itself confers disvalue. Thus, for example, being Jewish (or black, or a woman) may confer disvalue on being smart, which in turn may confer disvalue on being intellectually prolific: A person's intellectual prolificity may be seen as evidence of logorrhea, or lack of critical conscience, and may thus poison the evaluation of those intellectual products themselves. A first test for ascertaining whether the disvalue of some property of a person is to be explained as a case of higher-order political discrimination is to ascertain whether that property is disvalued uniformly across individuals, regardless of anything that might count as a primary disvalued property for a higher-order political discriminator. If someone is just as contemptuous of Fred Astaire's having rhythm as she is of Michael Jackson's, or just as contemptuous of intellectual pro-

22.
Of course there are other, more convoluted cases of higher-order political discrimination that represent epicyclic variations on the straightforward cases I shall be examining. For example, being black may wildly exaggerate the value attached to classical styling in a black dancer, if classical styling is perceived as something the person had to overcome great innate and cultural obstacles to achieve. In either case, being black functions as a primary disvalued property because it carries a presumption of inferiority into the evaluation of further properties of the person.

23.
Is it perhaps too strong to claim that a primary disvalued property poisons the higher-order political discriminator's evaluation of *all* the disvaluee's other properties? Can't a higher-order political discriminator respect a disvaluee's traits of character in a certain restricted area, *despite* his disvalued status? I am inclined to think not. For this seems to occur almost exclusively when the "valued" property itself conforms to the higher-order political discriminator's stereotypes. For example, a black man may be admired for his athletic prowess but encounter hostility when he runs for political office. In such cases the higher-order political discriminator's admiration and respect for the stereotypical trait is not unalloyed. It is tempered by a certain smug complacency at the disvaluee's confirmation of his disvalued status in the very cultivation and expression of that stereotypical trait. To sustain the previous objection, we would need to see a higher-order political discriminator exhibiting *unalloyed* admiration and respect for *non*stereotypical traits, such that *these positive feelings did not, in turn, positively reform the higher-order political discriminator's prejudicial attitude toward the person's primary disvalued property:* Someone who sincerely respects and admires a disvaluee for nonstereotypical reasons, without feeling threatened or invaded, has already begun to weaken the psychological edifice on which her politically discriminatory evaluation of the person as a disvaluee is based.

lificity in Balzac as in Isaac Asimov, then the charge of higher-order political discrimination may be defeated.[24]

Stereotypes change in accordance with changes in the objects of political discrimination, as different populations seek access to the goods, services, and opportunities enjoyed by the advantaged, and primary and higher-order disvalued properties change accordingly. For instance, the anti-Semitic response to the attempts of Jewish intellectuals to achieve full assimilation into the institutions of higher education in this country frequently found expression in the disvaluative description of assertively ambitious Jewish academics as pushy or opportunistic. Now similarly situated blacks and women frequently enjoy that title. Conversely, those with such primary disvalued properties who attempt to substitute diplomacy for assertion are characterized by higher-order political discriminators as manipulative, obsequious, or sycophantic. A second test for ascertaining whether or not the disvalue of some property of a person is to be explained as a case of higher-order political discrimination is to ascertain whether there is any alternative property, conduct, or manner, directed toward the same goal—of gaining access to unjustly withheld social advantages—that avoids or deflects the disvalue conferred by the primary disvalued property. If there is not—if, that is, whatever your strategy, you're damned if you do and damned if you don't—then the charge of higher-order political discrimination is prima facie justified.

Other arbitrary properties, not just the familiar political ones, can function as primary disvalued properties to a higher-order political discriminator. Physical appearance; style of diction; social bearing; familial, educational, or professional pedigree; circle of associates; and manner of dress are among the more familiar, if

24.
It might be thought that this first test is inherently self-limiting for the case in which the person happens to dislike just the property that is most typically associated with, for example, a certain race—say, dark skin—but nevertheless passes the first test in that she disvalues it uniformly across individuals, whether it occurs in blacks, East Indians, Jews, Arabs, Aborigines, or Coppertone-soaked Californians. I think what we should say about this kind of case is that it does not present a problem. The fact that someone is acquitted of being a racist doesn't imply that her evaluations are therefore admirable or enlightened. Any predicate or combination of predicates that *fails* the first test is either a rigged definite description of a particular disvalued group, such as "ova-producing featherless bipeds," or else describes a discriminatory stereotype, such as "dark-skinned, dark-eyed, woolly-haired individuals with rhythm." Of course, a person might just happen to disvalue only individuals who fit such a stereotype and not those who violate it. But because this disvaluation would not be independent of anything that might count as a primary disvalued property for such a person, it would not defeat the charge of higher-order political discrimination.

Note, however, that the first test does *not* work for identifying a distinct but related attitude, which we might call *generalized higher-order political discrimination,* in which a person comes to disvalue some constellation of higher-order properties across the board *specifically because of its original association with* a primary disvalued property stereotypically ascribed to a certain group. Someone who finds having rhythm vulgar in any dancer, regardless of racial or ethnic affiliation, because he associates having rhythm with blacks, whom he fears and despises, would exemplify such an attitude.

less widely acknowledged, objects of higher-order political discrimination. Some of these properties are often assumed to go hand-in-hand with, or even be partially definitive of, more widely recognized primary disvalued properties. For example, higher-order political discriminators may tend to assume that ethnic identity is inherently connected with a certain physical appearance (Jews have dark, curly hair and long noses), that racial identity is connected with a certain style of diction and class background (blacks speak Black English and come from the ghetto), or that gender identity is connected with a certain social bearing (women are sympathetic, passive, and emotional). This is how a stereotype is formed. But again I mean to call attention to a slightly different point: These properties themselves may be seen as sources of disvalue, *independently* of their possible connection with such stereotypically primary disvalued properties. Someone who has all the valued race, ethnic, religious, class, and gender properties but lacks the valued style of diction, mode of self-presentation, or educational or professional pedigrees may be subject to higher-order political discrimination just as fully as someone who lacks all of the former properties but has all of the latter. In both cases, this means that their other properties—their personality characteristics, interests, or achievements—will be seen as higher-order disvalued properties, by reason of their association with these equally arbitrary primary disvalued properties.

This shows that the first-order political discrimination with which we are familiar is merely a special case of a more general psychological phenomenon that is not limited to first-order *political* discrimination at all. However, higher-order political discrimination as defined earlier usually includes it, for it would be psychologically unusual, to say the least, to find an individual who is in general corrupt in his evaluations of a person's other properties in the ways just described, yet impartial and scrupulous in his evaluations of blacks, Jews, women, gays, and so on, and *their* properties. Someone who is apt to dislike a person because of her hair texture or accent or mode of dress can hardly be expected to be genuinely judicious when it comes to judging her gender, race, class, sexual orientation, or ethnic or religious affiliation. Hence we can expect that first-order political discrimination and higher-order political discrimination in general are to be found together.[25]

25.
There is another reason that favors retaining the label of higher-order *political* discrimination, despite its application to primary disvalued properties less widely recognized as political in nature, corresponding to a broader conception of political behavior. We can think of politically discriminatory stereotyping more generally as a means of sorting individuals into those with whom one is willing to share available power and resources versus those with whom one is not. In this broader sense, any disvalued property can become a criterion for excluding the disvaluee from the discriminator's circle of honorifically stereotyped valuees.

VI. Reciprocal Higher-Order Political Discrimination

Higher-order political discrimination as so far described implies a companion phenomenon, which I shall call *reciprocal higher-order political discrimination*. Here properties irrelevant to judgments of a person's competence or worth are seen as primary *valued* properties, as sources of value that confer value on the person's secondary, tertiary, etc., properties. Any one of the primary properties enumerated so far may have this function. For example, a person's gender may be perceived as conferring value on secondary properties, such as his competence to hold a certain professional position. Or a person's familial lineage may be perceived as conferring value on her admissibility to an institution of higher education. Or a person's class background may be perceived as conferring value on his manner of dress. Or a person's educational pedigree may be perceived as conferring value on her political pronouncements, which in turn confers value on her personal lifestyle, and so on. Each of these examples has an arbitrary and irrational quality to it. That is because reciprocal higher-order political discrimination, like higher-order political discrimination itself, is an arbitrary and irrational attitude.

Higher-order political discrimination and reciprocal higher-order political discrimination are materially interdependent. If a person's having a particular racial identity is a source of disvalue for a higher-order political discriminator, then if someone lacks that racial identity, she is not seen as tainted by that disvalue. For example, if a person's being Asian confers disvalue on his attempts at tact, that is, if he is therefore perceived as particularly evasive and inscrutable, then if he were white, he would not be perceived as similarly evasive and inscrutable. For if a higher-order political discriminator recognized that one can be just as evasive and inscrutable without being Asian, say, if one has a hidden agenda or lacks social skills, then it would have to be recognized that those properties, *rather* than his being Asian, might be conferring disvalue on his attempts at tact. Conversely, if a person's having a particular racial identity is a source of value for a higher-order political discriminator, then someone who lacks that racial identity is not blessed by that value. For example, if a person's being white confers value on his attempts at tact, that is, if he is therefore viewed as sensitive and reasonable, then if he were Asian, he would not be perceived as similarly sensitive and reasonable. For if a higher-order political discriminator recognized that one can be just as sensitive and reasonable without being white, say, if one has no personal investment in the issue or has thought hard about it, then it would have to be recognized that those properties, rather than his being white, might be conferring value on his attempts at tact.

The two tests for higher-order political discrimination apply analogously to reciprocal higher-order political discrimination: (1) Ascertain whether the higher-order valued property is valued uniformly across individuals, regardless of anything that might count as a primary valued property for the discriminator. If a person's perceived competence to hold a certain professional position would not be in any way diminished if she were black—if, that is, blacks with comparable competence have been hired to such positions—then the charge of reciprocal higher-order political discrimination may be defeated. (2) Ascertain whether there is any alternative property, conduct, or manner, directed toward the same goal—of gaining access to some social advantage—that avoids or deflects the value conferred by the primary valued property. If there is not—if, for example, whether you are assertively ambitious or carefully diplomatic, intellectually prolific or intellectually fallow, you can do no wrong—then the charge of reciprocal higher-order political discrimination is prima facie justified.[26] Henceforth I shall take higher-order political discrimination to include reciprocal higher-order political discrimination. These two phenomena demonstrate that one need not be a blatant racist, sexist, anti-Semite, or homophobe—let us describe such an individual as a *simple first-order political discriminator*—in order to practice political discrimination. Higher-order political discrimination is given fullest expression indirectly, by implication, in seemingly unrelated tastes, preferences, and behavior.

VII. Higher-Order Political Discrimination: A Case of Pseudorationality

So far I have used locutions like "seen as conferring value/disvalue on" and "by reason of its association with" to describe the relation between primary and higher-order disvalued or valued properties, without saying in any detail in what I

26.
Here it might be objected that the second test is inadequate to ascertain the existence of reciprocal higher-order political discrimination, because the explanation for why "you can do no wrong" may be not that all such higher-order properties receive value from primary valued properties but rather that all such higher-order properties are in any case irrelevant to judgments of a person's competence. However, remember that the second test applies specifically to properties directed toward the goal of gaining access to some social advantage. This includes not only properties irrelevant to the question of one's entitlement to that advantage, such as those pertaining to the manner or quality of one's self-promotion, but also properties directly relevant to that question, such as those pertaining to one's status, potential, training, experience, etc. The second test sifts out those cases in which irrelevant higher-order properties, such as one's manner of self-promotion, are made the basis for conferring the advantage, and in which relevant higher-order properties such as one's previous professional experience, are discounted as the bases for conferring the advantage. In both kinds of cases, higher-order political discrimination is marked by the *relaxation or modification* of the criteria of competence for receiving the advantage, in order to accommodate the particular properties of the valuee.

take that relation to consist. It does *not* consist in the set of beliefs held by the higher-order political discriminator to the effect that

(A) (1) agent *A* has primary disvalued property P;

(2) agent *A* has *n*-ary property *N;* and

(3) P confers negative value on . . . *N*.

(A) is faulty because of (3): Only the most perverse and unrepentant higher-order political discriminator would admit—even to herself—that it is P that confers negative value on N. On the other hand, only the most absurdly consistent higher-order political discriminator would affirm the belief that, in virtue of (A.1) and (A.2),

(3′) therefore *N* is of negative value, period.

This would be the plight of the higher-order political discriminator who, in virtue of his contempt for Isaac Asimov's intellectual prolificity, would feel compelled to abjure Balzac as well. Instead, (3) must be replaced by

(3″) *N,* in the way in which it is borne by *A,* is of negative value.

(3″) is better because it incorporates that locution that scrupled higher-order political discriminators are so reluctant or unable to further define: For the higher-order political discriminator, there is just something about *the way in which* a person dances rhythmically that is vulgar; something about the way in which a person manifests her intelligence that is glib or sophistical; something about the way in which people attempt to gain access to social advantages that is unctuous or opportunistic. The higher-order political discriminator would vehemently reject the suggestion that this "something" might have anything to do with the person's race, gender, class, sexual orientation, or ethnic or religious affiliation. But in fact, it is precisely this primary disvalued property from which the blemish spreads. Let us then take the following set of beliefs

(B) (1) agent *A* has primary disvalued property *P*;

(2) agent *A* has *n*-ary property *N*; and

(3″) *N,* in the way in which it is borne by *A,* is of negative value

plus the following stipulation

(4) For the higher-order political discriminator, *A*'s possession of *P* is what in fact confers negative value on *N*

as characteristic of the typical, that is, scrupulous, higher-order political discriminator.

What makes higher-order political discriminators so scrupulous? What, that is, explains the higher-order political discriminator's tendency to suppress (B.4)? Part of the answer lies in the nature of first-order political discrimination. As we have seen, first-order political discrimination can be understood as a species of pseudorationality that relies heavily on the mechanisms of rationalization and dissociation. The perception of someone's race, gender, class, sexual orientation, ethnic or religious affiliation, etc., as a source of disvalue or value is the consequence of applying value concepts such as "person," "human being," "citizen," "member of the community," "rational and responsible agent," and so on, too narrowly, to include only those individuals who have the primary valued property and exclude those individuals who lack it. And similarly, dissociating Jews as subhuman, blacks as childlike, gays as perverts, working-class people as animals, or women as irrational are ways of obscuring one's identification of these individuals as fully mature, responsible human beings, and thereby obscuring one's recognition of these individuals as full members of the community with which one identifies.[27]

Higher-order political discrimination then adds to this the pseudorational mechanisms of *denial,* in which we suppress recognition of an anomalous thing or property altogether, in order to preserve the internal consistency of our beliefs or theory about the world, ourselves, and other people. I have already argued that, typically, higher-order political discriminators are likely to be first-order political discriminators as well; that is, they have the same prejudices that incline them to view individuals with the primary disvalued properties as inferior, not fully members of their community. The simple first-order political discriminator experiences no conflict in categorizing disvaluees as inferior beings to be suppressed and exploited. Therefore, she has no need to exercise denial, either of her own discrimina-

27.
The irony in the case of racism is that there is a substantial literature in biology and the social sciences that indicates that almost all purportedly white Americans have between 5 and 20 percent black ancestry and hence are, according to this country's entrenched "just one trace" convention of racial classification, black. See F. James Davis, *Who Is Black?* (University Park: Pennsylvania State University Press, 1991); Virginia R. Dominguez, *White by Definition: Social Classification in Creole Louisiana* (New Brunswick: Rutgers University Press, 1986); Joel Williamson, *A New People* (New York: Free Press, 1980); L. L. Cavalli-Sforza and W. F. Bodmer, *The Genetics of Human Populations* (San Francisco: W. H. Freeman and Co., 1971), pp. 490–499; T. E. Reed, "Caucasian Genes in American Negroes," *Science* 165 (1969), pp. 762–768; P. L. Workman, B. S. Blumberg, and A. J. Cooper, "Selection, Gene Migration and Polymorphic Stability in a U.S. White and Negro Population," *American Journal of Human Genetics* 15, no. 4 (1963), pp. 429–437; Bentley Glass and C. C. Li, "The Dynamics of Racial Admixture—An Analysis of the American Negro," *American Journal of Human Genetics* 5 (1953), pp. 1–20; and in general, *Genetic Abstracts* from about 1950. For these references and discussion on this matter I am indebted to Monro S. Edmonson of Tulane University's Department of Anthropology.

tory responses or of the disvaluees' existence. By contrast, higher-order political discriminators must deny both, in order to preserve the consistency of their beliefs. Because they are deeply affected, but not fully reformed, by arguments and experiences that suggest that political discrimination is unjust, both their own discriminatory responses and the objects of those responses are anathema to higher-order discriminators. Because they do not want to believe that their responses are politically discriminatory, they deny them altogether. The higher-order political discriminator may deny, for example, that the primary disvalued property in question is a disvalue at all, and yet helplessly deplore the "fact" that nevertheless there are no competent or worthy candidates bearing this property to be found; or may hold any such candidate to a much higher standard of acceptance or performance than that he ordinarily applies, relative to which her secondary properties can be disparaged. He may denigrate her intelligence as cleverness, or ridicule her for working too hard when she exhibits energy and commitment to her work, or disparage her professional recognition as achieved through hustling or connections.

These discriminatory responses suggest that the higher-order political discriminator in fact categorizes such members of the disvalued group themselves in similarly demeaning terms with respect to their primary properties but experiences a conflict of conscience about doing so. Faced with the conflict between first-order politically discriminatory habits of thought and the dictates of conscience, the higher-order political discriminator exercises denial, above all in order to avoid this conflict, by eradicating its source from awareness. The higher-order political discriminator often fails to acknowledge the very existence or presence of members of the disvalued groups, in order to circumvent his own, first-order politically discriminatory responses to them.[28] For instance, he may ignore or fail to acknowledge a disvaluee's contribution to a general discussion, or respond to that contribution as though someone else had made it. Or he may relegate a disvaluee to marginal or peripheral tasks in a professional setting. Or he may simply ignore the disvaluee altogether, avoiding all social interaction not strictly required by social or institutional obligations. In behaving in this fashion, the higher-order political discriminator does not give vent to any sort of malevolent impulse. His aim is not to insult or injure the disvaluee in any way. Rather, his aim is to avoid the painfully conflict-

28.
This may contribute to an explanation of the phenomenon, noted by Schuman, Steeh, and Bobo (*Racial Attitudes in America: Trends and Interpretations* [Cambridge: Harvard University Press, 1985], that in the last twenty years, white support for the *principles* of equality and fairness for blacks have increased, concurrently with white opposition to the *implementation* of those principles.

ing feelings — of disgust or contempt, on one hand, and the pangs of conscience, on the other — that acknowledgement of the disvaluee provokes.[29]

When social or institutional obligations make denial of the disvaluee's presence impossible, denial of (at the very least) her primary disvalued property, and of its perceived disvalue, supplies a second-best resolution to this conflict of conscience: Denial of the disvaluee's primary disvalued property suppresses from awareness the discriminatory habits of thought elicited by it, hence similarly preserves consistency, by placating the requirements of conscience. Thus the higher-order political discriminator is guilty of an even greater failure of cognitive discrimination than that of the simple first-order political discriminator. For whereas the former fails merely to perceive the disvaluee's personhood through her difference, the former fails to perceive either her or her difference altogether. This is why the higher-order political discriminator tends to suppress (B.4). Unfortunately, to suppress habits of thought from awareness is not to eradicate their influence, any more than to suppress the disvaluee's existence from awareness is to eradicate her influence. Higher-order political discrimination is characterized by that attitude in which a certain habit of thought, namely, first-order political discrimination, poisons one's evaluations and behavior, whether one acknowledges this or not.

The higher-order political discriminator is inclined, moreover, *not* to acknowledge this, no matter how obviously incriminating his evaluations and behavior may be to a disinterested observer. For this would expose the painful conflict of conscience the higher-order political discriminator's behavior attempts to suppress. To acknowledge this conflict, in turn, would be to acknowledge the need to resolve it, that is, the need to work through and overcome the first-order prejudices that gave rise to it. But it is precisely in virtue of those first-order prejudices themselves that such a project of self-improvement stands very low on the higher-order political discriminator's list of priorities. Unlike the resolution of Oedipal conflicts, emotional problems, tensions in one's personal relationships, or career dilemmas,

29.
Here the joke characterizing the difference between first-order racism in the South and in the North is relevant: In the South, it is said, whites don't mind how close a black person gets, as long as he doesn't get too big; whereas in the North, whites don't mind how big a black person gets, as long as he doesn't get too close. Only the higher-order political discriminator of either region is compelled to deny the existence of the black person altogether.

Denial of a person's presence as a way of avoiding conflicting feelings about him is fairly common. A very handsome man may be the object of denial, when others' feelings of attraction to him conflict with their conviction that these feelings are inappropriate; a very fortunate or charismatic person may be the object of denial, when others' feelings of envy or resentment conflict with a similar conviction. Or a homely person may be the object of denial when others' feelings of repugnance conflict with their kindness or social good will. Higher-order political discrimination is most analogous to this last-described case.

coming to terms with one's prejudices and learning not to inflict them inadvertently on others just is not, in the last analysis, seen as terribly important by the higher-order political discriminator. That is part of what makes him a political discriminator in the first place.[30]

As I have painted it, then, higher-order political discrimination is peculiarly the sickness of thoughtful, well-intentioned, and conscientious individuals who nevertheless have failed adequately to confront and work through their own prejudices, or who perhaps have been too quickly satisfied by their ability to marshal arguments on behalf of doing so. Such individuals are being neither disingenuous nor hypocritical when they deny that a person's race, gender, class, sexual orientation, or ethnic or religious affiliation affects their judgment of her competence or worth. They vehemently insist that this is so, they want it to be so, and they genuinely believe it to be so. They are, nevertheless, mistaken. Their efforts to explain away each manifest expression of higher-order political discrimination on different and inconsistent grounds are unconvincing. And their behavior exhibits a degree of otherwise inexplicable arbitrariness and idiosyncrasy that severely strains our attempts to apply the principle of charity in making sense of it. Hence in order to understand the behavior of higher-order political discriminators, we must watch what they *do,* not what they *say.*[31]

For example, these attitudes may find expression in an expectation of greater deference or genuflection from a member of the disvalued group. The simple first-order political discriminator expresses his anger at the violation of this expectation in certain familiar stereotypes: the "uppity nigger" whose refusal to behave subserviently is seen as impudence or disrespect, or the "Jewish American Princess" whose assertiveness, presumption of self-worth, and expectation of attention and respect are seen as a sign of being spoiled, selfish, or imperious. But for the higher-order political discriminator, such anger is displaced into more subtle but similar reac-

30.
Here I think it would be wrong to interpret the higher-order political discriminator as concerned only with personal problems and not with social ones. Rather, the higher-order political discriminator belittles the importance of addressing a certain *personal* problem.

31.
One implication of characterizing higher-order political discrimination as a sickness rather than a fault is that higher-order political discriminators are, in the last analysis, not morally responsible for their behavior. This conclusion seems unpalatable in many respects. Nevertheless, I am reluctantly pessimistic about the efficacy of direct appeals to reason in higher-order political discriminators. Because their reason—or rather, their dogged pseudorationality—is so inherently a part of the problem, I am inclined to think that the solution should be sought in the adoption of some version of Strawson's "objective attitude" toward them; that is, that higher-order political discriminators must be *managed*—perhaps psychotherapeutically—rather than *addressed.* I suggest an explanation for this kind of intractability in "Two Conceptions of the Self" and "Pseudorationality," and suggest certain artistic strategies that may have a beneficial effect on higher-order political discriminators in section 8 of this chapter.

tions: Such an individual may just feel angered or personally affronted by a woman's presumption of equality—in personal, social, or intellectual status, or professional worth, or as a competitor for social or professional rewards—or unduly irritated by her failure to defer or back down in argument. She may be viewed as forward in conversation, when in fact she contributes no more and no less than anyone else; or stubborn, unresponsive, or impervious to well-intentioned criticisms, when in fact the only acceptable response to those criticisms, in the eyes of the higher-order political discriminator, would be for her to concur with them wholeheartedly and apologize for her dereliction. Or, to take another example, the higher-order political discriminator may feel invaded or compromised by a black person's jocularity or willingness to trade friendly insults that one accepts as a matter of course from those considered to be one's peers. The black person may be viewed as overly familiar, insolent, or presumptuous. In all such cases, the disvaluee's behavior is seen as a *presumption,* not a right or an accepted practice.[32] The higher-order political discriminator is tortured by the suspicion that he is somehow being ridiculed, or shown insufficient respect, or that the disvaluee's conduct bespeaks contempt.

In a compelling analysis of anger,[33] N. J. H. Dent suggests that anger is based ultimately on feelings of personal inferiority: These lead one to overestimate the importance of others' expressions of regard and esteem for one, which in turn multiplies the number of occasions upon which one feels slighted or demeaned when such expressions are not forthcoming, or of insufficient magnitude relative to one's importunate requirements. This oversensitivity to being slighted in turn provokes in one the desire to rectify one's situation through retaliation, by lashing out at the offender. This analysis by itself does not, I think, cover all cases of anger; nor does it explain the origins of simple first-order political discrimination. But it does provide insight into why higher-order political discriminators, like simple first-order political discriminators, are apt to become so angry, so often, at imagined slights from seemingly arrogant disvaluees. The more inferior one feels, the more expressions of esteem one requires. And the more inferior one perceives a disvaluee to be, the more elaborate the disvaluee's expression of esteem of one is required to be. Whereas a friendly nod from a perceived superior is sufficient to

32.
The view of the disvaluee's assumption of equality as a *pre*sumption may explain the higher-order political discriminator's otherwise inexplicable umbrage at being complemented by a disvaluee: An inferior is in no position to confer favors of any kind.

33.
N. J. H. Dent, *The Moral Psychology of the Virtues* (Cambridge: Cambridge University Press, 1984), pp. 155–160.

transport one to a state of grace, anything less than a full-length obeisance from a perceived inferior appears to be an insult.[34] In all such cases, irascibility regularly directed at particular members of disvalued groups should not be dismissed as simply an idiosyncrasy of character, even if it is not intentionally directed at members of disvalued groups *as such.* It is, nevertheless, an overt expression of higher-order political discrimination.

A second, related example of behavior and judgments distorted by higher-order political discrimination is the treatment of disvaluees in a way that would constitute a clear insult or faux pas, if the person so treated were one of one's recognized peers. For example, a white Gentile may privately make an anti-Semitic remark to a black colleague, in a misguided effort to establish rapport, when such a remark would be seen as a serious social lapse even among other white Gentiles. Or a heterosexual may make gratuitous disparaging remarks to a gay colleague about her work or job performance, of a sort designed to "cut her down to size" rather than provide constructive criticism. Or a man may make offensively personal remarks to a woman colleague about her physical appearance, personal life, or manner of dress, of a sort that would be highly inappropriate if they were made to another man. Or he might expect from a woman colleague extra forbearance for fits of temper, irresponsible conduct, or extraordinary professional demands that he would not from a man. The higher-order political discriminator, in other social contexts, may be acclaimed quite rightly as a "prince among men"; to disvaluees, however, he reveals himself as Mr. Hyde.[35] Yet unlike former President Lyndon Johnson, who conferred with his cabinet through an open bathroom door, while uninhibitedly and indiscreetly performing his morning ablutions, the higher-order political discriminator cannot be supposed to commit these boorish excesses with any offensive intent. Rather, he regards his response to a person's disvalued properties as socially innocuous; as an acceptable variation in social etiquette, keyed to the variations among personality traits of different individuals.

34.
In the Deep South up to the mid-1960s, for example, for a black person to meet the gaze of a white person was perceived as an offense, and for a black man even to look at a white woman was to invite lynching.

35.
This often creates additional difficulties in identifying cases of higher-order political discrimination for what they are. The testimony of a disvaluee suffers a credibility problem at the outset. This problem is severely exacerbated if the testimony concerns a higher-order political discriminator whom others have every reason to regard as a saint. Under these circumstances, any charge of inconsistency—whether it comes from others and targets the disvaluee, or comes from the disvaluee and targets the higher-order political discriminator—is in the eye of the beholder. For higher-order political discriminators regard coarse, tasteless, or brutal behavior toward disvaluees as called forth by them and so warranted; hence as fully consistent with the most highly refined manners and courtly civility toward others.

A third example of such distorted behavior is the implicit treatment of disvaluees as being obligated by different rules of conduct from those that govern oneself and those considered to be one's peers. One may apply different criteria of interpretation to the behavior of disvaluees: Whereas enigmatic behavior by valuees is excused, overlooked, or given the benefit of the doubt, similar behavior on the part of disvaluees is interpreted as proof of vice or malevolence. This interpretation motivates the higher-order political discriminator not only to avoid but also to justify the avoidance of direct interaction with the disvaluee, and thus avoid the conflict of conscience described earlier. Or one may apply rules of honor, loyalty, and responsibility only to those considered to be one's peers but may have no scruples about betraying the trust or confidentiality of a disvaluee, who is implicitly viewed as unentitled to such consideration. Alternately, one may hold disvaluees to far more stringent moral standards than the members of one's own community in fact practice among themselves. Any violation of these standards by the disvaluee then creates an irradicable moral blemish to which the valuees are invulnerable, by reason of their status as valuees. These cases express quite clearly the conviction that disvaluees just do not have quite that same status, hence are not to be subject to the same standards of treatment, as members of one's recognized community—at the same time that the higher-order political discriminator vehemently and in all honesty denies that any such discrimination is taking place. Indeed in all of these examples, the higher-order political discriminator may sincerely deny that the person's race, gender, sexual orientation, ethnic or religious affiliation, and so on, arbitrarily influences his evaluations, when his behavior shows patently that they do.

VIII. Failures of Cognitive Discrimination: Causes and Cures

There are many forces that may intensify higher-order political discrimination and its social consequences. Among them are, first and foremost, complicitous institutional practices. Individuals in positions of responsibility often rank their personal and social allegiances ahead of their professional obligation to protect disvaluees from the pernicious effects of higher-order political discrimination. Or they effectively reward it, by regularly interpreting instances of it as expressions of professional autonomy and refusing in principle to scrutinize suspected instances of it, on the grounds that doing so would be unwarranted interference in an organization's internal affairs. These institutions often comply with the letter of antidiscriminatory policies, by hiring members of disvalued groups to temporary positions of high public visibility. Because such individuals are regularly replaced by other equally competent but equally transient members of the same disvalued group, that group's visibility within the institution can be maintained, without infiltrating the entrenched system of political discrimination through permanent or seniority status. This is to abdicate the responsibility for enforcing those antidiscriminatory policies to which such institutions publicly claim to be committed.

Second, there is the intellectual resourcefulness of the higher-order political discriminator: Someone who is in fact deeply invested in the disvaluational status of some primary property may always recruit some further, equally irrelevant property to explain her seemingly irrational judgment, and thus deflect the charge of higher-order political discrimination: It may be said, for example, that the disvalued property is not a person's race, gender, sexual orientation, class, ethnic or religious affiliation, and so on, but rather his inability to "fit in," to "get along with others," or to "be a team player." This is a particularly familiar and dependable response, because the evidence for ascribing this property may be materially coextensive with the evidence for disvaluing the primary property at issue: Because the disvaluee is in theory held to the same standards of conduct that govern others in the community but in fact expected to conform to different ones, tailored to his disvalued status, his inability to "fit in" can be guaranteed at the outset.[36]

A third force that intensifies higher-order political discrimination is the repressive, pseudorational habits of rationalization, dissociation, and denial already discussed. Earlier I suggested that higher-order political discriminators were generally well-intentioned individuals who had failed to come to terms with their own prejudices. I also mentioned some possible reasons for this failure: avoidance of conflicts of conscience, feelings of personal inferiority, and first-order political discrimination among them. Another reason that should not be neglected is that higher-order political discriminators tend to rationalize, dissociate, or deny the very existence of higher-order political discrimination itself. They might claim, for example, that the phenomenon I have described is in truth perceptual sensitivity to subtle variations and qualities among individuals, all of which might be relevant to questions of value or competence in a sufficiently broad sense. Or they might agree that higher-order political discrimination exists, but dissociate it from their own motives and behavior, as an anomalous phenomenon that is too rare to merit further scrutiny. Or they might just flatly deny the existence of anything like what I have described as higher-order political discrimination, and deny as well the undeniably familiar in-

36.
Under these circumstances, the disvaluee, too, may be accused rightly of pseudorationality, if his personal investment in the theoretical standards of equal treatment is so great that he rationalizes, dissociates, or denies the facts of discrimination that blatantly confront him. But I argue elsewhere ("The Meaning of 'Ought' and the Loss of Innocence," manuscript, 1989) that self-preservation *requires* that, although such ideals ultimately must die, they must not do so without a long and painful struggle.

stances of it that I have invoked to anchor the foregoing analysis. These tactics reinforce the tendencies of higher-order political discriminators to deny their own collusion in the practice of higher-order political discrimination, and to deny or minimize their need to come to terms with it. Higher-order political discriminators are adept at the tactics of pseudorationality because they have so much self-esteem to lose by modifying their beliefs. But *we* must not be taken in. For above all, higher-order political discriminators need to understand that no one is fooled by their tactics. With the aid of this understanding, they may someday learn to stop fooling themselves.

How might higher-order political discriminators come to such an understanding? How might they achieve self-awareness of the pseudorational tactics that buttress their political discrimination? In closing, I want to limn a set of strategies for cultivating more fine-grained cognitive discriminations in general, through exposure to contemporary works of art, and suggest some ways in which these might provide an antidote to higher-order political discrimination in particular.[37] I will not mean to suggest that works of art are capable of *curing* higher-order political discrimination. As we have seen, higher-order political discrimination is supervenient on first-order political discrimination, and first-order political discriminators are ashamed not of their political discrimination but of themselves as inadequate to the honorific stereotypes they reciprocally impose on themselves. Insofar as a higher-order political discriminator retains a personal investment in that honorific stereotype, she will be unpersuaded by its deleterious effects on others to renounce it. This means that it is not just her cognitive habits that are in need of reform but her more central conception of herself. This is a task for social reconditioning or psychotherapy, not art. Nevertheless, art has an important role to play in intensifying a viewer's self-awareness of these matters. Art can highlight pseudorational failures of cognitive discrimination as themselves objects of aesthetic examination, and it can heighten a viewer's level of cognitive sensitivity to a wide range of complex situations, of which political discrimination is only one.

In the contemporary setting, galleries and museums announce themselves to the public as arenas in which cognitive alertness is required, and in which the viewer's capacity to understand and situate an anomalous object in its singularly appropriate context will be tested. In earlier historical periods, galleries and museums had different roles: pedagogical or inspirational, for example. But in this one, their

37.
None of my remarks here should be construed as an account of my own motivations, which are generally obscure to me, in producing the type of art I produce. Instead they should be regarded as providing a rationale for a certain kind of work, an interpretation that situates it in the context of my own conscious concerns.

primary role, and the role of the artworks they exhibit, is to challenge the limitations of the viewer's conceptual scheme—her presuppositions about reality, the human condition, and social and personal relationships, as well as her presuppositions about what art is and what an exhibition space is supposed to do. By introducing into a specialized cognitive context singular objects that defy easy categorization, galleries and museums signal themselves to their audience as purveyors of heightened awareness through the objects and artifacts they display. Generated by a culture that values innovation for its own sake as well as for its ability to create its own market, these contemporary artifacts function primarily to provoke or stimulate in the viewer more flexible and inclusive conceptualizations of reality that can encompass them. In this sense, contemporary art is a paradigmatic experience of cognitive anomaly. It offers one the opportunity to reorganize the conceptual structure of the self in order to accommodate it, and to test and develop one's capacity for cognitive discrimination in order to grasp it.

Some works of art satisfy this desideratum better than others. Some choose instead to reaffirm traditional values, or the social and political *status quo,* or prevailing comfortable convictions and perceptions of human nature. But since Impressionism and perhaps before, but most explicitly since Duchamp, the most significant works of art in the Western tradition[38] have taken seriously the challenge of heightened cognitive discrimination, that is, the challenge to compel the viewer to see what he did not see before, and to add these anomalous, newly discovered properties of objects and events to his permanent cognitive repertoire. Contemporary artists who are serious about art take seriously their responsibility to question and extend the limits of knowledge by offering anomalous objects, innovative in form, content, or both, as an antidote to provincial and conventional habits of thought.

Minimal art of the 1960s offers a particularly compelling example of this. For the first time in the history of modernism, artists were taken seriously as critics and theorists of contemporary art. And what many minimal artists explicitly averred in their writings was that no such theory was adequate to an understanding of the work; that the point of presenting geometrically, materially, and formally reductive objects was to draw the viewer's attention away from extrinsic associations and toward the specificity and materiality of the particular object itself. In its aesthetic strategies, minimalism repudiated the imposition of abstract theory—psychoana-

38.
By "the Western tradition" in art, I mean not only the Euroethnic canon itself but also the contributions of colonialized, marginalized, or non-Western cultures to it (as, for example, Tahitian art influenced Gauguin, Japanese art influenced van Gogh, African art influenced Picasso, or American Jazz influenced Stuart Davis).

lytic, social, or aesthetic—as cognitively inadequate to a full comprehension of the work. Instead it emphasized the uniqueness, singularity, and indexical immediacy of the art object itself. The category of art itself functioned as a catch-all term signifying the object's inherent resistance to extrinsic conceptualization, and so its aesthetic interest as an otherwise anomalous entity in its own right. This stance itself was, of course, a theoretical one. But minimalism differed from earlier theoretical stances in stipulating the properties of the specific object in question as the origin and locus of theorizing about it. It embedded the object in an abstract symbol system of its own making.

Conceptual and performance art of the late 1960s and early 1970s extended this strategy further, by subordinating the medium in which the work was realized to the concepts it embodied or explored. It was even more clearly the intrinsic meaning of the work, and not the cognitive preconceptions the viewer brought to it, that dictated its appropriate conceptualization. In subordinating medium to concept, conceptual art not only reaffirmed the conceptual fluidity and inclusiveness of art, as originally introduced by Duchamp's urinal. It also opened the door to the use of any medium, event, or object deemed appropriate to the particular concepts the artist chose to explore. Thus conceptual art repudiated all remaining traditional restrictions on content and subject matter as well as on medium. And in so doing, it created the possibility of seeing any object as a conceptual anomaly relative to the conceptual scheme within which it was conventionally embedded. Any such object became a potential locus of original conceptual investigation, and all such objects became potential threats to the conceptual unity of a rigidly or provincially structured self.

Under these circumstances, the gallery or museum as a site of cognitive provocation has become clear. Beyond a few extremely vague and uninformative terms of classification, such as "installation art," "performance art," "object art," and so on, there are no longer any expectations or preconceptions a viewer may legitimately bring to such work regarding what kind of viewing experience is in store—except that she will be required to discriminate cognitively a variety of elements, and fashion for herself a coherent interpretation of the experience that at the same time respects the intrinsic conceptual integrity of the work. A viewer of contemporary art must be prepared for media that include foodstuffs, bodily fluids, chemical compounds, and industrial materials, as well as traditional art media; and for content that may be highly autobiographical, social, sexual, political, or philosophical, as well as realistic or abstract. No viewer who insists on maintaining excessively rigid, provincial, or philistine views about art will survive in the contemporary art world for very long.

This is to suggest that the contemporary-art-going public is self-selected to consist, not in a specialized educational and economic elite, but rather of those individuals who are psychologically prepared and sophisticated enough to engage in the hard work of cognitive discrimination in general. For all the foregoing reasons, the contemporary-art-going public is likely to be particularly receptive to the conceptual challenge presented by cognitively anomalous objects or properties in general, and, a fortiori, by cognitively anomalous persons in particular. The arena of contemporary art, then, is a particularly apt one for addressing the cognitive failures of political discrimination.

Now return to the plight of the higher-order political discriminator, taken in by his own pseudorational attempts to eradicate from awareness his xenophobic attitudes and behavior. With its latitude in the use of media, content, and subject matter, contemporary art may offer a variety of approaches for reducing this cognitive disingenuity and enhancing self-awareness. Take, for example, *mimesis*: A work of art may incorporate into its subject matter these very pseudorationalizations as an ironic commentary or distancing device. These pseudorationalizations not only impose politically discriminatory stereotyping on others. They are themselves stereotypical reactions, conditioned habitual responses that are part of a behavioral repertoire as limited as that which the political discriminator imposes on anomalous others. Indeed, they embody such stereotypes even as they express them. It is in the nature of deeply instilled habits of thought and action to seem not only deeply private and individualized but also fixed, natural, and part of the objective order of things—so much so that voluntarily bringing them to light as objects of self-conscious scrutiny on one's own is exceedingly difficult. One scarcely knows what to question or scrutinize. But hearing or seeing them echoed back to one by an impersonal art object can make it clear to one that these phrases or habits of reasoning are not uniquely one's own but, rather, crude and common slogans that short-circuit the hard work of self-scrutiny. Thus mimesis can be an effective way of distancing oneself from such pseudorational slogans, and of illuminating their stereotypical character and function. By demonstrating their indiscriminate and simplistic application to a range of circumstances that clearly demand greater sensitivity to specifics, such a work can encourage greater cognitive discrimination of particular persons and circumstances for what they are.

A second device that may be useful as an antidote to higher-order political discrimination is *confrontation*: As we have seen, a higher-order political discriminator escapes from the meaning of her behavior into a thicket of abstract pseudorational theorizing that detaches her from the actual personal and social consequences of her actions. Because she denies the existence of the object of her higher-order political discrimination, in addition to her own responses to it, the higher-order political discriminator often lacks a sense of the hurtfulness of her behavior, or of the harmfulness of its consequences for others. An art object that confronts a higher-order political discriminator with the human repercussions of these consequences can help restore to the higher-order political discriminator a sense of reality, and a sense of cognitive responsibility for the human effects of her unreflective stereotyping of anomalous others. Moreover, a confrontative art object can draw the higher-order political discriminator's attention away from the abstract realm of theoretical obfuscation, and back to the reality of her actual circumstances at the moment. It can help resituate her in the indexical present of her immediate, one-to-one relation to the object and the issues it embodies.

Finally, consider the strategy of *naming*: We have seen that pseudorationality for the higher-order political discriminator consists in the construction of an elaborate edifice of euphemisms designed to obscure from himself and others the true meaning of his attitudes, actions, and policies toward others, and of the painful social realities to which his behavior in fact responds. This willed unconsciousness can be penetrated by concepts and symbols that speak plainly to the ugly realities these euphemisms conceal. An art object that draws the viewer's attention to these realities, and leaves no room for ambiguity in their identification, can be an assaultive and disturbing experience. It blocks escape into abstract speculation concerning the denotations and connotations of the terms or symbols deployed as referents, and may reinforce the vividness and objectivity of the realities brought forward through confrontation, with the legitimating imprimatur of linguistic or representational acknowledgment. At the same time, through repetition and repeated viewing, it can help accustom the higher-order political discriminator to the existence of these realities, and conceptually defuse them to psychologically manageable proportions.

Of course each of these strategies, as well as many others I have not mentioned, can be deployed outside the contemporary art context as well as within it: in psychotherapy, encounter groups, or organizational training sessions, for example. But one benefit of utilizing art objects in this role is that, unlike psychotherapists, group leaders, or other human subjects, an art object can elicit different reactions from different viewers *while maintaining exactly the same phenomenological presence to all of them*. It does not itself react personally to any particular viewer, or differently to one viewer than it does to another, or alter its presentational aspect to suit the tastes or dispositions of particular viewers. Because the logic of its internal structure and external appearance depends on its personal history and interactive relationship with the artist rather than with the viewer, its final form is fixed and immutable relative to any particular viewer in a way other human subjects cannot be. Thus a viewer's relation to an art object can be both direct and individual, on one hand, and *impersonal* on the other.

The impersonality, impenetrability, and inherent internal equilibrium of an art object can be a distinct advantage in attacking political discrimination through cognitive discrimination. A human subject who deploys these strategies in other interpersonal contexts is vulnerable to criticism by a participant who feels that the leader, trainer, or therapist is "reacting personally" to her: just doesn't like her, is personally attacking her, manipulating her, or projecting his own problems onto her. And in this type of situation, such criticisms may be justified. But in an art context, they cannot be. For unlike human subjects, an art object cannot have reactions to, intentions toward, or designs of any kind on a viewer and, a fortiori, cannot have *personal* reactions, intentions, or designs on any *particular* viewer. So although it may happen that a particularly insecure or provincial viewer initially may feel moved to accuse the work of art of manipulating him, ridiculing him, trying to pull the wool over his eyes, guilt-tripping him, attacking him, and so on, it will not require too much reflection on the viewer's part to conclude, finally, that this is not the kind of thing an art object, unlike a human subject, has the capacity to do. Nor will it require much more reflection on the viewer's part to conclude that, if he does indeed feel that the work is doing these things to him, these feelings can only be the result of magical thinking and personal projection of his own emotions onto the object, and that this response itself is worth his scrutiny.[39] An important benefit of utilizing art objects to combat higher-order political discrimination, then, is that they enable the viewer to discriminate cognitively between what he sees and what he is.

39.
Can the same claims be made for media advertising? Is it not clearly manipulative in intent? Here I think we need to distinguish, in the case of art as well as of advertising, between the creator's intentions in producing the work and its psychological effects on its viewers. Like advertisers, artists of course have intentions in producing a particular work. Typically, an advertiser's intention in producing a commercial is to get the consumer to buy the product, whereas an artist's intention in producing a work of art may be to get the viewer to reflect on his political or aesthetic attitudes. In both cases, these intentions can be distinguished from the psychological effects of the work on its recipient. An advertiser who pairs a beautiful woman with a certain make of car in order to get consumers to buy that make of car may intend to enhance the appeal of that make of car to consumers. That a particular consumer comes to hate his wife because he has a different make of car is not necessarily part of the advertiser's intention. Similarly, an artist who pairs depiction of the homeless with standard stereotypical rationalizations for ignoring them may intend to get viewers to reflect on their economic priorities. That a particular viewer feels guilt-stricken because she has been making contributions to her alma mater instead of to the homeless is not necessarily part of the artist's intention. Any individual who engages in an act of communication of any kind intends to have an effect on her audience, at least minimally that it understand her. This does not imply that she intends the actual effect on her audience her communication has. Consumers as well as art viewers may examine their reactions to a commercial and a work of art respectively, in order self-consciously to discern and differentiate their personal areas of vulnerability or uncertainty from the intended act of impersonal communication the object represents.

19.
The Grid (1989).
Courtesy Paula
Cooper Gallery,
collection Peter
Soriano.

Adrian Piper: A Biography

Solo Exhibitions

Three Untitled Projects (postal art exhibition) (New York: 0 to 9 Press, 1969)	March 1969
One Man (sic), One Work, New York Cultural Center, New York, N.Y.	February 1971
Adrian Piper, Gallery One, Montclair State College, Montclair, N.J.	February 1976
Adrian Piper at Matrix 56, Wadsworth Atheneum, Hartford, Conn.;	March 1980
in conjunction with	
Adrian Piper, Real Artways, Hartford, Conn.	March 1980
Adrian Piper, And/Or, Seattle, Wash.	February 1981
Adrian Piper: Reflections 1967–1987 (retrospective):	
The Alternative Museum, New York, N.Y.	April–May 1987
Nexus Contemporary Art Center, Atlanta, Ga.	November–December 1987
Goldie Paley Gallery, Philadelphia, Pa.	February–March 1989
University of Colorado Art Gallery, Boulder, Colo.	March 1990
Power Plant Gallery, Toronto, Canada	May–June 1990
Wooster Art Museum, Wooster, Ohio	August–October 1990
Lowe Art Museum, Coral Gables, Florida	December 1990–January 1991
Santa Monica Museum of Contemporary Art	February–March 1991
Washington Project for the Arts, Washington, D.C.	June–August 1991
John Weber Gallery, New York, N.Y.	March 1989
Matrix Gallery, University Art Museum, Berkeley, Calif.	August–November 1989
Williams College Art Museum, Williamstown, Mass.	January–March 1990
Why Guess, University of Rhode Island Art Gallery, Kingston, R.I.	February–March 1990
Pretend, John Weber Gallery, New York, N.Y.	September 1990
Why Guess, Exit Art, New York, N.Y.	October–November 1990
Out of the Corner, Whitney Museum of American Art, Film and Video Gallery, New York, N.Y.	October–November 1990
University of Iowa Art Gallery, Iowa City, Iowa	March–April 1990
What It's Like, What It Is, #1, Washington Project for the Arts, Washington, D.C.	June–August 1991
What It's Like, What It Is, #2, Hirshhorn Museum, Directions Gallery, Washington, D.C.	June–September 1991
Adrian Piper (European retrospective)	
Ikon Gallery, Birmingham, England	September–November 1991
Cornerhouse, Manchester, England	January–February 1992
Cartwright Hall, Bradford, England	March–May 1992
Kettle's Yard, Cambridge, England	July–September 1992
Kunstverein Munich, Germany	October–November 1992
Space, Time and Reference 1967–1970, John Weber Gallery, New York, N.Y.	October 1991
Political Drawings and Installations, 1975–1991 (retrospective):	
Cleveland Center for Contemporary Art, Cleveland, Ohio	November 1991–February 1992
Carver Center, San Antonio, Tex.	April 1992
Herron Gallery, Indianapolis Center for Contemporary Art, Indianapolis, Ind.	May–June 1992
Women & Their Work, Austin, Tex.	October–December 1992
What It's Like, What It Is, #2, Krannert Art Museum, Champaign, Ill.	January–February 1992
Ur-Madonna, Expo '92, Monasterio de Santa Clara, Moguer (Huelva), Spain	August 1992

Decide Who You Are:	
Grey Art Gallery, New York, N.Y.	September–October 1992
John Weber Gallery, New York, N.Y.	September–October 1992
Paula Cooper Gallery, New York, N.Y.	October 1992
Myers Fine Art Gallery, SUNY Plattsburgh Art Museum, Plattsburgh, N.Y.	February 1993
Art Awareness, Lexington, N.Y.	June–July 1993
City Gallery of Contemporary Art, Raleigh, N.C.	October–December 1993
Installations by Adrian Piper, New Langton Arts, San Francisco, Calif.	September–October 1993
The Hypothesis Series 1968–70, Paula Cooper Gallery, New York, N.Y.	March 1994
Cornered/Decide Who You Are, SUNY Buffalo, Buffalo, N.Y.	March–April 1995
Icons of One: Decide Who You Are, Savannah College of Art Gallery, Savannah, Ga.	October–November 1995
Galleria Emi Fontana, Milan, Italy	January 1997
Neue Gesellschaft für bildende Kunst, Berlin, Germany	January 1997

Group Exhibitions

Number Seven, Paula Cooper Gallery, New York, N.Y.	May 1969
Language III, Dwan Gallery, New York, N.Y.	May 1969
557,087, Seattle Art Museum, Seattle, Wash. (traveling)	September 1969
Concept Art, Stadtisches Museum, Leverkusen, West Germany	October 1969
Groups, School of Visial Arts Gallery, New York, N.Y.	November 1969
Plans and Projects as Art, Kunsthalle Berne, Berne, Switzerland	November 1969
Conceptual Art and Conceptual Aspects, New York Cultural Center, New York, N.Y.	April 1970
Art in the Mind, Allen Museum, Oberlin, Ohio	May 1970
Information, Museum of Modern Art, New York, N.Y.	June 1970
Language IV, Dwan Gallery, New York, N.Y.	June 1970
26 Contemporary Women Artists, Larry Aldrich Museum, Ridgefield, Conn.	April 1971
Paris Biennale, Musée d'Art Moderne, Paris, France	September 1971
Art without Limits, Memorial Art Gallery, Rochester, N.Y.	April 1972
Communications, Inhibodress Gallery, New South Wales, Australia	April 1972
Thought: Structures, Pace College Gallery, New York, N.Y.	January 1973
Nine New York Artists, Hartwick College, Oneonta, N.Y.	Apirl 1973
Artforms, Abstract Activities, Ideas, Pomona College, Claremont, Calif.	May 1973
c. 7,500, California Institute of the Arts, Valencia, Calif.	May 1973
Word Works, Mt. San Antonio College Art Gallery, Walnut, Calif.	April 1974
Woman's Work: American Art 1974, Philadelphia Civic Center, Philadelphia, Pa. (traveling)	April 1974–1976
In Her Own Image, Samuel S. Fleischer Art Memorial, Philadelphia, Pa.	April 1974
Bodyworks, Museum of Contemporary Art, Chicago, Ill.	March 1975
Word Works II, San Jose State University Art Gallery, San Jose, Ca.	April 1975
Eleven in New York, Women's Interart Center, New York, N.Y.	May 1975
Lives, The Fine Arts Building, New York, N.Y.	December 1975
Paris Biennale, Musée d'Art Moderne, Paris, France	September 1977
The Sense of the Self: From Self-Portrait to Autobiography, Newberger Museum, Purchase, N.Y.	September 1978
Untitled Exhibition, Artists' Space, New York, N.Y.	September 1978
Eventworks, Massachusetts College of Art, Boston, Mass.	March 1979

Both Sides Now, Artemesia Gallery, Chicago, Ill.	March 1979
A Decade of Women's Performance Art, National Women's Caucus for Art Conference, New Orleans, La.	February 1980
Speaking Volumes: Women's Artist Books, A. I. R. Gallery, New York, N.Y.	June 1980
Art of Conscience, Wright Gallery, Dayton, Ohio (traveling)	October 1980
Issue: Twenty Social Strategies by Women Artists, Institute of Contemporary Arts, London, England	November 1980
Events: Artists Invite Artists, The New Museum, New York, N.Y.	February 1981
The Gender Show, Group Material, New York, N.Y.	February 1981
The Page as Alternative Space, Franklin Furnace, New York, N.Y.	February 1981
Oppositions, And/Or, Seattle, Wash.	May 1981
Art at Ground Zero: Artists' Statements on Nuclear War, University of Michigan Residential College, Ann Arbor, Mich.	March 1983
The Black and White Show, Kenkeleba Gallery, New York, N.Y.	April 1983
Language, Drama, Source, and Vision, The New Museum, New York, N.Y.	October 1983
Disarming Images: Artists' Statements against Nuclear War, Newburger Museum, Purchase, N.Y. (traveling)	June 1984–1987
A Decade of New Art, Artists' Space, New York, N.Y.	June 1984
Tradition and Conflict, The Studio Museum in Harlem, New York, N.Y.	January 1985
Kunst mit Eigen-Sinn, Museum Moderner Kunst, Vienna, Austria	March 1985
The Art of Memory/The Loss of History, The New Museum, New York, N.Y.	November 1985
Floating Values, HallWalls, Buffalo, N.Y.	April 1987
Black Video: Performance/Document/Narrative, Gorman Museum, Davis, Calif.	April 1987
Past Time, Maryland Art Place, Baltimore, Md.	September 1987
Commitment to Print, The Museum of Modern Art, New York, N.Y. (traveling)	January 1988
Coast to Coast: A Women of Color National Artists' Book Project, WCA, Houston, Tex. (traveling)	February 1988
Autobiography: In Her Own Image, Intar Gallery, New York, N.Y. (traveling)	April 1988
Modes of Address, Whitney Museum Downtown, New York, N.Y.	July 1988
Unknown Secrets: Art of the Rosenberg Era (traveling). Curated by Nina Felshin	September 1988
Signs, Art Gallery of Ontario, Toronto, Canada (traveling)	September 1988
The Turning Point: Art and Politics in 1968, Cleveland Center for Contemporary Art, Cleveland, Ohio (traveling)	September 1988
Works on Paper, OneTwentyEight, New York, N.Y.	December 1988
Art as a Verb, Maryland Institute of Art, Baltimore, Md.	October 1988
Identity, Whitney Museum Downtown, New York, N.Y.	December 1988
Making Their Mark: Women Arists Move into the Mainstream 1970–85, Cincinnati Art Museum, Cincinnati, Ohio (traveling)	February–March 1989
Collecting, Organizing, Transposing, Maryland Art Place, Baltimore, Md.	February 1989
Art as a Verb, The Studio Museum in Harlem, New York, N.Y.	March–June 1989
Head, OneTwentyEight, New York, N.Y.	May 1989
American Resources, Bernice Steinbaum Gallery, New York, N.Y. (traveling)	June–July 1989
Some Choices, Long Beach Art Museum, Long Beach, Calif.	Summer 1989
Double Take: A Second Look at Advertising, Cincinnati Contemporary Arts Center, Cincinnati, Ohio	July–September 1989
Buttinsky, Feature, New York, N.Y.	September 1989
I Only Want You to Love Me, Feature, New York, N.Y.	October 1989
L'Art Conceptuel: Une Perspective, Musée d'Art Moderne, Paris, France (traveling)	November 1989–February 1990
Life is Wonderful, Simon Watson Gallery, New York, N.Y.	February 1990

Exotism, Zilkha Gallery, Wesleyan University, Middletown, Conn.	January–March 1990
Insect Politics, Hallwalls Contemporary Arts, Buffalo, N.Y.	March–April 1990
Signs of the Self: Changing Perceptions, Woodstock Artists Association, Woodstock, N.Y.	March–April 1990
Words and Images—with a Message, Women's Studio Workshop, Oneonta, N.Y.	April 1990
Sarah Charlesworth, Jeanne Dunning, Annette Messager, Adrian Piper, Laurie Simmons, Feigen Gallery, Chicago, Ill.	March–April 1990
Constructive Anger, Barbara Krakow Gallery, Boston, Mass.	May–June 1990
Art in Europe and America: The 1960s and 1970s, Wexner Center for the Visual Arts, Ohio State University, Columbus, Ohio	May–August 1990
Word as Image: American Art 1960–1990:	
Milwaukee Art Museum, Milwaukee, Wis.	June–August 1990
Contemporary Arts Center, Houston, Tex.	February 1991
The Power of Words: An Aspect of Recent Documentary Photography, P.P.O.W., New York, N.Y.	June–July 1990
The Thing Itself, Feature Gallery, New York, N.Y.	July–August 1990
Presumed Identities, Real Art Ways, Hartford, Conn.	November 1990
The Art of Drawing, Lehman College Art Gallery, New York, N.Y.	September–November 1990
Gender and Representation, Zoller Gallery, Penn State University, University Park, Pa.	February 1991
The Political Arm, John Weber Gallery, New York, N.Y.	February 1991
Show of Strength, Anne Plumb Gallery, New York, N.Y.	April–May 1991
The Art of Advocacy, The Aldrich Museum of Contemporary Art, Ridgefield, Conn.	May–September 1991
Awards in the Visual Arts:	
Hirshhorn Museum, Washington, D.C.	June–September 1991
The Albuquerque Museum of Art, History and Science, Albuquerque, N. Mex.	September–December 1991
The Toledo Museum of Art, Toledo, Ohio	December–January 1991
Visions/Revisions, Denver Art Museum, Denver, Colo.	April–August 1991
What It's Like, What It Is, #3, Dislocations, Museum of Modern Art, New York, N.Y.	October–December 1991
Open Mind: The LeWitt Collection, Wadsworth Atheneum, Hartford, Conn.	August–December 1991
Salvage Utopia, AC Project Room, New York, N.Y.	October 1991
Affrirmative Re-Actions, Iris and B. Gerald Cantor Art Gallery, Worcester, Mass.	November 1991
Artists of Conscience: 16 Years of Social and Political Commentary, New York, N.Y.	November–January 1991
Dispossessed Installations, Florida State University, Tallahassee, Fla.	August–September 1992
Dream Singers, Story Tellers: An African American Presence:	
Fukui Fine Arts Museum, Fukuyi-ken, Japan	November 1992–1993
New Jersey State Museum, Trenton, N.J.	August 1993–March 1994
Then & Now: A Selection of Artists Who Early in Their Museum Careers Exhibited at the Aldrich Museum of Contemporary Art of Ridgefield, Connecticut, Philippe Staib Gallery, New York, N.Y. Curated by Buzz McCall	April–May 1992
Book Works: A Women's Perspective, New Loom House, London, England	March–April 1992
Documenta 9, Kassel, Germany (declined)	May–August 1992
10: Artist as Catalyst, The Alternative Museum, New York, N.Y.	November 1992–February 1993
Will/Power, Wexner Center for the Arts, Ohio State University, Columbus, Ohio	September–December 1992
Mistaken Identities, University Art Museum, University of California at Santa Barbara, Santa Barbara, Calif.; Kunstverein, Graz, Austria	April–May 1993
Here's Looking at Me: Contemporary Self Portraits, Espace Lyonnais d'art contemporain, Lyon, France	January–April 1993

44th Annual Purchase Exhibition, American Academy and Institute of Arts and Letters, New York, N.Y.	November–December 1992
The Boundary Rider: 9th Biennale of Sydney, Gallery of New South Wales, Sydney, Australia	December 1992–March 1993
The Theater of Black Refusal: Black Art and Mainstream Criticism, University of California, Irvine, Fine Arts Gallery, Irvine, Calif.	April–May 1993
25 Years, Cleveland Center for Contemporary Art, Cleveland, Ohio	September–November 1993
Kontext Kunst, Neue Galerie, Graz, Austria	October 1993
Ciphers of Identity, Fine Arts Gallery, University of Maryland, Baltimore County (traveling)	November 1993–January 1994
L'Hiver de l'amour, Musée d'Art Moderne, Paris, France	February–March 1994
Can You Always Believe Your Eyes? Museum of Contemporary Art, De Beyerd, Breda, Holland	April–May 1994
Dignity for All: Reflections on Humanity, Artimo, Zeist, Holland	June–August 1994
Thirty Years, Larry Aldridge Museum of Contemporary Art, Ridgefield, Conn.	May–September 1994
Mappings, The Museum of Modern Art, New York, N.Y.	October–December 1994
The Winter of Love, Institute of Contemporary Art (P.S. 1), Long Island City, N.Y.	October 1994–January 1995
Articulate, Mary Delahoyd Gallery, New York, N.Y.	December 1994–January 1995
Gewalt/Geschäfte, Neue Gesellschaft für bildende Kunst e.V., Berlin, Germany	December 1994–February 1995
Black Male: Representations of Masculinity in Contemporary American Art. Curated by Thelma Golden, Whitney Museum of American Art, New York, N.Y.	November 1994–March 1995
Civil Rights Now, Southeastern Center for Contemporary Art, Winston-Salem, N.C.	January–April 1995
The Message Is the Medium: Issues of Representation in Modern Technologies, Castle Gallery College of New Rochelle, New Rochelle, N.Y.	February–April 1995
Public/Private: ARS 95, Museum of Contemporary Art, Finnish National Gallery, Helsinki, Finland	February–May 1995
Africus: South African Biennale, Johannesburg, South Africa	February–April 1995
Altered States: American Art in the 90s, Forum for Contemporary Art, St. Louis, Missouri	March–May 1995
Civil Rights Now, Cleveland Center of Contemporary Art, Cleveland, Ohio	May–August 1995
It's Not a Picture, Galleria Emi Fontana, Milan, Italy	May–June 1995
Options 2: Selections from the Modern and Contemporary Permanent Collection, Stanton Gallery, Denver Art Museum, Denver, Col.	June 1995–
Cornered, The Paula Cooper Gallery, New York, N.Y.	July–August 1995
Reconsidering the Object of Art: 1965–1975, Museum of Contemporary Art, Los Angeles, Calif. (withdrawn due to Philip Morris sponsorship)	October 1995–January 1996
Art with Conscience, Newark Art Museum, Newark, N.J.	November 1995–February 1996
Now Here, Louisiana Museum of Modern Art, Humlebaek, Denmark	May–September 1996
Hidden in Plain Sight: Illusion in Art from Jasper Johns to Virtual Reality, Los Angeles County Museum of Art, Los Angeles, Ca.	October 1996–January 1997
Devant l'histoire, Centre Georges Pompidou, Paris, France	December 1996–April 1997

Performances

Meat into Meat, loft performance, New York, N.Y.	October 1968
Untitled Catalysis, Max's Kansas City, New York, N.Y.	April 1970
Streetworks, New York, N.Y.	May 1970
Catalysis Series, streets of New York, N.Y.	1970–1971
Streetworks II, New York, N.Y.	April 1971
Food for the Spirit, Private Loft Performance, New York, N.Y.	June–July 1971
Untitled Streetworks, streets of New York, N.Y.	1971–1973
Two Untitled Streetworks, Rochester, N.Y.	April 1972

Untitled Streetwork, Rhode Island School of Design, Providence, R.I.	October 1973
Being Mythic on the Street, for "Adrian Piper: The Mythic Being," in *Other Than Art's Sake,* a film by Peter Kennedy	October 1973
Some Reflective Surfaces, The Fine Arts Building, New York, N.Y.	December 1975
Some Reflective Surfaces, The Whitney Museum, New York, N.Y.	February 1976
The Mythic Being, streets of Cambridge, Mass.	1975–1976
Danke(sehr)schon, Kurfurstendamm, West Berlin, West Germany	September 1977
Collegium Academicum Freischrei, Hauptstrasse, Heidelberg, West Germany	February 1978
It's Just Art:	
Allen Memorial Museum, Oberlin, Ohio	April 1980
Contemporary Art Institute of Detroit, Detroit, Mich.	July 1980
Wright Gallery, Dayton, Ohio	October 1980
The Western Front, Vancouver, B.C., Canada	February 1981
And/Or, Seattle, Wash.	February 1981
Artists' Space, New York, N.Y.	April 1981
Penn State University, University Park, Pa.	May 1981
Wide Receiver, streets of Menlo Park, Calif.	October 1982
Invasion, Streets of Palo Alto, Calif.	December 1982
Funk Lessons:	
Nova Scotia College of Art and Design, Halifax, Nova Scotia	March 1983
Walker Art Center and the Minneapolis College of Art and Design, Minneapolis, Minn.	October 1983
University of California at Berkeley, Berkeley, Calif.	November 1983
San Francisco Art Institute, San Francisco, Calif.	February 1984
The Women's Building, Los Angeles, Calif.	March 1984
California Institute of Art, Los Angeles, Calif.	March 1984
New Langton Arts, San Francisco, Calif.	March 1984
Funk Lessons (videotape), *What's Cooking, VI,* Center for Music Experiment, University of California at San Diego, La Jolla, Calif.	February 1985
My Calling (Card) #1, dinner/cocktail party reactive guerrilla performance	April 1986–1990
My Calling (Card) #2, disco/bar reactive guerrilla performance	May 1986–1990
My Calling (Cards) #1 and #2: A Meta-performance I, Randolph Street Gallery, Chicago, Ill.	February 1987
My Calling (Card) #1 and #2: A Meta-performance II, The Studio Museum of Harlem, New York, N.Y.	May 1988

Videotapes

The Mythic Being (1973) in *Other Than Art's Sake,* by Peter Kennedy

Some Reflective Surfaces (1975; edited by Bob Boilen, 1987)

Funk Lessons (1984; produced by Sam Samore), distributed by The Kitchen, New York, N.Y.

Funk Lessons: A Metaperformance (1987; edited by VQ Productions)

My Calling (Cards) #1 and #2: A Meta performance I (1987; edited by Bob Boilen)

My Calling (Cards) #1 and #2: A Meta performance II (1988; edited by Videosphere)

Cornered, video installation (1988; edited by Bob Boilen)

The Big Four-Oh, video installation (1988; edited by Bob Boilen)

My Calling (Card) #1: A Double Metaperformance, (1987–1988; edited by Videosphere)

Out of the Corner, video installation (1990; edited by Dekart)

Please God (1991; produced by Videosphere)

What It's Like, What It is #1 (video installation; produced by Videosphere/WPA)

What It's Like, What It is #3 (video installation; produced by Videosphere/GWTV)

Ur-Madonna (1992; produced by Plus Ultra, Seville)

Publications in Art and Art Criticism

"Untitled," *0 to 9*, no. 5 (December 1968).

"Untitled," *0 to 9*, no. 6 (July 1969).

"Untitled," *Streetworks* (July 1969).

"Untitled," *Art Press*, no. 1 (August 1969).

"Three Models of Art Productions Systems," in *Information* (New York: Museum of Modern Art, 1970); reprinted in *Conceptual Art*, ed. Ursula Meyer (New York: E. P. Dutton, 1972)

"Untitled," *Free Media Bulletin* (London: Ted Hawke Press, 1971), No. 12.

"Groups" (collated by Lucy Lippard), *Studio International* (March 1970), 95.

"An Ongoing Essay," *Art and Artists* (March 1972), 42–46.

"Selections from 'An Ongoing Essay,'" in *Six Years: The Dematerialization of the Art Object*, ed. Lucy Lippard (New York: Praeger, 1973). Reprinted in Blake Stimson and Alex Alberro, Eds. *Conceptual Art* (Cambridge, MA.: MIT Press, forthcoming)

"Untitled," in *Six Years: The Dematerialization of the Art Object*, ed. Lucy Lippard (New York: Praeger, 1973).

"Withdrawal Statement (from New York Cultural Center), in *Six Years: The Dematerialization of the Art Object*, ed. Lucy Lippard (New York: Praeger, 1973).

"In Support of Meta-Art," *Artforum* 12, no. 2 (October 1973), 79–81.

"A Political Statement," *Art-Rite* 6 (Summer 1974).

"Notes on the Mythic Being," *Tri-Quarterly* (Winter 1974).

Talking to Myself: The Ongoing Autobiography of an Art Object (published in English-Italian in Bari, Italy: Marilena Bonomo, 1975; published in English-French in Brussels, Belgium: Fernand Spillemaeckers, 1974).

"To Art (Reg. Intrans. V.)," *The Fox* 1, no. 1, (1975).

"A Proposal for Pricing Works of Art," *The Fox* 1, no. 2 (1975).

"The Mythic Being: I/You (Her)," in *Individuals: Post-Movement Art*, ed. Alan Sondheim (New York: E. P. Dutton, 1976).

"Notes on the Mythic Being, I–II," in *Individuals: Post-Movement Art*, ed. Alan Sondheim (New York: E. P. Dutton, 1976).

"Some Reflective Surfaces," *Sun and Moon* 2 Spring 1976), 18–20.

"Untitled (1968)," in *Essaying Essays: Alternative Forms of Exposition*, ed. Richard Kostelanetz (New York: Out of London Press, 1976).

"Untitled (1969)," in *Essaying Essays: Alternative Forms of Exposition*, ed. Richard Kostelanetz (New York: Out of London Press, 1976).

"Cheap Art Utopia," *Art-Rite* 14 (Winter 1976–1977), 11–12.

"I Embody," in *From The Center: Feminist Essays on Women's Art*, ed. Lucy Lippard (New York: E. P. Dutton, 1976).

"This Is Not the Documentation of a Performance," *Studio International* 193, no. 987 (Summer 1978), 200–201.

"Critics' Delight," in *A Critical Assembling*, ed. Richard Kostelanetz (New York: Participation Project Foundation, 1979).

"Political Self-Portrait #2 (Race)" (text only), *Heresies 2: Third World Women,* no. 4 (1979), 37–38.

"Where's the Art?" *Matrix 56: Adrian Piper* (Hartford, Conn.: Wadsworth Atheneum, 1980).

"Is the Alternative Space a True Alternative?" (compiled by Rudolph Baranik), *Studio International* 195, no. 990, (1980), 72.

"Some Political Self-Reflections (July 1980)," in *Issue* (London: Institute of Contemporary Art, November 1980).

"Some Thoughts on the Political Character of This Situation," in *Art of Conscience* (Dayton, Ohio: Wright University, November 1980).

"Untitled Art-Political Meditation," *The Village Voice* (February 4, 1981), 62.

"Food for the Spirit," *High Performance* 4, no. 1 (Spring 1981).

"It's Just Art," *High Performance* 4, no. 1 (Spring 1981).

"Ideology, Confrontation, and Political Self-Awareness: An Essay," *High Performance* 4, no. 1 (Spring 1981); reprinted in *Blasted Allegories: An Anthology of Writings by Contemporary Artists,* ed. Brian Wallis (New York: New Museum Of Contemporary Art/MIT Press, 1987).

"Performance and the Fetishism of the Art Object," *Vanguard* 10, no. 10, (December 1981–January 1982), 16–19; reprinted in *Essays on Performance and Cultural Politicization: Open Letter, 5–6,* ed. Bruce Barber, Fifth Series, (Summer–Fall 1983), 7–17.

"Critical Hegemony and the Division of Labor in Art," *Position Paper for the Visual Arts Seminar on Art Criticism,* September 19–20, 1983, Proceedings of the National Endowment for the Arts 1983 (Washington, D.C.: The National Endowment for the Arts, 1984).

"Letter to Thomas McEvilley," *Artforum* 22, no. 2 (October 1983), 2–3.

"Selected Funk Lessons: A Page Project by Adrian Piper," *Artforum* 22, no. 5 (January 1984), 64.

"Untitled Statement," in *The Art of Memory/The Loss of History* (New York: New Museum of Contemporary Art, 1985), 34.

"A Tale of Avarice and Poverty," *WhiteWalls* 15 (Winter 1987), 70–81.

"Flying," *Adrian Piper: Reflections 1967–1987* (retrospective catalog; New York: Alternative Museum, 1987); reprinted in *Adrian Piper* (catalog to accompany exhibition at Ikon Gallery, Birmingham, England, September 1991).

"It's Not All Black and White" (Letters to the Editor), *The Village Voice,* June 9, 1987, 4, 6.

"Who Is Safely White?" *Women Artists News* 12, no. 2 (June 1987), 6.

"An Open Letter to Donald Kuspit," *Real Life* 17–18 (Winter 1987–Spring 1988), 2–11.

"Xenophobia and the Indexical Present," and "Funk Lessons," in *Re-Imaging America: The Arts of Social Change,* ed. Mark O'Brien (Philadelphia: New Society Press, 1990); reprinted in *Kontext Kunst,* ed. Peter Weibel (Köln: DuMont Buchverlag, 1994), 490–498 (and cover).

"That Was Then/This Is Now" (incorporating selections from "Form and Idea" [1968], "Concrete Space-Time-Infinity Piece" [1968], "Ways of Adverting One's Gaze" [1988], and "My Calling [Card] #1" [1986–1988]), *Flashart* 143 (November–December 1988).

"On Conceptual Art," *Flashart* 143 (November–December 1988).

"A Paradox of Conscience," *The New Art Examiner* 16, no. 8 (April 1989), 27–31.

"Cornered," *Balcon* 4 (1989), 122–135.

"How Can Anybody Want to Wipe You Out Just for Being Different?" (Wonder Project), *Artforum* 28, no. 10 (Summer 1989), 135.

"The Triple Negation of Colored Women Artists," *Next Generation,* catalog (Chapel Hill: University of North Carolina, 1990); reprinted in *At the Crossroads* 3 (Summer–Fall 1994), 14–18.

"Girl Talk (#1–#3)," *ArtVu* 4, no. 1 (July 1990).

"Goodbye to Easy Listening," in *Adrian Piper: PRETEND* (New York: John Weber Gallery, 1990).

"The Joy of Marginality," *Art Papers* 14, 4 (July–August 1990), 12–13; reprinted in *Ikon 12–13: The Nineties* (1991–1992), 3–7.

"Introduction to Epistemology," *Real Life* 20 (1990), 18–19.

"Artist Statement," in *Words and Images with a Message* (catalog to accompany exhibition at the Women's Studio Workshop, 1990).

"Xenophobia and the Individual Present," *Cover* (September 1990), 14.

"Letter to the Editor," *Art in America,* November 1990, 39.

"Untitled Statement," in *Reimaging America: A Voice of Dissent Project,* catalog (Philadelphia: Momenta Art Gallery, 1991).

"Vanilla Nightmares 1986–," *Drawings,* catalog (New York: John Weber Gallery, 1991), 34–35.

"A Transition into Solipsism October 1971," in *The Political Arm* (New York: John Weber Gallery, 1991), 32–33.

"Letter to the Editor," *Artforum* 29, no. 9 (May 1991), 27–28.

Colored People (London: Bookworks, 1991).

"Aspekte des liberalen Dilemmas," *Texte zur Kunst* 1, Jahrgang Nr. 3 (Summer 1991), 54–57.

"Letter to the Editor: Angle Dangle," *City Paper* 11, no. 29 (July 19–25, 1991), 4.

"Goodbye to Easy Listening," in *Adrian Piper: Pretend* (New York: John Weber Gallery, 1990); reprinted in *Aphros Review* (Pace University) 31 (Spring–Summer 1991), 34–40.

"Brenson on Quality," *Art Papers* 15, no. 6, (November–December 1991), 68–73.

"What It Isn't #2," *The City Paper* 11, no. 33 (August 16–22, 1991), 4.

"Adrian Piper," *MOMA Members Quarterly* (Fall 1991), 8.

"Cornered: A Video Installation Project By Adrian Piper," *Movement Research Performance Journal* 4, (Winter–Spring 1992), 10.

Artists of Conscience, Alternative Museum Publication (December 1991–January 1992), 65.

"Art and Politics: A Pre-Election Symposium" *Art in America* 10 (October 1992), 41.

"Government Support for Unconventional Works of Art," in Andrew Buchwalter, Ed. *Culture and Democracy: Social and Ethical Issues in Public Support for the Arts and Humanities* (Boulder: Westview Press, 1992); reprinted in *Recommendations to the Clinton Administration on the NEA.*

Decide Who You Are (texts) (New York: Paula Cooper Gallery, 1992).

"Passing for White, Passing for Black" *Transition* 58 (1992), 4–32; reprinted in *New Feminist Criticism: Art-Identity-Action,* ed. Joanna Frueh, Cassandra L. Langer, and Arlene Raven (New York: Harper Collins 1994), 216–247; excerpted in *Utne Reader* (November–December 1994), 87–88. Reprinted in Elaine K. Ginsberg, Ed. *Passing and the Fictions of Identity* (Durham: Duke University Press, 1996); and in Rebecca Kaminsky, Ed. *Cross Talk: A Multicultural Feminist Symposium* (Cambridge, MA: MIT Press, 1996).

"The Logic of Modernism," *Flashart* 26, no. 168 (January–February 1993), 56–58, 118, 136; reprinted in *Callaloo* 16, no. 3 (Summer 1993); *Kontext Kunst,* ed. Peter Weibel (Köln: DuMont Buchverlag, 1994), 282–288, cover.

"Xenophobia and the Indexical Present II: Lecture," *Place Position Presentation Public,* ed. Ine Gevers (Den Haag, Netherlands: Jan Van Eyck Akademie, 1993), 24, 136–157.

Introductory essay, *New Observations* 97 (September–October 1993), 2–4.

"What's Art? (What's Not?)," *The Washington Post,* Sunday, October 24, 1993, G-6.

"On Louise Bourgeois," *Louise Bourgeois* (Washington, D.C.: Corcoran Gallery, 1993).

"The Great War for Control of Reality," *Ethics of Change: Women in the '90s—Sex, Power and Politics* [with Patricia Ireland and Phyllis Schlafly], ed. Barbara J. Raines. *The Proceedings of the February Forums, Volume VII* (New Smyrna Beach: The Atlantic Center for the Arts, 1993), 95–161.

Modern Art and Society, ed. Maurice Berger (New York: Harper Collins, 1994); cover.

"Vanilla Nightmares #17" (cover), in David Roediger, *Towards the Abolition of Whiteness* (New York: Verso, 1994).

"You Don't Want Me Here," *Ik + De Ander* (Amsterdam: Beurs van Berlage, 1994), 119.

"Political Self-Portrait #3;" Selections from *Talking to Myself: The Ongoing Autobiography of an Art Object; Notes on the Mythic Being; Political Self-Portraits #1, 2, 3; My Calling (Card) #1; Cornered;* "Higher-Order Discrimination," in *Voicing Today's Visions: Writings by Contemporary Women Artists,* ed. Mara Witzling (New York: Universe, 1994), 286–308.

"My Calling (Cards) #1 and 2," *Long News in the Short Century* 5 (1994), 86–87.

"Four Intruders plus Alarm Systems," "Safe" (monologues), in *Feminism and Tradition in Aesthetics,* ed. Peggy Zeglin Brand and Carolyn Korsmeyer (University Park: Pennsylvania State University Press, 1995), 235–244.

"On 1980s Feminist Theorizing," *October* 71 (Winter 1995), 35–36.

"Decide Who You Are," *Reframings: New American Feminist Photographers,* Ed. Diane Neumaier (Philadelphia: Temple University Press, 1995)

"Mortal Remains," *Mortal Remains,* ed. Ricardo Bloch and Don Celender (Minneapolis: Intermedia Arts Minnesota, 1996).

"Withdrawal Clarified," (letter) *Art in America 84,* 4 (April 1996), 29.

Publications in Philosophy

"Utility, Publicity, and Manipulation," *Ethics* 88, no. 3 (April 1978), 189–206.

"Property and the Limits of the Self," *Political Theory* 8, no. 1 (February 1980), 39–64; reprinted in *The International Library of Legal and Political Philosophy,* ed. Thomas Campbell (London: Dartmouth Press, 1992).

"A Distinction without a Difference," *Midwest Studies in Philosophy 7: Social and Political Philosophy* (1982), 403–435.

"The Rationality of Military Service," in *Conscripts and Volunteers: Military Requirements, Social Values, and the All-Volunteer Force,* ed. Robert Fullinwider, Maryland Studies in Public Philosophy (Totowa, N.J.: Rowman and Allenheld, 1983), 126–147.

"Critical Hegemony and Aesthetic Acculturation," *Nous* 19, no. 1 (1985), 29–40.

"Two Conceptions of the Self," *Philosophical Studies* 48, no. 2 (September 1985), 173–197; reprinted in *The Philosopher's Annual* 8 (1985), 222–246.

Review of *Goods and Virtues,* by Michael Slote, *The Journal of Philosophy* 83, no. 8 (August 1986), 468–473.

"Instrumentalism, Objectivity, and Moral Justification," *American Philosophical Quarterly* 23, no. 4 (October 1986), 373–381.

"Moral Theory and Moral Alienation," *The Journal of Philosophy* 84, no. 2 (February 1987), 102–118.

"Personal Continuity and Instrumental Rationality in Rawls' Theory of Justice," *Social Theory and Practice* 13, no. 1 (Spring 1987), 49–76.

"Pseudorationality," in *Perspectives on Self-Deception,* ed. Amelie O. Rorty and Brian McLaughlin (Los Angeles: University of California Press, 1988), 297–323.

Review of *The Emergence of Norms* by Edna Ullmann-Margalit, *The Philosophical Review* 97, no. 1 (January 1988), 99–107.

"Hume on Rational Final Ends," *Philosophy Research Archives* 14 (1988–1989), 193–228; reprinted in *Hume on Reason and the Passions,* ed. Marcia Lind (forthcoming).

"Higher-Order Discrimination," in *Identity, Character and Morality,* ed. Owen Flanagan and Amelie O. Rorty (Cambridge, Mass.: MIT Press, 1990), 285–309; reprinted in condensed form in the monograph series Studies on Ethics in Society (Kalamazoo: Western Michigan University, 1990).

"Seeing Things,'" *Southern Journal of Philosophy* 29, Supplementary Volume: Moral Epistemology (1990), 29–60.

"Impartiality, Compassion, and Modal Imagination," *Ethics* 101, no. 4, Symposium on Impartiality and Ethical Theory (July 1991), 726–757.

"Government Support for Unconventional Works of Art," in *Culture and Democracy: Social and Ethical Issues in Public Support for the Arts and Humanities,* ed. Andrew Buchwalter (Boulder: Westview Press, 1992).

"Xenophobia and Kantian Rationalism," *Philosophical Forum* 24, no. 1–3 (Fall–Spring 1992–1993), 188–232. Reprinted in *Feminist Interpretations of Kant,* ed. Robin M. Schott (University Park: Pennsylvania State University Press, forthcoming).

"Two Kinds of Discrimination," *Yale Journal of Criticism* 6, no. 1 (1993), 25–74.

"Kant on the Objectivity of the Moral Law," in *Reclaiming the History of Ethics: Essays for John Rawls,* Ed. Andrews Reath, Christine M. Korsgaard, and Barbara Herman (New York: Cambridge University Press, 1996).

"Making Sense of Value," *Ethics 106,* 2 (April 1996), 525–537.

"The Form of Self-Knowledge in Kant's Metaethics," *Diskursparadigma: Form,* Ed. Georg Schölhammer (Vienna: Suhrkamp Verlag, forthcoming).

Invited Lectures and Conferences on Art

Mount Holyoke College, South Hadley, Mass.	November 1971
"Art and Politics" panel, The Art Students' League, New York, N.Y.	May 1972
Creative Artists Public Service Grants panel, New York, N.Y.	January 1973
"Conceptual Art" panel, The New School for Social Research, New York, N.Y.	March 1973
Skidmore College, Saratoga Springs, N.Y.	May 1973
Rhode Island School of Design, Providence, R.I.	April 1974
Massachusetts College of Art, Boston, Mass.	March 1977
Wadsworth Atheneum, Hartford, Conn.	March 1980
Oberlin College, Oberlin, Ohio	April 1980
NEA Conference on Art and Social Change, Contemporary Arts Center, Cincinnati, Ohio	June 1980
And/Or, Seattle, Wash.	February 1981
Emily Carr College of Art, Vancouver, B.C., Canada	February 1981
Franklin Furnace, New York, N.Y.	April 1981
Penn State University, University Park, Pa.	May 1981
NEA Conference on Funding the Visual Arts, Los Angeles Museum of Contemporary Art, Los Angeles, Calif.	October 1982
Banff Centre, School of Fine Arts, Banff, Canada	November 1982
National Exhibition Centre, Castlegar, B.C., Canada	November 1982
Panel on Dance and the Other Arts, Stanford University, Stanford, Calif.	February 1983
Nova Scotia College of Art and Design, Halifax, N.S.	March 1983
NEA Visual Artists' Fellowship Selection Panel (Conceptual/Performance/New Genres), Washington, D.C.	April 1983
Berkeley Art Department, University of California at Berkeley, Berkeley, Calif.	May 1983
NEA Seminar on Art Criticism, Washington, D.C.	September 1983
NEA Policy Panel, Washington, D.C.	October 1983
University of Wisconsin, Madison, Wis.	October 1983
Moderator and Panelist for Symposium, "The Power of Art: The Language of Images," Walker Art Center and the Minneapolis College of Art and Design, Minneapolis, Minn.	October 1983
Minneapolis College of Art and Design, Minneapolis, Minn.	October 1983
San Francisco Art Institute, San Francisco, Calif.	February 1983
California Institute of Art, Los Angeles, Calif.	March 1984

The Women's Building, Los Angeles, Calif.	March 1984
Foundation for Art Resources, Los Angeles, Calif.	March 1984
The Kitchen, New York, N.Y.	March 1984
University of California at San Diego, La Jolla, Calif.	March 1984
NEA Art Critics' Fellowship Selection Panel, Washington, D.C.	April 1984
Panelist, Ohio Arts Council, Columbus, Ohio	March 1986
Symposiast, "What Do Artists Read?" ARLIS/College Art Association Convention, New York, N.Y.	March 1986
Symposiast, "Tracking the Avant-Garde," Chicago Art Institute, Chicago, Ill.	April 1986
Antioch College, Yellow Springs, Ohio	May 1986
Martin Luther King Commemorative Lecture, Cleveland Museum of Art, Cleveland, Ohio	January 1987
Panelist, "Identity, The Politics of," WCA Conference, Boston, Mass.	February 1987
Time Arts Seminar, Chicago Art Institute, School of the Arts, Chicago, Ill.	February 1987
Dialogue Criticism Workshop: "The Impact of Criticism," Contemporary Arts Center, Cincinnati, Ohio	May 1987
Maryland Art Place, Baltimore, Md.	September 1987
Nexus Gallery, Atlanta, Ga.	November 1987
Feminist Art Institute, New York, N.Y.	January 1988
Maryland Arts Council, Baltimore, Md.	February 1988
"Modernist Controversies," Vancouver Art Gallery, University of British Columbia, Vancouver, B.C., Canada	February 1988
Rutgers University, New Brunswick, N.J.	March 1988
University of Akron, Akron, Ohio	April 1988
Panelist, Art Matters, Inc., New York, N.Y.	April 1988
Panelist, "The Ideology of the Margin," The New Museum of Contemporary Art, New York, N.Y.	May 1988
International Design Conference, Aspen, Colo.	June 1988
Panelist, The Artists' Foundation, Boston, Mass.	June 1988
Panelist, "The End of the Decade," The New Museum, New York, N.Y.	July 1988
Orcas Conference, Seattle, Wash.	November 1988
Panelist, Art Matters, Inc., New York, N.Y.	November 1988
"Xenophobia and the Indexical Present," Moore College of Art, Philadelphia, Pa.	March 1989
City Sites: Artists and Urban Strategies, California College of Arts and Crafts, Oakland, Calif.	March 1989
Artists Advisory Panel, The New Museum of Contemporary Art, New York, N.Y.	April 1989
Western Washington University, Bellingham, Wash.	April 1989
Commencement Address, Nova Scotia College of Art and Design, Halifax, N.S., Canada	April 1989
"Art and Politics" panel, The Jewish Museum, New York, N.Y.	May 1989
"Ideology, Confrontation," Readings from *Blasted Allegories,* The New Museum, New York, N.Y.	June 1989
Public Art Dialogue: Southeast, Durham, N.C.	June 1989
Matrix Gallery, University Art Museum, Berkeley, Calif.	September 1989
University of Washington, Seattle, Wash.	September 1989
University of Colorado, Boulder, Colo.	October 1989
Second Feminist Art History Conference, Barnard College, New York, N.Y.	October, 1989
Art Department, University of Arizona, Tucson, Ariz.	November 1989
Hunter College, New York, N.Y.	November 1989
Dia Art Foundation, New York, N.Y.	November 1989
Maryland Institute College of Art, Baltimore, Md	November 1989
Art Department, Franklin and Marshall College, Lancaster, Pa.	November 1989

Williams College, Williamstown, Mass.	January 1990
Art Department, Western Michigan University, Kalamazoo, Mich.	January 1990
Fresno State University, Fresno, Calif.	February 1990
Art Department, Illinois State University, Normal, Ill.	February 1990
"De Facto Racism in the Visual Arts," College Art Association Convention, New York, N.Y.	February 1990
Women's Caucus for Art, College Art Association Convention, New York, N.Y.	February 1990
University of Colorado, Boulder, Colo.	March 1990
Williams College, Williamstown, Mass.	March 1990
Seminars With Artists, Whitney Museum, New York, N.Y.	March 1990
Whitney Museum Independent Study Program Seminar, New York, N.Y.	March 1990
Power Plant Gallery, Toronto, Canada	May 1990
NEA Interarts: New Forms Grant Selection Panel, Washington, D.C.	May 1990
Installations Grants Panel, Franklin Furnace, New York, N.Y.	May 1990
"The Next Generation," Southeastern Center for Contemporary Art, Winston-Salem, N.C.	July 1990
Panelist, "Another Look at the Art Journals," Whitney Museum of American Art, New York, N.Y.	October 1990
Exhibition Lecture, Film and Video Gallery, Whitney Museum of American Art, New York, N.Y.	October 1990
Wooster Art Museum, Wooster, Ohio	October 1990
Keynote Address, Society for Photographic Education Annual Convention, New Orleans, La.	March 1991
"Brenson on Quality," Panel on Quality, Smithsonian Institution, Washington, D.C.	May 1991
Hirshhorn Museum, Washington, D.C.	June 1991
"Xenophobia and the Indexical Present," Andrew J. Cardiff Ritchie Lecture, Yale University, New Haven, Conn.	September 1991
Ikon Gallery, Birmingham, England	November 1991
"Xenophobia and the Indexical Present," Museum of Modern Art, New York, N.Y.	January 1992
Brown University, Providence, R.I.	January 1992
Walker Art Center, Minneapolis, Minn.	February 1992
"Place Position Presentation Public," Jan Van Eyck Akademie, Maastricht, Holland	April 1992
Bard College, Annandale-on-Hudson, N.Y.	April 1992
Keynote Address, "Xenophobia and the Indexical Present," "Preparing for Pluralism: Meeting the Challenges for an Inclusive Society," The Multicultural Institute, Washington, D.C.	May 1992
Commencement Address, California Institute of the Arts, Valencia, Calif.	May 1992
Documenta IX, Kassel, Germany	July 1992
Kettles Yard, Cambridge, England	July 1992
Expo '92/Plus Ultra, Moguer, Spain	July 1992
"Xenophobia and the Indexical Present," Conference: *What Does The Critique of Pure Reason Have to Do with the Pure Critique of Racism? A Look at the Work of Adrian Piper,* New York University Philosophy Department, Performance Studies Department, and Grey Art Gallery, New York, N.Y.	October 1992
Opening Plenary Address, American Society for Aesthetics 50th Anniversary Meeting, Philadelphia, Pa.	October 1992
Kunstverein Munich, Munich, Germany	November 1992
Wexner Center, Columbus, Ohio	November 1992
Sydney Biennale, Sydney, Australia	December 1992
Main Speaker (with Patricia Ireland and Phyllis Schlafly), Conference, "Women in the 90's: Women, Sex, and Power," Atlantic Center for the Arts, New Smyrna Beach, Fla.	February 1993
"The Great War for Control of Reality" (multimedia event), Atlantic Center for the Arts, New Smyrna Beach, Fla.	February 1993

California University of Pennsylvania, California, Pa.	February 1993
Seminar on "Passing for White, Passing for Black," Committee on Culture and Society, New York University, New York, N.Y.	March 1993
Keynote Address, Conference: *Feminism and Art History,* University of Leeds, Leeds, England	September 1993
The City Gallery, Raleigh, N.C.	October 1993
"The Great War for Control of Reality" (multimedia event), Marquette University, Milwaukee, Wis.	October 1993
Baltimore Museum of Art, Baltimore, Md.	November 1993
Panel, "The Visual Arts Encounter: African Americans and Europe," Palais du Luxembourg, Paris, France	February 1994
State University of New York at Plattsburg, Plattsburg, N.Y.	February 1994
Wellington Gray Gallery, East Carolina State University, Greensboro, N.C.	March 1994
"Decide Who You Are" (reading), High Museum, Atlanta, Ga.	March 1994
Seminole Community College, Sanford, Fla.	April 1994
University of Washington, Seattle, Wash.	April 1994
Contemporary Art Institute, Paris, France	May 1994
"Alternative Spaces," panel, Museum of Modern Art, New York, N.Y.	May 1994
Commencement Address, Massachusetts College of Art, Boston, Mass.	May 1994
Rijksakademie, Amsterdam, Holland	June 1994
Panel, Beurs van Berlage, Amsterdam, Holland	June 1994
Panel, "Histories Properly Told," Alma Matthews House, New York, N.Y.	November 1994
"Kann Kunst eine soziale Wirkung haben?" (graduate seminar), Kunstakademie München, Munich, Germany	January 1995
"Wie beschreiben Sie Ihre Kunst?" (graduate seminar), Kunstakademie München, Munich, Germany	January 1995
"Form, Inhalt, und Mitteilungsstratagien" (public lecture), Kunstakademie München, Munich, Germany	January 1995
"Gewalt/Geschäfte" (panel), Neue Gesellschaft für bildende Kunst, Berlin, Germany	January 1995
Rice University, Houston, Tex.	February 1995
Syracuse University, Syracuse, N.Y.	February 1995
University of Maryland at Baltimore County, Baltimore, Md.	March 1995
"Recent Work 1988–1992," Savannah College of Art, Savannah, Ga.	October 1995
Modernist Utopias Conference, Musée d'Art Contemporain, Montréal, Quebec	December 1995
"Recent Work 1988–1992," Museum of Contemporary Art, Chicago, Il.	December 1995
Whitney Independent Study Program, New York, N.Y.	January 1996
Scripps College, Claremont Graduate School, Claremont, Ca.	February 1996
"Where Are We Going?" *Art at the End of the Century: A Dialogue,* Albright-Knox Art Gallery/SUNY Art Gallery, Buffalo, N.Y.	February 1996
Panel: "Who Is She? Conversations with Multi-Talented Women," Brandeis University, Rose Art Museum, Waltham, Mass.	March 1996
"Writing the Arts: When Language Meets Form," Pratt Institute, Brooklyn, N.Y.	June 1996
Panel: "Multikulturalismus und die Populärkultur," Universität zu Köln, Köln, Germany.	July 1996
Inaugural Ian Burn Memorial Lecture, Monash University Gallery, Melbourne, Australia.	July 1996
Inaugural Ian Burn Memorial Lecture, Museum of Contemporary Art, Sydney, Australia.	July 1996
Panel: "Conceptual Art," American Society for Aesthetics, Montreal, Canada.	October 1996

Invited Lectures and Conferences in Philosophy

"Good Reasons to Serve," Society for Philosophy and Public Affairs, American Philosophical Association Eastern Division Convention, Boston, Mass.	December 1980
Comments on Bart Gruzalski's "Utilitarianism, Slavery, and the Facts," Moral Philosophy Colloquium, American Philosophical Association Eastern Division Convention, Boston, Mass.	December 1980
"Good Reason to Serve," Military Conscription Working Group, The Center for Philosophy and Public Policy, Washington, D.C.	May 1981
"The Rationality of Military Conscription," Collective Action/ Social History Group, University of Michigan, Ann Arbor, Mich.	January 1982
"Two Conceptions of the Self," Stanford University Philosophy Department, Stanford, Calif.	December 1982
"Two Conceptions of the Self," University of California at Berkeley Philosophy Department, Berkeley, Calif.	February 1983
"Two Conceptions of the Self," University of Minnesota Philosophy Department, Minneapolis, Minn.	October 1983
Comments on Richard Galvin's "Act Individuation and Deontological Theories," Moral Philosophy Colloquium, American Philosophical Association Eastern Division Convention, Boston, Mass.	December 1983
"Performance: The Problematic Solution," Conference: *Philosophical Problems of the Self-Consciously Invented Arts,* The Kitchen, New York, N.Y.	March 1984
"Two Conceptions of the Self," University of Pennsylvania Philosophy Department, Philadelphia, Pa.	March 1984
"Creative Autonomy and Aesthetic Acculturation," Philosophy of Art Symposium, American Philosophical Association Western Division Convention, Chicago, Ill.	April 1985
"Narcissism and Moral Alienation," Wayne State Philosophy Department, Detroit, Mich.	November 1985
"Instrumentalism, Objectivity, and Moral Justification," Moral Philosophy Colloquium, American Philosophical Association Pacific Division Convention, Los Angeles, Calif.	March 1986
Comments on Lawrence Hinman's "Emotion, Morality, and Understanding," Moral Philosophy Colloquium, American Philosophical Association Central Division Convention, St. Louis, Mo.	May 1986
"Higher-Order Discrimination," George Washington University Philosophy Department, Washington, D.C.	November 1986
"Rationality and the Structure of the Self," Association for the Philosophy of the Unconscious, American Philosophical Association Eastern Division Convention, Boston, Mass.	December 1986
"Higher-Order Discrimination," Kennedy Institute of Ethics, Georgetown University, Washington, D.C.	January 1987
"The Meaning of 'Ought' and the Loss of Innocence," Conference: *The Personal Turn in Ethics,* University of Minnesota Philosophy Department, Minneapolis, Minn.	April 1987
"The Meaning of 'Ought' and the Loss of Innocence," Vassar College Philosophy Department, Poughkeepsie, N.Y.	October 1987
"Higher-Order Discrimination," Howard University Philosophy Department, Washington, D.C.	October 1987
"The Meaning of 'Ought' and the Loss of Innocence," University of Mississippi Philosophy Department, Oxford, Miss.	November 1987
"Higher-Order Discrimination," University of Mississippi Philosophy Department, Oxford, Miss.	November 1987
"Rationality and the Structure of the Self," University of Minnesota Philosophy Department, Minneapolis, Minn.	November 1987
"Rationality and the Structure of the Self," Columbia University Philosophy Department, New York, N.Y.	March 1988
"Higher-Order Discrimination," Conference: *Character and Morality,* hosted by Radcliffe and Wellesley Colleges, Cambridge, Mass.	April 1988
"Higher-Order Discrimination," Symposium: *Feminism and Racism,* American Philosophical Association Eastern Division Convention, Washington, D.C.	December 1988
Comments on Walter Schaller's "Should Kantians Care about Moral Worth?" Moral Philosophy Colloquium, American Philosophical Association Central Division Convention, Chicago, Ill.	April 1989
"The Meaning of 'Ought' and the Loss of Innocence," University of California, Los Angeles Philosophy Department, Los Angeles, Calif.	April 1989

"The Meaning of 'Ought' and the Loss of Innocence," University of Colorado at Boulder Philosophy Department, Boulder, Colo.	October 1989
"Impartiality, Compassion, and Modal Imagination," Wellesley College, Wellesley, Mass.	November 1989
"Higher-Order Discrimination," Franklin and Marshall College, Lancaster, Pa.	November 1989
"The Meaning of 'Ought' and the Loss of Innocence," Invited Address on Ethics, American Philosophical Association Eastern Division Convention, Atlanta, Ga.	December 1989
"Higher-Order Discrimination," Williams College, Williamstown, Mass.	January 1990
"Impartiality, Compassion, and Modal Imagination," Western Michigan University Philosophy Department, Kalamazoo, Mich.	January 1990
"Higher-Order Discrimination," Western Michigan University, Kalamazoo, Mich.	January 1990
"Impartiality, Compassion, and Modal Imagination," Purdue University Philosophy Department, West Lafayette, Ind.	March 1990
Impartiality, Compassion, and Modal Imagination," Illinois State University Philosophy Department, Normal, Ill.	March 1990
"Higher-Order Discrimination," Conference: *Ethics and Racism,* Brown University, Providence, R.I.	March 1990
"Impartiality, Compassion, and Modal Imagination," Conference: *Impartiality,* Hollins College, Roanoke, Va.	June 1990
"Seeing Things,'" Spindell Conference: *Moral Epistemology,* Memphis State University, Memphis, Tenn.	October 1990
"Impartiality, Compassion, and Modal Imagination," University of Connecticut Philosophy Department, Storrs, Conn.	December 1990
"Is There a Future for African-American Women in Philosophy?" Panel: *Problems Facing Women Philosophers: Towards an Agenda for the Nineties,* American Philosophical Association Central Division Convention, Chicago, Ill.	April 1991
Comments on Andrew Buchwalter's "Philosophy, Culture and Public Policy," Political Philosophy Colloquium, American Philosophical Association Eastern Division Convention, New York, N.Y.	December 1991
"Xenophobia and Kantian Rationalism," Cornell University Philosophy Department, Ithaca, N.Y.	February 1992
"Xenophobia and Kantian Rationalism," Conference: *What Does the Critique of Pure Reason Have to Do With the Pure Critique of Racism? A Look at the Work of Adrian Piper,* New York University Philosophy Department, Performance Studies Department, Grey Art Gallery, New York, N.Y.	October 1992
Comments on Stephen Beck's "Moral Considerability and the Goodness Principle," Moral Philosophy Colloquium, American Philosophical Association Eastern Division Convention, Washington, D.C.	December 1992
"The Meaning of 'Ought' and the Loss of Innocence," Mt. Holyoke Philosophy Department, S. Hadley, Mass.	September 1993
"The Meaning of 'Ought' and the Loss of Innocence," Marquette University of Philosophy Department, Milwaukee, Wis.	October 1993
Comments on Claudia Mills's "Goodness as Weapon," Moral Philosophy Colloquium, American Philosophical Association Eastern Division Convention, Atlanta, Ga.	December 1993
"The Obligations of Philosophical Performance," Philadelphia Philosophical Consortium, (co-speaker: Joyce Carol Oates), Philadelphia, Pa.	February 1994
"The Meaning of 'Ought' and the Loss of Innocence," Georgia State University Philosophy Department, Atlanta, Ga.	September 1994
"A Philosophical Analysis of Xenophobia," Public Lecture, Georgia State University, Atlanta, Ga.	September 1994
"The Meaning of 'Ought' and the Loss of Innocence," Oberlin College Philosophy Department, Oberlin, Ohio	October 1994
"Making Sense of Value," Author Meets Critics: Elizabeth Anderson's *Value in Ethics and Economics,* American Philosophical Association Pacific Division Convention, San Francisco, Calif.	March 1995
"Rationality and the Structure of the Self," Conference: *Moral Psychology and Moral Identity,* Oberlin College Philosophy Department, Oberlin, Ohio	April 1995
"The Form of Self-Knowledge in Kant's Metaethics," Symposium: *Diskursparadigma: Form,* University of Vienna, Vienna, Austria	June 1995

"A Kantian Analysis of Xenophobia," Plenary Address, VII. Symposium der Internationalen Assoziation von Philosophinnen, Vienna, Austria
September 1995

"The Meaning of 'Ought' and the Loss of Innocence," University of Utah Philosophy Department, Salt Lake City, Utah
November 1995

"The Meaning of 'Ought' and the Loss of Innocence," Scripps College, Claremont Graduate School, Claremont, Ca.
February 1996

"A Kantian Analysis of Xenophobia," New York Institute for the Humanities at New York University, New York, N.Y.
March 1996

"Rationality and the Structure of the Self: Kant's Two Standpoints on Action," Midwest Study Group of the North American Kant Society, Loyola University, Chicago, Ill.
April 1996

"A Kantian Analysis of Xenophobia," State University of New York at Stonybrook, Stonybrook, N.Y.
September 1996

"Judgment and Practice," Author Meets Critics: Barbara Herman's *The Practice of Moral Judgment,* American Philosophical Association Eastern Division Convention, Atlanta, Ga.
December 1996

Critical Reviews

"Adrian Piper," *The New Yorker* (October 29, 1990).

"Adrian Piper," *Downtown Express* 4, no. 23 (October 31, 1990).

"Adrian Piper," *American Visions* 6, no. 4, (August 1991), 12.

"Adrian Piper," *Dialogue* (November–December 1991), 35.

"Adrian Piper's Black Box/White Box," *Morning Edition,* WOSU Columbus, National Public Radio (September 28, 1992).

"Adrian Piper," *The Late Show,* British Broadcasting Company 2 Television (January 1992).

"Adrian Piper," *Today's Monitor,* Monitor Television (July 22, 1991).

"Adrian Piper," *Around Town* WETA-Washington, Public Broadcasting Service (February 11, 1993).

"The Artist," *The Renaissance,* Public Broadcasting Service (February 8, 1993).

"Art: Carl Andre/Group Show," *The New Yorker* (March 22, 1993), 18.

"Art: Piper Pulls Out of MOCA Show," Morning Report, *The Los Angeles Times,* Wednesday, November 22, 1995, F2

Adler, Sabine, "Wer hat Angst vorm schwarzen Mann?" Ausstellung, Adrian Piper im Munchener Kunstverein, *TZ München* (October 7, 1992).

Aletti, Vince, "The Power of Words," *The Village Voice* (July 13, 1990).

"Aletti, Vince, "Choices: The Political Arm," *The Village Voice* (February 19, 1991).

Als, Hilton, "Spotlight: Adrian Piper," *Flash Art* 147 (Summer 1989), 142–143.

Als, Hilton, "Adrian Piper's Ways of Seeing," *The Village Voice* (September 25, 1990), Arts Section cover, 55, 95.

Als, Hilton, "Choices, Video: Adrian Piper," *The VIllage Voice* (October 23, 1990), 124.

Anglesey, Zoe, "Putting Out the Word," *Reflex* (September–October, 1991).

Appiah, Anthony, "Art Beat," *The Village Voice Literary Supplement* (October 1992), 12.

Aquin, Stephane, "Pour la suite du monde: Histoire à suivre," *Voir* (June 4–10, 1992).

Art in America (editorial board), "1987 in Review," *Art in America Annual 1988–89* 76, no. 8 (August 1988), 53.

Avgikos, Jan, "Adrian Piper: John Weber Gallery, Paula Cooper, Grey Art Gallery," *Artforum* (December 1992), 91.

Babha, Homi, "Focus: Black Male: Representations of Masculinity in Contemporary American Art," *Artforum* (February 1995), 86.

Bailey, David A., "Adrian Piper: Aspects of the Liberal Dilemma," *Frieze* (October 1991), 14–15.

Baker, Kenneth, "NY MOMA'S 'Dislocations' Sets Its Ties, Distance from High Modernism," *San Francisco Chronicle* (December 8, 1991).

Baldauf, Anette, "Everybody Is Trying to Look Black," *Die Musikbox* (Vienna Radio, March 23, 1993).

Baldauf, Anette, "Rassismus und Fremdenangst: Gesprach mit der Konzeptkunstlerin und Philosophin Adrian Piper," *Wiener Zeitung Kulturmagazin* (Freitag 30, 1993), 16.

Barber, Bruce, "Adrian Piper," *Parachute* (Summer 1981), 45–46.

Barber, Bruce, "Performance as Social Intervention: Interview with Adrian Piper," *Parachute* (Fall 1981), 25–28.

Barden, Lane, "Mechanisms of Marginalization: Theater of Refusal at UCI Fine Arts Gallery," *Artweek* (May 6, 1993), 22.

Barr, Barbara, "Reply to Piper," *Women Artists News* 12, no. 2 (June 1987), 6; also see two subsequent issues for responses to Barr from Alicia Faxon, May Stevens, Judith Wilson, Howardena Pindell, and Josephine Withers.

Barrie, Lita, "Shedding Her Male Identity," *Artweek* (March 14, 1991).

Barrow, Claudia, "Adrian Piper: Space, Time, and Reference 1967–1970," in *Adrian Piper* (catalogue to accompany exhibition at Ikon Gallery, Birmingham, England, September 1991).

Becker, Von Jochen, "Politische Selbst-Portraits: Adrian Piper im Munchener Kunstverein," *Die Tagaszeitung*. Kultur, Berlin (Saturday, November 21, 1992), 17.

Berger, Maurice, "The Critique of Pure Racism: An Interview with Adrian Piper," *Afterimage* 18, no. 3 (October 1990), cover, 5–9.

Berger, Maurice, "Black Skin, White Masks: Adrian Piper and the Politics of Viewing," in *How Art Becomes History* (New York: Harper Collins, 1992), and cover, frontispiece.

Berger, Maurice, "Displacements," in *Ciphers of Identity* (Catonsville: University of Maryland Baltimore County, 1993), 13–41.

Berger, Maurice, "Skowhegan Medal for Sculpture/Installation: Adrian Piper," *Skowhegan Forty-Ninth Anniversary Awards* (New York: Skowhegan School of Painting and Sculpture, 1995), p.6

Berland, Dinah, "Black's a Color in Exhibit at the Museum of Art," *Long Beach Press-Telegram,* spotlight (Sunday June 25, 1989), D1-D3.

Biller, Gerry, Russell Bowman, and Dean Sobel, *Word as Image: American Art 1960–1990* (catalog to accompany exhibition at Milwaukee Art Museum, Milwaukee, Wis.).

Bishton, Derek, "Fear of the Other," *Creative Camera* (February–March 1992), 48–49.

Blase, Christophe, "Sezierte Angst -Eine politische Kunstlerin: Adrian Piper in Munchen," *Frankfurter Allgemeine Zeitung* (November 3, 1992).

Bode, Peter M., "Wer ist Schwarz und Wer is Weiss? Kunstverein, Die provozierende Anti-Rassismus-Schau der New Yorkerin Adrian Piper" *Abendzeitung* (October 8, 1992).

Bogardi, Georges, "Pour la suite de monde," *Canadian Art* (Fall 1992), 94–96.

Bonami, Francesco, "Dislocations: The Place of Installation," *Flash Art* 25, no. 162 (January–February 1992), 128.

Bond, Ruth M., "Piper's Philosophy," *City Paper* (June 28, 1991), 38.

Bonet, Eugeni, "Art Noves tecnologies: side i critica social en l'Art contemporani," *Avui* (September 23, 1992).

Bonetti, David, "Art Poser: Adrian Piper's Work Raises Racial Questions," *San Franciso Examiner* (Sunday, October 16, 1989), F1, F4.

Borger, Irene, "Funk Lessons: A Guerrilla Performance," *L.A. Weekly,* (March 28, 1984), 63–64.

Borger, Irene, "The Funk Lessons of Adrian Piper," *Helicon Nine* 14–15 (1986), 150–153.

Botterbusch, Vera, "Der Virus Rassismus: Adrian Pipers provokante Installation im Kunstverein," *Suddeutsche Zeitung Munchen* (October 14, 1992).

Boyd, Wallace, "Image Reveals Personal Art," *The Emory Wheel* (October 18, 1988), 8.

Brand, Peggy Zeglin, "Revising the Aesthetic-Nonaesthetic Distinction: The Aesthetic Value of Activist Art," in *Feminism and Tradition in Aesthetics,* ed. Peggy Zeglin Brand and Carolyn Korsmeyer (University Park: Pennsylvania State University Press, 1995), 245–272.

Brandon, Dolores, "Adrian Piper," *Crossroads,* National Public Radio (December 18, 1992).

Bremner, Ann, "Black Box/White Box," in *Will/Power* (catalog); (Columbus: Wexner Center for the Arts of Ohio State University, 1993), 54–61. Reprinted by New Langton Arts (1993).

Brenson, Michael, "Adrian Piper," *The New York Times* (May 1, 1987), C31.

Brenson, Michael, "Black Artists: A Place in the Sun," *The New York Times* (Sunday, March 12, 1989), C1.

Brenson, Michael, "Split Show of Black Artists Using Nontraditional Media," *The New York Times,* (Friday, April 7, 1989).

Brenson, Michael, "Adrian Piper's Head-On Confrontation of Racism," *The New York Times* (Friday, October 26, 1990), C36.

Brentano, Robyn, "Outside the Frame: Performance, Art and Life," in *Outside the Frame: Performance and the Object* (catalogue) (Cleveland: Cleveland Center for Contemporary Art, 1994).

Brumfield, John, "Marginalia: Life in a Day of Black L.A. or, The Theater of Refusal," *Art Issues* 29 (September–October, 1993), 24–27.

Buck, Louisa, "Women in Art," *Kaleidescope,* British Broadcasting Company Radio (June 29, 1992).

Buchanan, Nancy, "Collective Funk," *High Performance* 26 (September 1984), 69.

Carriere, Daniel, "Entre tolerence et acceptation," *Le Devoir* (July 16, 1992).

Cantor, Judy, "Seville: Carmen on a Motorcycle," *ArtNews* 91, no. 2 (February 1992), 32–33.

Chambers, Eddie, "Adrian Piper," *Art Monthly* (1991), 13–15.

Chambers, Eddie, "Introduction," *History and Identity* (Norwich, England: Norwich Gallery, 1991).

Checefsky, Bruce, "Ohio: Adrian Piper," *The New Art Examiner* 18, no. 4 (December 1990), 45.

Chideya, Farai, "Stars Artist: Adrian Piper," *Nar* 2 (Spring 1992), 12–13.

Christensen, Judith, "Artistic Tribute to King . . ." *The San Diego Union,* Arts Section (April 1, 1991), D4.

Colby, Joy, "Horse Packs Quite a Wallop," *The Detroit News* (Friday, January 10, 1992), D4.

Coleman, Wanda, "A Second Heart: Racism, Identity, and the Blues Aesthetic," *High Performance* 52 (Winter 1990), 24–26 (cover)

Cotter, Holland, "Black Artists: Three Shows," *Art in America* 78 (March 1990), 164–217.

Cotter, Holland, "Dislocating the Modern," *Art in America* (January 1992), 100–107.

Cottingham, Laura, "Adrian Piper," *Journal of Contemporary Art* 5, no. 1, (Spring 1992), 88–136.

Crichton, Fennela, "London Newsletter," *Art International* 23, no. 6 (Summer 1974), 42.

Croft, Brenda, "Black Like Me," *Art and Australia* (March 1993), 63–67.

Cron, Marie-Michele, "Miroir de la société du spectacle," *Le Devoir* (July 18, 1992).

Crow, Thomas, "I'll Take the High Road, You Take the Low Road," *Artforum* 29, no. 5 (January 1991).

Crowley, Madeline, "Adrian Piper: Talking to Myself: The Ongoing Autobiography of An Art Object," *Whitney Symposium on American Art* (May 1, 1989).

Cullinan, Helen, "Two Black Women Artists Travel on Parallel Paths," *The Cleveland Plain Dealer* (February 1, 1987), 7H.

Curtiss, Cathy, "Seeing in Black and White," *Los Angeles Times* (April 20, 1993), F1–2.

Danto, Arthur, C., "Dislocationary Art," *The Nation* (January 6, 1992).

Dattenberger, Simone, "Alptraum der Rassisten: Münchens Kunstverein zeigt Arbeiten von Adrian Piper," *Munchener Merkur* (October 7, 1992).

Davenport, Kimberly, "Impossible Liberties: Contemporary Artists on the Life of Their Work over Time," *Art Journal 54*, 2 (Summer 1995), 40–52.

Deak, Edit, "Pencil Moustache Makes Up," *Art-Rite* 11–12 (Winter 1975).

Deitcher, David, "Drawing from Memory," in *The Art of Memory/The Loss of History* (New York: The New Museum of Contemporary Art, 1985), 15–21.

Deitcher, David, "Art on the Installation Plan," *Artforum* 30, no. 5 (January 1992), 78–84.

De Lometar, Catherine, "Delayed Exposure Contemporary Aboriginal Photography," *Art and Australia* (March 1993), 57–62.

Desmond, Jane, "Mapping Identity onto the Body," *Women and Performance* 6, no. 2 #12 (1993), 102–126.

De Yampert, Rick, "Piper's Art Drawn from Controversy," *Daytona Beach News Journal* (February 14, 1993), 3H.

Dimling, Rebecca, "Review," *Art Papers* (January–February 1993).

Dimling, Rebecca, "Will/Power," *Art Papers* (January–February 1993), 58–59.

Dorsey, John, "Video and Audio in a Show of Ego," *The Baltimore Sun* (September 15, 1987), C1–3

Dreher, Thomas, "Adrian Piper, Cindy Sherman: Zwei amerikanische Kunstlerinnen," *Kritik* (January 1993), 4–10.

Emenhiser, Karen, "Art at the End of the Century: A Dialogue," (brochure) University at Buffalo Art Gallery/Albright-Knox Art Gallery, Winter 1996.

Engberg, Kristen, "Marketing the (ad)just(ed) cause," *New Art Examiner* (May 1991), 22–28.

Failing, Patricia, "Black Artists Today: A Case of Exclusion?" *Art News* (March 1989), 124–131.

Farver, Jane, "Adrian Piper," *Adrian Piper: Reflections 1967–87* (retrospective catalog) (New York: The Alternative Museum, 1987).

Fass, Matthew, "Confrontational Art," *The Antioch Record* 14, no. 17 (May 16, 1986), 8.

Feigenbaum, Nancy, "Artist Who Meets Racism Head-On Will Analyze Her Work in Lecture," *Orlando Sentinel* (April 7, 1994), A2.

Flam, Jack, "Armchair Activism at MOMA," *The Wall Street Journal* (December 31, 1991).

Fleming, Jeff, "This is real. And it has everything to do with you," *Adrian Piper* (brochure to accompany exhibition at Southeastern Center for Contemporary Art).

Fleming, Lee, "Galleries: Adrian Piper at Brody's," *The Washington Post* (Saturday, February 13, 1993), G2.

Fox, Catherine, "Art," *Atlanta Journal-Constitution* (Sunday, December 27, 1987), 5f.

Fox, Catherine, "Artist Pushes Viewers to Confront Racism," *Atlanta Journal-Constitution* (Wednesday, November 17, 1993), B11.

Frank, Peter, "Performance Diary," *Soho Weekly News* (April 1, 1976), 18.

Frank, Peter, "The Self and Others," *The Village Voice* (November 27, 1978), 102.

Fryer-Kohles, Jeanne C., "Ohio: Art in Europe and America: The 1960's and 1970's," *The New Art Examiner* 18, no. 2 (October 1990), 44–45.

Gaines, Charles, "The Theater of Refusal: Black Art and Mainstream Criticism," in *The Theater of Refusal* (catalog) (Irvine: University of California, 1993), 13–22.

Gewalt/Geschäfte (Berlin: Neue Gesellschaft für bildende Kunst, 1994), 49.

Giddings, Paula, "Black Males and the Prison of Myth," *The New York TImes* (Arts and Leisure Section Sunday, September 11, 1994).

"Goings on about Town: The Political Arm," *The New Yorker* (February 25, 1991).

Goldberg, Roselee, "Recent Performance Work," *Studio International* 191, no. 1981 (May–June 1976), 288.

Goldberg, Roselee, "Public Performance, Private Memory" (with Laurie Anderson, Julia Heyward, and Adrian Piper), *Studio International* 192, no. 982, (July–August 1976), 19–23.

Goldberg, Roselee, *Live Art: Performance from 1900 to the Present* (New York: Harry N. Abrams, 1980).

Golden, Thelma, "Black Male: Representations of Masculinity in Contemporary American Art," *Black Male* (catalogue) (New York: Whitney Museum of American Art, 1994).

Goldstein, Ann, "Adrian Piper," *Reconsidering the Object of Art: 1965–1975* (catalogue) (Los Angeles: The Museum of Contemporary Art, 1995), 196–199.

Goode-Bryant, Linda, and Phillips, Marcy, *Contextures* (New York: Just Above Midtown, 1978), 33.

Gopnik, Adam, "Goings on about Town: 'The Thing Itself,'" *The New Yorker* (July 30, 1990), 13.

Gopnik, Adam, "The Art World: Empty Frames," *The New Yorker* (November 25, 1991).

Green, Ellen Renee, "Adrian Piper," in *No Title: The Collection of Sol LeWitt,* The Wadsworth Atheneum (Middletown, Conn.: Wesleyan University, 1981).

Grigsby, Darcy Grimaldo, "Dilemmas of Visibility: Contemporary Women Artists' Representations of Female Bodies," *Michigan Quarterly Review* 29, no. 4 (Fall 1990), 584–618; reprinted in *The Female Body: Figures, Styles, Speculations,* ed. Leonard Goldstein, 83–102.

Grimley, Terry, "Paper Tigress's Powerful Roar," *The Birmingham Post* (Tuesday, October 22, 1991), 39–64.

Hacket, Regina, "Demanding Works Challenge Viewers of 'Bad Politics,'" *Seattle Post-Intelligencer* (Wednesday, August 7, 1991), C4.

Hall, Jacqueline, "Show's Viewers Face Many Truths," *The Columbus Dispatch* (September 23, 1992).

Hall, James, "False Colours," *The Independent* (Tuesday, August 18, 1992), Arts 13.

Hall, James, "The Five Best Exhibitions," *The Independent* (Sunday Preview, 16 August 1992).

Hammond, Marsha, "Adrian Piper," *Art Papers* 12, no. 2 (March–April 1988), 40–41.

Hanhardt, John G., "Adrian Piper: 'Out of the Corner,'" *Whitney Museum of American Art: New American Film and Video Series* 53 (October 1990).

Hanna, Deirdre, "Piper Probes Roots of Racism," *Now Magazine* (Toronto, May 10, 1990).

Hanson, Bernard, "Matrix Art Engages Spectator," *The Hartford Courant* (Sunday March 2, 1980), 2G.

Harris, Patty, "Four Summer Downtown Art Shows," *Downtown* (August 29, 1990), 12A–13A.

Hayt-Atkins, Elizabeth, "The Indexical Present: A Conversation with Adrian Piper," *Arts Magazine* (March 1991), 48–51.

Heartney, Elinor, "On View: New York," *The New Art Examiner* 18, no. 4 (December 1990), 36–37.

Heartney, Elinor, "New York—Dislocations: Museum of Modern Art," *Art News* (January 1992).

Heath, Jennifer, "Retrospective Exposes Viewers' Racism, Sexism," *Rocky Mountain News* (March 25, 1990), 72.

Hedlund, Keith, "Piper Discusses Subtle Discrimination," *The Williams Record* (January 16, 1990).

Heisler, Eva, "Will/Power," Exhibition Review, *Columbus Art* (September 1992).

Hermes, Manfred, "Vanilla Nightmares, Funk Lessons," *Spex,* (Cologne, October 1992).

Hess, Elizabeth, "Art Apocalypse," *The Village Voice* (October 28, 1986), 94.

Hess, Elizabeth, "Ways of Seeing Adrian Piper," *The Village Voice* (May 26, 1987), 100.

Hess, Elizabeth, "White Cube Crumbling," *The Village Voice* 36, no. 45 (November 5, 1991), 110.

Hess, Elizabeth, "Visible Man," *The Village Voice* (November 22, 1994), 31, 33–34.

Hewitt, John, "Pandora's Box That's Packed with Politics," *T&A* (Thursday, April 23, 1992), 15.

Hirsh, Linda Blaker, "Stretching the Boundaries," *The Hartford Advocate* (March 26, 1980).

"Hit by Racism, Artist Designs Cards for Bigots," *Jet* 80, no. 14 (July 22, 1991), 35.

Hixson, Kathryn, "AVA 10: 1991," *Awards in the Visual Arts* (catalog to accompany traveling exhibition at Hirshhorn Museum, Washington, D.C.; The Albuquerque Museum of Art, History, and Science, N.Mex.; and the Toledo Museum of Art, Ohio, 1991).

Hoffman, Justin, "Adrian Piper," *Artis* Bern u. Stuttgart, (December–January 1993), S.64.

Hopkins, Mary, "Women's Caucus for Art," *Women Artists News* 12, no. 2 (June 1987), 3–4.

Howell, John, "Exegisis of the Phenomenon of Written Art by Women," *Art Rite* 14 (Winter 1976–1977).

Hulme, Alan, "The Art of Stirring Things Up," *Manchester Evening News* (January 16, 1992).

Hulme, Alan, "Exhibitions," Manchester Evening News (January 24, 1992).

Jacques, Geoffrey, "'The Decade Show' Colors the Art World," *The City Sun* (August 15–21, 1990), 26.

Jinkner-Lloyd, Amy, "Women Artists Expose Raw Emotions in 'Autobiography' Exhibition at Nexus," *Atlanta Journal-Constitution* (October or November 1989).

Johnson, Hans, "Frick Art: Piper Exhibit offers 'no hiding place,'" *The Wooster Voice* (September 17, 1990), 4.

Johnson, Ken, "Being and Politics," *Art in America* 78, no. 9 (September 1990), cover and 154–161.

Johnson, Ken, "'The Political Arm' at John Weber," *Art in America* 79, no. 6 (June 1991), 48.

Johnson, Mark I., "Schlafly, Piper Up to Bat at Forum," *New Smyrna Beach Observer* (February 20, 1993).

Johnson, Patrica C. "Ambiguity, Directness Contrast in Rice Show," *Houston Chronicle* (Thursday, February 9, 1995), 6C.

Johnson, Vivien, "The Unbounded Bienalle: Contemporary Aboriginal Art," *Art and Australia* (March 1993), 49–56.

Jones, Jim, "Women in the 90's: Sex Power and Politics," *New Smyrna Beach Observer* (February 19, 1993).

Jones, Jim, "Her Words Were Her Weapons," *New Smyrna Beach Observer* (March 23, 1993), 1A, 3A.

Jones, Kellie, "Interrogating Identity: A Roundtable Discussion," *Interrogating Identity* (catalog, New York University Grey Art Gallery, 1991).

Jordan, James, "A Critic Reveal(ed)(ing)," *Dialogue* (November–December 1980), 4–5.

Joselit, David, "Object Lessons," *Art in America 84*, 2 (February 1996), 68–71, 107.

Jouannais, Jean-Yves, "Pour la suite du monde," *Art Press Montreal* 171 (July–August 1992), 75.

Kalil, Susie, "Art on the Borderline," *Houston Press* 7, No. 8 (February 21–March 1995), p. 33.

Karcher, Eva, "Jeder Mensch hat Angst vor dem Fremden. Ein Interview mit der amerikanischen Kunstlerin und Philosophin Adrian Piper uber Rassismus," *Suddeutsche Zeitung* Nr. 261 (1992), Seite 15.

Karmel, Pepe, "The Corner as Trap, Symbol, Vanishing Point, History Lesson," *The New York Times*, July 21, 1995, p. C25.

Kaufman, Jason, "Musée d'Art Contemporain de Montreal," *Atelier* 789 (Tokyo, November 1992), 77–90.

Keller, Andrea-Miller, "Le musée comme oeuvre et artefact," *Les Cahiers du Musée National d'Art Moderne* (Centre Georges Pompidou, 1989), 66.

Keziere, Russell, "Less Medium, More Message: Adrian Piper," *Vanguard* 10, no. 4, (May 1981), 36–37.

Kimmelman, Michael, "In Los Angeles, the Making of a Better Mood," *The New York Times*, Sunday, January 14. Section 2.

King, Elaine, A., "Art in the Age of Information," brochure accompanying exhibition, The Wood Street Galleries & 808 Penn Modern, Pittsburgh, Pa. (February 26–April 17, 1993).

Kingsley, April, "Art Goes Underground," *The Village Voice* (October 16, 1978), 122.

Knight, Christopher, "Looking Racism in the Face," *Los Angeles Times* (March 5, 1991), F1, F6.

Kohn, Barbara, "Piper in Performance," *Dialogue* (September–October 1980), 9–10.

Kokich, Kim, "Adrian Piper," *Morning Edition,* National Public Radio (July 8, 1991).

Kolpan, Steve, "Self Service: Self Portraits Bare Social Issues at WAA," *The Woodstock Times* (March 29, 1990).

Koniger, Maribel, "Adrian Piper," *Tema Celeste* (Spring 1993), S94.

Kornblau, Gary, "1965–1975: Reconsidering the Object of Art," *Art Issues* (January/February 1996), 36–37.

Kosuth, Joseph, "Art After Philosophy II," *Studio International* (November 1969), 161.

Koussev, Rachel, "Art Can Combat Xenophobia, Says Feminist Artist," *Yale Daily News* 114, no. 17, (Thursday, September 26, 1991), 3.

Kronthaler, Helmut. "Der Rassismus im Kopf, Retrospektive der US-Amerikanerin Adrian Piper im Münchner Kunstverein," *Landshuter Zeitung* (October 30, 1992).

Kuspit, Donald, "Art of Conscience: The Last Decade," *Dialogue* (September–October 1980), 19–20.

Kuspit, Donald, "Adrian Piper: Self-Healing through Meta-Art," *Art Criticism* 3, no. 3, (September 1987), 9–16.

Kuspit, Donald, "Art and the Moral Imperative," *The New Art Examiner* 18, no. 5 (January 1991), 18–25.

Lalonde, Joanne, "Video mise en scene du quatrième mur," *ETC Montreal* 2015 (November 1992–February 1993), 58–59.

Lammers, Dufflyn, "Welcome to the struggle," *The Georgia Guardian 4,* 45 (November 3–9, 1995), 1A and 11B

Langdon, Ann R., "Women Visual Artists You Might Like to Know," *Women in the Arts* (1990), 39.

Langer, Cassandra L., "Autobiography: In Her Own Image," *Women Artists News* 13, no. 3 (Fall 1988), 26–27.

Langer, Cassandra L., "Feminist Art Criticism: Turning Points and Sticking Places," *Art Journal* 50, no. 2 (Summer 1991), 21–28.

Larson, Kay, "The Human Condition," *New York Magazine* (November 4, 1991), 122–123.

Larson, Kay, "Dislocations," *Galleries Magazine* (December–January 1991).

Lasch, Christopher, *The Minimal Self* (New York: W. W. Norton, 1984), 150–151.

Ledes, Richard C., "Adrian Piper at John Weber," *Artscribe* (January–February 1991), 81–82 (illus.).

Lepage, Jocelyne, "Un coup de gran fury et du MAC aux Montrealais," *La Presse Montreal* (Saturday, May 30, 1992), E1–3.

Levin, Kim, "Choices: Art 'The Thing Itself,'" *The Village Voice* (August 7, 1990), 102.

Levin, Kim, "Choices: Art 'Adrian Piper,'" *The Village Voice* (September 25, 1990), 104.

Lewis, Jo Ann, "Tantalizing Reflections," *The Washington Post* (June 12, 1991), F9.

Lewis, Jo Ann, "Racism's Unwilling Witness," *The Washington Post* (June 22, 1991), G1, G5.

Lewis, Jo Ann, "Images That Get Under the Skin," *The Washington Post* (June 27, 1991), G1, G5–6.

Lida, Marc, "Outside Looking In," *108 Review* 12, (May–June 1988), 1, 5.

Lippard, Lucy, "Catalysis: An Interview with Adrian Piper," *NYU Drama Review* (March 1972), 76–78.

Lippard, Lucy, "Jonathan Borofsky at 2,096,974," *Artforum* (November 1974), 63n.

Lippard, Lucy, "Transformation Art," *Ms.* (October 1975), 33–39.

Lippard, Lucy, *From The Center: Feminist Essays on Women's Art* (New York: E. P. Dutton, 1976).

Lippard, Lucy, "Women's Body Art: The Pains and Pleasures of Rebirth," *Art in America* (May–June 1976), 73–82.

Lippard, Lucy, "Caring: Five Political Artists," *Studio International* 193, no. 987 (Summer 1978), 197–207.

Lippard, Lucy, *Get the Message? A Decade of Art for Social Change* (New York: E. P. Dutton, 1984).

Lippard, Lucy, *Mixed Blessings: New Art in a Multicultural America* (New York: Pantheon Books, 1990).

Lippard, Lucy, "Intruders: Lynda Benglis and Adrian Piper," in *Breakthroughs: Avant Garde Artists in Europe and America,* ed. John Howell (New York: Rizzoli, 1991), 125–132.

Lippard, Lucy, "Escape Attempts," *Reconsidering the Object of Art: 1965–1975* (catalogue) (Los Angeles: The Museum of Contemporary Art, 1995), 16–38.

Litt, Steven, "Confronting Raw Reality," *The Plain Dealer* (December 12, 1991), E14.

Litt, Steven, "A Cornucopia of New Artistic Talent in Toledo," *The Cleveland Plain Dealer* (December 29, 1991), H3.

Litten, Laura, "Both Sides Now," *New Art Examiner* (April 1979), 13–14.

Loupias, Barnard, "Art noir au Palais du Luxembourg," *Le nouvel Observateur* 1258 (February 17–23, 1994).

MacGregor, Elizabeth, introduction essay in *Adrian Piper* (Ikon Gallery and Cornerhouse catalog), (September 1991), 7–9.

Mahler, Gwen, "Awards in the Visual Arts 10 (AVA 10)," *Metropolitan Muse* (August 1991), 7–8.

Marks, Laura U., "Adrian Piper: Reflections 1967–87," *Fuse* (Fall 1990), 40–42.

Marks, Laura U., "The Blue Flame of Reason," *Adrian Piper: Cornered/Decide Who You Are,* in *University at Buffalo Art Gallery Overview 1994–1995* (catalogue) (Buffalo, N.Y.: University at Buffalo Art Gallery, 1995), 43–44.

Matheny, Dave, "Lesson in Funk Isn't Just Dancing; It's an Artistic Leap," *Minneapolis Star and Tribune* (November 1, 1983), 1C, 3C.

Mayer, Rosemary, "Performance and Experience," *Arts* (December 1972), 33–36.

Mays, John Bentley, "Practicing the Art of Being Seen," *The Globe and Mail* (Saturday May 30, 1992), C4.

McCracken, David, "Market Jitters Hit Art Expos and Auctions," *Chicago Tribune* (May 3, 1991), 66 (illus.).

McEvilley, Thomas, "Adrian Piper," *Artforum* 26, no. 1 (September 1987), 128–129.

McWilliams, Martha, "Gallery Panel Discussion," *The Washington City Paper* (February 19, 1993), 44.

Menaker, Deborah, "Adrian Piper: Artworks," brochure for Williams College Museum of Art, January 1990.

Mendelssohn, Joanna, "Collusion Course," *The Bulletin with Newsweek* (Australia, December 22, 1992), 78.

Merritt, Lissa, "Interview: Adrian Piper," *Aurora* (Yale University: Winter 1992), 6–8, 21–22.

Metzger, Rainer, "Collagiertes Elend: Adrian Piper im Kunstverein Munchen," *Der Standard* (Kultur, November 19, 1992).

Metzger, Rainer, "Adrian Piper," *Kunstforum* 121, 435, Band 121 (1993?), 435–436.

Miller, Donald, "Artists Master Technologies at City Galleries," *Pittsburgh Post-Gazette* (Saturday, March 13, 1993).

Miller-Keller, Andrea, "Adrian Piper," *Matrix* 56 (Hartford, Conn.: Wadsworth Atheneum Press, March 1980).

"Mistaken Identities: 'a politically extremely correct exhibition,'" [*ruimte*] 10, 4 (1993), Holland.

Morgan, Robert, "Adrian Piper," *Arts Magazine* 63, no. 10 (Summer 1989), 99.

Morisiani, Paola, "New York," *Juliet Art Magazine* (December–January 1991), 56.

Morrison, Ewan, "Vote/Emote," *Variant* (Winter 1991), 22–23.

Moss, Karen, "Altered Egos: Making Art as an Other," in *Altered Egos* (Santa Monica: Santa Monica Museum of Art, 1994), 5–14.

Mullis, Melissa, "'Lay On Top of Me' and Other Art Works at the Nexus Center," *The Technique* (Friday, October 28, 1988), 17.

"Museum of Contemporary Art at the Temporary Contemporary," *The Print Collector's Newsletter* (January/February 1996).

Myers, Terry R., "Route 66 to Kassel," *Fort/Myers Publication Number One* (July 1992).

Nalley, Jon, "What We Pretend Not To Know: The Power of Adrian Piper," *Downtown* 212 (October 3, 1990), cover, 20.

"National Art News, Los Angeles: Artists Protest Sponsorship," *ARTnews* (February 1996), 53.

Nochlin, Linda, "Learning from 'Black Male'," *Art in America* 83, 3 (March 1995), 86–91.

Norklun, Kathi, "An Art Problem," *Art Week* 15, no. 18 (May 5, 1984), 12.

Norton, Eleanor Holmes, "The Movement Grows Up At the Corcoran: Reflections on the Civil Rights Struggle," *The Washington Post* (Sunday August 29, 1993).

O'Grady, Lorraine, "Olympia's Maid: Reclaiming Black Female Subjectivity," *AfterImage* 20, no. 1 (Summer 1992), 14–15.

Olander, William, "Art and Politics: Of Arms and the Artist," *Art in America* (June 1985).

Olander, William, "Fragments," in *The Art Memory/The Loss of History* (New York: The New Museum of Contemporary Art, 1985), 7–12.

O'Toole, Denise, "Feminism Baffled Men Schlafly Says at Forum," *Dayton News-Journal* (Sunday,February 21, 1993), 1D, 8D

Ottmann, Klaus, *Exotism* (catalog to accompany exhibition at Wesleyan University, 1990).

Paoletti, John, "Adrian Piper," *Adrian Piper: Reflections 1967–1987,* (New York: The John Weber Gallery, 1989).

Patterson, Tom, "Statement: Exhibition Is Coolly Confrontational," *Winston-Salem Journal* (Sunday, April 26, 1992), C4.

Perl, Jed, "Dismodern," *The New Criterion* (December 1991), 46–51.

Perkins, Hetti, "Beyond the Year of Indiginous Peoples," *Art and Australia* (March 1993).

Perreault, John, "Art," *The Village Voice* (March 27, 1969), 15–17.

Perreault, John, "Art," *The Village Voice* (May 1, 1969), 14–16.

Perreault, John, "Art," *The Village Voice* (June 5, 1969), 16–18.

Perreault, John, "Art," *The Village Voice* (November 20, 1969), 34.

Perreault, John, "Art," *The Village Voice* (May 14, 1970), 16.

Perreault, John, "Art," *The Village Voice* (July 16, 1970), 31.

Perreault, John, "Art," *The Village Voice* (April 29,1971), 31.

Perreault, John, "Art," *The Village Voice* (February 8, 1973), 28.

Perree, Rob, "Adrian Piper: plaatst de waarheid boven de schoonheid," *Kunst Beeld Nr. 11,* 15e Jaargang (November 1991), 32–34.

Philippi, Desa, "Politics in the Indexical Present," *Artscribe* 81.

Phillips, Deborah C., "New Faces in Alternative Spaces," *Art News* 80, no. 9, (November 1981), 99–100.

Phillpot, Clive, "Arts Magazines and Magazine Art," *Artforum* 18, no. 6 (February 1980), 52–54.

Phillpot, Clive, "Talking to Myself," *Art Journal* 39, no. 3 (Spring 1980), 213–217.

Phillpot, Clive, "Adrian Piper: Talking to Us," *Adrian Piper: Reflections 1967–87* (retrospective catalog, New York; The Alternative Museum, 1987).

Picard, Charmaine, and Potter, Sarah, "Corpus Delicti," *PhotoVision* 23 (1992), 10–14, 54–57.

Pincus, Robert L. "Perspectives on an Era Painted Red," *The San Diego Union* (Sunday, September 17, 1989).

Pindell, Howardena, "Breaking the Silence," *The New Art Examiner* 18, no. 3 (November 1990), 23–27, 50–51.

Plagens, Peter, "557,087," *Artforum* (November 1969), 67.

Pontbriand, Chantal, "Pour la suite du monde," *Parachute* 68 (October–December 1992), 52–53.

Prevallet, Kristen, "CU Art Show Gives Views of 'Real World,'" *Colorado Daily* (March 15, 1990).

Prevallet, Kristin, "Challenging Basic Truths," *Icons* (April 1990), 3–4.

Princenthal, Nancy, "Artist's Book Beat," *The Print Collector's Newsletter* 21, no. 6 (January–February 1991), 235.

Purchase, Steve, "13 Artists Act Out Their Work," *The Baltimore Evening Sun* (Thursday, November 24, 1988).

Quatman, Christian, "Mittlerin zwischen Mainstream und Marginalitat," *Kunstforum International* 118, 229–232, 221.

Raven, Arlene, "Colored," *The Village Voice* (May 31, 1988), 92.

Raven, Arlene, "I to Eye," *The Village Voice* (January 31, 1989), 86.

Raven, Arlene, "In Tongues," *The Village Voice* (May 30, 1989), 89.

Raven, Arlene, "Civil Disobedience," *The Village Voice* (September 25, 1990), Arts Section, and cover, 55, 94.

Raven, Arlene, "Adrian Piper: You and Me," *Adrian Piper* (catalog to accompany exhibition at Ikon Gallery, Birmingham, England, September 1991), 17–19.

Raven, Arlene, "The Language of Virtue: What Makes Art Valuable?" *High Performance* (Fall 1994), 46–47.

Raven, Arlene, "Word of Honor," chapter 10 of *Mapping the Terrain: New Genre Public Art,* ed. Suzanne Lacy (Seattle: Bay Press, 1995), 167.

Reid, Nick, "Re-View: Adrian Piper," *Northern Star* (April 16–23, 1992).

Reinblatt, Melanie, "Musée d'Art Contemporain Exhibit not the Kind of Art you Take Home," *The Montreal Downtowner* (Wednesday, August 26, 1992), 18.

Rifkin, Ned, *Directions: Adrian Piper,* "What It's Like, What It Is #2" (brochure to accompany exhibition at Hirshhorn Museum, Washington, D.C., June 1989).

Rinder, Lawrence, "Adrian Piper: Racism Confronted," MATRIX/BERKELEY 130 (University Art Museum, Berkeley, August 1989), 3.

Robinson, Deborah, "Adrian Piper," *Ikon Education* (Birmingham, England, September–November 1991).

Robinson, Walter, "Artworld: Tobacco Road, Part II," *Art in America 84,* 1 (January 1996), 126.

Rosen, Miriam, "Les Refuseurs de Kassel," *Liberation* (Nouvelle Serie #3443, Wednesday June 17, 1992), 39–40.

Roth, Moira, "Adrian Piper," in *The Amazing Decade: Women and Performance in America, 1970–1980,* ed. Moira Roth, (Los Angeles: Astro Artz, 1983).

Roulette, Todd, "Adrian Piper," *Thing* (Spring 1991), 33.

Rubin, David S., "Adrian Piper," exhibition brochure for *Adrian Piper: Political Drawings and Installations, 1975–1991* (Cleveland Center for Contemporary Art, 1991).

Sabin, Selma, "Piper's 'Vanilla Nightmares' on View at WCMA," *The Advocate* (January 17, 1990).

Sanchez, Annette B. "Art in the Age of Information: Thought-Provoking," *New Pittsburgh Courier* (Saturday, April 17, 1993), B6.

Sanconie, Maica, "Noire Amerique," *Beaux Arts* (October 1992).

Schwendenwein, Jude, "A Look at Privilege, Presumption," *The Hartford Courant* (November 18, 1990).

Schwendenwein, Jude, "Outtakes: Out of the Corner," *High Performance* 53 (Spring 1991), 65, 67.

Scott, Martha B., "Post-Everything Angst," in *The Art of Advocacy* catalog (Ridgefield, Conn.: The Aldrich Museum of Contemporary Art, 1991), 5–7.

Serlis, Effie, "Adrian Piper," in *Interviews with Women in the Arts* (New York: School of Visual Arts Press, 1975).

Shortal, Helen, "Action Works," *The Baltimore City Paper* (December 16, 1988), 14.

Shuter, Marty, "Adrian Piper confronts the world's racism," *Savannah Morning News and Evening Press,* Sunday, October 29, 1995, 1G and 3G.

Siegel, Suzie, "Forum Mixes Art, Politics," *Tampa Tribune* (Friday, February 5, 1993).

Siegel, Suzie, "Sometimes You've Got to be Radical . . . ," *Tampa Tribune* (Monday, March 1, 1993), Baylife 1, 5.

Sims, Lowery Stokes, "Art as a Verb: Issues of Technique and Content," *Art as a Verb* (Baltimore: Maryland Institute, College of Art, 1988).

Sims, Lowery Stokes, "Aspects of Performance in the Work of Black American Women Artists," in *Feminist Art Criticism* ed. Arlene Raven, Cassandra Langer, and Joanna Frueh (Ann Arbor: UMI Research Press, 1988).

Sims, Lowery Stokes, "Mimicry, Xenophobia, Etiquette and Other Social Manifestations: Adrian Piper's Observations from the Margins," *Adrian Piper: Reflections 1967–1987* (New York: John Weber Gallery, 1989).

Sims, Lowery Stokes, "The Mirror the Other," *Artforum* 27 (March 1990), 111–115.

Smallwood, Lyn, "The Art of Agitprop," *Seattle Weekly* (August 14, 1991), Arts and Leisure.

Smith, Roberta, "Adrian Piper," *The New York Times* (Friday, September 14, 1990), C24.

Smith, Roberta, "At the Modern, Works Unafraid to Ignore Beauty," *The New York Times* (Friday, October 18, 1991), C1, C18.

Smith, Virginia Warren, "The Art of Confrontation," *Atlanta Journal-Constitution* (December 6, 1987), 12J–13J.

Solomon-Godeau, Abigail, *Mistaken Identities,* (catalog, University of Washington Press, 1992–1993).

Soutif, Daniel, "Adrian Piper, l'Amérique noire sur blanche," *Liberation* (November 20, 1990), 40.

Sozenski, Edward J., "Artist's Themes Are Sexism, Racism," *The Philadelphia Inquirer* (Thursday, March 16, 1989).

Sozenski, Edward J., "Entering Their Worlds, We Confront Our Own," *The Philadelphia Inquirer* (Sunday, December 1, 1991), 1E, 5E.

Spivak, Gayatri Chakravorty, "Franzosischer Feminismus im internationalen Rahmen," *Texte zur Kunst* 1, 4 (Fall 1991), 52–79.

Stals, Jose Lebrero, "Adrian Piper—Convento de Santa Clara, Moquer, Spain," *Flash Art* News, (November–December 1992), 135.

Staniszewski, Mary Anne, "Conceptual Art," *Flash Art* 143 (November–December 1988), 88.

Staniszewski, Mary Anne, "Piper Pipes Up," *Elle* V, 7 (March 1990), Faces/Art: 92.

Staniszewski, Mary Anne, "Race against Time," *Adrian Piper: PRETEND* (New York: John Weber Gallery, 1990).

Sterritt, David, "Watching TV Creatively—In a Video Installation," *The Christian Science Monitor* (November 19, 1990).

Stevens, Mitchell, "Chicago: Sarah Charlesworth, Jeanne Dunning, Annette Messager, Adrian Piper, Laurie Simmons," *The New Art Examiner* 17, no. 11 (Summer 1990), 37.

Storr, Robert, "Devil on the Stairs: Looking Back on the Eighties" (catalog to accompany exhibition, Philadelphia Institute of Contemporary Art, University of Pennsylvania, 1991).

Storr, Robert, *Dislocations* (catalog essay, New York: Museum of Modern Art, 1992).

Storr, Robert, "The Map Room: A Visitor's Guide," *Mapping* (catalog, New York: The Museum of Modern Art, 1994), 5–23.

Storr, Robert, "Between a Rock and a Hard Place," Paper #3 in the *Paper Series on the Arts, Culture and Society* (New York: The Andy Warhol Foundation for the Visual Arts, 1994).

Sullivan, Meg, "Creative Confrontation of Racism," Art News & Notes, *Daily News,* L.A. Life, (February 15, 1991, 49).

"Summer Priorities: Adrian Piper at the WPA & Fig Leaves in the 90s," *Baltimore Alternative* (July 1991), 25, 26.

Swartz, Anne, "'Adrian Piper: Icons of African-American Identity'," *The Georgia Guardian,* October 20–26, 1995, 1B and 8B.

Sweeney, Louise, "Controversial Show Salutes Top Ten in the Visual Arts," *Christian Science Monitor* (July 19, 1991), 10.

Sydell, Laura, "Exit Art," *All Things Considered,* National Public Radio (June 29, 1992).

Szakacs, Dennis, "Adrian Piper," brochure essay, City Gallery of Art, Raleigh, N.C. (October–December 1993).

Taubin, Amy, "Self-Life," *The Village Voice* (March 1, 1987), 55–56.

Taubin, Amy, "Adrian Piper," Choices: Video, *The Village Voice* (March 28, 1989), 45.

Taubin, Amy, "Dislocations," *The Village Voice* 36, no. 53, (December 31, 1991), 68.

Thompson, Mildred, "Interview: Adrian Piper," *Art Papers* 12, no. 2 (March–April 1988), 27–30.

Thorson, Alice, "Worthy Winners," *City Paper* (July 5, 1991), 25.

Tipper, Andy, "Piping Up," *What's On* (September 14–27, 1991), 35.

Tsatsos, Irene, "A Dialogue with Adrian Piper," *P-Form* 2, no. 2 (April–May 1987), 22–25.

Twardy, Chuck, "Present Tension," *The Raleigh News and Observer,* Weekend Section (Friday, October 1, 1993), 14–15.

Upson, Nicola, "Smiling at Strangers," *Second Shift* I, no. 1 (Spring 1993, United Kingdom), 6–9.

Vallongo, Sally, "Art with a Modern Message," *The Blade* (December 8, 1991), 1–2.

Vallongo, Sally, "A Sneak Preview of Tomorrow's Art," *The Peach* (December 18, 1991), P1.

Van Tuyl, Laura, "Artist Adrian Piper Mounts Urgent Challenge to Racism in Society," *Christian Science Monitor* (July 19, 1991), 10.

Verdino-Sullwood, Carla Maria, "Dislocations: Dialogue of Disparate Visions," *The Crisis* 99 (January 1992), 7–8.

Verdino-Sullwood, Carla Maria, "Generous with Our Uniqueness: Forging New Directions for African-American Women in the Arts," *Crisis* 99, no. 7, 29–36

Vogel, Carol, "Inside Art: Philip Morris Loses an Artist," *The New York Times,* Friday, November 24, 1995.

Walker, Alexia, "Adrian Piper: Endless Loop Record/Erase," *L'hiver de l'amour* Bis, Musée d'Art Moderne de la Ville de Paris (February–March 1994), 73.

Walker, Maxine, "Maxine Walker in Conversation with Adrian Piper," *Autograph* (December 1991).

Wallach, Amei, "Art with a Wallop," *New York Newsday* (Monday, April 10), section 2, 4.

Wallach, Amei, "Artists and Identity," *The MacNeill/Lehrer Report* (September 8, 1989).

Wallach, Amei, "Making Trouble in the Galleries," *New York Newsday* (Sunday, September 23, 1990), 14–16.

Wallach, Amei, "Artful Assault on Sensibilities," *New York Newsday* (Friday, October 18, 1991), 74, 99.

Wallach, Amei, "New Voices," *New York Newsday* (December 29, 1991).

Wallach, Amei, "Images of Black Males: A Reflection on Society," *New York Newsday* (Friday, November 11, 1994).

Wallis, Brian, "Will/Power at Wexner Center," *Art in America* (February 1993), 116–117.

Watkin, Mel, "Adrian Piper: The Racist Within: Some Personal Observations," *What It's Like, What It Is, #1* (brochure to accompany exhibition at the Washington Project for the Arts, June 1991).

Weil, Benjamin, "Interview with Adrian Piper," *Purple Prose* 3 (Paris: Summer 1993), 74–79.

Weintraub, Joanne, "College Philosopher's Artwork Anything but Black and White," *The Milwaukee Journal* (Thursday, October 14, 1993), B3.

Welish, Marjorie, "In This Corner, Adrian Piper's Agitprop," *Arts Magainze* 65, no. 7 (March 1991), cover, 43–47.

Weser, Marcia Goren, "Artist's Work Deals with Society's Prejudices and Fears," *San Antonio Light* (March 29, 1992), L5.

Wetzel, Anita, *Words and Images with a Message* (catalogue to accompany exhibition at the Women's Studio Workshop, 1990).

Willemson, Roger, "Adrian Piper," *Premiere* (November 5, 1992, Hamburg Cable TV).

Wilson, Judith, "Adrian Piper," *Black Arts Annual 1987/1988,* ed. Donald Bogle (New York: Garland Press, 1989).

Wilson, Judith, "Optical Illusions: Images of Miscegenation in Nineteenth and Twentieth Century Art," *American Art* (Summer 1991), 88–107.

Wilson, Judith, "'In Memory of the News and of Ourselves': The Art of Adrian Piper," *Third Text* 16/17, (Autumn–Winter 1991), 39–62.

Wilson, Judith, "Beauty Rites: Towards an Anatomy of Culture in African American Women's Art," in Image and Identity: The African American Experience in 20th Century Art, *The International Review of African American Art* 11, no. 3 (1994), 11–18.

Wilson, Rhonda, "Angry Art," *Everywoman* (December 1991–January 1992)

Williams, Val, "Adrian Piper," *Creative Camera,* 27.

Wood, Joe, "Talking Back to Malcolm," *Elle* (November 1992), 130.

Wooster, Ann-Sargent, "Making Their Mark," *Making Their Mark: Women Enter the Mainstream 1970–1985* (New York: Abbeville Press, 1989).

Zelanski, Paul, and Fisher, Mary Pat, *Shaping Space: The Dynamics of Three-Dimensional Design* (Second Edition) (New York: Harcourt Brace College Publishers, 1995), 192.

Zimmer, William, "Perceptions of the Other," *The New York Times* (February 11, 1990), 32.

Zimmer, William, "The Public and the Private in Robust Dialogue," *The New York Times* (Westchester Edition, Sunday, October 28, 1990).

Index

Note: Page numbers followed by *f* refer to illustrations.

A.–A (Piper) V.I:141–146
Abstract; Abstraction, V.I:271
 in art for art's sake, V.II:196
 artist's advantages with, V.I:242
 cognitive discrimination and, V.II:254–255
 cognitive inaccessibility and, V.II:210
 conceptualism and, V.I:227, 242
 dichotomy between concrete and, V.II:94, 98–99
 as flight, V.I:xxiii, 224–225, 227; V.II:xxi
 as flying, V.I:xxiii, 224, 227; V.II:xxi
 generalization in, V.I:224
 identity and, V.I:227–232
 of objects, V.I:225, 257–258
 in performance art, V.II:94, 96
 symbolism and, V.I:259, 261
 transformation failure and, V.II:97–98
"Abstract Expressionism: Weapon of the Cold War" (Cockcroft) V.II:212n1
Academia; Academics, V.I:232; V.II:149
 one-upmanship in, V.I:228
 philosophical tradition in, V.II:149
 provincialism in, V.I:229
 racism in, V.I:229, 230, 280–281; V.II:150–151
 responsibility of, V.II:185–187
 sexism in, V.I:229, 281; V.II:150–151
 social hierarchy in, V.I:264
 success in art world vs., V.II:79
Academic point of view, V.I:xiv; V.II:xii
Acceptance, V.I:173, 199; V.II:201
 by "passed" relatives, V.I:288
 in ideal society, V.I:246–247
 in relationships, V.I:256
 toleration vs., V.I:245
Access, V.II:201
 to Other as person, V.II:225–227
Accessibility, V.I:53, 122
 in "cheap art utopia," V.II:33–34
 as condition for art production, V.I:159
 of Funk music, V.I:198
 importance of, V.I:138
 ontological status of work and, V.II:98
 to public, V.I:115
Acconci, Vito, V.I:xxxvi, 37, 113; V.II:xxxiv
 Points, Blanks Way, V.II:12*f*
Accountability
 division of labor and, V.II:71–73
 intellectual conscience and, V.II:154
Acculturation, V.I:217
 aesthetic, V.II:63, 66–67, 68
 shared art making and, V.II:132
"Action painting," V.II:212
Actions, as art product, V.II:13
Activism, individualism and, V.I:xv; V.II:xiii
Activity, art, V.I:51–52. *See also* Art making
Ade, King Sonny, V.I:200
Adrian Piper: PRETEND, V.II:175
Adrian Piper: Reflections 1967-1987, V.I:223; V.II:134n3
"Adrian Piper" (Morgan) V.II:165n13
"Adrian Piper, Self-Healing Through Meta-Art" (Kuspit) V.II:134n2, 162n3, 186n9
 critique of, V.II:107–125
"Adrian Piper" (Smith) V.II:184.1, 186n8
Advertising
 effect on art of, V.II:214
 intellectual conscience and, V.II:154
 intention in, V.II:258.39
 use of in art, V.I:273
Aesthetic acculturation, V.II:63
 art education and, V.II:66–67, 68
 division of labor and, V.II:72
Aesthetic bias, V.II:66
Aesthetic dogma, audience response and, V.II:95
Aesthetic emotion, V.II:190–198
 defined, V.II:190
 harmony and, V.II:192, 193, 194
 quality and, V.II:190–196
 as self-awareness, V.II:193
 spiritual content and, V.II:192–193
 subjectivity in, V.II:197–198
 transcendence and, V.II:192–193, 194–195, 196, 198–199
Aesthetic empiricism, V.I:xvii; V.II:xv
Aesthetic evaluation, self-transcendence and, V.I:204
Aesthetic experience, V.I:37, 204
 artist and viewer in, V.I:37
 continuity of with living, V.I:39
 expectations and, V.II:54
 mainstream art and, V.I:xxxvii, xxxviii; V.II:xxxv, xxxvi
 in performance art, V.I:204
 relinquishment of power in, V.II:196
Aesthetic integrity, V.I:240
Aesthetic isolation, politics and, V.I:31
Aestheticizing Response, V.I:181, 266
Aesthetic judgment, appropriateness of, V.I:265
Aesthetic language, suppression of anomaly through, V.I:265
Aesthetic literalism, V.I:xx; V.II:xviii
Aesthetic motivation, V.I:52
Aesthetic obliteration, as cultural racism goal, V.II:146
Aesthetic quality of artist, V.II:20–21
Aesthetics, V.I:96, 145, 183; V.II:70, 185
 acculturation in, V.II:63, 67–68
 art context and, V.I:95
 art vs. nonart objects and, V.I:41, 42
 in "cheap art utopia," V.II:33, 34
 decision making and, V.I:225
 dichotomy between personal and, V.II:94–98, 99
 ethics and, V.I:xx; V.II:xviii
 experience and, V.I:204
 formalism as, V.II:210
 politics and, V.I:164, 167, 169, 181, 183, 202–203
 power concerns vs. cultural racism and, V.II:146n16
 and production value, V.II:31–32
 in stereotyped response, V.I:164
 See also Aesthetic value; Standards; Value(s)
Aesthetic self-consciousness, V.I:96
Aesthetic sensibility, art in nonart situations and, V.I:37
Aesthetic significance, personal significance vs., V.II:93
Aesthetic universals, subjectivity of artist vs., V.II:95, 96
Aesthetic value, V.I:xvii, 41–42, 267; V.II:xv, 66
 deformation and, V.II:76–78
 demand for innovation vs., V.II:77–78
 economic value vs., V.I:121; V.II:31, 32, 77–78
 exchange value and, V.II:31, 32
 function and, V.II:59
 humanistic value vs., V.II:25–27
 ideal determinants of, V.II:59–60
 market value as, V.II:170
 overproduction and, V.II:75
 in political art, V.I:267
 political value vs., V.I:247–248
 uniqueness vs., V.II:57–58, 59
 See also Aesthetics
Affirmative action, V.I:279
 in art world, V.II:183, 184, 186, 187
 in art world welfare system, V.II:186, 187
 power of words and, V.II:199
Africa, European culture's debt to, V.I:206
African-American ancestry, in white families, V.I:288–289, 291
African-American art
 appropriation of, V.II:183–184, 209
 art historians' view of, V.I:xvi–xvii; V.II:xiv–xv
 "discovery" of, V.II:183
 excluded from mainstream, V.II:162, 163–164
 growing attention to, V.II:163–164
 ignored by critics, V.II:161
African American culture, V.II:197
African-American music, V.I:195
African Americans; Afro-Americans
 American Dream and, V.I:xxiv; V.II:xxii
 art and, V.I:xvii; V.II:xv
 as colonized people, V.II:171
 cultural knowledge about, V.II:197
 cultural racism and, V.II:127
 cultural roots and, V.I:199–200
 repressed fears about, V.I:273
 separation from "passed" relatives, V.I:284, 286, 287
 shared culture of, V.I:206
 social wisdom of, V.I:298–299
 stereotyping of. *See* Stereotyping
 terms used for, V.I:305
 use of terms, V.II:127n1, 161n1
 See also Blacks; Colored

African art
  aesthetic emotion and, V.II:198
  appropriated by Picasso, V.II:209
"African Influence on the Music of the Americas" (Waterman) V.I:216
"African Music" (Merriam) V.I:216
African Rhythm and African Sensibility (Chernoff) V.I:216
Africans, V.I:199–200
African tribal imagery, appropriation of, V.II:70
Agent; agency, V.I:143
  catalytic, V.I:33–34
Agents, in "cheap art utopia," V.II:33
Aggression
  artist accused of, V.II:118
  Mythic Being series and, V.I:47
AIDS, V.I:57
  artistic censorship and, V.II:166
  funding withheld from exhibit on, V.II:162
Alice in Wonderland (Carroll) V.I:59
Alienation
  artist accused of, V.II:137, 139
  of artists, V.II:75, 76, 80
  of artwork from creator's intention, V.II:70
  cultural, V.I:41
  as cynicism result, V.II:87
  division of labor as cause of, V.II:75
  in *Mythic Being* series, V.I:147
  overcoming sense of, V.I:204
  overproduction and, V.II:76
  positive aspects of, V.I:245
  of product from process, V.I:33, 36
  race and, V.I:233, 278
  racial identity and, V.I:285
  self-acceptance accompanied by, V.I:173
  self-conscious, in Euroethnic art, V.II:211
  suggested remedies for, V.II:80–81
Alien(s) V.I:xx, 91; V.II:xviii
  artwork dismissed as, V.II:139
  fear of. *See* Xenophobia
  Mythic Being as, V.I:138
  Other as, V.I:206, 208
  persons vs., V.II:227
Allegiance to group, V.I:233
Allen Memorial Art Museum, V.I:176
Aloofness of artist, V.I:xv; V.II:xiii
Alter egos, V.I:xviii; V.II:xvi
  personal history for, V.I:103
  See also Mythic Being
Alternative Museum, V.I:xvi, 237; V.II:xiv, 134n3
Altruism, V.I:145
Ambiguity
  appearance and, V.I:17
  as value in art world, V.I:203
Ambivalence, about art world success, V.I:239
Ambrosian chant, V.II:175
American art
  contemporary, V.II:209–214
  Greenbergian formalism in, V.II:209, 211–212
  influence on European art of, V.II:213, 214
  social content in European art vs., V.II:211–212
American Bandstand, V.I:xv; V.II:xiii
American cultural imperialism, V.II:213, 214
American culture, V.I:209
American Dream, tragic dimension of, V.I:xxiv; V.II:xxii
American Express, V.I:273
"American Painting during the Cold War" (Kozloff) V.II:212n1
American vs. European modernism, V.II:211–212
Amos, Emma, V.II:185
Analysis
  conceptual, V.II:186
  of presuppositions, V.II:17–18
Analytic tradition
  artists and, V.I:xiv, xxxv; V.II:xii, xxxiii
  philosophy and, V.II:149–152, 153
Anderson, Poul, *Tau Zero,* V.I:58–59, 60
Andre, Carl, V.I:3, 29
Androgyny, V.I:123, 124
Angelico, Fra, V.II:209
Anger, V.I:147
  as barrier to art, V.I:230
  bases for, V.II:249–250
  of blacks, V.I:277
  dialogue about, V.I:82–86
  first-order political discrimination and, V.II:248, 249
  frustration and, V.I:65, 66
  at game playing, V.I:64
  higher-order political discrimination and, V.II:248–250
  object vs. cause of, V.I:82, 83–84
  reactions to, V.I:277
  as topic, V.I:184, 185
  value distortions and, V.I:251
Anomalous behavior, as subject matter, V.I:261
Anomalous objects, categorization and, V.I:255
Anomaly, V.II:129–130
  avant-garde form as, V.II:129
  denial as reaction to, V.II:222
  dismissal or suppression of, V.I:265
  innovation dismissed as, V.II:168
  mainstream responses to, V.II:129, 132
  resistance to integration of, V.II:220
  response to Other as, V.I:129
  xenophobia as reaction to, V.II:220, 222, 223, 226
Another Present Era (Perry) V.I:277, 281, 288, 306, 307
Antihumanism, in conceptual art, V.II:3
Anti-Semitism, V.I:219, 229, 233
  higher-order political discrimination and, V.II:240, 241
  pseudorationality and, V.II:222
  racism and, V.I:281
Antithesis, in dialectic analysis, V.II:18
Antiwar movement, ideological doublethink in, V.II:86
Anxiety
  artist accused of, V.II:118
  at presence of other, V.I:246
  unconscious, V.I:xx; V.II:xviii
Appearance, pertinence of, V.I:17
Approach-avoidance, confronting, V.I:177
Appropriating Response, V.I:266–267
Appropriation, V.I:266–267
  of African American art, V.II:183–184, 209
  in art, V.I:217; V.II:211
  by art institutions, V.II:75
  in Euroethnic art, V.II:209, 210, 211
  formalism as result of, V.II:210
  of idiolects of Other, V.II:209
  innovation of form and, V.II:211
Appropriation response, V.I:181
Area Relocation Series (Piper) V.II:12*f*
"Are Art Museums Racist?" (Berger) V.II:185n2
Arena. *See* Art context
Aretha Franklin Catalysis, V.I:151, 152, 201
Aristotle, V.I:99
  Kantian rationalism and, V.II:216–217
  Metaphysics, V.I:32
Arrogance, V.I:203
  illusion of omniscience as, V.II:50
  illusion of perfectability as, V.II:49
  political artists accused of, V.II:177
  self-esteem seen as, V.I:298
Art, V.I:228
  abstract, for art's sake, V.II:196. *See also* Abstract; Abstraction
  aesthetic bias and, V.II:66
  aesthetic value of. *See* Aesthetic value
  African-American. *See* African-American art
  artists as definers of, V.I:32, 33, 51–52
  avant-garde. *See* Avant-garde
  career commitment to, V.II:63–64
  cognitive provocation through, V.II:255
  as communication medium, V.I:xxxi–xxxii, 234; V.II:xxix–xxx
  compensation for, V.I:121–123
  conceptual. *See* Conceptual art
  confrontational, V.I:43–44. *See also* Confrontation
  as confrontation vs. escape, V.I:xxxi; V.II:xxix
  consciousness and, V.I:47
  contemporary. *See* Contemporary art
  contexts for, V.I:xxix–xxx, xxx, xxxi–xxxii, 31, 44–45, 95, 120, 121, 159; V.II:xxvii–E-xxviii, xxviii, xxix–xxx, 6–12, 13, 70, 165n13, 186. *See also* Art context(s)
  criteria for, V.II:64–65
  cultural racism and, V.II:128
  in daily existence, V.I:xvii; V.II:xv
  defensive reactions to, V.I:249, 251
  definition of, V.II:65–66
  as didactic tool, V.I:40, 249; V.II:26, 27, 203
  documentation and, V.I:35, 36–37
  Easy Listening, V.I:xxxii; V.II:xxx, 176–177, 178, 181

economics and, V.I:xxxii, 40; V.II:xxx
environmental, ideas in, V.II:10*f*
Euroethnic. *See* Euroethnic art
as exploration medium, V.I:xxxi; V.II:xxix
folk, V.II:65, 127
formalist. *See* Formalism
form in, V.II:6–12
function and, V.II:25
government support issues, V.II:201–206
graffiti, V.II:171n22, 209
"High," V.II:67, 127
ideas in, V.I:239; V.II:5, 8–12. *See also* Conceptual art
insinuating in nonart situations, V.I:37
instructive role of, V.I:xiv; V.II:xii
as intuitive process, V.II:4
language as subject of, V.I:91; V.II:213
mainstream. *See* Mainstream art
marginality of, V.I:234, 236
minimalist. *See* Minimalism
miscommunication in, V.I:185–186
modern, V.II:52, 53–55
performance. *See* Performance(s) Performance art
political contexts for, V.I:xxix–xxx, xxxi–xxxii, 31–32, 161–167; V.II:xxvii–xxviii, E-xxix–xxx. *See also* Political art; Politics, and art
politics separated from, V.II:212–213
and popular culture, V.I:268–269
pricing proposal for, V.II:31–32
process, intellectual conscience and, V.II:154n5
production of. *See* Art making; Production of art
production systems for, V.II:13
purpose of, V.I:32–33
quality issues, V.II:189–200
racial identity and, V.I:234
racism and, V.I:253–254
racism as target of, V.I:246
"rational," V.II:3
reaction of viewers to, V.I:xxxi–xxxii; V.II:xxix–xxx
"reductive," V.II:3
as reflection, V.I:xxiii; V.II:xxi
religious, V.II:193
reproduction implications, V.II:57
self-transcendence through, V.I:232
selling, V.I:270–271
social awareness throught, V.II:253
socialist, V.II:39
social role of, V.II:203, 253
as societal reflection, V.II:20
support for, V.I:xxxii–xxxiii, 239; V.II:xxx–xxxii
as tool for change, V.I:xx, xxi, 240; V.II:xviii, xix
value of, V.II:65
values and, V.II:25–26
See also Art criticism; Art history; Artists; Meta-art; *specific genres*
"Art" (Perreault) V.II:22.2, 22n2
Art activity. *See* Art making
"Art as a Hobby," V.I:115
Art as Experience (Dewey) V.I:39
"Art Beat: "Darky' Chic" (Goldstein) V.II:65n2
"Art Beat: Race and the State of the Arts" (Goldstein) V.II:65n2
"Art Beat: The Romance of Racism" (Goldstein) V.II:73n6
"The Art Biz" (Myers) V.II:72n5
Art category, V.I:51–53
Art collectors, V.II:64, 71–72
protest movement and, V.I:31
Art of Conscience: The Last Decade, V.II:43
Art context, formalist aesthetic judgment and, V.II:195
Art context(s) V.I:xxix–xxx, xxxi–xxxii, 31, 95; V.II:xxvii–xxviii, xxix–xxx, 186
aesthetics and, V.I:95
alternative, V.I:45
appropriation and, V.I:217
art world as, V.II:24
avoidance responses in, V.I:177
categorization and, V.I:50
choice of, V.I:142–143
consciousness as, V.I:100–101
criticism as independent of, V.II:70
dynamic vs. static, V.I:137
expectations and, V.II:54
function as independent of, V.II:70
importance of, V.II:8
independence from, V.I:159
institutional determinants of, V.II:65
legitimacy and, V.II:81–82
limitations of, V.I:44–45
media and, V.II:6, 7
politics and, V.I:122–123, 161–167; V.II:43
problems with, V.I:39–42
product and, V.II:13
subject matter as independent of, V.II:70
varying responses and, V.I:209–211
Art-contextual legitimacy, political effectiveness and, V.II:81–82
Art criticism, V.II:29, 41–42, 68–69, 108, 125
African-American art and, V.II:161
by artist of own work, V.I:xxix; V.II:xxvii
artists and, V.II:21–22, 68–69, 70–71
artist's definition of, V.I:xiii; V.II:xi
artist's rebuttal of, V.II:107–125
artist's role in, V.I:xv–xvi; V.II:xiii–xiv
artist's views on, V.I:236
of artist vs. work, V.II:164–166
biography vs., V.II:143–146, 186
in "cheap art utopia," V.II:33
conflict of interest and, V.II:68–69
as context-independent, V.II:70
critical hegemony and, V.II:65, 66
cultural knowledge and, V.II:165
cultural racism in, V.II:135–143, 146
dealers' role in, V.II:71–72
division of labor and, V.II:67–69
ethnocentricity of, V.II:184–185
formalism and, V.II:64–65, 69–70
inadequacy of psychoanalysis in, V.II:125
incompetence in, V.II:182
inflated theorizing in, V.I:236
intellectualism in, V.II:196
intellectual radicalism and, V.II:152
Marxist viewpoint on, V.II:213
meta-art and, V.I:xxx–xxxi; V.II:xviii-xxix, 2.22, 2.24
parochialism in, V.I:236
as parody, V.I:xvi; V.II:xiv, 121
political correctness and, V.I:236
politically self-aware, V.I:xxix; V.II:xxvii
power of, V.II:68, 69
questions about, V.II:186–187
responsibility of, V.II:184–187
socioeconomic conditions and, V.II:23–24, 72
xenophobia in, V.II:143, 145, 146
Art Criticism, V.II:107
Art critics
art establishment and, V.I:53
artists as, V.I:xv–xvi; V.II:xiii–xiv
as closet artists, V.II:69
cultural racism of, V.II:140–141
dealers as, V.II:71–72
formalist values and, V.II:64
mainstream, V.I:xvi–xvii; V.II:xiv–xv
meta-art misunderstood by, V.II:108, 109, 111
meta-art perspective for, V.I:xxix; V.II:xxvii
myth of objectivity, V.I:xxix; V.II:xxvii
power of, V.II:68
responsibility of, V.II:184–185
viewpoints of, V.I:xvi; V.II:xiv
zero-sum game and, V.II:167
Art education, V.II:66–68
aesthetic acculturation and, V.II:66–67, 68
Euroethnicity and, V.II:66–67
intellectual radicalism and, V.II:152
judgments of quality and, V.II:196, 197
marketing and, V.II:71
positive aspects of, V.II:66–67
production and, V.II:71
sociocultural context and, V.II:72
Arte povera, appropriation and, V.II:183
Art establishment
art category vs., V.I:52–53
artist's participation in, V.I:52
See also Art world
"Art for art's sake," V.I:xiv, xvii, 237; V.II:xii, xv, 43, 189, 196
Art forms, choice of, V.I:3
Art for people's sake, V.II:43
Art for the Art-World Surface Pattern (Piper) V.I:161, 165*f*, 228, 265
description of, V.I:162–164, 167
Artforum (magazine) V.I:29, 100
in author's dream, V.I:100
Art history, V.II:168
and art criticism, V.II:22, 23–24
artist's place in, V.I:xxix; V.II:xxvii
division of labor and, V.II:72
Easy Listening Art and, V.II:176–177
emphasis on Euroethnic art in, V.II:186
ethnocentrism in, V.I:xiv; V.II:xii

Artifacts, V.I:146; V.II:168
cultural, V.I:217
outlaw, V.I:217
as tool for transcendence, V.II:192–193
Artificial context, for presenting idea, V.II:6–7
Artificial relationships, expressing dualism through, V.I:18
Art institutions, V.II:72–77, 89
appropriation by, V.II:75, 183–184
artists as investors in, V.II:80–81
complicity of artists with, V.II:85
formalist values in, V.II:64–65
ideological indoctrination by, V.I:xxxvi; V.II:xxxiv
politics and, V.II:81–83
success and, V.II:167–173
See also Art education
Artist-audience relationships, V.I:47; V.II:95–99, 100–101
catalysis through, V.II:177–178
as collaborative, V.I:205; V.II:100
as confrontational, V.I:xx, 177, 178–179; V.II:xviii. *See also* Confrontation
Artistic encounter, aesthetic emotion and, V.II:195–196
Artistic expression, V.II:74
Artistic independence, as myth, V.II:78
Artistic success, as zero-sum game, V.II:167, 169–172
Artistic temperament, romanticism and, V.II:24
Artistic vs. moral standards, V.II:154–158
Artist(s) V.I:xiii, 35, 42, 239–240; V.II:xi, 56
accessibility and, V.I:115
admittance to mainstream from margins, V.II:185–186
aesthetic quality of, V.II:20–21
aesthetic vs. personal significance of work to, V.II:93
alienation of. *See* Alienation
analytic philosophy and, V.I:xxxv; V.II:xxxiii
art criticism and, V.II:21–22, 68–69, 70–71, 164–166
art critics as, V.II:69
art defined by, V.I:32, 33
and art history, V.II:23, 186
and art market, V.II:71–72, 75–76
as art object. *See* Art object(s) artist as
as audience, V.I:53
audience awareness needed by, V.II:94–95
author's exposure to, V.I:3
autonomy issues among, V.II:63, 87–88
black. *See* Black artists
career commitment by, V.II:63–64, 66–67
as catalytic agents, V.I:34–55
in "cheap art utopia," V.II:33–34
classification of, V.I:248
colored, V.I:xxxviiin3; V.II:xxxvin3, 183–184. *See also* Black artists; Colored women E-artists
competition among, V.II:167
complicity of with art institutions, V.II:85
concretizing vision of, V.I:94
criticism and, V.II:64–65, 68–69
dealers and, V.II:71–72
detachment of, V.II:3
dialogue between audience and, V.II:102
dialogue as goal of, V.II:144
division of labor and, V.II:67–69, 71–73
ego of, V.I:264
epistemic nature of, V.II:20–21
ethics and, V.II:73–75
feminist, V.I:xxxvii; V.II:xxxv
formalist values and, V.II:64–65
historian compared with, V.II:79
ideological fictions and, V.II:85–86, 87–89
innovation pressures on, V.II:78–79
inscrutability of, V.II:20
investment in institutions by, V.II:80–81
isolation of, V.I:39, 122; V.II:26
mainstream. *See* Mainstream artists
marginalized. *See* Marginality; Marginalization
meta-art as occupation for; V.II:17, 18, 20–21, 22
motivations of, V.II:19
motivation vs. effects of, V.II:139–140, 144
objectivity of, V.II:3
as observers, V.I:95–96
opacity and uniqueness of, V.II:19–20, 21
otherness of, V.II:165–166
as parasites, V.I:40
passivity of assumed, V.II:101
persona and, V.I:112
personality vs. objectivity and, V.II:3
personal vs. aesthetic significance of work and, V.II:93
political statement for, V.II:29
politics and, V.I:40–41, 202–203; V.II:81–85, 86–87, 86–89
power of, V.I:203; V.II:101
production rate of, V.II:76–77
production role of, V.II:72–73, 79–80
quality judgment and empowerment of, V.II:198
relationship of with audience, V.I:47; V.II:95–99, 100–101
responsibility of, V.I:xv, 203; V.II:xiii, 74–75
right of to communicate, V.I:203
roles of, V.I:xv, xxxvi–xxxvii, 9, 39, 40; V.II:xiii, xxxiv–xxxv, 70–71, 72–73, 95. *See E-also specific types of roles*
separating work from, V.I:33
social role of, V.II:25–27, 50, 89
socioeconomic constraints on, V.II:78
as spectators, V.I:94
as subject-object, V.II:129
as subject, V.II:101–102, 118, 120. *See also* Artist(s) as art object
success determinants for, V.II:153–154, 167–168, 169–172
supplementary occupations for, V.II:80
training of. *See* Art education
vocational role for, V.II:23, 24. *See also* Artist(s) meta-art as occupation for
women. *See* Women artists
as workers, V.II:32
Artist's books, V.I:259
"Artists Grapple with New Realities" (Brenson) V.I:277n7
Artists' Space, V.II:162
Art journals, responsibility of, V.II:184–187
Art-Language (Atkinson) V.I:11
Art-Language group, V.II:213
Art lovers. *See* Audience; Viewers
Art making, V.I:94–95; V.II:18–20
abstraction and, V.I:225
conditions on, V.I:159
conflict with philosophy, V.I:92–93
decision making in, V.I:119–120
economics and, V.I:121–123, 234, 239
fear and, V.I:94
inner conflicts and, V.I:92–93
as lifeline to integrity, V.II:132
methodological considerations, V.I:119–120
motivation and, V.I:52, 245
opacity in, V.II:19–20
philosophy as influence on, V.I:242
philosophy vs., V.I:105
political constraints on, V.I:120–121, 122–123
political context and, V.I:40
political neutrality of, V.II:82–84
production and exchange value in, V.II:31
purpose of for artist, V.II:132
reason and, V.I:119–120
self-transcendence through, V.I:232
stress and, V.I:239
uniqueness in, V.II:19–20
See also Works
Art market, V.I:239–240
academia compared to, V.II:79–80
artists and, V.II:71–72
ideological indoctrination for, V.I:xxxvi; V.II:xxxiv
pressure of, V.II:76
standards of excellence defined by, V.II:154–155, 156
value determined by, V.II:169–170
Art News (magazine) V.I:29
Art object(s) V.I:9–10, 34–35, 118
as aesthetic vs. epistemic, V.II:19
appropriation of by art institutions, V.II:75
artist as, V.I:35–36, 42–45, 49–51, 53, 89–90, 91, 92, 94, 95, 100–102, 261, 262; V.II:21, E-100, 101, 102, 129, 213–214
as art product, V.II:13
as catalytic agents, V.I:34–35, 36, 262
cognitive discrimination and, V.II:257–258
as commodities, V.II:55, 59
as communication medium, V.II:93
confrontation with, V.II:177–178, 256–257
consciousness as arena for, V.I:100–101
deformation of, V.II:76–78
as enigmatic exemplars, V.II:26

equilibrium of, V.II:257–258
function and, V.II:25
generalization of, V.II:55–56
humans as, V.I:19, 262
identity of, V.II:51–56, 58, 59, 60
ideological restrictions and, V.I:115
instrumentalizing conception and, V.II:52
isolation of, V.I:39–40, 42; V.II:58
language as, V.I:259; V.II:213
media as, V.I:258–259
in minimalism, V.I:257; V.II:213, 254–255
mystery of, V.II:51, 52–53, 56, 58
nonart objects vs., V.I:41–42
nonmaterial, V.I:118
passivity of assumed, V.II:101
pricing proposal for, V.II:31–32
reproduction implications, V.II:57–58
text as, V.I:263–264
uniqueness and aesthetic value of, V.II:57–58
See also Art product
Art product
defined, V.II:13
uniqueness of, V.II:79–80
See also Art object(s)
Art production systems, V.II:13. *See also* Production of art
Art professionals, as funding decision makers, V.II:203–204
Art Selector, artist as, V.I:9
"Art Self-Consciousness Consciousness," V.I:27
Art Students' League, V.I:29
Art subject(s) *See* Subject matter
Art world, V.I:265
aesthetics vs. economics in, V.I:121
affirmative action welfare in, V.II:183, 184
artist's relationship with, V.II:137
artist's view of, V.I:32
bestowing of significance by, V.II:156, 157–158
black self-awareness and communication with, V.I:180
blind review proposals and, V.II:171
catalysis as limited by, V.I:44–45
colored male artists and, V.II:170–171
colored women artists and, V.II:163–173
competition in, V.II:167
as context for art, V.II:24
entropy in, V.I:39–40
Euroethnicity in, V.II:65, 67, 161, 165, 167, 168, 171–172, 183–184, 186
heterosexual white male aesthetic in, V.II:161
ideology in, V.I:xxxvi, xxxviii; V.II:xxxiv, xxxvi, 167–169
isolation in, V.I:41
male focus of, V.II:161, 169–170
marginality in, V.I:234, 236, 237
money and status in, V.I:114–115
Mythic Being as confrontation with, V.I:138
performance for, V.I:151
political events and, V.I:30–31
political statement on, V.II:29
politics and, V.II:44, 81–82
power relationships in, V.I:190; V.II:43
quality issues in, V.II:189–200
racism in, V.I:xxxv, xxxvi; V.II:xxxiii, xxxiv, 163–164, 185
reactions to artist in, V.I:262, 265
repression in, V.II:161, 162–163
response to external pressure, V.I:xxxviii; V.II:xxxvi
sexism in, V.I:xxxv, xxxvi; V.II:xxxiii, xxxiv
standards of excellence in, V.II:154–158
success determinants in, V.II:153–154, 167–168, 169–172
value of originality in, V.II:153
welfare system in, V.II:183, 184, 186, 187
withdrawal from, V.I:227
women artists and, V.II:168
See also Art establishment; Art institutions
"Art World Racism: A Documentation" (Pindell) V.II:164
Asimov, Isaac, V.II:240, 244
Foundation Series, V.I:59
As One (Kool and the Gang) V.I:215
Aspects of the Liberal Dilemma (Piper) V.I:171*f*, 266; V.II:140
description of, V.I:169–170
Asphalt Rundown (Smithson) V.II:10*f*
Assault, perceptual, V.II:55
Assimilation, V.I:51, 53, 174
conceptual, V.II:132
cultural integrity vs., V.II:141
higher-order political discrimination and, V.II:240
limits of, V.I:201–202
realization about, V.I:80
as subject for artist, V.I:xv; V.II:xiii
Assorted Anti-Postmodernist Artifacts (Piper) V.I:217
Assumptions
in *A.~A,* V.I:145
attacking work through, V.II:136
of audience, V.I:203
of "avant-garde," V.I:203
biographical viewpoints and, V.II:143, 144
as limits, V.I:142
and limits of assimilation, V.I:201–202
Astaire, Fred, V.I:199; V.II:239
Asymmetry, first-/third-person, V.II:223–224
Atkinson, Terry
Art-Language, V.I:11
letter to, V.I:15
Audience, V.I:47; V.II:154
accessibility of artist to, V.I:115
artist as, V.I:53
artist's awareness of, V.II:94–95
artist's relationship with. *See* Artist-audience relationships
assumptions of, V.I:203
awareness in, V.I:143
in "cheap art utopia," V.II:33
collaboration with, V.I:205. *See also* Artist-audience relationships
communication with, V.I:210; V.II:84, 93, 98. *See also* Communication
confrontation with, V.I:xx, 177, 178–179; V.II:xviii. *See also* Confrontation
construction of image with, V.I:156
and contemporary art, V.II:255–256
critical feedback role of, V.II:98–99
defense mechanisms of, V.I:164
dialogue between artist and, V.II:102
listening to vs. hearing music by, V.II:175–176
for meta-art, V.II:18
miscommunication with, V.II:93
misevaluation by, V.II:93
for music meant to be heard, V.II:176
mutilation by artist for, V.I:189, 192
participation by. *See* Participation by audience
and performance, V.I:49–50, 177–180, 205–206; V.II:60–61
political art and, V.II:83–84
reactions of, V.I:xxxi–xxxii, 7, 32–33, 124, 205–206, 249, 251, 268–270; V.II:xxix–xxx
role of, V.I:51
self-discovery as goal for, V.II:130, 132
Some Reflective Surfaces and, V.I:151
xenophobia of, V.I:268
See also Viewers
Audio tape, V.I:48, 49, 144
in *Art for the Art-World Surface Pattern,* V.I:265
Just Gossip and, V.I:141
as medium, V.I:141
as medium for abstraction, V.I:227
Auerbach, David, V.I:147
Aural information contexts, V.II:7
Authenticity
adherence to role and, V.I:208
in friendship, V.I:300–301
passing and, V.I:276
Authority, V.I:189; V.II:83
Autobiographical material, V.I:89–90, 91; V.II:94
artwork misinterpreted as, V.II:139
in Mythic Being, V.I:117
rationale for using, V.I:246
"Autobiography: In Her Own Image" exhibit, V.II:166
The Autobiography of an Ex-Coloured Man (Johnson) V.I:282, 285, 295, 305, 307
The Autobiography of Malcolm X (Malcolm X) V.I:293, 295, 301, 307
Autonomy, V.I:115; V.II:186
art as career and, V.II:63
creative, V.II:87–88
maintaining, V.I:27
Avalanche interviews, V.II:22
Avant-garde
assumptions of, V.I:203

end of claimed, V.II:163n8
existence of, V.I:236
marginalized artists and, V.II:183, 185–186
moving from, V.II:185
response to anomaly in, V.II:129, 130
Average White Band, *Shine,* V.I:215
Avoidance
confronting, V.I:177
as response to racism, V.I:181
Awards in the Visual Arts, V.II:162
Awe, aesthetic emotion and, V.II:191, 192

Baader-Meinhof gang, V.II:35
Baca, Judy, V.I:236
Bach, Johann Sebastian, V.II:175
Prelude and Fugue, V.I:91
"Backing Down Behind Closed Doors at the NEA" (Hess) V.II:201n2
Bad faith
acknowledgment of racial identity and, V.I:300–301
in mainstream art world, V.I:xxxvii, xxxviii; V.II:xxxv, xxxvi
"Bad Painting" exhibition, V.II:154n5
Baer, Jo, V.II:52
Balance, aesthetic emotion and, V.II:192, 193
Balzac, Honoré de, V.II:240, 244
Bars and discos, calling card for, V.I:221, 272
Beauty, content vs., V.I:249. *See also* Quality; Taste
Beckett, Samuel, V.I:258
Beethoven, Ludwig van, V.I:268, 293; V.II:175
Behavior, self-consciousness and, V.I:92
Behavioral codes, street performances and, V.I:262
Behavioral norms, V.I:246–247
disvaluees and, V.II:250–251
See also Conventions
Being and Nothingness (Sartre) V.I:117
Beliefs
higher-order political discrimination and, V.II:243–245
ideology and, V.II:48–50
self-examination and, V.II:47–48
Berger, Maurice, V.I:273; V.II:185
"Are Art Museums Racist?," V.II:185n2
"Speaking Out: Some Distance to Go," V.II:185n2
Berkeley, *Funk Lessons* performance in, V.I:202*f,* 269
Berlin, author's visit to, V.II:35–39
Berry, Chuck, V.I:199
Betrayal
anger at, V.I:82–83
sense of, V.I:300
Beuys, Joseph, V.I:xv; V.II:xiii
Bhagavad Gita, V.I:9
Bias
aesthetic, V.II:66
socioculturally determined, V.II:65–66
Bibliography of Funk, V.I:216, 269
Billboard, *Think About It,* V.I:272
Biography of artist, art criticism vs., V.II:143–146, 186
Bittner, Rüdiger, V.II:231n18
"Black Artists: A Place in the Sun" (Brenson) V.II:170.21, 185n3
Black artists, acceptance by art world of, V.I:xxxvii, xxxviii; V.II:xxxv, xxxvi
"Black Artists Today: A Case of Exclusion?" (Failing) V.II:170.21, 185n3
Black culture, richness of, V.I:203. *See also* Black popular culture
Black Like Me (Griffin) V.I:285, 296, 297, 299, 307
Black music and dance, V.I:195–196
Blackness, V.II:134n4
rejection of, V.I:206
self-awareness and, V.I:175*f*
Suffering Test of, V.I:276, 278, 303, 305
See also Racial identity
Black Panthers, V.II:70n4
Black popular culture, V.I:198, 199–201
richness of, V.I:203
xenophobia and, V.I:198, 199, 200, 201
See also Black working-class culture
Black power movement, V.I:xvii; V.II:xv
Blacks
in academic philosophy, V.II:151
acknowledgment of mixed ancestry among, V.I:292–293
and civil rights movement, V.I:199, 262
culture of, V.I:201, 203, 206. *See also* Black popular culture; Black working-class culture
discrimination against, V.II:222, 247n29, 250.34
experience of racism among, V.I:263
first- vs. higher-order racism against, V.II:247n29
and Funk music, V.I:195, 196, 197, 198–199, 270
higher-order political discrimination and, V.II:240, 241
identity as, V.I:229–230, 233, 272, 275–306. *See also* Racial identity
legal definition of, V.I:291–292
middle-class, V.I:277, 278
"one-drop" classification of, V.I:291–292
as Other, V.I:208
politics and, V.I:199, 284
popular culture of. *See* Black popular culture; Black working-class culture
pseudorationality and discrimination against, V.II:222
racism and, V.I:169, 181, 219–220, 266–267, 273; V.II:127. *See also* Racism
reactions of, V.I:249
stereotypes of, V.I:xviii, 253, 266–268; V.II:xvi
terms used for, V.I:204, 305
use of term, V.II:127n1
xenophobic reactions to, V.I:198–199
See also African Americans; Colored
Black self-awareness, communication with art world and, V.I:180
Black Skins, White Masks (Fanon) V.II:137n10
Black working-class culture, V.I:201, 206, 207–208, 229; V.II:197
appropriation of artifacts from, V.I:217
art world's reaction to, V.I:268
cultural racism and, V.II:127
Funk Lessons and, V.I:195–196, 198–200
Funk music and, V.I:203
richness of, V.I:203
See also Black popular culture
Blindfolding, ideological, V.II:214
Blindness
commitment and, V.I:69, 72–73
to needs of others, V.II:50
Blind review, art world and, V.II:171
Block Area Enlargement Series (Piper) V.I:16*f,* 17, 18
"Blue Rhythm and Hot Notes" (Jones) V.I:216
Blumberg, B. S., "Selection, Gene Migration and Polymorphic Stability," V.II:245n27
Bobo, Lawrence, *Racial Attitudes in America: Trends and Interpretations,* V.II:246n28
Bodmer, W. F., *The Genetics of Human Populations,* V.II:245n27
Body, as self-conscious object, V.I:19
Body art, V.II:129. *See also* Performance art
Boll, Heinrich, *Group Portrait with Lady,* V.I:141
Books
artist's, V.I:259
distributing art in, V.II:34
as unsituated information contexts, V.II:7
Bootsy (William Collins) V.I:212*f,* 268
Bootsy's Rubber Band (Bootsy) V.I:214, 215
The One Giveth, V.I:214
Player of the Year Award, V.I:214
"Shejam (Almost Bootsy Show)" V.I:215
Ultra Wave, V.I:214
Borges, Jorge-Luis, V.I:xviii–xix; V.II:xvi–xvii
Borough map location series, V.I:17, 18
Boundaries
fear of violation of, V.I:254, 255, 256; V.II:132
language as conveyor of, V.I:15
The Bounds of Sense (Strawson) V.II:217n6
Brand, Peggy Zeglin, *Feminism and Tradition in Aesthetics,* V.I:181
Brenson, Michael, V.I:xiv; V.II:xii, 127, 163, 185, 187n12
article on quality reviewed, V.II:189–200
"Artists Grapple with New Realities," V.II:77n7
"Black Artists: A Place in the Sun," V.II:170.21, 185n3
"Is Quality an Idea Whose Time Has Gone?," V.II:189.1
The Brothers Johnson, *Light Up the Night,* V.I:215
Brown, James, V.I:214
Browne, Tom, *Love Approach,* V.I:214
Buchanan, Nancy, V.II:108

Buchwalter, Andrew, V.II:204
Culture and Democracy: Social and Ethical Issues in Public Support for the Arts and E-Humanities, V.II:201
"Philosophy, Culture, and Public Policy," V.II:204n3
Burnham, Linda, V.II:108
Burroughs, William, V.II:193
Burton, Scott, V.I:xxxv; V.II:xxxiii
Bush, George, V.I:299
Business cards. *See* Calling cards
Byzantine religious art, appropriation of, V.II:209

Califia, Pat, "Feminism and Sadomasochism," V.II:47n1
Calling cards, V.I:xix, 219–221, 230, 245, 249, 271–272; V.II:xvii
Cambodia, V.I:xvii, 30, 177, 178, 227, 262; V.II:xv
Cambridge (Mass.) V.I:147
Canonization of artist, market vs. aesthetic value and, V.II:77
Canons
admittance from margins to, V.II:185–186
art world's refusal to modify, V.II:169
of Easy Listening Art, V.II:176, 177
expropriation of innovation into, V.II:171
power of words and, V.II:199
Capitalism
art criticism and, V.II:23
artist's role and, V.I:39
art-making context and, V.I:122–123
art production and, V.II:32
art world's decline and, V.I:40
meta-art and, V.II:27
Career, art as, V.II:63–89
autonomy issues in, V.II:63
commitment to, V.II:66–67
financial issues in, V.II:63–65
Carroll, Lewis
Alice in Wonderland, V.I:59
Through the Looking Glass, V.I:59
Catalysis, V.I:32–33, 45
confrontation and, V.I:42–44
through music meant to be heard, V.II:175
through political art, V.II:178
Catalysis series (Piper) V.I:143, 151, 227
Catalysis I, V.I:42
Catalysis III, V.I:43–44, 44*f,* 262
Catalysis IV, V.I:43
Catalysis V, V.I:44
Catalysis VI, V.I:43
Catalysis VII, V.I:45
fear and, V.I:94
Mythic Being series and, V.I:147
random variables in, V.I:143
Spectator Series and, V.I:104
symbology in, V.I:262–263
Catalytic agents
artists as, V.I:34–55
art objects as, V.I:34–35, 36, 262

Categorical imperative, V.I:191
Categorization, V.I:255–256; V.II:133
art context and, V.I:50
of experience, V.I:255
functional, resistance to, V.II:52–53
racism in, V.I:281
social comfort and, V.I:xix; V.II:xvii
Catholic Counter-Reformation, role of art in, V.II:25, 26
"Caucasian Genes in American Negros" (Reed) V.II:245n27
Cavalli-Sforza, L. L., *The Genetics of Human Populations,* V.II:245n27
Cayou, Dolores Kirton, V.I:213
"The Origins of Modern Jazz Dance," V.I:216
CCNY. *See* City College of New York
Censorship, V.I:266, 273; V.II:161
by intimidation, V.II:162
changing subject as, V.II:165
de facto, of male artists vs. CWAs, V.II:163
elitism as result of, V.II:203
as McCarthyism legacy, V.II:209
passive, V.I:xxxv, xxxvi; V.II:xxxiii, xxxiv, 201–202
people with AIDS and, V.II:166
political art and, V.I:266
See also Self-censorship
Center. *See* Marginality
Certainty, epistemology and, V.I:74
Cézanne, Paul, V.II:3
Chaka Khan (Chaka Khan) V.I:215
Change. *See* Social change
Chaos
aesthetic emotion and, V.II:193–194
ideas obstructed by, V.II:6
Charts. *See* Media
Chaucer, Geoffrey, V.I:201, 269
"Cheap art utopia," V.II:33
Chernoff, John Miller, *African Rhythm and African Sensibility,* V.I:215
Chess, V.I:77
Chestnutt, Charles Waddell, *Journals,* V.I:279, 307
Chicanos; Chicanas, political engagement vs. professional success and, V.II:81–82
Chinese art, aesthetic emotion and, V.II:198
Chisholm, Roderick, *Perceiving,* V.I:92
Church Street Post Office, V.I:48
Cimabue, V.II:209
City College of New York (CCNY) V.I:xvii, 31, 228, 262; V.II:xv
protest movement at, V.I:30, 31
Civil rights movement, V.I:xvii, 195, 199; V.II:xv
ideological doublethink in, V.II:86
Civil society, state vs., V.II:206
Clarity, V.I:3, 17; V.II:3, 6
as aesthetic value, V.I:267
existential, V.I:258
Clarke, Arthur, V.I:58, 60
The Clash, "Overpowered by Funk" (*Combat Rock*) V.I:215

Classification, as instrument of racism, V.I:305
Class, social
higher-order political discrimination and, V.II:240–241, 243, 245, 249
reciprocal higher-order political discrimination and, V.II:242, 243
status and, V.I:147
support for artist and, V.I:xxxiii; V.II:xxxi
Claustrophobia, V.I:162
in *Four Intruders. . .,* V.I:181
Clinton, George, V.I:xv, 268; V.II:xiii, 175
Close to Home (Piper) V.I:246
Close to Home II.B (Piper) V.I:243*f*
Close to Home #IV.B (Piper) V.I:250*f*
Closet artists, art critics as, V.II:69
Cockcroft, Eva, "Abstract Expressionism: Weapon of the Cold War," V.II:212n1
Cocktail parties, confronting racism at, V.I:219–220
Coe, Sue, V.II:193
Cognition
and categorization, V.I:255, 281
and experience, V.II:219–220
Cognitive discrimination
art objects and, V.II:257–258
definition of, V.II:215
experience and, V.II:217–220
failures of, V.II:251–258
political discrimination and, V.II:216–217
strategies for cultivating, V.II:253–258
xenophobia and, V.II:220–228
Cognitive dissonance, V.I:230
categorization for prevention of, V.I:255
Cognitive errors
personal investment in, V.II:228–229
xenophobia and, V.II:223–228
Cognitive inaccessibility, V.II:210
Cognitive structuring
experience and, V.II:217–220
language and, V.II:217
Coherence, as performance goal, V.I:155
Cold war, role of art in, V.II:212–213
Coles, Robert, "Shrinking History Part 1," V.II:18n1
Collaboration
artist-audience, V.I:205; V.II:100–102
catalysis through, V.II:177–178
of dealer and collectors, V.II:71–72
in *Funk Lessons,* V.I:195–211
morality and, V.I:145
objecthood vs., V.I:27
overproduction and, V.II:76–77
power relationships and, V.I:190, 191–192
Collections, success as admission to, V.II:167
Collective past, V.I:295
Collectors
art criticism and, V.II:23
collaboration with dealers by, V.II:71–72
formalist values and, V.II:64
protest movement and, V.I:31
relationship with, V.I:270
success defined by, V.II:167

Collins, William. *See* Bootsy
Colonized people, African Americans as, V.II:171
Color
burden of, V.I:xxiv; V.II:xxii
persons of, use of term, V.II:127n1, 161n1
Colored
stereotyping of, V.II:135
use of term, V.I:204, 305; V.II:127, 127n1
See also African Americans; Blacks
Colored artists
biographical viewpoints and, V.II:143, 144–145
mainstream artists and, V.I:xxxviiin3; V.II:xxxvin3
plagiarism from, V.II:183–184
poststructuralism and, V.II:169n19
research questions on, V.II:186–187
stereotyped as Other, V.II:186
See also Colored women artists
Colored male artists, Euroethnic art world and, V.II:170–171
"Colored" (Raven) V.II:162n4
Colored women, marginalization of, V.I:xxxiv, xxxv; V.II:xxxii, xxxiii
Colored women artists (CWAs)
art world and, V.II:161, 163–173
dual battle of, V.II:166
intellectual integrity and, V.II:169
seen as Other, V.II:165–166
seen as threat, V.II:168–169
stereotyping of, V.II:164–165
zero-sum game and, V.II:172
Combat Rock (The Clash) V.I:215
Comic books, accessibility of, V.II:33–34
Commercialism, as substitute for history, V.II:214
Commitment
to art career, V.II:63–64
conversation about, V.I:67–80
rationality and, V.I:67, 80
Commodities, art objects as, V.I:40; V.II:59, 214
Commodity consumption, marginal utility of, V.II:54–55
Communal activism, individual imagination and, V.I:xv; V.II:xiii
Communal nature of art, V.II:190
Communication, V.I:210; V.II:84, 93, 98
and alienation, V.I:256–257
artist's right to, V.I:203
art as medium for, V.I:xxxi–xxxii, 234; V.II:xxix–xxx
breakdown of in here and now, V.I:257
comprehending-uncomprehending dichotomy, V.II:97–98
conventionality and, V.I:77
cross-cultural, V.I:180
in dance, V.I:177
in declaratives, V.I:xxxiv; V.II:xxxii–xxxiii
and form, V.II:6
idiom of, importance of sharing, V.II:96
language used for power vs., V.I:265
misunderstandings and, V.I:185–186
one-way mechanism of, V.II:49
shared lexicon of symbols and, V.II:96
See also Audience, communication with
Communications media, internal activity and, V.I:38
Communism. *See* McCarthyism
Community
dissemination of art in, V.II:88
politics and, V.I:202–203
sense of, V.I:174
support of, V.II:77–78
Compensation, V.I:121–123
Competence, intellectual independence and, V.II:151–152
Competition
between women, V.I:126
cooperative model vs., V.II:173
funding sources and, V.II:203
marketing and, V.I:239
Composing, by author, V.I:89, 90
Composite masses, V.I:21
Concept; Conceptualization
cognitive discrimination and, V.II:217, 218, 219
elasticity of, V.I:142
misinterpretation of, V.II:96
as preproduct discipline, V.I:4
Conception
empirical, V.II:222–223, 224–225
errors of. *See* Cognitive errors
personal investment in, V.II:228–229
rational failure of, V.II:227–228
Conceptual analysis, V.II:186
Conceptual art, V.I:xxxiv–xxxvi, 241–242, 249, 262; V.II:xxxiii
abstraction in, V.I:227, 242
alienation in, V.I:38
analytic philosophy and, V.I:xxxv; V.II:xxxiii
antihumanism in, V.II:3
artist as art object in, V.I:19; V.II:213–214
artist's definition of, V.I:248
cognitive discrimination and, V.II:255
defense of process in, V.II:3–4
first-generation context, V.I:xxx; V.II:xxviii
going beyond, V.I:31
idea as primary in, V.I:4–5, 38, 258–259; V.II:11
intellectual conscience and, V.II:154n5
language and, V.I:xxxv, 241–242; V.II:xxxiii
marginalization of artist and, V.I:xxxv–xxxvi; V.II:xxxiii–xxxiv
marginalization of women in, V.I:xxxv; V.II:xxxiii
Meat into Meat as, V.I:261–262
media in, V.I:248–249
objectivity in, V.II:3–4
role of, V.I:xvii; V.II:xv
self-reflexivity in, V.II:213–214
shared vocabulary for, V.I:xxx; V.II:xxviii
social content in, V.II:213–214
symbology in, V.I:257–258, 259, 261
See also Conceptualism
"Conceptual Art and Conceptual Artists" exhibit, V.I:30
Conceptual artist, author as, V.I:248–249
Conceptual distance, for functional objects, V.II:52
Conceptualism
abstraction and, V.I:227, 242
aesthetic values in, V.I:267
generalization in, V.I:224
historical background, V.I:xiii–xiv; V.II:xi–xii
nonart situations and, V.I:xvii; V.II:xv
philosophical roots of, V.I:xiv; V.II:xii
See also Conceptual art
Conceptualization, V.II:96
"Conceptualized Conflicts" (Thorson) V.II:186n8
Concrete, dichotomy between abstract and, V.II:94, 98–99
Concrete forms, V.II:6
Concrete Infinity 6" Square (Piper) V.I:14*f*
Concrete particulars, distortion of, V.I:248
Concrete Space-Time Infinity 8" Square (Piper) V.I:258–259
Concrete Space-Time-Infinity Pieces (Piper) V.I:241–242
Concretized form of ideas, V.II:3–4
Concretizing of artist's vision, V.I:94
Condescension
audience's feelings of, V.II:101
in culture, V.II:88
Conditions on art making, V.I:159. *See also* Life conditions; Socioeconomic conditions; E-Spatiotemporal conditions
Conflict of interest, art criticism and, V.II:68–69
Conformity
art career and, V.II:64
to social categories, V.I:255
social comfort and, V.I:233
Confrontation, V.I:34, 178–179
An Open Letter from Adrian Piper, V.II:45
as antidote for ideology, V.II:50
art as, V.I:9–10, 43–44, 266–267
art as escape vs., V.I:xxxi; V.II:xxix
catalysis and, V.I:42–44
for cognitive provocation, V.II:256–258
in collaborative political art, V.II:177–178
dance as, V.I:177
of economic exploitation, V.II:130
of ideological fiction, V.II:87
in indexical present, V.I:xx; V.II:xviii
interpretive control and, V.II:100, 101
in *Mythic Being* series, V.I:138, 147
in performance art, V.I:9–10, 155–156, 180; V.II:99, 100, 101
of racism, V.I:xx, 169, 220, 266–267, 271–272; V.II:xviii

ritualized, disco dancing as, V.I:151
of stereotyping, V.I:xxi, 242; V.II:xix
as theme, V.I:137, 141
of xenophobia, V.I:234, 242
ConFunkShun,
Spirit of Love, V.I:214
To the Max, V.I:214
Confusion, as barrier to art, V.I:230
Conscience, V.I:xxxix, 9; V.II:xxxvii, 187
higher-order political discrimination and, V.II:216, 246–247
intellectual, V.II:151–152, 154–155
Consciousness, V.I:102
aesthetic emotion and, V.II:190
art as arising from, V.I:47
as art context, V.I:100–101
artist as object of, V.I:50
in art production systems, V.II:13
cognitive discrimination and, V.II:218–219
documenting contents of, V.I:19–23
failure to perceive in Other, V.II:227–228
and objects, V.I:94, 95, 100–101
self-conscious, V.I:27
sensory, V.I:20–21
subjective, V.II:223
subjective limits of, V.I:142
See also Self-consciousness
Consciousness-raising, call for, V.II:89
Conscripts and Volunteers (Fullinwider) V.II:49n2
Conservatism
in analytic philosophy, V.II:150
ideological fictions and, V.II:86, 87, 88
positive aspects of, V.II:151–152
Consistency
Kantian Rationalism Thesis and, V.II:219
as value in philosophy, V.II:150
Consumption
defined, V.II:54
marginal utility of, V.II:54–55
Contemporary art, V.II:168, 169–170, 209–214, 255–256
accessibility and, V.I:122
cognitive provocation through, V.II:255
sources on, V.I:29
Contemporary Heterosexuality and Lesbian Existence (Rich) V.II:49n3
Contempt, as result of ostracism, V.I:173
Content, V.II:214
aesthetic emotion and, V.II:195
cognitive provocation through, V.II:255
form vs., V.II:110, 111, 193–196, 210, 214
Greenbergian formalism and, V.II:209
modernism and, V.II:212
priority of over media, V.I:249
quality based on form vs., V.II:189, 191–192, 194
self-reflexive, V.II:213–214
spiritual, V.II:192–193
style as vehicle for, V.II:150
See also Social content
Context(s)
for art. *See* Art context
in conceptual art, V.II:11
in environmental art, V.II:10
in formal art, V.II:9
and ideas, V.II:6–12
importance of, V.II:8
language and, V.I:209–211
problems with, V.I:39–42
public. *See* Public context
quality judgments and, V.II:197, 198–199
social, xenophobia and, V.I:256
sociopolitical, V.I:xxix; V.II:xxvii
Continuity
in European and American art, V.II:209
willful amnesia vs., V.II:214
Control
attributed to artist, V.II:116–117
as responsibility of artist, V.I:xvi; V.II:xiv
See also Interpretive control
Conventions
behavioral, failure to conform to, V.I:199. *See also* Behavioral norms
communication and, V.I:77
of individuality, V.II:205
performance art and, V.II:204
repression and, V.II:205
rules and, V.I:79
stereotyping and, V.II:224–225
violation of in public interest, V.II:204–205
Cooper, A. J., "Selection, Gene Migration and Polymorphic Stability," V.II:245n27
Cooper, Paula, V.I:xxxvi; V.II:xxxiv
Cooperation, as zero-sum game alternative, V.II:173
Co-optation
by mainstream, V.I:236
intervention to prevent, V.I:219
seeming inevitability of, V.II:87
Corcoran Gallery, V.II:162
Cornered (Piper) V.I:xix, 272–273, 304*f;* V.II:xvii
Corporate funding, V.II:205
exhibition decision and, V.II:202, 203
Cottingham, Laura, V.II:214n2
Courtesy, norms of, V.I:246
Covert racism, V.I:229, 230, 292, 293, 301–302
Craft(s) V.II:65, 127
Creative autonomy issues, V.II:87–88
Creative expression, self-conscious acknowledgment with, V.I:92
Creative process, V.I:5, 7
artist as embodiment of, V.I:34
economic pressures and, V.II:78
importance of concept in, V.I:4, 5
overproduction and, V.II:76–77
problems with, V.I:38
product alienated from, V.I:33, 36
product as part of, V.I:35
Creativity, V.I:200
Criteria
for acceptance as truth, V.I:74, 76
for commitment, V.I:80–81
A Critical Assembling (Kostelanetz) V.II:41
Critical distance, moral perspective and, V.II:157
Critical hegemony, V.II:65, 66
condescending assumptions of, V.II:88
cultural interpretation of artwork and, V.II:69–71
demoralizing effect of, V.II:67
division of labor and, V.II:69, 70
formalism and, V.II:70
suggested remedies for, V.II:80
Critical integrity, V.II:112
Critical matrix, supplied by artist, V.I:xxxix; V.II:xxxvii
Critical self-consciousness, V.I:98
Critical subjectivity, V.II:22n2
Criticism
eliciting from friends, V.I:144–145
interpretation vs., V.II:124
See also Art criticism
Critics. *See* Art critics
The Critique of Judgment (Kant) V.II:191n3
The Critique of Pure Reason (Kant) V.I:55, 71, 228, 255, 256; V.II:17, 216–217, 216n4
Cross-cultural appropriation, in Euroethnic art, V.II:211
Cross-cultural judgments, quality criteria, V.II:197, 198, 199
Cruising White Women. See Mythic Being series
Cruz, Celia, V.II:175
Cryptic viewpoint, art for art's sake and, V.II:196
Cubists, appropriation by, V.II:183
Cultural alienation, V.I:41
Cultural artifacts, V.I:217
Cultural communication, problems with, V.I:180
Cultural context, quality judgments and, V.II:197, 198–199
Cultural conventions. *See* Conventions
Cultural dissonance, dance and, V.I:268
Cultural identity, syndrome of the Other and, V.I:208, 209
Cultural idioms, V.I:202–203; V.II:102
dissonance among, V.II:102
Cultural imperialism, V.II:213, 214
Cultural inferiority complex, racism and, V.I:206
Cultural integrity, assimilation vs., V.II:141
Cultural interpretation, control of, V.II:93
Cultural knowledge, art criticism and, V.II:165
Cultural memory, social content of art and, V.II:214
Cultural Other
ideal vision for, V.I:245–248
as target of art, V.I:246–247
Cultural parity, requirements for, V.I:199–200

Cultural racism, V.II:127–146
aesthetic obliteration as goal of, V.II:146
in art criticism, V.II:135–143, 146
biographical viewpoints and, V.II:144–145
ethnicity and, V.II:145
invisibility and, V.II:128, 133
language and, V.II:133
legal racism and, V.II:127
racial identity and, V.II:138
stereotyping in, V.II:134
Culture
American, V.I:209
art and, V.II:69, 189, 199–200
artifacts and, V.I:217
black working-class. *See* Black working-class culture
condescension in, V.II:88
dance and, V.I:195
ethnocentricity and legitimation of, V.II:88
exploitation by, V.I:240
Funk music and, V.I:197, 198
"High," V.II:78, 202
influence of white vs. black, V.II:127
marginalization and, V.II:128–130
popular. *See* Popular culture
roots of, V.I:206
self-awareness and, V.II:210
visual, censorship of, V.II:213
xenophobia and, V.I:199, 200
See also Mainstream culture
Culture and Democracy: Social and Ethical Issues in Public Support for the Arts and E-Humanities (Buchwalter) V.II:201
CWAs. *See* Colored women artists
Cynicism, alienation as result of, V.II:87

Dada. *See* Duchamp, Marcel
Dada show, in Berlin, V.II:37
Dance; Dancing, V.I:48, 90
as confrontation, V.I:80, 177
cultural dissonance and, V.I:268
culture and, V.I:195
discotheque, V.I:89, 91, 96–98, 151
Funk, V.I:197–198, 200–201, 213
performance, V.I:154
as performance medium, V.I:177, 180, 195–196
self-transcendence through, V.I:195
sociopolitical significance of, V.I:151–152
stereotyping and, V.II:137
Dance, social expectations and, V.I:200
DANCE Black Africa, V.I:216
Danger, in power, V.I:154
Darboven, Hanne, *Untitled Drawing,* V.II:11*f*
Darkness, symbolism of, V.I:xxiii–xxiv; V.II:xxi–xxii
David, V.II:211
Da Vinci, Leonardo, V.I:29
Davis, F. James, *Who Is Black? One Nation's Definition,* V.I:284, 287, 288, 289, 291–292, 297, E-307; V.II:245n27
Davis, Stuart, V.II:209
Dealers, V.II:29, 33, 75
collaboration with collectors by, V.II:71–72
deformation of art products and, V.II:77
formalist values and, V.II:64
manipulation by, V.II:75–76, 77
political statement on, V.II:29
"Dear Friend" calling cards, V.I:xix; V.II:xvii
See also Calling cards
Death, readiness for, V.I:90
de Baere, Bart, V.II:214n2
Decision making, V.I:119–120
aesthetic, V.I:225
Declaratives
communication in, V.I:xxxiv; V.II:xxxii–xxxiii. *See also* Objective declarative voice
Defaced Funk Lessons Poster (Piper) V.I:207*f*
Defense mechanisms
impersonality, V.I:286
of personal ideology, V.II:48–50
political art and, V.I:164, 167
self-reflection against, V.II:48–49
as target of artist, V.I:253
Defensiveness
cutting through, V.I:234
as response to art, V.I:249, 251
Deference
academia and, V.I:229
politics of, V.I:228
Defiance, V.I:151
Deformation, V.II:76–78
Dehumanization
of artists by critics, V.II:125
as cultural racism, V.II:129
Dejeuner sur l'herbe (Manet) V.II:211
de Kooning, Willem, V.II:211, 212
Delacroix, Ferdinand-Victor-Eugene, V.II:211
Delusion, aesthetic vs. socioeconomic imperatives, V.II:84
Democracy, responsibility of government in, V.II:206
Denial
catalog of methods, V.I:xx; V.II:xviii
definition of, V.II:222
in higher-order political discrimination, V.II:245–248, 252–253
self-stereotyping and, V.II:232, 233
Dennis, Donna, V.II:52
Denotation, Kantian Rationalism Thesis and, V.II:219
Dent, N. J. H., *The Moral Psychology of the Virtues,* V.II:249n33
Dependence, intellectual, V.II:154
Depoliticization, confronting, V.I:164
Derek, Bo, V.I:199
Derogation, V.II:229–230
Desastres de la guerra (Goya) V.II:211
Descartes, Ren), V.II:110, 111, 191
Meditations on First Philosophy, V.II:191
Detachment
abstraction and, V.I:224
of artist, V.II:3
engagement vs., V.I:xvii; V.II:xv
as response to black anger, V.I:277
Devaluation of art objects, reproduction and, V.II:57–58
Deviance, honorific stereotype of self and, V.II:231, 232, 233
Dewey, John, V.I:xvii, 39; V.II:xv
Diagrams
as forms, V.II:6, 7
information context for, V.II:7
See also Media
Dialectic analysis of art, V.II:18
Dialogue
art as, V.I:xxxii; V.II:xxx
and audience participation, V.I:196–198
between artist and audience, V.II:102
calling card and, V.I:220
in Funk music, V.I:214
as goal of artist, V.II:144
initiating, V.I:271
The Diary of Anne Frank, V.I:89, 91
Didacticism, V.I:xiv; V.II:xii
in artist-audience relationship, V.II:99, 100
interpretive control and, V.II:99, 100, 101
Didactic role of art, V.I:40, 249; V.II:26, 27, 203
Difference and Pathology: Stereotypes of Sexuality, Race and Madness (Gilman) V.II:134, E-138n11
Dignity, racial vs. individual, V.I:285
Dijkstra, Bram, *Idols of Perversity: Fantasies of Feminine Evil in Fin-de-Siécle Culture,* E-V.II:134n4, 135n7, 137n10
Dimensionality, object of art as, V.I:xvii; V.II:xv
Dinner parties, V.I:271
confronting racism at, V.I:219–220, 271
funk music at, V.I:268–270
Disco dancing, V.I:177, 180, 196, 201, 215
in *It's Just Art,* V.I:177, 180
sociopolitical context of, V.I:151–152
Discography of Funk, V.I:214–215, 269
Disco-jazz, V.I:151
Disco music, V.I:215
reactions to, V.I:201
Discontinuity, aesthetic emotion and, V.II:193–194
Discotheque dancing, V.I:89, 91, 96–98, 272
Some Reflective Surfaces and, V.I:151, 152
Discotheques, calling card for, V.I:221, 272. *See also* Calling cards
Discrete forms
ideas vs., V.I:38
limitations of, V.I:36, 37, 38, 42
political constraints and, V.I:120
See also Form
Discrimination
cognitive, V.II:251–258
cognitive discrimination failures and, V.II:252–253
first-order political, V.II:228–233
generalized higher-order political, V.II:240n24

higher-order political, V.II:237–241, 243–251, 252–253, 256–257
political. *See* Political discrimination
and rationalism, V.II:216–220
reciprocal first-order, V.II:233–237
reciprocal higher-order, V.II:242–243
second-order political, V.II:237, 238, 239
types of, V.II:215–216. *See also specific types*
Discriminatory stereotype, inductive generalization vs., V.II:230
Disentitlement, institutionalized, V.I:291–292
Dispersion: The Mythic Being (Piper) V.I:107–114
Disruption, aesthetic emotion and, V.II:193–194
Dissent, marginalization of, V.I:xvi; V.II:xiv
Dissociation
definition of, V.II:222
in first-order political discrimination, V.II:245
in higher-order political discrimination, V.II:252
Distance; Distancing
distortion as result of, V.I:248
self-awareness and, in European art, V.II:213
from subject matter, V.II:211
Distortion, as result of distance, V.I:248
Distribution, as condition for art production, V.I:159
Disvaluation
anti-discrimination policies and, V.II:251–252
discrimination and, V.II:229–230, 233, 237, 238–239, 241, 242, 245, 250
higher-order political discrimination and, V.II:246
malevolence vs., V.II:246–247, 251
Disvaluees, V.II:230, 231
criteria of behavior and, V.II:250–251
higher-order political discrimination against, V.II:246–247
perceptions of behavior of, V.II:248–249
pseudorationality of, V.II:252n36
in second-order political discrimination, V.II:237
treatment of, V.II:250–252
Division of labor, V.II:67–69
aesthetic acculturation and, V.II:72
alienation of artists caused by, V.II:75
critical hegemony and, V.II:69, 70
performance art and, V.II:99–100
power and, V.II:73
responsibility and, V.II:73, 74–75
"Doctor Lawyer Indian Chief: "Primitivism' in 20th Century Art," (McEvilley) V.II:143n12, E-185n4
Documentation, V.I:30, 33, 35–37, 55
confused with art, V.I:34, 36–37
photography in, V.I:35
posters as, V.I:264
Dogma, aesthetic, audience response and, V.II:95
Dogmatism
arrogance and, V.II:49
ideological self-deception and, V.II:86
Dolphins
dialogue about, V.I:73, 74, 75, 76, 77
as Other, V.I:206
Dominguez, Virginia R., *White by Definition: Social Classification in Creole Louisiana,* V.I:286, E-289, 307; V.II:245n27
Dorsey, Tommy, V.I:268
Double standard, V.I:292
Doubt
of beliefs, V.II:47
misunderstanding about, V.II:110–111
"Do You Love What You Feel?" (Rufus and Chaka Khan) V.I:177
Draft avoidance, V.II:48–49
Draft counseling, illusion of perfectability and, V.II:49
Drawing
figurative, V.I:99–100
self-discovery through, V.I:91
in *Vanilla Nightmares,* V.I:253
See also Media
Drawing of Phillip Zohn (Piper) V.I:56*f*
Drawings (catalog) V.I:253
Dreams, V.I:223–224
as objects, V.I:100
Drip painting, V.II:53, 54
Duality; dualism, V.I:xxiii; V.II:xxi
misinterpretation of, V.II:122
as subject matter, V.I:17–18
Duccio, V.II:209
Duchamp, Marcel, V.I:95; V.II:52, 157, 185, 193, 254, 255
Dugway Proving Grounds (Utah) V.I:259
Duplication, as condition for art production, V.I:159
Dürer, Albrecht, V.II:193
The Dynamics of Creation (Storr) V.II:18n1
"The Dynamics of Racial Admixture-An Analysis of the American Negro" (Glass and Li) E-V.II:245n27

Earthworks. *See* Media
East Berlin, author's visit to, V.II:38–39
Easy Listening Art, V.I:xxxii; V.II:xxx, 176–177, 178
art that is meant to be seen vs., V.II:181
Easy Listening Music, V.II:175, 176
Economics of art, V.I:xxxii, 40, 199; V.II:xxx
alienation of artist and, V.II:75, 76
art as career and, V.II:63–65
art criticism and, V.II:23
art making and, V.I:121–123, 234, 239
in art world vs. academia, V.II:79–80
exploitation, V.II:130
overproduction and, V.II:75–76
pricing proposal for artwork, V.II:31–32
production and, V.I:159; V.II:71, 72
racial identity and, V.I:291–292
standards of excellence and, V.II:154–155, 156
zero-sum game and, V.II:167
See also Marketing; Market value
Economic vs. professional rewards, V.I:239, 240
Edelman, Gerald M.
Neural Darwinism: The Theory of Neuronal Group Selection, V.II:218n7
The Remembered Present: A Biological Theory of Consciousness, V.II:218n7
Edmonson, Monro S., V.II:245n27
Education
of artist, V.I:3–7
elitism and, V.I:202–203
peer review qualifications and, V.II:203–204
in philosophy, V.II:151
quality judgments and, V.II:196, 197
sense of entitlement and, V.I:xviii; V.II:xvi
See also Art education
Educator, author as, V.I:xiv, xv; V.II:xii, xiii
Ego, of artists, V.I:264
Egypt, African culture disseminated through, V.I:206
Elements of Style (Strunk and White) V.II:149
Eliot, George, V.I:155
Elitism; Elitists, V.II:222
in academia, V.I:229–230
in art world, V.I:122
education and, V.I:202–203
intellectual, V.I:229–230, 275
McCarthy era and, V.II:203
one-way communication as, V.II:49
Elizabeth, Queen, V.I:299
Ellison, Ralph, *The Invisible Man,* V.I:xxiii; V.II:xxi, 195
Embarrassment
Funk Lessons and, V.I:198
as weapon against racism or sexism, V.I:247
Emecheta, Buchi, *The Joys of Motherhood,* V.II:195
Emotion, aesthetic, V.II:190–198
Empathy, failure of, V.I:246
Empiricism, aesthetic, V.I:xvii; V.II:xv
Empowerment
judgment and, V.II:198
through valorization, V.II:198
Empty Thought Balloon (Piper) V.I:102*f*
"Empyrrhical Thinking (and Why Kant Can't) (McEvilley) V.II:185n4
Engagement by artist
detachment vs., V.I:xvii; V.II:xv
individual vs. communal, V.I:xv; V.II:xiii
with society, V.II:214
Enigma, Other seen as, V.II:138
Enigmatic exemplar, artwork as, V.II:26
Enigmatic Other, appropriation of idiolects of, V.II:209
Enlightenment, harmony and, V.II:194
Entertainment, participatory culture vs., V.I:213

Entitlement, V.I:xxxix; V.II:xxxvii
in ideal society, V.I:246
marginalization vs. sense of, V.I:xxxiv–xxxv; V.II:xxxiii–xxxiv
racial identity and, V.I:291
sense of, V.I:xviii, xxxiii–xxxiv; V.II:xvi, xxxii–xxxiii
sense of, writing as reinforcement to, V.I:xl; V.II:xxxviii
Entity, quality vs., V.I:93
Entrepreneurship, as motivator, V.II:169
Entropy, in art world, V.I:39–40
Environment, V.I:162; V.II:10, 25
in *Art for the Art-World Surface Pattern,* V.I:162
"Art Self-Consciousness Consciousness," V.I:27
as object of perception, V.I:9
space conditions, V.I:21
spatial contexts, V.II:7
in *What It's Like, What It Is #3,* V.I:xxi; V.II:xix
Environmental ideas, V.II:10
Envy, V.I:67
racist remarks about, V.I:281
Epistemic complacency, V.II:128
Epistemic inscrutability, V.II:226–227
Epistemic insecurity
advantages of, V.I:xxxix; V.II:xxxvii
writing and, V.I:xl; V.II:xxxviii
Epistemic judgment, normative judgment vs., V.II:234–237
Epistemic nature of artist, V.II:20–21
Epistemic rules of thumb, as stereotypes, V.II:234–237
Epistemic transparency, V.II:21
Epistemology, certainty and, V.I:74
Equilibrium of art objects, advantages of, V.II:257–258
"Erotic Art Show," V.II:161
Escape, art as confrontation vs., V.I:xxxi; V.II:xxix
Esche, Charles, V.II:214.2
Esotericism, as McCarthy era legacy, V.II:203
Estrangement, V.I:137
Ethical dilemma, relatives and, V.I:284
Ethical parochialism, V.II:73–75
Ethics
aesthetics and, V.I:xx; V.II:xviii
art and, V.I:189
commitment to, V.I:80
feminism and, V.I:228
Ethnic art, primacy of formalism over, V.II:88
Ethnic groups, V.I:xv, xix, 251; V.II:xiii, xvii
Ethnic identity
higher-order political discrimination and, V.II:240–241, 243, 245, 249
reciprocal higher-order political discrimination and, V.II:242, 243
Ethnicity, V.II:234
cultural racism and, V.II:145
exclusion and, V.II:70
status and, V.I:147, 149
Ethnic other, as target of art, V.I:246–247
Ethnocentricity; Ethnocentrism
in analytic philosophy, V.II:150
in art education, V.II:67
in art history, V.I:xiv; V.II:xii
legitimacy and, V.II:88
in mainstream art world, V.II:161
quality judgments and, V.II:198
Etiquette, norms of, V.I:246–247, 251
calling cards and, V.I:271
higher-order political discrimination and, V.II:250
Euroethnic art, V.II:88, 152–158, 168–169, 171
appropriation in, V.II:183–184, 209, 210, 211
content over form in, V.II:195
ethnocentrism in, V.II:161
fiction of preeminence of, V.II:88
formalism in, V.II:209, 210
heterosexual white male aesthetic and, V.II:161
ideology and, V.II:169
intellectual standards in, V.II:152
modernism and, V.II:209–214
originality in, V.II:153
self-awareness in, V.II:209, 210
self-consciousness in, V.II:210
social content in, V.II:209, 210–211
standards of excellence in, V.II:154–158
See also European art
Euroethnicity, V.II:164, 177
aesthetic vs. market value of art and, V.II:169–170
art education and, V.II:66–67
art world and, V.II:65, 67, 161, 165, 167, 168, 171–172, 183–184, 186
bias as result of, V.II:73
biographical information and, V.II:143
condescension and, V.II:88
contemporary art and, V.II:169–170
cultural interpretation based on, V.II:69
demoralizing effect of, V.II:67
Easy Listening Art and, V.II:176
exposure of, V.II:163
ideological commitment to, V.II:167
ideological myth and, V.II:166
legitimacy and, V.II:65
modernism and, V.II:209–214
postmodernism and, V.II:167–169, 172–173
of viewers, V.II:164
Europe, V.II:214
African culture disseminated through, V.I:206
reactions to author in, V.I:262
European art
distanced self-awareness in, V.II:213
political tradition in, V.I:265
social content in American art vs., V.II:211–212
See also Euroethnic art
Evaluation of art
aesthetic vs. political, V.I:247–248
formalist values and, V.II:64–65
Event contexts, for presenting idea, V.II:7
Events
dreams and, V.I:100
limitations of, V.I:34, 37, 42
production systems for, V.II:13
Excellence, defined by art market, V.II:154–155, 156
Exchange value
aesthetic value and, V.II:31, 32
pricing proposal, V.II:31
Exclusion
of colored women artists, V.II:161, 163–173
ethnicity and, V.II:70
Exhibits; Exhibitions, V.I:xvi, 30; V.II:xiv
retrospective, V.I:237
standards of excellence and, V.II:155–156
See also exhibits by name
Existential clarity, V.I:258
Exorcism, in *Mythic Being* series, V.I:147
Expectations
art context and, V.II:54
artist-audience contact and, V.II:98–99
disvaluation and, V.II:248–249
interpretive control problems and, V.II:93, 98
racial identity and, V.I:297–298
Experience
of aesthetic emotion, V.II:190
aesthetic. *See* Aesthetic experience
categorization of, V.I:255
cognitive structuring and organization of, V.II:217–220
perception limited by, V.II:224–225
transformation through, V.I:247–148, 247–248
universal, V.II:89
viewing, V.I:34
Experiential input, in art production systems, V.II:13
Exploitation, V.I:191; V.II:85, 86
accusations of, V.I:303–304
confronting through art, V.II:130
context and, V.I:209
cultural, V.I:240
economic, V.II:130
responsibility for, V.I:295
sexual, V.I:209
voluntary, V.I:190–191
Exploration, art as medium for, V.I:xxxi; V.II:xxix
Expression, freedom of, V.II:73–75
External. *See* Realization
"External" world, appropriation from, V.I:217

Failing, Patricia, V.II:185
"Black Artists Today: A Case of Exclusion?," V.II:170.21, 185n3
Familiarity, of Mythic Being, V.I:138
Family, V.I:286
acceptance by, V.I:287–288
rejection of by passing, V.I:284
See also Relatives

Family background, V.I:281–282, 284, 297–298, 302–303
status and, V.I:147
Fanon, Frantz, *Black Skins, White Masks,* V.II:137n10
Fantasy, V.I:48, 59–60
as barrier to art, V.I:229
racist, V.I:254
Farver, Jane, V.I:237; V.II:134n3
Fashion modeling, V.I:89, 90, 91, 98–99
Faulkner, William, *Go Down, Moses,* V.I:295, 306, 307
Fauvists, appropriation by, V.II:183
Fear
art in climate of, V.I:xxxi; V.II:xxix
art making and, V.I:94, 230
intellectualism as response to, V.II:196
racism and, V.I:xx, 254, 263, 273; V.II:xviii
as reaction to anomaly, V.II:220, 221
of the Other, V.II:128–129, 132, 133
unconscious, V.I:xx; V.II:xviii
xenophobia as reaction to, V.II:220, 221
Female; Femaleness
malevolence linked with, V.II:137n10, 138–139
See also Gender
"Female Trouble" (Schjeldahl) V.II:186n11
Feminism, V.I:9, 261
art criticism and, V.I:xv; V.II:xiii
awareness of exploitation in, V.II:86
dancing and, V.I:154
interpersonal impact of, V.I:228
marginalization of, V.II:138–139
one-way communication and, V.II:49
"Feminism and Sadomasochism" (Califia) V.II:47n1
Feminism and Tradition in Aesthetics (Brand and Korsmeyer) V.I:181
Feminist artists, acceptance of "women artists" and, V.I:xxxvii; V.II:xxxv
Fetishism
art objects and, V.II:58–59
biographical viewpoint of critic and, V.II:144
in performance art, V.II:60–61
Fiction. *See* Ideological fictions
Figurative art, going beyond commitment to, V.I:29
Figurative drawing, V.I:99–100
Film
event context for, V.II:7
as form, V.II:6
in *It's Just Art,* V.I:177
Financial evaluation, art criticism and, V.II:23
Financial issues
art as career and, V.II:63–64
overproduction and, V.II:75–76
Fine Arts Building (New York) V.I:155
Finite systems, construction of, V.I:5, 7
Finley, Karen, V.II:204, 205
First-order political discrimination, V.II:228–233, 245
higher-order discrimination vs., V.II:216, 247
First-order variables, V.I:143, 144
First-/third-person asymmetry, V.II:223–224
Fitzgerald, Ella, V.I:199
Five Full Thought Balloons (Piper) V.I:106
Five Unrelated Time Pieces (Piper) V.I:9, 261
See also Meat into Meat
Flash of the Spirit: African and Afro-American Art and Philosophy (Thompson) V.I:216
Flight
abstraction as, V.I:xxiii, 224–225, 227; V.II:xxi
dreams of, V.I:223–224
Flirtation, accusation of, V.I:228
Flying, V.I:223–232
abstraction as, V.I:xxiii, 224, 227; V.II:xxi
dreams about, V.I:223–224
"Flying" (Piper) V.I:xxiii; V.II:xxi
Folders, as unsituated information contexts, V.II:7
Folk art
cultural racism and, V.II:127
definition of art and, V.II:65
Food for the Spirit series (Piper) V.I:51–55, 54*f*
Mythic Being series and, V.I:147
Form
aesthetic emotion and, V.II:193–195, 196
commitment and, V.I:73
in conceptual art, V.II:11
concretized, V.II:3–4
content vs., V.II:110, 111, 193–196, 210, 214
discrete, V.I:42
in environmental art, V.II:10
essential, V.I:47
in formal art, V.II:9
ideas and, V.I:38, 45; V.II:3–4, 6–12
innovation and, V.II:210
originality and, V.II:153
quality based on content vs., V.II:189, 191–192, 194
translating concept to, V.I:4–5
See also Discrete forms
Formal ideas, defined, V.II:9
Formalism, V.II:67, 74, 195
aesthetic emotion and, V.II:191–192, 195
avant-garde, V.II:130
demoralizing effect of, V.II:67
in Euroethnic art, V.II:209, 210
fiction of preeminence of, V.II:88
Greenbergian, V.II:209, 211–212, 213, 214
impersonality as result of, V.II:69–70
limitations of, V.I:41
social content and, V.II:211–212
universality and, V.II:69, 70
Formalist aesthetic judgment, art context and, V.II:195
Formalist values, art institutions and, V.II:64–65
Formalist works, defined, V.I:17
Forty-nine Three-Part Variations on Three Different Kinds of Cubes (LeWitt) V.II:11*f*, 208*f*
"46 Variations on Three Different Kinds of Cube" exhibit (LeWitt) V.I:29, 258
Foundation Series (Asimov) V.I:59
Foundations, funding by, V.II:202–203
"Four Conceptual Artists" exhibit, V.I:30
Four Intruders plus Alarm Systems (Piper) V.I:182*f*, 229, 249; V.II:44
description of, V.I:181–186, 266–267
Fragmentation, aesthetic emotion and, V.II:193
Framework. *See* Context
Frank, Anne, V.I:89, 91
Frankenthaler, Helen, V.II:52
Franklin, Aretha, V.I:151
Jump To It, V.I:215
"Respect," V.I:48, 152
Fraser, Andrea, V.I:266
Fraud, passing and accusations of, V.I:276, 278–279
Frazier, Alice, V.I:299
Free #2 (Piper) V.II:179*f*
Freedom
abstraction as, V.I:xxiii, 224; V.II:xxi
dispersion of personal history and, V.I:113, 114
in masculine guise, V.I:263
overcoming obstacles to, V.I:145
from self-censorship, V.I:217
Freedom of expression, V.II:73–75
funding sources and, V.II:203
tolerance for unconventional and, V.II:206
Freedom of thought, constraints on thinker vs, V.I:xiii, V.II:xi
French masters, V.I:187
Freud, Sigmund, V.II:212
Fried, Michael, V.I:262
Friendliness, calling card and, V.I:221
Friendship, V.I:125–126, 141
A.~A and, V.I:145
in Berlin, V.II:36, 37
racial identity and, V.I:233–234, 294–295
sexual attraction and, V.I:190
stereotypes as basis for, V.II:235
trust and, V.I:300–301
Frohnmayer, John, V.II:201
Frustration, anger and, V.I:82–83
Fullinwider, Robert, *Conscripts and Volunteers,* V.II:49n2
Full Thought Balloon (Piper) V.I:105*f*
Function
aesthetic value and, V.II:59
art and, V.II:25
art context expectations and, V.II:54
as context-independent, V.II:70
resisting categorization by, V.II:52–53
unperceived, as subject matter, V.I:18
Functional categorization, resistance to, V.II:52–53
Functional context, mystery in isolation from, V.II:58
Functional objects, individuality of, V.II:52
Funding
freedom of expression and, V.II:203
government, V.II:201–206
peer review for, V.II:202

political art and, V.I:240
politics and, V.II:201–206
power and, V.II:203
self-censorship and, V.I:xxxi; V.II:xxix
Funk, bibliography of, V.I:216
Funk Lesson Discography and Bibliography (Piper) V.I:269
Funk Lessons: Berkeley Performance, V.I:202*f*, 269
Funk Lessons: Nova Scotia College of Art and Design Performance (Piper) V.I:197*f*, 269
Funk Lessons with Adrian Piper (Samore)(video) V.I:196
Funk Lessons Performance Handout (Piper) V.I:213–214, 269
Funk Lessons Poster of Bootsie (Piper) V.I:212*f*
Funk Lessons series (Piper) V.I:229, 245
background of, V.I:268–269, 270
defaced poster from, V.I:207*f*
descriptions of, V.I:195–198, 269
goals of, V.I:195, 198–199
notes on, V.I:198–211
performance hand-out summary, V.I:213–214
relationships and, V.II:114
Funk music, V.I:151, 196
black working-class culture and, V.I:203
characteristics of, V.I:213–214
context for, V.I:211
described, V.I:195
discography of, V.I:214–215
in *Four Intruders. . .*, V.I:181
in *It's Just Art,* V.I:177, 180
reactions to, V.I:197–199, 200–201, 268–269
sexism and, V.I:209
sexuality and, V.I:214, 269
status and, V.I:204
"Funky Town" (Lipps, Inc.) V.I:215

Galileo, V.II:197n5
Galleries, V.II:29, 255
artist's relationship with, V.I:239
art segregated from life in, V.I:39, 40
as cognitive provocation sites, V.II:253–254, 255
CWAs and, V.II:162
decision-making criteria of, V.II:76
ethics of, V.II:73–75
overproduction and, V.II:75–76
political statement on, V.II:29
protest movement and, V.I:31
as public spaces, V.II:43–44
sociopolitical climate and, V.I:xxxvi; V.II:xxxiv
as spatial context, V.II:7
zero-sum game and, V.II:167
Game playing
anger at, V.I:64
as commitment to rules, V.I:80
communication and, V.I:77
provisional commitment as, V.I:78, 79
Games, zero-sum, V.II:167, 169–172
Games and Decisions (Luce and Raiffa) V.II:167n17
Gap Band, *Gap Band IV,* V.I:215
Gaucho (Steely Dan) V.I:215
Gauguin, Paul, V.II:209
Gaye, Marvin, *Midnight Love,* V.I:215
Gays, V.I:151
calling cards for, V.I:272
Gender
as obstruction, V.I:xxiii; V.II:xxi
as primary disvalued property, V.II:225
race and, V.I:xviii; V.II:xvi
reaction of art world to, V.I:262
recognition by art world and, V.II:162
status and, V.I:147, 149
stereotypes of race and, V.II:166
Gender identity, V.I:xxiii; V.II:xxi
false preconceptions about, V.I:233
higher-order political discrimination and, V.II:240–241, 243, 245, 249
reciprocal higher-order political discrimination and, V.II:242, 243
Genealogy, V.I:282
discoveries of black ancestry, V.I:289
passing and, V.I:286
research difficulties, V.I:287
General, V.II:94
Generality, V.I:37
excessive, V.II:95
mainstream art world and, V.I:xxxvii; V.II:xxxv
in performance art, V.II:60
Generalization
in abstraction, V.I:224
of art objects, V.II:55–56
conceptual, V.I:224
Generalized higher-order political discrimination, V.II:240n24
Genetic Abstracts, V.I:288
The Genetics of Human Populations (Cavalli-Sforza and Bodmer) V.II:245n27
Genius, self-indulgence vs., V.II:95–96
Genre, generalization of art objects by, V.II:56
Gericault, Théodore, V.I:265; V.II:211
German language, in *Vanilla Nightmares,* V.I:253
Germany
author's visit to, V.II:35–39
psychological intimacy in, V.II:36
Germinal (Zola) V.II:195
Gershwin, George, *Porgy and Bess,* V.I:xix, 240; V.II:xvii
Getting Back. See Mythic Being series
Gevers, Ine, *Place Position Presentation Public,* V.I:255
Ghettoization
all-African-American shows and, V.II:166n15
diversity in, V.II:146n16
in Euroethnic art world, V.II:184
Giacometti, Alberto, V.II:211, 212
Gilman, Sander, *Difference and Pathology: Stereotypes of Sexuality, Race and Madness,* V.II:134n4, 138n11
Gingold, Hermione, V.I:52
Giotto, V.II:209
Girl with Teeth (Piper) V.I:193*f*
Glass, Bentley, "The Dynamics of Racial Admixture-An Analysis of the American Negro," E-V.II:245n27
Glass, Phillip, V.I:114, 201
"Global" political art, V.I:234
Glueck, Grace, "'Racism' Protest Slated over Title of Art Show," V.II:73n6
Goals of artists, dialogue, V.II:144
Go Down, Moses (Faulkner) V.I:295, 306, 307
Goldstein, Richard
"Art Beat: 'Darky' Chic," V.II:65n2
"Art Beat: Race and the State of the Arts," V.II:65n2
"Art Beat: The Romance of Racism," V.II:73n6
"Goodbye to Easy Listening" (Piper) V.I:xvi; V.II:xiv
Goodman, Nelson, *The Language of Art,* V.II:57
Government
arts funding issues, V.II:201–206
social community vs., V.II:206
Goya, Francisco Jos) de, V.I:265; V.II:193, 211
Desastres de la guerra, V.II:211
Graduate school
family background and, V.I:281–282
racism in, V.I:275, 278–279, 280–281
Graffiti art, V.II:171n22, 209
Grandmaster Flash, "The Message," V.II:197
Graphics. *See* Media
Graph-paper reduction series, V.I:17, 18
Greco-Roman sculptures, as political art, V.I:265
Greece, African culture disseminated through, V.I:206
Greek art, appropriated in Renaissance, V.II:209
Greenberg, Clement, V.I:xvi; V.II:xiv, 196, 214
Greenbergian formalism, V.II:209, 211–212, 213, 214
Griffin, John Howard, *Black Like Me,* V.I:285, 296, 297, 299, 307
Group Portrait with Lady (Boll) V.I:141
Growth, commitment and, V.I:69, 70
Guernica (Picasso) V.I:251; V.II:211
Guerrilla performance, V.I:219–221
Guilbaut, Serge, *How New York Stole the Idea of the Avant-Garde,* V.II:212n1
Guilt
passing and, V.I:219
reform and, V.I:247
of whites, V.I:277
Guilt-trip, "professional black" and, V.I:219
Guitar playing, V.I:60, 89, 90

Haacke, Hans, V.II:203, 205, 213
Hagiography, research vs., V.II:184, 185
Haley, Alex, V.I:293
Hall and Oates, *Private Eyes,* V.I:215
Hammons, David, V.II:193
Handy, W. C., V.II:175

Hanley, Charles, *Psychoanalysis and Philosophy,* V.II:18n1
Happenings, limitations of, V.I:34, 37, 42
Harassment, racial or sexual
in academia, V.I:281
racial identity and experience of, V.I:295–296
Haring, Keith, V.II:209
Harlem, experiences in, V.I:276, 278
Harmony, aesthetic emotion and, V.II:192, 193, 194
Harper, Frances E. W., *Iola Leroy; or, Shadows Uplifted,* V.I:278, 280, 288, 289, 292, 293, 303, E-307
Harvard University, V.I:147, 149, 264
Hearing, listening vs., V.II:175–176
Heartney, Elinor, "On View: New York," V.II:186n10
Hegel, Georg Wilhelm Friedrich, *The Philosophy of Fine Art,* V.I:47
Hegelian method of analysis, V.II:18
Hegemony, critical. *See* Critical hegemony
Hellenic art, appropriated in Renaissance, V.II:209
Helms, Jesse, V.II:162, 202
Henderson, Michael, *Wide Receiver,* V.I:215
Here and Now (Piper) V.I:241*f,* 247, 259
Here and now. *See* Indexical present
Herman, Woody, V.I:268
Hess, Elizabeth, V.II:135n8, 136n9, 139, 140
"Backing Down Behind Closed Doors at the NEA," V.II:201n2
"Reply," V.II:134n2
responses to criticism by, V.II:134–142
"Ways of Seeing Adrian Piper," V.II:134n2, 186n9
Hesse, Eva, V.II:52
Repetition Nineteen, V.II:9*f*
Heterogeneous society, disruptive work and, V.II:194
Heterosexual (HET)white males, upper middle class, V.I:xxxvi, xxxviii; V.II:xxxiv, xxxvi
affirmative action and, V.II:183, 184, 186, 187
Euroethnic aesthetic and, V.II:161, 168, 169–170
sense of entitlement and, V.I:xxxiii–xxxiv, xxxix; V.II:xxxii, xxxvii
vision of parity with, V.I:246
See also Male(s) WASPs; Whites
Hierarchies, V.I:148–149
academic, V.I:264
socioeconomic, V.I:147
"High art," V.II:67, 127
"High culture," V.II:78
funding sources and, V.II:202
"Higher-Order Discrimination" (Piper) 237n21
Higher-order political discrimination, V.II:237–241, 243–251
anger as expression of, V.II:250
art as antidote to, V.II:256–257
cognitive discrimination failures and, V.II:252–253
first-order discrimination vs., V.II:216, 247
generalized, V.II:240n24
intention and, V.II:248
strategies for ameliorating, V.II:253–258
High Performance, photo-text presentation in, V.II:108
Hindu art, appropriation and, V.II:209, 210
Hispanic artists, political engagement vs. professional success and, V.II:81–82
Historians
artists as, V.I:xv; V.II:xiii
success of artists compared to, V.II:79
Historical background
author's view of art and, V.I:xvii–xviii; V.II:xv–xvi
conceptualism, V.I:xiii–xiv; V.II:xi–xii
social role of artist, V.II:25–26
History. *See* Art history
History Lesson (Straub) V.I:103
Hoffman, Abbie, V.I:40
Holliday, Billie, V.II:175
Homogeneity, of artwork/activity/artist, V.II:20
Homophobia
calling card responses to, V.I:272
disco dancing and, V.I:151
pseudorationality and, V.II:222
Homosexuals. *See* Gays; Homophobia; Lesbianism
Honesty, intellectual, V.II:155
Honorific stereotype, V.II:229, 230
deviance and, V.II:231, 232, 233
in self-conception, V.II:231–233
Hostility, V.I:183
artist accused of, V.II:137, 139
of critic, V.II:140–141
in *Mythic Being* series, V.I:147
provocation of, V.I:233
unconscious, V.I:xx; V.II:xviii
Hotel piece, V.I:91
How New York Stole the Idea of the Avant-Garde (Guilbaut) V.II:212n1
Hughes, Langston, V.I:xxiv; V.II:xxii
Huguenot mass, attendance at, V.I:111
Hulten, Pontus, V.I:187–190, 187*f,* 191, 192
Humanistic values
aesthetic values vs., V.II:25–27
meta-art and, V.II:24, 26
Human objects as subjects, V.I:19, 262. *See also* Artist(s) as art object
Humiliation
for passing, V.I:277
for racist remarks, V.I:219
Hunsecker, J. J., V.II:163n10
Hybridization, V.I:206
Hypocrisy, in political art, V.II:85–88
Hypothesis: Situation #10 (Piper) V.I:22*f*–23*f*
Hypothesis series (Piper) V.I:9, 19–23, 35, 227, 261
Hypothesizing a work, thought processes for, V.II:17, 18
Icarus, image of artist as, V.II:96
Iconography
in Mythic Being, V.I:123–124, 125
in *Vanilla Nightmares,* V.I:253
"I could do that" responses to art, V.II:22n
Ideal, context over form in, V.II:12
Ideals
commitment and, V.I:73
creative process and, V.I:5, 7
Ideal society, V.I:245–246
response to racism in, V.I:251
Ideas, V.I:xiii; V.II:xi
in art, V.I:239; V.II:8–12. *See also specific types of art*
as art product, V.II:13
basic kinds of, V.II:5–6
in conceptual art, V.I:4–5, 38, 258–259; V.II:11
and context, V.II:6–7
contexts for presenting, V.II:7, 8
environmental, V.II:10
in finite systems, V.I:5, 7
and form, V.I:38, 45; V.II:6
in formal art, V.II:9
images and, V.I:38
objective reality of, V.II:3–4
as preproduct discipline, V.I:4
realization of, V.I:17–18
as response to reason, V.II:5
Identity, V.I:112, 256
abstraction from, V.I:227–232
American vs. Other, V.II:161
black, V.I:229–230, 285. *See also* Racial identity
cultural, syndrome of the other and, V.I:208, 209
"dispersion" of, V.I:107
false identity mechanism, V.II:48
focus on work vs., V.II:166
and friendship, V.I:233–234
gender and, V.I:xxiii, 233; V.II:xxi
generalization and, V.II:55–56
in ideal society, V.I:245
of objects, V.II:51–56, 58, 59, 60
personal, V.I:90
political, V.I:174
preconceptions about, V.I:233
professional, V.I:233
pseudorationality and, V.II:222
racial. *See* Racial identity
sexual, V.I:118
social, restructuring of, V.I:198
as theme, V.I:141
Ideological art, cultural racism and, V.II:130
Ideological blindfolding, V.II:214
Ideological commitment, in Euroethnic mainstream, V.II:167
Ideological fictions, V.II:87–88
conservatism and, V.II:86, 87, 88
definition of success, V.II:78
Euroethnicity and, V.II:166

as self-defeating, V.II:89
social responsibility of artists, V.II:84–85
See also Ideology
Ideology, V.I:xvii; V.II:xv
art education and, V.II:72
artist's condemnation of, V.I:xvii; V.II:xv
art used for, V.II:212–213
blindfolding of visual arts by, V.II:214
confrontation as antidote for, V.II:50
in definition of success, V.II:78
in Euroethnic art world, V.II:169
indoctrination with, V.I:xxxvi, xxxviii; V.II:xx-xiv, xxxvi
mainstream, V.I:236; V.II:167–169
mechanisms of, V.II:48–50
personal, V.II:48
of postmodern art, V.II:161
racism and, V.I:181; V.II:48, 166
self-deception and, V.II:86
self-imposed restrictions and, V.I:115
unconventional art and, V.II:205, 206
uniqueness of artwork as, V.II:79–80
See also Ideological fictions
"The Ideology of the Margin: Gender, Race, and Culture" (panel) V.I:233
Idiolects
mainstream, adopted by marginalized, V.II:133
of Other, appropriation of, V.II:209
Idiom of communication, importance of sharing, V.II:96
Idioms
cultural, V.I:202–203; V.II:102
of Funk, V.I:211
Idols of Perversity: Fantasies of Feminine Evil in Fin-de-Siécle Culture (Dijkstra) V.II:134n4, E-135n7, 137n10
I Embody (Piper) V.I:139*f*, 245, 264
"If I Was a Dancer (Dance Part 2) (Rolling Stones) V.I:215
Ignorance, V.I:xvii, 202; V.II:xv
as barrier to art, V.I:230
in ideal society, V.I:246
institutional prejudice and, V.I:xvii; V.II:xv
". . .I-know-what-I-like" statements, V.II:22n2
Illusion of omniscience, V.II:50
Illusion of perfectability, V.II:48–49
Image, V.I:117
construction of with audience, V.I:156
ideas and, V.I:38
of Mythic Being, V.I:125
Imagery, as subject matter, V.I:121
Imagination, failure of, V.I:246
Immediate here-and-now. *See* Indexical present
"Impartiality, Compassion and Modal Imagination" (Piper) V.II:227n16
Imperialism, American cultural, V.II:213, 214
Impermanence, performance and, V.I:121
Impersonality
as cultural racism, V.II:129
as defense, V.I:286
formalism and, V.II:69–70
Impressionism, intellectual radicalism and, V.II:152
Inaccessibility, as stereotype, V.II:138
Inclusivity, metaphysical, V.II:98
Incompetence, in art criticism, V.II:182
Incongruity, planned, V.I:xv; V.II:xiii
Independence, intellectual, V.II:151–152
Independence of artist, as myth, V.II:78
Indexical present (Immediate here-and-now) V.I:241–242, 247–248
communication breakdown in, V.I:257
confrontational art and, V.II:257
confronting racism in, V.I:xx; V.II:xviii
experiencing other in, V.I:248
in *I/You/Us,* V.I:264–265
in *Meat into Meat,* V.I:261
response to racism in, V.I:267
Individual dignity, racial dignity vs., V.I:285
Individualism, V.I:257
methodological, V.I:246
Individuality
community and, V.I:174
conventions on, V.II:205
"dispersion" of, V.I:107
of functional objects, V.II:52
Individual preferences, unconventional art and, V.II:204–205
Individuals: Post-Movement Art (Sondheim) V.I:117
Individuals
responsibility of for social change, V.I:247
See also Audience
Inductive generalization
discriminatory stereotype vs., V.II:230
stereotype vs., V.II:235
Inferiority, primary disvalued property and, V.II:215–216
Inferiority complex, cultural, racism and, V.I:206
Infinity
object of art as, V.I:xvii; V.II:xv
race and gender as limits on, V.I:xxiii; V.II:xxi
Information, V.I:115; V.II:6
in art production systems, V.II:13
art as source of, V.II:203
dissemination of, art contexts for, V.I:121
forms conveying, V.II:6
ordering of, V.I:20
sensory, V.I:20
uniqueness of art object and, V.II:19
Information contexts, V.II:7
aural, V.II:7
unsituated, V.II:7
"Information" show, V.I:30
Ingres, Jean-Auguste-Dominique, V.I:29
Inheritance, racial identity and, V.I:291–292
Injustice, V.I:285
Innovation
aesthetic value vs. demand for, V.II:77–78, 156, 157, 158, 161
of content vs. form, V.II:210
dismissal of, V.II:168
postmodernism's attitude toward, V.II:168, 169
punishment of, V.II:187
self-consciousness required for, V.II:210
as threat to mainstream, V.II:169
See also Originality
Input-output art, V.I:100
Inquiry (Into Meaning and Truth) (Russell) V.I:92
Insanity, V.I:50–51
Inscrutability
of artist, V.II:20
of Mythic Being, V.I:125
of Other, V.II:138
Insensitivity
acknowledgment of racial identity and, V.I:300–301
failure of empathy and, V.I:246
Inspiration
African American art as source of, V.II:184
non-Euroethnic art as source of, V.II:209
as thought process, V.II:17, 18
Installations, V.I:xxi; V.II:xix
Aspects of the Liberal Dilemma, V.I:266
See also Exhibits; Media
Institutionalized disentitlement, V.I:291–292
Institutional politics, support for artist and, V.I:xxxii–xxxiii; V.II:xxxi–xxxii
Institutional prejudice, V.I:xvii; V.II:xv
Institutional racism, interpersonal racism vs., V.I:246, 247
Institutions
higher-order political discrimination and, V.II:251–252
support for artist and, V.I:xxxii–xxxiii; V.II:xxxi–xxxii
See also Art institutions
Instrumentality, in performance art, V.II:60
Instrumentalizing conception of objects, V.II:52
Intar Gallery, V.II:162
Integrated society, vision for, V.I:245–246
Integration, V.I:255
author's experience of, V.I:279
Integration of anomaly, resistance to, V.II:220
Integrity
art making as lifeline to, V.II:132
critical, V.II:112
cultural, assimilation vs., V.II:141
importance of, V.I:240
Intellect
attacks on, V.II:135
masculinity equated with, V.I:xxxv; V.II:xxxiii
passions and, V.I:63–64
Intellectual conscience, V.II:151–152
lack of, V.II:154–155
values and, V.II:157–158
violation of standards and, V.II:158
Intellectual conservatism, in philosophy, V.II:151–152

Intellectual curiosity, entrepreneurship vs., V.II:169
Intellectual dependence, V.II:154
Intellectual elitism, V.I:229–230
Intellectual honesty, V.II:155
Intellectual input, in art production systems, V.II:13
Intellectual integrity, CWAs and, V.II:169
Intellectualism, as response to fear, V.II:196
Intellectual provincialism, V.I:203
Intellectual radicalism, V.II:152–153
Intellectual responsibility, V.II:154
 independence and, V.II:151–152
Intellectuals, philosphy and, V.II:149–150
Intent; Intention
 alienation of artwork from, V.II:70
 in art vs. advertising, V.II:258n39
 ascription of malevolence and, V.II:226–227
 cultural racism and, V.II:128
 form and, V.I:5
 higher-order political discrimination and, V.II:248
 justification vs., V.II:25
 translating to physical reality, V.I:4
Interiority, V.I:xxxix, xl; V.II:xxxvii, xxxviii
 attacks on, V.I:246
 in creative process, V.I:38
Interlopers, moral outrage of, V.I:210–211
Interpersonal interaction, as target of art, V.I:246
Interpersonal racism, institutional racism vs., V.I:246, 247
Interpretation, criticism vs., V.II:124
Interpretive control, V.II:93, 95–96, 98–99
 artist as art object and, V.II:100–101
 confrontation as aid to, V.II:99
 ontological status of work and, V.II:98–99
Intervention, calling card as, V.I:219
"In This Corner: Adrian Piper's Agitprop" (Welish) V.II:186n10
Intimacy, sexism and, V.I:247
Intimate relationships, xenophobia in, V.I:256
Intimate space, Funk music and, V.I:214
Intuition
 making form work with, V.I:5–6
 systematic approach vs., V.I:96
Intuitive process, art as, V.II:4
Invasion of the Body Snatchers, V.I:219
Inventive form, aesthetic emotion and, V.II:192, 193–195
Investment, by artists in art institutions, V.II:80–81
Investment, personal
 in cognitive error, V.II:228–229
 in self-conception, V.II:231
Investment value, V.I:121
 art criticism and, V.II:23
 pricing proposal and, V.II:32
Invisibility, cultural racism and, V.II:128, 133
The Invisible Man (Ellison) V.I:xxiii; V.II:xxi, 195
Iola Leroy; or, Shadows Uplifted (Harper) V.I:278, 280, 288, 289, 292, 293, 303, 307
IQ, power of words and, V.II:199
Irony, in political art, V.I:267
Irrationality, commitment and, V.I:67, 80
Irresponsibility
 artists accused of, V.I:203
 division of labor as cause of, V.II:73, 74–75
Isherwood, Christopher, V.II:165n14
Islamic art, appropriated by Europeans, V.II:209
Isolation
 aesthetic, politics and, V.I:31
 of artist, V.I:39, 122; V.II:26
 of art objects, V.I:39–40, 42; V.II:58
 in art world, V.I:41
 from functional context, V.II:58
 sociopolitical awareness vs., V.I:xvii; V.II:xv
"Is 'Quality' an Idea Whose Time Has Gone?" (Brenson) V.II:189n1
Issue (catalog) V.I:173
Italy, African culture disseminated through, V.I:206
It's Just Art (Piper) V.I:179*f*, 201
 description of, V.I:177–180
 disco dancing in, V.I:177, 180
It's Just Art Announcement Poster (Piper) V.I:176*f*
I/You (Her) (Piper) V.I:125–126, 127*f*–136*f*
I/You (Us) (Piper) V.I:249, 264–265

Jackson, Michael, V.II:155, 239
Jackson State University, V.I:xvii, 30, 262; V.II:xv
Jamaica, racial mix in, V.I:289
Japanese art, Van Gogh and, V.II:209
Jazz, V.I:198; V.II:209
"Jesus freaks," commitment and, V.I:69–70, 72
Jews
 anti-Semitic remarks about, V.I:229. *See also* Anti-Semitism
 dissociation and, V.II:222
 racism toward, V.I:281
 status and, V.I:147, 149
Johnson, James Weldon, *The Autobiography of an Ex-Coloured Man,* V.I:282, 285, 295, 305, 307
Johnson, Lyndon, V.I:299; V.II:250
Jolson, Al, V.I:199
Jones, A. M., "Blue Rhythm and Hot Notes," V.I:216
Jones, Michael, V.II:127
Jonestown (Guyana) V.II:197n5
The Journal of Philosophy, V.II:116
Journals, art, V.II:186–187
Journals (Chestnutt) V.I:279, 307
Journal writing
 by author, V.I:89, 90, 91
 in *Dispersion* series, V.I:107, 108
 mantras from, V.I:103, 109–110, 117, 263
 Mythic Being and, V.I:113, 114, 137, 147, 263
 self-discovery through, V.I:91
 in *Spectator Series* and, V.I:102, 103–105
The Joys of Motherhood (Emecheta) V.II:195
Judd, Donald, V.I:xvi, 29; V.II:xiv
 Untitled, V.II:9*f*
Judgment
 discrimination and, V.II:215–216, 220
 empowerment and, V.II:198
 epistemic rules of thumb and, V.II:234–237
 institutional, V.I:xxxii–xxxiii; V.II:xxxi–xxxii
 moral, V.I:210–211
 of quality, V.II:189, 195, 197–198
 universal standards for, V.II:197–198
Jump To It (Franklin) V.I:215
Jupiter Symphony (Mozart) V.II:195
Just Gossip (Piper) V.I:141, 146
Justification
 intention vs., V.II:25
 for meta-art, V.II:27
 pragmatic value and, V.II:25

Kaiser Wilhelm Gedächtnis-Kirche, V.II:53–54
Kaltenbach, Steve, V.I:37
Kant, Immanuel, V.I:xv, xvi, 50, 189, 191; V.II:xiii, xiv, 39, 69, 223, 224, 225, 226, 227
 The Critique of Judgment, V.II:191n3
 The Critique of Pure Reason, V.I:55, 71, 228, 255, 256; V.II:17, 216n4
 formalist aesthetic judgment and, V.II:195
 Logic, V.II:217n6
 Observations on the Feeling of the Beautiful and the Sublime, V.II:191n3
 rationalism of, V.II:216–220
Kantian Rationalism Thesis (KRT) V.II:216–220, 221
Kant's Theory of Mental Activity (Wolff) V.II:216n5
Kaprow, Allan, V.I:xv, xvi; V.II:xiii, xiv
Kemp Smith, Norman, V.II:216n4
Kennedy, Peter, V.I:113
Kent State University, V.I:xvii, 30, 227, 262; V.II:xv
Khan, Chaka, V.I:209
 Chaka Khan, V.I:215
 "Do You Love What You Feel?," V.I:177
Khmer Rouge, V.I:177
King, Martin Luther, V.I:272
Kissinger, Henry, V.I:272
Kitt, Eartha, V.I:299
Kohut, Alexander, V.II:123
Kool and the Gang, *As One,* V.I:215
Korsmeyer, Carolyn, *Feminism and Tradition in Aesthetics,* V.I:181
Kostelanetz, Richard, *A Critical Assembling,* V.II:41
Kosuth, Joseph, V.II:213
Kovay, Don, V.I:199
Kozloff, Max, "American Painting during the Cold War," V.II:212n1
Kozlov, Christine, V.I:xxxv; V.II:xxxiii
Kramer, Hilton, V.II:162
 "A Times Critic's Piece about Art Amounts to Political Propaganda," V.II:187n12
Krasner, Lee, V.II:52, 192
Krauss, Rosalind, V.I:xvi–xvii; V.II:xiv–xv, 161

Kris, Ernst, *Psychoanalytic Explorations in Art* (Kris) V.II:18n1
Krishnamurti, V.I:57
Kropotkin, Prince, V.I:189
KRT. *See* Kantian Rationalism Thesis
Kruger, Barbara, V.I:xix; V.II:xvii, 184n1
Kuffler, Suzanne, V.I:114
Kuhn, Thomas, V.II:220
  The Structure of Scientific Revolutions, V.II:220n11
Kuspit, Donald, V.I:xvi; V.II:xiv, 135n6, 139, 140, 161–162
  "Adrian Piper, Self-Healing Through Meta-Art," V.II:107, 134n2, 162n3, 186n9
  critique of, V.II:107–125, 134–142
Kuspit Extermination Fantasy (Piper) V.II:106*f*
Kuspit Strangulation Fantasy (Piper) V.II:119*f*

Labeling; Labels. *See* Categorization
Labor
  as condition for art production, V.I:159
  costs of in art production, V.II:31
  See also Division of labor
Landshoff, Andreas, V.I:113
Language, V.II:6
  aesthetic emotion as resistant to, V.II:199
  as art object, V.I:259; V.II:213
  boundaries conveyed by, V.I:15
  cognitive structuring and, V.II:217
  conceptual art and, V.I:xxxv, 241–242; V.II:xxxiii
  and context, V.I:209–211, 253; V.II:7
  cultural racism and, V.II:133
  event context for, V.II:7
  generalizing concepts in, V.II:55–56
  information context for, V.II:7
  limitations of, V.II:199
  in *Mythic Being* series, V.I:263–264
  of performance art, V.II:95–96
  power and, V.I:265; V.II:133–134, 199
  public perceptual, V.I:5
  racism and, V.I:305
  self-transcendence and, V.II:133
  as subject of art, V.I:91; V.II:213
The Language of Art (Goodman) V.II:57
Larsen, Nella
  Passing, V.I:286, 307
  Quicksand, V.I:307
Law, V.I:60–61
"Laws of Falling Bodies" (Raven) V.II:185n5
Lazerowitz, Morris, *Psychoanalysis and Philosophy,* V.II:18n1
Lee, Peggy, V.I:199
Leftist ideology, artist's condemnation of, V.I:xvii; V.II:xv
Legal issues in miscegenation, V.I:291–292
Legal racism, cultural racism and, V.II:127
Legitimacy; legitimation
  art-contextual, political effectiveness and, V.II:81–82
  ethnocentricity and, V.II:88
  Euroethnicity and, V.II:65
  passing and, V.I:276
  of personal attacks, V.II:143
Lesbianism, one-way communication and, V.II:49
Letter to Terry Atkinson (Piper) V.I:11, 15
LeWitt, Sol, V.I:xx, xxxvi, 7, 11, 102, 225, 264; V.II:xviii, xxxiv, 213
  conceptual art aesthetic developed by, V.II:11
  conceptual art defined by, V.I:248
  European art and, V.II:214
  Forty-nine Three-Part Variations on Three Different Kinds of Cubes (LeWitt) V.II:11*f*, 208*f*
  "46 Variations on Three Different Kinds of Cube" exhibit, V.I:29, 258
  influence of on artist, V.I:29–30, 241
  minimal art and, V.I:257–258
  "Notes on Conceptual Art," V.I:29
  "Paragraphs on Conceptual Art," V.I:xiii, 4n2, 248; V.II:xi
  "Sentences," V.I:xiii; V.II:xi
Lexicon of symbols, shared by artist and audience, V.II:96
Li, C. C., "The Dynamics of Racial Admixture-An Analysis of the American Negro," V.II:245n27
Liberalism, V.I:266
Liberal Response, V.I:266
Liberation, from syndrome of the Other, V.I:208–209
Life conditions
  contexts for presenting, V.II:7
  ideas and, V.II:5
Light Up the Night (Brothers Johnson) V.I:215
Limitations, V.I:142
Limits, overstepping of, V.I:86
Lingner, Michael, V.II:214n2
Linguistic pigeonholing, V.II:133
Lippard, Lucy, V.I:xxxvi; V.II:xxxiv, 127
  "Sol LeWitt: Non-Visual Structures," V.I:4n2
Lipps, Inc, "Funky Town" (*Mouth to Mouth*) V.I:215
Listening, hearing vs., V.II:175–176
Literalism, aesthetic, V.I:xx; V.II:xviii
Literature, aesthetic emotion and, V.II:195
Logic
  in analytic philosophy, V.II:149
  as antidote to myth, V.I:xxiv; V.II:xxii
Logic (Kant) V.II:217n6
Loneliness, self-acceptance accompanied by, V.I:173
Look but Don't Touch (Piper) V.I:158*f*
Los Angeles Museum of Contemporary Art, V.I:187
Loudspeakers, as aural information context, V.II:7
Louisa Picquet, The Octoroon Slave and Concubine: A Tale of Southern Slave Life (Mattison) E-V.I:276, 307
Louisiana, V.I:289, 291
Love Approach (Browne) V.I:214
Lozano, Lee, V.I:37
LSD, V.I:89
Luce, R. Duncan, *Games and Decisions,* V.II:167n17

McCarthy, Joseph, V.II:212
McCarthyism
  Greenbergian formalism and, V.II:209
  legacy of, V.II:201, 203, 212–213, 214
McCoy, Terry, V.II:162
Mace, V.I:61–62
McEvilley, Thomas, V.II:185
  "Doctor Lawyer Indian Chief: 'Primitivism' in 20th Century Art," V.II:143n12, 185n4
  "Empyrrhical Thinking (and Why Kant Can't)" V.II:185n4
Machaut, Guillaume de, V.II:175
"Magiciens de la Terre" exhibit, V.II:166
Magisterial form, aesthetic emotion and, V.II:192, 193–195
Mainsream idioect, adoption of by marginalized, V.II:133
Mainstream, V.II:163
  admittance from margins to, V.II:185–186
  Euroethnic, V.II:168–169
  expropriation of, V.II:171
  fear of the Other in, V.II:128, 129, 130
  marginality and, V.I:245
  See also Mainstream art
Mainstream academic philosophy, V.II:149
Mainstream art, V.I:236
  admittance of marginalized artists, V.II:185–186
  African-American art excluded from, V.II:162
  co-optation by, V.I:236
  critical viewpoints in, V.I:xvi–xvii; V.II:xiv–xv. *See also* Art criticism
  CWAs and, V.II:168–169
  economics and, V.I:122
  education and, V.II:66–68
  Euroethnic expropriation in, V.II:171
  Euroethnicity of, V.II:161, 163
  feminist art and, V.II:138–139
  ideological commitment in, V.II:167
  marginality and, V.I:234, 236, 237, 245
  solipsism in, V.II:45
  trivial concerns in, V.II:45
  See also Mainstream
Mainstream artists, appropriation by, V.I:xxxvii, xxxviii; V.II:xxxv, xxxvi
Mainstream culture
  blacks and, V.I:199
  social dance in, V.I:195
Mainstream ideology, V.I:236
Makeba, Miriam, V.II:175
"Making Flippy Floppy" (Talking Heads) V.I:215
Malcolm X, *The Autobiography of Malcolm X,* V.I:293, 295, 301, 307
Male(s)
  affirmative action and, V.II:183, 184, 186, 187
  attention paid to CWAs vs., V.II:163

colored, Euroethnic art world and, V.II:170–171
confronting stereotypes of, V.I:181
Mythic Being as, V.I:117–118, 147
racial fears of, V.I:298–299
See also Gender; Heterosexual white males; WASPs
Malevolence
ascription of, V.II:226–227
disvaluation vs., V.II:246–247, 251
Manet, Édouard
Dejeuner sur l'herbe, V.II:211
Olympia, V.II:155
Mangold, Sylvia, V.II:52
Manipulation
accusations of, V.I:268, 296, 303–304
audience's feelings of, V.I:205
by dealers, V.II:75–76, 77
Mantras
from journal, V.I:103, 109–110
Mythic Being and, V.I:xviii, 112, 113, 114, 117, 123, 137, 263; V.II:xvi
in *Spectator Series,* V.I:103–105
See also Meditation
Mapplethorpe, Robert, V.II:162, 163
Maps
as forms, V.II:6
information context for, V.II:7
See also Media
Marat, Jean-Paul, V.II:211
Marginality; Marginalization, V.I:xxxiv–xxxvi; V.II:xxxiii–xxxv
admittance to mainstream from, V.II:185–186
in art world, V.I:234, 236, 237
and avant-garde, V.II:183, 185–186
conceptual artists and, V.I:xxxv–xxxvi; V.II:xxxiii–xxxiv
cultural racism and, V.II:128–129
of dissent, V.I:xvi; V.II:xiv
for economic reasons, V.II:77
of feminist art, V.II:138–139
gaining sense of, V.I:164
innovation dismissed as, V.II:168
mainstream idiolect and, V.II:133
as plagiarism rationale, V.II:183–184
positive aspects of, V.I:217, 233–234, 236–237, 245
proposal to overcome, V.II:142
sense of entitlement vs., V.I:xxxiv–xxxvi; V.II:xxxiii–xxxiv
social benefit discouraged by, V.II:205–206
sociocultural categorization and, V.I:xxxiv, xxxv; V.II:xxxii, xxxiii
universal quality standards and, V.II:199
of women artists, V.I:xxxv; V.II:xxxiii
Marginal utility of commodity consumption, V.II:54–55
Marketing, V.I:270–271
art criticism in service of, V.II:22–23
art education and, V.II:71
artists and, V.II:71–72
art vs. academic work, V.II:79–80
author's views on, V.I:239
competition and, V.I:239
self-censorship and, V.I:xxxii; V.II:xxx
sociopolitical status and, V.I:xxxvi; V.II:xxxiv
success defined by, V.II:169
zero-sum game and, V.II:167
See also Economics of art
Market value
aesthetic value vs., V.II:170
government funding as antidote to, V.II:201
preventing fluctuations in, V.II:32
pricing proposal, V.II:31–32
success determined by, V.II:169–170
See also Economics of art
Marriage, V.I:71, 72, 78
Marsalis, Wynton, V.II:195
Marshall Plan, V.II:39, 213
Martin, Agnes, V.II:52
Marx, Karl, V.II:39, 48, 59
Marxism, V.I:9
art criticism from viewpoint of, V.II:213
behavior anomalous to, V.I:261
Masculine; Masculinity, V.I:104, 117–118
art world and, V.I:xxxv; V.II:xxxiii
freedom in, V.I:263
Mythic Being and, V.I:147
Master of the Osservanza, V.II:210
Saint Anthony Abbot series, V.II:194
Material, riding with, V.I:4–5
Material form, as tool for public perceptual language, V.I:5
Materiality, abstraction from, V.I:225, 227
Matisse, Henri-Émile-Benoît, V.II:192, 211
Matrix, supplied by artist, V.I:xxxix; V.II:xxxvii
Mattison, H., *Louisa Picquet, The Octoroon Slave and Concubine: A Tale of Southern Slave Life,* E-V.I:276, 307
Max's Kansas City, V.I:27, 37, 262
Mayer, Bernadette, V.I:37
Mayer, Rosemary, V.I:51, 89–90, 100; V.II:52
"Performance and Experience," V.I:89–90; V.II:18n1
Mazlish, Bruce, *Psychoanalysis and History,* V.II:18n1
M. B. *See* Mythic Being
Meaning, V.I:xxxix–xl; V.II:xxxvii–xxxviii
Kantian Rationalism Thesis and, V.II:219
motivation vs., V.II:139–140, 144
uniqueness of art object and, V.II:19
Means of expression, choice of, V.I:3
Meat into Meat (Piper) V.I:9–10, 261
Meat into Meat #5 (Piper) V.I:8*f*
Meat into Meat #9 (Piper) V.I:8*f*
Media
artist's books, V.I:259
as art objects, V.I:258–259
artwork inhibited by, V.I:36–37
changes in use of, V.I:30, 31
choice of, V.I:38, 121, 248
cognitive provocation through, V.II:255
in conceptual art, V.I:248–249
CWAs ignored in, V.II:162
documentation, impact of work diminished by, V.I:33
idea vs., V.I:17
installation, V.I:162–168, 177–180
language as, V.I:91
limitations of, V.I:41
political effectiveness and, V.II:83, 84
politics and choice of, V.I:120
price of recognition by, V.II:141, 142
priority of content of, V.I:249
two-dimensional, V.I:227
See also Art context(s) Communications media; *various types*
Medieval music, V.II:197
Meditation, V.I:9, 123
self-control through, V.I:91
See also Mantras
Meditations on First Philosophy (Descartes) V.II:111, 191n4
"Mediumistic" translation of idea to form, V.I:5
Memory, distortions of, V.I:294
Men. *See* Gender; Male(s)Merriam, Alan P., "African Music," V.I:216
Message, in music meant to be heard, V.II:175
"The Message" (Grandmaster Flash) V.II:197
Meta-art, V.I:xvii; V.II:xv
as art, V.II:115
art criticism and, V.I:xxx–xxxi; V.II:xviii–xxix, 22, 24
artist's definition of, V.I:xiii, xxix; V.II:xi, xxvii, 17, 24
described, V.II:17–18
epistemic vs. aesthetic analysis in, V.II:21
humanistic values and, V.II:24, 26
justification for, V.II:27
misunderstandings about, V.II:108, 109, 111, 115–116, 123–124
objections to, V.II:117
as occupation for artists, V.II:17, 18, 20–21, 22
performance art and, V.II:116
as perspective for art critics, V.I:xxix; V.II:xxvii
textual performance seen as, V.II:115
Metamorphosis
of Mythic Being, V.I:123–125
revelation of racial identity and, V.I:299–301
Metaphysical Deduction, V.II:216–217
Metaphysical inclusiveness, problems caused by, V.II:98
Metaphysical pretensions, V.II:98
Metaphysics, V.II:98
abstraction and, V.I:227
aesthetic emotion and, V.II:190–191
sociopolitical role of art and, V.I:xvii; V.II:xv
truth and, V.I:74
Metaphysics (Aristotle) V.I:32
Method; methodology, V.I:119–120
dialogue with critic about, V.II:124–125
Methodological individualism, V.I:246
Michael Sternschein (Piper) V.I:225, 226*f*

Michelangelo, V.I:265
Middle-class, art lovers as, V.I:xx; V.II:xviii
Middle-class blacks, V.I:277, 278
Midnight Love (Gaye) V.I:215
Mimesis, cognitive discrimination encouraged by, V.II:256
Mimicry, V.I:49
Mind, reality and, V.II:5
Minimalism, V.I:225, 257
  aesthetic values in, V.I:267
  alienation in, V.I:38
  author's background in, V.I:258
  cognitive discrimination and, V.II:254–255
  limitations of, V.I:41
  social content and, V.II:213, 214
Minorities, V.I:164, 166; V.II:130
  See also Cultural racism; Ethnic groups; *specific minorities*
Minority status, myth of, V.II:166
"The Mirror the Other" (Sims) V.II:185n6
Miscegenation, V.I:xix; V.II:xvii
  extent of, V.I:288–289, 291, 305–306
  legal definitions, V.I:291–292
  results of, V.I:287
Miscommunication, misinterpretation and, V.II:93
Misevaluation, V.II:93
  lack of shared lexicon and, V.II:96
Misinterpretation
  of artwork as autobiography, V.II:139
  shared communication idiom and, V.II:96
  of subject matter, V.II:118, 120
Missa Prolationem (Ockeghem) V.II:195
Mistrust, V.I:230
Misunderstandings
  about identity, V.I:233
  quality judgments and, V.II:197–198
Modeling experience, V.I:89, 90, 91, 98–99
Modern art, V.II:52, 53–55
Modernism, V.I:xx; V.II:xviii
  artist's purpose and, V.I:xv; V.II:xiii
  conceptualism and, V.I:xvii; V.II:xv
  content and, V.II:212
  development of, V.II:209–214
  European vs. American, V.II:211–212
  ideological commitment in, V.II:167
MOMA. *See* Museum of Modern Art
Mondrian, Piet, V.II:209
Monetary value
  art criticism and, V.II:23
  pricing proposal, V.II:31–32
  standards of excellence and, V.II:154–155, 156
Money problems, V.I:102
Monk, Meredith, V.II:193
Monologue, V.I:48, 266–267, 272–273
  in *Art for the Art-World Surface Pattern,* V.I:162–164, 265
  in *Aspects of the Liberal Dilemma,* V.I:169–70, 170, 266
  by author compared to "crazy" man, V.I:92
  in *Four Intruders. . .,* V.I:181, 183–186, 266–267
  in *It's Just Art,* V.I:178
  Phillip Zohn Catalysis, V.I:58–88
  in *Spectator Series,* V.I:107
Montclair State College (New Jersey) V.I:158, 159
Monteverdi, Claudio, V.I:201
  Orfeo, V.II:197
Moore, G. E., V.I:145
"Moral cretins," V.I:229, 230, 232
Moral outrage, V.I:210
The Moral Psychology of the Virtues (Dent) V.II:249n33
Morals; Morality, V.I:120, 230
  art as guide for, V.I:240
  artistic conventions and, V.II:205–206
  and artists, V.II:82–83
  of artist and viewer, V.I:xx; V.II:xviii
  collaborative work and, V.I:145
  critical distance and, V.II:157
  funding decisions and, V.II:205–206
  judgment and, V.I:210–211
  moral vs. artistic standards, V.II:154–158
  philosophy and, V.I:230, 232
  politically correct involvement and, V.II:86–87
  racism and, V.I:186
  standards for disvaluees and, V.II:251
  as subject matter, V.I:9–10
Morgan, Robert, "Adrian Piper," V.II:165n13
Morris, Errol, V.I:189
Motivation; Motives
  aesthetic, V.I:52
  for art making, V.I:245
  art making and, V.I:52
  misascription of, V.II:227, 228
  public meaning and, V.II:139–140, 144
  values and, V.II:74
Motor City Affair (Parliament) V.I:214
Motown, V.I:151
Mourning, by mainstream art world, V.II:167, 168, 169
Mouth to Mouth (Lipps, Inc.) V.I:215
Movement, generalization of art objects by, V.II:56
Movies, inhibition of art in, V.I:37
Mozart, Wolfgang Amadeus, V.I:201, 268
  Jupiter Symphony, V.II:195
Multiculturalism, and art, V.II:183–187
Murphy, Eddie, V.I:300
Murray, Elizabeth, V.II:185
Musée d'Art Moderne (Paris) V.I:87
Museum of Modern Art (MOMA) V.I:xxi, xxiii, 30; V.II:xix, xxi, 167
Museums, V.I:40; V.II:255
  art segregated from life in, V.I:39, 40
  as cognitive provocation sites, V.II:253–254, 255
  power of funding sources for, V.II:202
  protest movement and, V.I:31
  as public spaces, V.II:43–44
  racism in, V.II:185
  role of, V.II:253–254
  sociopolitical climate and, V.I:xxxvi; V.II:xxxiv
  zero-sum game and, V.II:167
Music, V.I:48, 266
  aesthetic emotion and, V.II:195
  African-American, V.I:195
  in *Assorted Anti-Postmodernist Artifacts,* V.I:217
  author and, V.I:89, 90, 91
  disco, V.I:201, 215
  disco-jazz, V.I:151
  Easy Listening, V.II:175, 176
  in *Four Intruders. . .,* V.I:266
  in *It's Just Art,* V.I:177
  listening to vs. hearing, V.II:175–176
  Medieval, V.II:197
  Muzak, V.II:175
  Renaissance, V.II:197
  soul, V.I:214
  use of, V.I:185
  See also Funk music
Music meant to be heard, V.II:175–176
Musicology, author's study of, V.I:11, 228, 268
Mutilation, self-, V.I:189, 192
Muzak, V.II:175
My Calling (Card)Number One: A Reactive Guerrilla Performance for Dinners and Cocktail Parties (Piper) V.I:271
My Calling (Card)Number Two: Reactive Guerrilla Performance for Bars and Discos (Piper) V.I:272
My Calling (Cards)#1 and #2 (Piper) V.I:219–221, 230, 245, 249, 271–272
Myers, John Bernard, "The Art Biz," V.II:72n5
"My Rival" (Steely Dan) V.I:215
Mystery of the object, V.II:51, 52–53
  aesthetic emotion and, V.II:192, 193
  generalization and, V.II:56
  uniqueness and, V.II:57–58
Myth
  of artistic independence, V.II:78
  of critical objectivity, V.I:xxix; V.II:xxvii
  logic as antidote to, V.I:xxiv; V.II:xxii
  of minority status, V.II:166
Mythic Being (M.B.) V.I:xviii–xix; V.II:xvi–xvii
  described, V.I:108, 109
  iconography in, V.I:123–124, 125
  in *It's Just Art,* V.I:177, 180
  meaning of, V.I:118–119
  metamorphosis of, V.I:123–125
  mythology and, V.I:113
  notes on, V.I:112–114, 117–126, 137–138
  performances of, V.I:117–118, 138, 147, 263–264, 272
  personal history and persona, V.I:107, 109, 113, 114, 115, 117, 118, 123
  preparatory notes for, V.I:91–114
  privilege and, V.I:112
  public nature of, V.I:124–125

reactions of audience to, V.I:124
See also Mythic Being series
Mythic Being series (Piper) V.I:108–109, 115, 137, 143n2, 147, 164, 177, 227, 228, 266
Cruising White Women, V.I:147, 148*f*, 264
Cycle I: 4/12/68, V.I:116*f*
Cycle I: 6/6/70, V.I:110*f*
Cycle II, V.I:111
Cycle XII, V.I:113n9
Getting Back, V.I:147, 148*f*, 264
I Embody, V.I:139*f*, 245, 264
I/You (Her) V.I:125–126, 127*f*–136*f*
symbology in, V.I:263–264
See also Mythic Being (M.B.)
Mythology
Mythic Being and, V.I:113
of witness, V.I:103

"Naked City: The *Times*" (Hunsecker) V.II:163n10
Naming
power of, V.II:133–134, 142–143
as pseudorationality antidote, V.II:257
Narcissism
acknowledgment of other-orientation vs., V.II:122
author accused of, V.II:116, 117, 120, 124
solipsism vs., V.II:116
Narrow-mindedness, commitment and, V.I:69, 72–73
National Endowment for the Arts (NEA) V.II:161, 162, 201
Native Americans, legal identification of, V.I:291
NEA Art Criticism Symposium, V.II:161
NEA. *See* National Endowment for the Arts
Negation, of colored women artists, V.II:161, 163–173
Negro, use of term, V.II:127n1
Negro Slavery in Louisiana (Taylor) V.I:287, 307
Nengudi, Senga, V.II:193
Neograffitists, V.II:171n22
appropriation by, V.II:183
Neural Darwinism: The Theory of Neuronal Group Selection (Edelman) V.II:218n7
"Neurology and the Soul" (Sacks) V.II:218n7
Neurosis, Otherness dismissed as, V.II:134–135
Neutrality, political, as ideological fiction, V.II:82–84
New Art Examiner, V.II:164
Newman, Barnett, *Stations of the Cross,* V.II:196
New Museum, V.I:233; V.II:154n5
Newness, desire for, V.II:55
A New People (Williamson) V.I:206; V.II:245n27
News, in *Vanilla Nightmares,* V.I:253
New Wave music, V.I:215
Funk and, V.I:196
New York, V.I:263–264
Mythic Being and, V.I:147
in *Utah-Manhattan Transfer,* V.I:259
New York Cultural Center, V.I:30
New York Observer, V.II:162
New York Times
colored women's art reviewed in, V.II:163
and *Vanilla Nightmares* series, V.I:253, 273
Next Generation: Southern Black Aesthetic, V.II:161
"Night People" (War) V.I:181, 266
Nihilistic view of art, women artists and, V.II:168
"19th Nervous Breakdown," V.I:96
Nixon, Richard, V.I:227, 262
Noblesse oblige, V.I:246–247
Noland, Kenneth, V.I:29
Nonfunctional nature of art, V.II:25
Nonmaterial art objects, V.I:118
Normative judgment, epistemic judgment vs., V.II:234–237
Norms
etiquette, V.I:246–247
fear of Other as, V.II:133
outlaw artifacts as violation of, V.I:217
"Notes on Conceptual Art" (LeWitt) V.I:29
Nova Scotia College of Art and Design, V.I:197*f*, 269
Now. *See* Indexical present

Objecthood, objectness, V.I:xvii; V.II:xv
abstraction and, V.I:227
artist as, V.I:89–90
"dispersion" of, V.I:107
representativeness and, V.I:17
self-consciousness of, V.I:90–91
self-definition and, V.I:91
sentient vs. nonsentient, V.I:262
as subjecthood, V.I:27
as theme, V.I:141
Objectification, V.I:137
of blacks, V.I:263
of environment, V.I:9
of self, V.I:154
Objectified perceptions, as subject matter, V.I:9
Objectifying experience, in psychotherapy, V.I:89
Objective declarative voice, V.I:xxxiv, xxxix–xl, 253; V.II:xxxii–xxxiii, xxxvii–xxxviii
Objective truth, expression of, V.I:xxxiv; V.II:xxxii
Objective universality, V.I:xxxi, xxxiv; V.II:xxix, xxxii
artist's commitment to, V.I:xxxix–xl; V.II:xxxvii–xxxviii
epistemic insecurity and, V.I:xxxix; V.II:xxxvii
Objectivity
of artist, V.II:3
myth of, in art criticism, V.I:xxix; V.II:xxvii
quality issues, V.II:189, 196–197
subjective reactions of viewers and, V.I:7
Object(s) V.I:xvii, 92; V.II:xv
abstract, V.I:225, 227
aesthetic values of, V.I:41, 95; V.II:59–60
of anger, cause vs., V.I:82, 83–84
anomalous, V.I:255
art. *See* Art objects
as art product, V.II:13
in conceptual art, V.I:257–258
dance, V.I:152
dependent single, V.I:21
detachment of from self, V.I:224
devaluation of, V.II:57–58
drawing, V.I:91, 99–100
dreams as, V.I:100
human, V.I:19, 261, 262
identity of, V.II:51–56, 58, 59, 60
instrumentalizing conception of, V.II:52
media as, V.I:258–259
in modern art, V.II:53–55
mystery of, V.II:51, 52–53
Mythic Being as, V.I:138
perception of, V.I:99–100
private, construction of with audience, V.I:156
seeing others as, V.II:50
self as, V.I:19, 261
self-consciousness and, V.I:50–51, 90–91, 94
three-dimensional, V.I:227
transcendence of, V.II:193
Obliterated collective past, acknowledging, V.I:295
Obliteration, aesthetic, V.II:146
O'Brien, Mark, *Reimaging America: The Arts of Social Change,* V.I:245
Observations on the Feeling of the Beautiful and the Sublime (Kant) V.II:191n3
Observer, artist as, V.I:95–96
Obsession; Obsessive
Mythic Being and, V.I:138
with Other, V.II:132
Occupation, commitment to art as, V.II:63–64
Occupational choice
socioeconomic status and, V.II:23
supplementary, V.II:80
Ockeghem, Johannes, *Missa Prolationem,* V.II:195
Oldenburg, Claes, V.II:53–54
Olympia (Manet) V.II:155
Omniscience, illusion of, V.II:50
The One Giveth (Bootsy) V.I:214
One-upsmanship, academic, V.I:228
Ontological status of work
accessibility and, V.II:98
interpretive control and, V.II:98–99
Opacity; opaque, V.I:125; V.II:227
of artist, V.II:19–20, 21
of art product, V.II:19
interpretive control problems and, V.II:98
third-personal, V.II:225–226
An Open Letter from Adrian Piper (Piper) V.II:45

Opportunism
  accusations of, V.II:82
  lack of intellectual conscience and, V.II:154
Orfeo (Monteverdi) V.II:197
Originality
  in analytic philosophy, V.II:149
  in analytic philosophy vs. art, V.II:153. *See also* Innovation
Original Photo for Political Self-Portrait #1 (Piper) V.I:173f
Original Photo for Political Self-Portrait #2 (Piper) V.I:174f
Original Photo for Political Self-Portrait #3 (Piper) V.I:173f
"The Origins of Modern Jazz Dance" (Cayou) V.I:216
Orr-Cahall, Christine, V.II:162
Osservanza, Master of the, V.II:210
  Saint Anthony Abbot series, V.II:194
Ostracism, V.I:173
  social expectations and, V.I:200
Osumare, Halifu, V.I:206, 213
Other, V.I:147; V.II:185
  aesthetic of Otherness, V.II:185
  as alien, V.I:206
  American identity vs., V.II:161
  appropriation of idiolects of, V.II:209
  artists as, V.II:165–166
  averting one's gaze from, V.II:127. *See also* Cultural racism
  categorization and, V.I:255, 256
  colored artist stereotyped as, V.II:186
  concealed, V.II:135n5
  confrontation with self, V.I:141
  CWAs seen as, V.II:165–166
  disempowerment of, V.II:165–166
  dismissed as neurotic, V.II:134–135
  as enigmatic, V.II:138
  Eurocentrism and, V.II:165–168
  experiencing in indexical present, V.I:248
  failure to rationally conceive of, V.II:227–228
  fear of, V.II:128–129, 132, 133, 135n5
  formalism and, V.II:70
  ideal vision for, V.I:245–248
  identification with, V.I:206
  innovation and, V.II:185
  liberation from syndrome of, V.I:208–209
  misrepresentation of, V.II:133–134
  as object, V.II:50
  power abdicated to, V.I:253–254
  as target of art, V.I:246–247
Out of the Corner (Piper) V.II:208f
Outdoor environment, as spatial context, V.II:7
"Outing," of blacks passing as white, V.I:286
Outlaw artifacts, V.I:217
"Overpowered by Funk" (The Clash) V.I:215
Overproduction, V.II:75
Overstimulation, marginalization and, V.II:129

Painting
  action, V.II:212
  drip, V.II:53, 54
  pattern, V.II:127
Paper, as media for abstraction, V.I:227
"Paragraphs on Conceptual Art" (LeWitt) V.I:xiii, 4n2, 248; V.II:xi
Parallel Grid Proposal for Dugway Proving Grounds (Piper) V.I:11, 15
Parasites, artists as, V.I:40
Paris Biennale (1977) V.I:161, 265
"Paris-Moscow" exhibition, V.I:187
Parker, Charlie, V.II:175
Parks, Rosa, V.I:299
Parliament
  Motor City Affair, V.I:214
  Trombipulation, V.I:214
Parochialism
  in art criticism, V.I:236
  ethical, V.II:73–75
Parody, art criticism as, V.I:xvi; V.II:xiv, 121
Participation by audience, V.I:195–198
  spectatorship vs., V.I:213
  transformation through, V.II:102
Particulars, distortion of, V.I:248
Passing, V.I:xix, 204; V.II:xvii
  calling cards and, V.I:219
  as cause for shame, V.I:275–276, 280, 285, 296–297
  ethical challenges in, V.I:284
  guilt and, V.I:219
  and racial identity, V.I:275–306
  racism and, V.I:230
  separation required for, V.I:284, 286, 287
Passing (Larsen) V.I:286, 307
Passions, intellect and, V.I:63–64
Passive censorship, V.I:xxxv, xxxvi; V.II:xxxiii, xxxiv, 201–202
Pattern painting
  appropriation and, V.II:183
  cultural racism and, V.II:127
Peacock, Mary, V.I:xxx, 11; V.II:xxviii
Pear, Robert, "Reagan's Arts Chairman Brings Subtle Changes to the Endowment," V.II:65n2
Peer review, funding and, V.II:202–204
Pendulum Music (Reich) V.II:10f
People, confusion of personhood with, V.II:223–225
People with AIDS (PWAs) artistic censorship and, V.II:166
Perceiving (Chisholm) V.I:92
Perception, V.I:96
  art as source of, V.II:203
  and categorization, V.I:255
  of objects, V.I:99–100
  See also Sensory consciousness
Perceptual assault, V.II:55
Perfectibility, illusion of, V.II:48–49
Performance(s) V.I:261–263; V.II:108
  of art object, V.II:60
  attacked as neuroses, V.II:135
  audience and, V.I:49–50; V.II:60–61
  collaborative, V.I:195–211
  confrontational, V.I:9–10, 45–59, 155–156, 180; V.II:99, 100, 101
  critique of writings about, V.II:107–125
  explanation and, V.II:112–113
  Funk Lessons, V.I:195–216, 268–269
  impermanence and, V.I:121
  of *It's Just Art,* V.I:177–180
  Mythic Being, V.I:xviii–xix, 117–118, 137, 138, 147–148, 263–264; V.II:xvi–xvii
  problems of, V.II:93–104
  purpose of, V.I:203–204
  reactive guerrilla, V.I:219–221
  signals in, V.I:155
  signs in, V.I:156
  of *Some Reflective Surfaces,* V.I:152, 154, 155–156
  "Spectator" series, V.I:103–105
  standards of, V.II:158
  subversive nature of, V.I:155–156
  textual, meta-art mistaken for, V.II:108, 109, 111
  See also Media; Performance art
Performance art, V.I:248; V.II:60–61, 93–104, 116, 204
  appropriation and, V.II:183
  cognitive discrimination and, V.II:255
  cultural adjustment to, V.II:101
  ethical issues, V.I:189
  fear of the Other and, V.II:129
  interpretive control problems, V.II:93
  meta-art and, V.II:116
  power of, V.II:101
  transformation problems, V.II:93–94
  transformation as self-transcendence in, V.II:103
  violation of convention in, V.II:204
  warning about, V.II:61
  writing about, V.II:112–113
Performance artist, misclassification of author as, V.I:248
"Performance and Experience" (Mayer) V.II:18n1
  notes for, V.I:89–90
Performers, V.I:151
Performing objects, types of, V.I:89–90
Permutations, in creative process, V.I:7
Perreault, John, V.I:262
  "Art," V.II:22n2
Perry, Elaine, *Another Present Era,* V.I:277, 281, 288, 306, 307
Persona
  artist and, V.I:112
  "performing self" vs. "personal self," V.II:108, 109
  in *Spectator Series,* V.I:103, 104, 105, 107, 109; V.II:108, 109
Personal
  dichotomy between aesthetic and, V.II:94–98, 99
  interdependence of with political, V.I:161

Personal history
Mythic Being persona and, V.I:107, 109, 113, 114, 115, 117, 118, 123
revisionism in, V.I:294
sexuality in, V.I:104, 109, 110
Personal ideology, V.II:48
mechanisms of, V.II:48–49
Personal investment
in cognitive error, V.II:228–229
in self-conception, V.II:231
Personality
definition of, V.II:220
effects of xenophobia on, V.II:227–228
honorific self-stereotype and, V.II:231–232
personhood equated with, V.II:230, 231
value judgments about, V.II:221
works dealing with, V.I:46–47
Personal meaning, transcending through aesthetic emotion, V.II:198–199
Personal preferences, violation of in public interest, V.II:204–205
Personal significance of work, aesthetic significance vs., V.II:93
Persona (Piper) V.I:105
Personhood
confusion of people with, V.II:223–225
definition of, V.II:220–221
failure to perceive in Other, V.II:228
judgments about people and, V.II:221
personality equated with, V.II:230, 231
pseudorational cognition and, V.II:222
xenophobia and, V.II:220–221, 233
Person(s)
aliens vs., V.II:227
definition of, V.II:220–221
misconception of Other as, V.II:226
value judgments about, V.II:234–237
Persons of color, use of term, V.II:127n1, 161n1
Perspective, spatiotemporal, V.I:225
PESTS, V.I:236
Philip Morris Tobacco Company, V.II:202, 203
Philistinism, conventions as protection for, V.II:205
Phillip Zohn Catalysis (Piper)
background of, V.I:57–58
text of, V.I:58–88
Philosophy, V.I:57
aesthetic emotion and, V.II:195–196
analytic, V.II:149–152, 153
artists' repudiation of, V.I:xxxv; V.II:xxxiii
art making vs., V.I:105
author's study of, V.I:xxx, xxxi, 11, 89–90, 228, 264; V.II:xxviii, xxix
as conceptual tool, V.I:228
conflict of art making with, V.I:92–93
influence on art making of, V.I:242
intellectual conservatism in, V.II:151–152
morality and, V.I:230, 232
negative criticism of, V.II:121
preproduct discipline and, V.I:4
reflective technique in, V.I:89–90
relevance of to artist, V.I:41
roots of conceptualism in, V.I:xiv; V.II:xii
self-transcendence through, V.I:55
value of originality in, V.II:153
Vedanta, V.II:165n14
"Philosophy, Culture, and Public Policy" (Buchwalter) V.II:204n3
The Philosophy of Fine Art (Hegel) V.I:47
Phipps, Susie Guillory, V.I:291
Photodocumentation, V.I:35, 264–265
Food for the Spirit, V.I:55
in *Mythic Being* series, V.I:147
See also Media
Photographs
in *Aspects of the Liberal Dilemma,* V.I:170, 266
in fictionalized family narrative, V.I:282
as forms, V.II:6
in *Four Intruders. . .,* V.I:266
in *Hypothesis* series, V.I:261
information context for, V.II:7
in *It's Just Art,* V.I:178
in *Mythic Being* series, V.I:114, 123–124
in *Spectator Series,* V.I:101–102
See also Media
Physical properties
as primary disvalued properties, V.II:240–241
as subject matter, V.I:18
of truth, V.I:74
Piano playing, V.I:89, 90, 91
Picasso, Pablo, V.I:265; V.II:70, 209, 212
Guernica, V.I:251; V.II:211
Pigeonholing, linguistic, V.II:133. *See also* Categorization; Stereotyping
Pindell, Howardena, V.II:162n4
"Art World Racism: A Documentation," V.II:163–164
Piper, Adrian
A.~A, V.I:141–146
Area Relocation Series, V.II:12*f*
Art for the Art-World Surface Pattern, V.I:161, 162–164, 165*f*, 167, 228, 265
Aspects of the Liberal Dilemma, V.I:169–170, 171*f*, 266; V.II:140
Assorted Anti-Postmodernist Artifacts, V.I:217
Block Area Enlargement Series, V.I:16*f*, 17, 18
Catalysis. See Catalysis series
Close to Home, V.I:246
Close to Home II.B, V.I:243*f*
Close to Home #IV.B, V.I:250*f*
Concrete Infinity 6" Square, V.I:14*f*
Concrete Space-Time Infinity 8" Square, V.I:258–259
Concrete Space-Time-Infinity Pieces, V.I:258–259
Cornered, V.I:xix, 272–273, 304*f*; V.II:xvii
Cruising White Women, V.I:147, 148*f*, 264
Defaced Funk Lessons Poster, V.I:207*f*
Dispersion: The Mythic Being, V.I:107–114
Drawing of Phillip Zohn, V.I:56*f*
Empty Thought Balloon, V.I:102*f*
Five Full Thought Balloons, V.I:106
Five Unrelated Time Pieces, V.I:9, 261
"Flying," V.I:xxiii; V.II:xxi
Food for the Spirit series, V.I:51–55, 54*f*, 147
Four Intruders plus Alarm Systems, V.I:181–186, 182*f*, 229, 249, 266–267; V.II:44
Free #2, V.II:179*f*
Full Thought Balloon, V.I:105*f*
Funk Lesson Discography and Bibliography, V.I:269
Funk Lessons: Berkeley Performance, V.I:202*f*, 269
Funk Lessons: Nova Scotia College of Art and Design Performance, V.I:197*f*, 269
Funk Lessons Performance Handout, V.I:213–214, 269
Funk Lessons Poster of Bootsie, V.I:212*f*
Funk Lessons series. *See Funk Lessons* series
Getting Back, V.I:147, 148*f*, 264
Girl with Teeth, V.I:193*f*
"Goodbye to Easy Listening," V.I:xvi; V.II:xiv
Here and Now, V.I:241*f*, 247, 259
"Higher-Order Discrimination," 237n21
Hypothesis: Situation #10, V.I:22*f*–23*f*
Hypothesis series, V.I:9, 19–23, 35, 227, 261
I Embody, V.I:139*f*, 245, 264
"Impartiality, Compassion and Modal Imagination," V.II:227n16
It's Just Art, V.I:177, 177–180, 179*f*, 180, 201
It's Just Art Announcement Poster, V.I:176*f*
I/You (Her) V.I:125–126, 127*f*–136*f*
I/You (Us) V.I:249, 264–265
Just Gossip, V.I:141, 146
Kuspit Extermination Fantasy, V.II:106*f*
Kuspit Strangulation Fantasy, V.II:119*f*
Letter to Terry Atkinson, V.I:11, 15
Look but Don't Touch, V.I:158*f*
Meat into Meat, V.I:9–10, 261
Meat into Meat #5, V.I:8*f*
Meat into Meat #9, V.I:8*f*
Michael Sternschein, V.I:225, 226*f*
My Calling (Card)Number One: A Reactive Guerrilla Performance for Dinners and Cocktail Parties, V.I:271
My Calling (Card)Number Two: A Reactive Guerrilla Performance for Bars and Discos, V.I:272
My Calling (Cards)#1 and #2, V.I:219–221, 230, 245, 249, 271–272
Mythic Being series. *See Mythic Being* series
An Open Letter from Adrian Piper, V.II:45
Original Photo for Political Self-Portrait #1, V.I:173*f*
Original Photo for Political Self-Portrait #2, V.I:174*f*
Original Photo for Political Self-Portrait #3, V.I:173*f*
Out of the Corner, V.II:208*f*
Parallel Grid Proposal for Dugway Proving Grounds, V.I:11, 15

Persona, V.I:105
Phillip Zohn Catalysis, V.I:57–58, 58–88
Political Self-Portrait #1 (Sex) V.I:247
Political Self-Portrait #2, V.I:173*f*, 174*f*, 175*f*
Portrait, V.I:244*f*
"Power Relations," V.I:xvi; V.II:xiv
"Pseudorationality," V.II:220n10
"Rationality of Military Service," V.II:49n2
"Rationality and the Structure of the Self," V.II:218n8
Relocated Planes, V.I:265
Self-Portrait Exaggerating My Negroid Features, V.I:230, 231*f*, 245, 267–268
Situation series, V.I:227–228. *See also Hypothesis* series
Sixteen Permutations on the Planar Analysis of a Square, V.I:6*f*
16 Planar Variations, V.I:258
A Slave to Art, V.I:190–191
Some Reflective Surfaces, V.I:151–152, 153*f*, 154–156, 201
Space, Time, Language, Form, V.I:12–13*f*
Spectator Series, V.I:101–105
Strutting, V.I:147
Surfaces, V.I:137. *See also Some Reflective Surfaces*
A Tale of Avarice and Poverty, V.I:230, 270, 283*f*
"Talking to Myself," V.I:xvii; V.II:xv
10.00/Hour Drawing of Pontus Hulten, V.I:188*f*
Think About It, V.I:272, 290*f*
This Is Not the Documentation of a Performance, V.I:xix, 160*f*, 265; V.II:xvii
Three Political Self-Portraits, V.I:228
Twelve-Part Grid Proposal for Dugway Proving Ground, V.I:30
"Two Conceptions of the Self," V.II:220n10
Untitled Catalysis for Max's Kansas City, V.I:262
Untitled Construction, V.I:258
Untitled Drawing, V.I:225
Untitled Performance for Max's Kansas City, V.I:27, 27*f*
Untitled Three-Part Painting, V.I:225
Ur-Mutter #2, V.II:160*f*
Utah-Manhattan Transfer, V.I:227, 259–260
Utah-Manhattan Transfer #1 (Piper) V.I:260*f*
Utah-Manhattan Transfer #2, V.I:260*f*
Vanilla Nightmares #3, V.I:252*f*
Vanilla Nightmares #16, V.II:131*f*
Vanilla Nightmares #18, V.I:235*f*, 273
Vanilla Nightmares series, V.I:229, 245, 253–254, 273
What It's Like, What It Is #3, V.I:xxi, xxii*f*; V.II:xix, xx*f*
Why Guess? #2, V.II:147*f*
"Xenophobia and Kantian Rationalism," V.II:220n12
Place Position Presentation Public, (Gevers) V.I:255
Plagiarism
from colored artists, V.II:183–184
in Euroethnic art world, V.II:183–184
Planned incongruity, V.I:xv; V.II:xiii
Plato, V.I:93
The Republic, V.I:92
Timaeus, V.I:92
Player of the Year Award (Bootsy) V.I:214
Points, Blanks Way (Acconci) V.II:12*f*
Political, interdependence of with personal, V.I:161
Political action
art as means of, V.I:234
by artists, V.I:40–41
incitement to, V.I:174
Political art, V.I:xix, 169–186, 202–203, 234, 248; V.II:xvii, 201
aesthetic emotion and, V.II:193
abstraction from identity in, V.I:228
accessibility as challenge in, V.I:267
audience and, V.II:83–84
censorship and, V.I:266
contexts for, V.I:xxix–xxx, xxxi–xxxii, 31–32, 161–167; V.II:xxvii–xxviii, xxix–xxx
defense mechanisms and, V.I:164, 167
Four Intruders plus Alarm Systems (Piper) V.I:181–186, 182*f*
funding and, V.I:240
"global," V.I:234
Greco-Roman sculptures as, V.I:265
hypocrisy in, V.II:85–88
It's Just Art (Piper) V.I:177–180
legitimation of, V.I:265–267
other functions of art and, V.II:181
Paris-Moscow exhibition and, V.I:187
potential for healing in, V.II:177–178
professional acceptance and, V.II:81–84
racist responses to, V.I:201
repudiation of, V.II:209
sociocultural context for, V.II:181
Political beliefs, illusion of omniscience and, V.II:50
Political correctness
affiliation of artist and, V.II:82–83
art criticism and, V.I:236
audience responses and, V.I:251
covert racism and, V.I:302
ideological self-deception and, V.II:86
realism vs., V.I:xxi; V.II:xix
Political discrimination, V.II:216, 220, 228–258
cognitive discrimination and, V.II:216–217
definition of, V.II:215
first-order, V.II:228–233, 245
first-order vs. higher-order, V.II:216, 247
higher-order, V.II:237–241, 243–251, 252–253, 256–257
reciprocal first-order, V.II:233–237
reciprocal higher-order, V.II:242–243
second-order, V.II:237–238, 239
third-order, V.II:238–239
xenophobia and, V.II:216, 222
Political effectiveness, self-awareness and, V.II:86
Political encounter, aesthetic emotion and, V.II:195–196
Political identity, V.I:174
Political intention, cultural racism and, V.II:128
Political neutrality, of art making, V.II:82–84
Political self-awareness, in art criticism, V.I:xxix; V.II:xxvii
Political Self-Portrait #1 (Sex) (Piper) V.I:247
Political Self-Portrait #2 (Piper) V.I:173*f*, 174*f*, 175*f*
Political value, aesthetic value vs., V.I:247–248
Political vs. personal values, V.I:161
Politics
aesthetics and, V.I:164, 167, 169, 181, 183, 202–203
and art, V.I:xiii, xxi, 120–121, 236; V.II:xi, xix, 73, 203. *See also* Political art
art criticism and, V.I:xv; V.II:xiii
artists and, V.I:40–41, 202–203; V.II:81–85, 86–87, 86–89
arts funding and, V.II:201–206
art world and, V.I:30–31, 40–41; V.II:44
blacks and, V.I:199
commitment and, V.I:69, 72
constraints on art making and, V.I:120, 121, 122–123
as context for art, V.I:122–123, 161–167; V.II:43
of deference, V.I:228
discrimination and. *See* Political discrimination
Funk music and, V.I:214
Greenbergian formalism and, V.II:209
identity and, V.I:174
ignoring vs. avoiding, V.I:161
illusion of omniscience and, V.II:50
institutional, V.I:xxxii–xxxiii; V.II:xxxi–xxxii
quality issues, V.II:189–200
racism and, V.I:253–254, 279
separated from art, V.II:212–213
struggle to transcend, V.I:227
Pollock, Jackson, V.II:53, 54
Popular culture, V.I:200, 268
aesthetic interest and, V.II:157
formalist values and, V.II:65
Porgy and Bess (Gershwin) V.I:xix, 239, 240; V.II:xvii
Portrait (Piper) V.I:244*f*
Posters, V.I:228
as documentation, V.I:264
Look but Don't Touch, V.I:158
as media, V.I:137, 138
Postmodernism, V.I:xix; V.II:xvii
cultural racism and, V.II:130
as Easy Listening Art, V.II:176
Euroethnicity and, V.II:167–169, 172–173
ideology of, V.II:161, 167
innovation and, V.II:168

institutional prejudice and, V.I:xvi; V.II:xiv
mainstream art and, V.I:236
social content and, V.II:212
Poststructuralism, colored artists and, V.II:169n19
Poverty, V.I:102
positive aspects of, V.I:240
Power, V.II:133, 199
abdication of required for success, V.II:78–79
aesthetic experience and, V.II:146n16, 196
of art criticism, V.II:68, 69
art institutions and, V.II:66
of artists, V.I:203; V.II:101
in art world, V.I:190; V.II:43
disempowerment of Other, V.II:165–166
division of labor and, V.II:73
funding sources and, V.II:203
institutional constraints on, V.II:84
language and, V.I:265; V.II:133–134, 199
Mythic Being and, V.I:147
of naming, V.II:133–134, 142–143
of performance art, V.II:101
political statement about, V.II:29
price of participation in, V.II:146
racism and, V.I:253–254
reflection and, V.I:152
and relationships, V.I:189–190, 191–192
sexuality and, V.I:154, 190, 191
unconventional art and, V.II:206
universal quality standards and, V.II:199
voluntary self-objectification and, V.I:154
"Power Relations" (Piper) V.I:xvi; V.II:xiv
Pragmatic value, justification of activity and, V.II:25
Preconceptions
about identity, V.I:233
art as challenge to, V.I:249
transcending, V.II:133
Preferences, individual, unconventional art and, V.II:204–205
Prejudice
faith in reason over, V.I:xiii; V.II:xi
institutional, V.I:xvii; V.II:xv
social constraints and, V.I:xxiv; V.II:xxii
Prelude and Fugue (Bach) V.I:91
Present. *See* Indexical present
Presley, Elvis, V.I:199
Presumption, behavior of disvaluee seen as, V.II:249
Presuppositions
nalysis of, V.II:17–18
in meta-art, V.II:17
in recognition of truth, V.I:76
Pricing proposal, V.II:31–32
See also Economics of art; Market value
Primary disvalued properties, V.II:215
as basis for judgment, V.II:233–236
physical properties as, V.II:240–241
race and gender as, V.II:225
reactions to deviance from, V.II:232–233
valuee and, V.II:229
Primary valued properties, V.II:215, 233–236, 238, 239–241, 242
as basis for judgment, V.II:233–236
Primitivism, cultural racism and, V.II:127
Privacy
artistic, V.I:39, 40
calling card as plea for, V.I:221
Private Eyes (Hall and Oates) V.I:215
Private sector, funding decisions in, V.II:202–203
Privilege
Mythic Being persona and, V.I:112
racism as protection for, V.I:305–306
social class and, V.II:xxxiii
Procedures, in meta-art, V.II:17
Process, V.I:38
product as alienated from, V.I:33, 36
product as, V.I:42–45
unperceived, as subject matter, V.I:18
See also Creative process; Thought processes
Process art, intellectual conscience and, V.II:154n5
Product, defined, V.II:13
Production of art, V.II:84
alienation of artist and, V.II:75–76
conditions for, V.I:159
education and, V.II:71
ideological fictions about, V.II:79–80
market pressures and, V.II:75–78
pricing proposal, V.II:31–32
systems for, V.II:13
Product(s) V.I:42; V.II:75
alienation of from process, V.I:33, 36
deformation of, V.II:76–78
as part of process, V.I:35
process as, V.I:42–45
Profession; professionals, V.I:233
as funding decision makers, V.II:203–204
Professional identity, false preconceptions about, V.I:233
Professional vs. economic rewards, V.I:239, 240
Progressive Labor Party, V.II:86
Propaganda, V.II:38, 212–213
Properties
primary valued or disvalued, V.II:215, 233–236, 238, 239–241, 242
secondary valued or disvalued, V.II:237
tertiary disvalued, V.II:238
Protest movement, V.I:31
impact on artist, V.I:30, 262
Provincialism
in academia, V.I:229
conventions as protection for, V.II:205
in Euroethnic art world, V.II:184
in first-order political discrimination, V.II:229, 230
intellectual, V.I:203
xenophobia and, V.II:222–223
Provisional commitment, V.I:78, 79
Pryor, Richard, V.I:206
Pseudorationality, V.II:221–222, 252–253, 256
definition of, V.II:221
of disvaluees, V.II:252n36
first-order political discrimination and, V.II:245
higher-order political discrimination and, V.II:243–251, 252–253
"Pseudorationality" (Piper) V.II:220n10
Psychic split, limits and, V.I:xxiii; V.II:xxi
Psychoanalysis, inadequacy of as critical tool, V.II:125
Psychoanalysis and History (Mazlish) V.II:18n1
Psychoanalysis and Philosophy (Hanley and Lazerowitz) V.II:18n1
Psychoanalytic Explorations in Art (Kris) V.II:18n1
Psychological encounter, aesthetic emotion and, V.II:195–196
Psychological intimacy, in Germany, V.II:36
Psychological uniqueness, limits of, V.II:4
Psychologist, artist's work with, V.I:48
Psychotherapy, V.I:111
author's experience with, V.I:89
confrontational art vs., V.II:257–258
objectifying experience in, V.I:89
Publications, success as appearance in, V.II:167
Public context, independence of art from, V.I:47
Public good, public interest vs., V.II:204
Public interest, violation of conventions in, V.II:204–205
Publicity
in "cheap art utopia," V.II:34
quality concerns in, V.I:236
as success, V.II:167
Public meaning
biographical viewpoint of critic and, V.II:143–144
motivation of artist and, V.II:139–140, 144
Public nature, of Mythic Being, V.I:124–125
Public perceptual language, material form as tool for, V.I:5
Public space, V.II:43–44
calling card for women in, V.I:272
Mythic Being and, V.I:138
use of, V.I:121
Pudd'nhead Wilson (Twain) V.I:298, 307
Punishment, for black identity, V.I:280–281
Punishment for asserting ideas, positive effects of, V.I:xxxix; V.II:xxxvii
Punishment of supporters, V.I:xxxii–xxxiii; V.II:xxxi–xxxii
Punk, V.I:215
Puritanism, V.I:269
PWAs. *See* People with AIDS

Quality
aesthetic emotion and, V.II:190–196
Brenson analysis reviewed, V.II:189–200
in "cheap art utopia," V.II:33

entity vs., V.I:93
marginalized artists and, V.II:185
objective judgment of, V.II:196–197
race and gender issues separated from, V.II:162
standards of, V.II:189, 195, 198, 199, 200
varying definitions of, V.II:189
Quicksand (Larsen) V.I:307

Race
aesthetic quality and, V.II:162
gender and, V.I:xviii; V.II:xvi
as obstruction, V.I:xxiii; V.II:xxi
as primary disvalued property, V.II:225
stereotypes exposed, V.I:xviii; V.II:xvi
stereotypes of gender and, V.II:166
terms used for, V.II:127n1
Racial Attitudes in America: Trends and Interpretations (Schuman, Steeh, and Bobo) E-V.II:246n28
Racial harassment
in academia, V.I:281
self-identification and experience of, V.I:295–296
Racial identity, V.I:xxiii, 233, 268, 272–273, 275–306; V.II:xxi
accusations of fraud and, V.I:276, 278–279
acknowledgment of, V.I:292–293
costs of acknowledging, V.I:303–304
cultural racism and, V.II:138
dignity and, V.I:285
economics and, V.I:291–292
entitlement and, V.I:291
expectations and, V.I:297–298
extent of admixture, V.II:245n27
friendship and, V.I:233–234, 294–295
higher-order political discrimination and, V.II:240–241, 242, 243, 245, 249
legal definitions of, V.I:291–292
public acknowledgment and, V.I:299–301
reciprocal higher-order political discrimination and, V.II:242, 243
self-awareness and, V.I:175*f*, 233
self-worth and, V.I:294–295, 302
status and, V.I:292–293, 295, 306
stereotypes and, V.I:268
Think About It and, V.I:290*f*
whites and, V.I:233, 272–273, 275, 278–279, 287, 288–289, 291–293, 294–295, 298–E-299, 306
Racism, V.I:xx, 206; V.II:xviii, 48, 222
in academia, V.I:229, 230, 280–281; V.II:150–151
anger as response to, V.I:251
in art criticism, V.II:140, 143
artist's witnessing of, V.I:xix; V.II:xvii
art as tool for ending, V.II:178. *See also* Social change
in art world, V.I:xxxv, xxxvi; V.II:xxxiii, xxxiv, 163–164, 185
awareness of identity and, V.I:233
basis for. *See* Racism, roots of
black popular culture and, V.I:198–199, 200, 201
calling cards as response to, V.I:219–221
classic text on, V.II:137n10
classification as instrument of, V.I:305
class privileges and, V.I:xxxiii; V.II:xxxi
confronting, V.I:xix–xx, xxiii–xxiv, 169, 181–186, 220, 271–272; V.II:xvii–xviii, xxi–E-xxii
confronting through art, V.I:234, 245, 249, 266–267; V.II:130
covert, V.I:229, 230, 292, 293, 301–302
cultural. *See* Cultural racism
cultural inferiority complex and, V.I:206
denial patterns, V.II:246
difference between sexism and, V.I:247
disco dancing and, V.I:151
dissociation and, V.II:222
etiquette norms and, V.I:246–247
in Euroethnic art, V.II:156
false identity mechanism and, V.II:48
fear and, V.I:xx, 254, 263, 273; V.II:xviii
from fellow blacks, V.I:276
freedom of expression and, V.I:273–75
Funk Lessons and, V.I:197
gratuitous, V.II:73–75
ideology and, V.I:181; V.II:48, 166
interpersonal vs. institutional, V.I:246, 247
irony of racial admixture and, V.II:245n27
language and, V.I:305
last outpost of, V.I:293
legal, V.II:127
liberation from, V.I:245–246, 247
light-skinned blacks and, V.I:277–278
morality and, V.I:186
in museums, V.II:185
objectification in, V.I:263
passing and, V.I:230, 275–306
political art and, V.I:201
popular culture and, V.I:199–200
in *Porgy and Bess,* V.I:240
as protection for privilege, V.I:305–306
pseudorationality and, V.II:222
in responses to art, V.I:201, 203
responses to, V.I:xx–xxi, 181, 219–220, 267, 297–298, 302; V.II:xviii–xix
roots of, V.I:246, 263, 291–292, 298–299
scope of xenophobia and, V.II:223
self-hatred and, V.I:292
sexism vs., as subject matter, V.I:247, 251
sexuality and, V.I:201, 229, 253–254, 298–299
as subject, V.I:255–273
as tragedy, V.I:xxiv; V.II:xxii
types of political discrimination and, V.II:247n29
unacknowledged, V.I:301–302
in unguarded situations. *See* Racism, covert
as visual pathology, V.II:177
See also Cultural racism
"'Racism' Protest Slated over Title of Art Show" (Glueck) V.II:73n6
Radicalism, intellectual, V.II:152–153
Radio, as aural information context, V.II:7
Raffaele, Joseph, V.I:29
Raiffa, Howard, *Games and Decisions,* V.II:167n17
Ramayana Monkey Chant, V.I:200
Raphael, V.I:29
Rap music
Funk and, V.I:196, 269
as outlaw mode of expression, V.I:217
"Rational" art, V.II:3
Rationalism, Kantian thesis on, V.II:216–220
Rationality, V.II:252
art making and, V.I:119–120
commitment and, V.I:67, 80
cultural conventions and, V.II:224–225
failure to perceive in Other, V.II:227–228
"Rationality of Military Service" (Piper) V.II:49n2
"Rationality and the Structure of the Self" (Piper) V.II:218n8
Rationalization
defensive, V.II:130
definition of, V.II:222
in first-order political discrimination, V.II:245
in higher-order political discrimination, V.II:252
Raven, Arlene, V.II:162, 185
"Colored," V.II:162n4
"Laws of Falling Bodies," V.II:185n5
"Reagan's Arts Chairman Brings Subtle Changes to the Endowment" (Pear) V.II:65n2
Realism
political correctness vs., V.I:xxi; V.II:xix
social, V.I:187
Reality, V.II:5
abstraction and, V.I:227
ideas vs., V.II:7
translating idea to, V.I:4
Realization of ideas, V.I:17–18
Realization of piece, separation of idea and form in, V.I:38
Reason
artist's passion for, V.I:xxiv; V.II:xxii
art making and, V.I:119–120; V.II:17, 18
faith in over prejudice, V.I:xiii; V.II:xi
ideas as response to, V.II:5
Reasoning, about presuppositions, V.II:17–18
Receptivity, in dialogue, V.I:73
Reciprocal first-order political discrimination, V.II:233–237
Reciprocal higher-order political discrimination, V.II:242–243
Reciprocal privileges, art critic and, V.II:124–125
Recitals, author's feelings about, V.I:89, 90
Recognition
desire for, V.I:173
self-conscious, eliciting, V.II:130, 132
Recognition of artist
by art etablishment, V.I:52–53

price of, V.II:141, 142
sociopolitical climate and, V.I:xxxvi; V.II:xxxiv
Recognition of truth, V.I:76, 77
Records
aural information context for, V.II:7
as forms, V.II:6
Red-baiting. *See* McCarthyism
"Reductive" art, V.II:3
Reductivism, V.II:212, 213
Reed, T. E.: "Caucasian Genes in American Negroes," V.II:245n27
Referential vs. physical qualities, V.I:17–18
Reflection, V.II:18
art as, V.I:xxiii; V.II:xxi
Mythic Being as, V.I:125
power and, V.I:152
representation vs., V.I:225
Reflective technique, in philosophy, V.I:89–90
Reflective vs. involved vision of work, V.I:34–35
Reform; Reformation, V.II:89
as goal of artist, V.I:248
Regressive proof, V.II:17–18
Reich, Steve, V.I:200; V.II:175
Pendulum Music, V.II:10*f*
Reimaging America: The Arts of Social Change (O'Brien) V.I:245
Reinhardt, Ad, V.I:3n1
Reise, Barbara, V.I:15
Rejection, gaining strength from, V.I:277–278
Relationships
artist-audience, V.I:47; V.II:95–99, 100–101
in performance art, V.II:113–114
power and, V.I:189–190
trust and, V.I:300–301
unconventional art and, V.II:206
xenophobia in, V.I:256
Relatives, V.I:281–282
black identity and, V.I:284
tracing history of, V.I:287–288
welcoming of, V.I:306
See also Family
Relativity, quality issues, V.II:189
Religion. *See* Spiritual; Spirituality
Religious art, V.II:193
appropriation of, V.II:209
Relocated Planes (Piper) V.I:265
Rembrandt, V.II:79, 193
The Remembered Present: A Biological Theory of Consciousness (Edelman) V.II:218n7
Renaissance art, V.II:167
difference as source of inspiration in, V.II:209
Renaissance music, V.II:197
Repetition Nineteen (Hesse) V.II:9*f*
"Reply" (Hess) V.II:134n2
Representation, reflection vs., V.I:225
Representative qualities, V.I:17–18
"Representing Miscegenation Law" (Saks) V.I:289, 307
Repression
in art world, V.II:161, 162–163
attempts at justifying, V.II:171
Reproduction
as condition for art production, V.I:159
implications of, V.II:57–58
Reproduction media, V.I:121
The Republic (Plato) V.I:92
Research
hagiography vs., V.II:184, 185
questions on, V.II:186–187
Resentment, racist remarks about, V.I:281
Resistance, as subject for artist, V.I:xv; V.II:xiii
"Respect" (Franklin) V.I:48, 152
Responsibility
art as reminder of, V.I:234
asserting control as, V.I:xvi; V.II:xiv
for collective past, V.I:295
danger of abdicating, V.II:87
division of labor and, V.II:73, 74–75
for exploitation, V.I:295
freedom of expression and, V.II:73–74
intellectual independence and, V.II:151–152
personhood and, V.II:220–221
for social change, V.I:247
See also Responsibility; Responsibility of artists
Responsibility of artists, V.I:xv, 203; V.II:xiii
in "cheap art utopia," V.II:34
Retrospective exhibits, V.I:237
Revisionism, in personal history, V.I:294
Rewards, economic vs. professional, V.I:239, 240
Rhode Island School of Design (R.I.S.D.) V.I:114, 115
Rhythm and blues, in *It's Just Art,* V.I:177
Rich, Adrienne, *Contemporary Heterosexuality and Lesbian Existence,* V.II:49n3
"Riding with the material," V.I:4–5
Ringgold, Faith, V.I:236
R.I.S.D. *See* Rhode Island School of Design
Ritualized communication, in dance, V.I:177
Ritualized confrontation, disco dancing as, V.I:151
Ritualized repetition, in *Mythic Being* series, V.I:147
Rockefeller, Nelson, V.II:57
Rock music, Funk and, V.I:195, 215
Rodin, Auguste, V.I:29
Rolling Stones, V.I:96, 199
"If I Was a Dancer (Dance Part 2) (*Sucking in the Seventies*) V.I:215
Romanticism, artistic temperament and, V.II:24
Rosner, David, V.I:8*f,* 9, 10, 261
Rufus, "Do You Love What You Feel?," V.I:177
Russell, Bertrand, V.I:93
Inquiry (Into Meaning and Truth) V.I:92
Russian artists, V.I:187

Saar, Betty, V.II:166
Sacks, Oliver, "Neurology and the Soul," V.II:218n7
Saint Anthony Abbot series (Master of the Osservanza) V.II:194
St. John's Church, V.I:265
Saks, Eva, "Representing Miscegenation Law," V.I:289, 307
Salience, of formal properties over alien cultural meaning, V.II:210
Salient features of conceptual art, V.I:249
Salient interpretations of Easy Listening Art, V.II:178
Salle, David, V.II:154n5
Salsa, V.I:151
Samore, Sam, *Funk Lessons with Adrian Piper,* V.I:196
Sanctions, social, V.II:205–206
Sarraute, Nathalie, V.I:264
Sartre, Jean Paul, *Being and Nothingness,* V.I:117
Satire, of stereotypes, V.I:266
Sawyer, Diane, V.I:272
Schamlos, V.I:253
Schjeldahl, Peter, "Female Trouble," V.II:186n11
Schleier, Hans-Martin, V.II:35
Scholarship, art world's responsibility for, V.II:185–187
Schoenberg, Arnold, V.II:175
Schooling, status and, V.I:147
School of Visual Arts, V.I:3, 29, 225
Schuman, Howard, *Racial Attitudes in America: Trends and Interpretations,* V.II:246n28
Science, V.I:255
Science fiction, V.I:58–60
Science and the Modern World (Whitehead) V.I:92
Scientology, V.I:66
Scrutiny, self-conscious, cultural racism and, V.II:128
Sculpture
ideas and image in, V.I:38
as political art, V.I:265
Secondary valued or disvalued properties, V.II:237
Second-order political discrimination, V.II:237–238, 239
Second-order variables, V.I:143–144
Segregation, cognitive errors and, V.II:228
Sélavy, Rrose, V.I:117
"Selection, Gene Migration and Polymorphic Stability" (Workman et al.) V.II:245n27
Self, V.I:55; V.II:120
assumptions about artist's sense of, V.II:107–25
attempts at control by, V.II:116–117
cognitive discrimination and, V.II:216
coherence threatened by anomalous data, V.II:216
confrontation with Other, V.I:141
detachment of objects from, V.I:224
dispersion of, V.I:107
Kantian Rationalism Thesis and, V.II:219
Mythic Being and, V.I:125
as object, V.I:261

"performing" vs. personal, V.II:108, 109
privileged access to, V.II:225–227
transcending. *See* Self-transcendence
voluntary objectification of, V.I:154
See also Solipsism
Self-acceptance, V.I:251
Self-actualization, social stability and repression of, V.II:205
Self-affirmation, V.II:111
Self-aggrandizement, V.I:145
for artistic success, V.II:167
failure of transformation and, V.II:97
Self-alienation, author accused of, V.II:122
Self-awareness, V.I:249; V.II:xxvi
aesthetic emotion as, V.II:193
in art criticism, V.I:xxix; V.II:xxvii
communication with art world and, V.I:180
degrees of, V.II:47
distanced, in European art, V.II:214
eliciting, V.II:130, 132
in Euroethnic art, V.II:209, 210
generating in viewer, V.I:251
higher-order political discrimination and, V.II:253
intellectual, V.I:191
intellectual conscience and, V.II:151, 152
political action and, V.I:174
political effectiveness and, V.II:86
racial identity and, V.I:175*f*, 233
racism and, V.I:xix; V.II:xvii
strategies for attaining, V.II:253
Self-censorship, V.I:xxxi, xxxix; V.II:xxix, xxxvii, 212–213
freedom from, V.I:217
funding problems and, V.I:xxxi; V.II:xxix
interiority as result of, V.I:xxxix; V.II:xxxvii
intimidation and, V.II:162
Self-conception, V.II:222
honorific self-stereotype and, V.II:232–233
xenophobia and, V.II:221
Self-consciousness, V.I:102, 118; V.II:213
aesthetic, V.I:96
anger and, V.I:82
artist as object for, V.I:94
behavior and, V.I:92
critical, V.I:98
dancing and, V.I:97, 98, 151, 152
in Euroethnic art, V.II:210
of human objects, V.I:19
moving from solipsism to, V.I:47–51
of objecthood, V.I:90–91, 94
political consciousness and, V.I:31–32
and "Spectator" series, V.I:103–104
spectatorship and, V.I:101–102
as theme, V.I:141
transcendence and, V.I:55, 142–143
un-self-conscious, V.I:114
Self-conscious recognition, eliciting, V.II:130, 132
Self-containedness, disco dancing and, V.I:151
Self-control, V.I:63
Self-deception
on aesthetic vs. economic imperatives, V.II:84
avoidance of in art world, V.II:155
readings in, V.I:92
Self-defeating allegiances, V.II:89
Self-defense, strategies for, V.I:245
Self-determination, social stability and repression of, V.II:205
Self-discovery
as goal for audience, V.II:130, 132
methods of, V.I:91
Self-doubt, misunderstanding about, V.II:110–111
Self-esteem
art world's welfare system and, V.II:184
false identity mechanism and, V.II:48
higher-order political discrimination and, V.II:253
ideological self-deception as prop to, V.II:86
racial identity and, V.I:302
seen as arrogance, V.I:298
See also Self-worth
Self-examination, V.II:47–48
See also Self-reflection
Self-expression
attacks on as cultural racism, V.II:134
attention to act vs. product of, V.II:165
Self-hatred, V.I:173
racial identity and, V.I:292
Self-image, V.I:47
cultural racism and, V.II:127–128
objecthood and, V.I:91
self-worth and, V.I:294–295
Self-indulgence
excessive subjectivism as, V.II:95
genius vs., V.II:95–96
Self-knowledge, artist charged with search for, V.II:111
Self-mutilation, V.I:189, 192
Self-objectification, voluntary, V.I:154
Self-Portrait Exaggerating My Negroid Features (Piper) V.I:230, 231*f*, 245, 267–268
Self-protectiveness, sexism and, V.I:247
Self-reflection, V.II:213
art as impetus to, V.II:130, 132
dance and, V.I:151
defense mechanisms against, V.II:48–49, 50
generating in viewer, V.I:251
Self-reflexive content, V.II:213–214
Self-representation, recommendation for, V.II:22
Self-respect, V.I:214, 286
in face of racism, V.I:298–300
Self-revelation, in *A.~A*, V.I:145
Self-righteousness, condemnation of, V.I:xvii; V.II:xv
Self-scrutiny. *See* Self-examination
Self-transcendence, V.I:55; V.II:130
aesthetic evaluation and, V.I:204
art as means to, V.I:232
of audience and artist, V.I:143–144
barriers to, V.I:230
dance as means to, V.I:195
in friendship, V.I:57
Funk dance and, V.I:213
Funk music and, V.I:214
language and, V.II:133
in *Mythic Being* series, V.I:147
obstructions to, V.I:xxiii; V.II:xxi
philosophy as means to, V.I:55
as theme, V.I:142–143
transformation as, V.II:102–103
universal quality standards and, V.II:198
See also Transcendence
Self-worth, V.I:276, 306
as armor, V.I:279
maintaining in face of racism, V.I:297–298
racial identity and, V.I:294–295, 302
See also Self-esteem
Selling art, V.I:270–271
Sensory consciousness, V.I:20–21
Sensory data, organization of, V.II:217
Sensory input, in art production systems, V.II:13
Sensory overload, V.II:55
"Sentences" (LeWitt) V.I:xiii; V.II:xi
Sentient vs. nonsentient objects, V.I:262
Serrano, Andres, V.II:162, 163, 193
Seth Siegelaub Gallery, V.I:30
Sex. *See* Gender
Sexism, V.II:177
in academia, V.I:229, 281; V.II:150–151
in art criticism, V.II:140, 143
in art world, V.I:xxxv, xxxvi; V.II:xxxiii, xxxiv
confronting through art, V.II:130
context and, V.I:209
difference between racism and, V.I:247
dissociation and, V.II:222
etiquette norms and, V.I:246–247
in Euroethnic art, V.II:156
interpersonal vs. institutional, V.I:246, 247
liberation from, V.I:245, 246
racism vs., as subject matter, V.I:247, 251
as visual pathology, V.II:177
Sexual harassment, in academia, V.I:281
Sexuality, V.I:287
artistic conventions and, V.II:204, 205
disco dancing and, V.I:151
Funk music and, V.I:214, 269
higher-order political discrimination and, V.II:244, 245
Mythic Being and, V.I:118, 124
in personal history, V.I:104, 109, 110
power and, V.I:154, 190, 191
racism and, V.I:201, 229, 253–254, 298–299
repression of, V.II:161
white society's reactions to, V.I:201
Sexual morality, miscegenation and, V.I:292
Shakespeare, William, V.I:201
Shame
deviance from self-stereotype and, V.II:231, 232, 233

experience of, V.I:94
passing and, V.I:275–276, 280, 285, 296–297
political discrimination and, V.II:253
as weapon against racism or sexism, V.I:247
Shamelessness, V.I:253
Shankar, Ravi, V.I:268
"Shape Shifter" (Storr) V.II:185n7
Shared vocabulary, search for, V.I:xxx; V.II:xxviii
Shaw, Artie, V.I:268; V.II:175
Shawcross, William, V.I:177
"Shejam (Almost Bootsy Show) (Bootsy) V.I:215
Sherman, Cindy, V.I:xviii; V.II:xvi
Shine (Average White Band) V.I:215
"Shrinking History Part 1" (Coles) V.II:18n1
Signals, in performance, V.I:155
Signs, in performance, V.I:156
Simplicity, as aesthetic value, V.I:267
Sims, Lowery, V.II:127, 185
"The Mirror the Other," V.II:185n6
Singing, playing an instrument vs., V.I:90
Singularity
abdication of, V.II:146
complex, V.II:142
eradication of, V.II:133–134
stereotyping and, V.II:230
Situation series (Piper) V.I:227–228
See also Hypothesis series
Sixteen Permutations on the Planar Analysis of a Square (Piper) V.I:6*f*
16 Planar Variations (Piper) V.I:258
Slavery
family histories and, V.I:287
pseudorationality and, V.II:222
A Slave to Art (Piper) V.I:190–191
Slides
event context for, V.II:7
as forms, V.II:6
in *It's Just Art,* V.I:178
Smith, Roberta, V.II:162
"Adrian Piper," V.II:184.1, 186n8
Smithson, Robert, V.I:264
Asphalt Rundown, V.II:10*f*
Smith, Tony, V.I:29; V.II:192
Snow, Michael, V.I:37
Social categorization
comfort levels and, V.I:xix; V.II:xvii
conformity to, V.I:255
Social change
artist as agent of, V.I:xv, 32–33; V.II:xiii, 89
art as tool for, V.I:xx, xxi, 240; V.II:xviii, xix, 177–178, 181
as goal of artist, V.I:249, 251
individual responsibility for, V.I:247
recognition of universality and, V.II:89
vision for, V.I:245–246
Social class
institutional support and, V.I:xxxiii; V.II:xxxi
status and, V.I:147
Social comfort
categorization and, V.I:xix; V.II:xvii
conformity and, V.I:233
insistence on, V.I:306
stereotyping and, V.I:xix; V.II:xvii
Social community, government vs., V.II:206
Social constraints, prejudice and, V.I:xxiv; V.II:xxii
Social content
in conceptual art, V.II:213–214
cultural memory and, V.II:214
in Euroethnic art, V.II:209, 210–211
in European vs. American art, V.II:211–212
formalism and, V.II:211–212
form vs., V.II:214
Greenbergian formalism and, V.II:209
in minimalist art, V.II:213, 214
postmodernism and, V.II:212
Social context
need for research on, V.II:186
xenophobia and, V.I:256
Social contract, V.I:xx; V.II:xviii
Social conventions. *See* Conventions
Social dance, culture and, V.I:195
Social disease, V.I:246
Social hierarchy, in academia, V.I:264
Social identity, restructuring of, V.I:198
Social interaction
ideal vision of, V.I:246
as target of art, V.I:246
Socialist art, V.II:39
Socialization
etiquette norms and, V.I:247
performance effects and, V.II:101, 102
Social meaning, biographical viewpoint of critic and, V.II:143–144
Social parity, conventional behavior and, V.I:199
Social realism, V.I:187
Social responsibility, in "cheap art utopia," V.II:34
Social role of art, V.II:203, 253
Social roles
of artist, V.II:25–27, 50, 89
strict adherence to, V.I:208
Social sanctions, V.II:205–206
Social space, Funk music and, V.I:214
Social stability, as entrenching repression, V.II:205
Social status
passing and, V.I:284
racial identity and, V.I:292–293, 295, 306
Social structure, logical failures in, V.I:xx; V.II:xviii
Social wisdom, of African Americans, V.I:298–299
Society, V.I:199, 285; V.II:72, 186
artist's role in, V.II:25–27
art as reflection of, V.II:20
categorization in, V.I:xix, 255–256, 291–292; V.II:xvii
etiquette norms in, V.I:246–247
ideal, vision of, V.I:245–246
public good vs. public interest in, V.II:204
response to racism in, V.I:302
white, V.I:201–202
Sociocultural categorization, marginalization and, V.I:xxxiv, xxxv; V.II:xxxii, xxxiii
Sociocultural context
alienation of artist from, V.II:75
art education and, V.II:72
of civil rights movement, V.I:199
CWAs' art and, V.II:169
of *Funk Lessons,* V.I:195
need for research on, V.II:186
for political art, V.II:181
Socioculturally determined bias, V.II:65–66
Socioeconomic conditions
art accessibility and, V.I:122
art career and, V.II:63–65
art criticism and, V.II:23–24, 72
artist as subject to, V.I:78
definition of art and, V.II:65–66
Socioeconomic dynamics, communication with audience and, V.II:84
Socioeconomic hierarchies, V.I:147
Socioeconomic status
black popular culture and, V.I:200
higher-order political discrimination and, V.II:240–241, 243, 245, 249
reciprocal higher-order political discrimination and, V.II:242, 243
vocational choice and, V.II:23
Sociopolitical context, V.I:xxix, 9; V.II:xxvii
in *Art for the Art-World Surface Pattern,* V.I:161–167
artist and, V.I:xxxvi, xxxviii; V.II:xxxiv, xxxvi
of dancing, V.I:151–152
isolation vs. awareness of, V.I:xvii; V.II:xv
Sociopolitical engagement, advantages of, V.I:xxxviii; V.II:xxxvi
Sociopolitical influences on arts, V.II:20
The Soho Weekly News, V.II:41
Solidarity, in racial identity, V.I:233
Solipsism, V.I:xxxix, 51; V.II:xxxvii
in art criticism, V.I:236
beginning of author's interest in, V.I:90
definition of art and, V.II:66
exploration of subjectivity and, V.I:57
failure of transformation and, V.II:97
illusion of omniscience and, V.II:50
in mainstream art, V.II:45
moving to self-consciousness from, V.I:47–51
narcissism vs., V.II:116
quality art and, V.II:192
as theme, V.I:142
transcendence of, V.I:144
transition into, V.I:45–47
See also Self
Solitary works, V.I:48, 49, 51
Solitude, in public space, V.I:272
"Sol LeWitt: Non-Visual Structures" (Lippard) V.I:4n2

Some Reflective Surfaces (Piper) V.I:153*f*, 201
description of, V.I:151–152, 154–156
Sondheim, Alan, V.I:114
Individuals: Post-Movement Art, V.I:117
Sorrow, self-acceptance accompanied by, V.I:173
Soul music, V.I:151, 214
Soul Train, V.I:xv; V.II:xiii
South Africans, V.I:169
Southeast Center for Contemporary Art, V.II:162
Soviet Union, V.I:187
Space
activating, V.I:262
in event context, V.II:7
See also Public space; Social space; Spatial contexts
Space, Time, Language, Form (Piper) V.I:12–13*f*
Spatial contexts, V.II:7
Spatial forms, V.II:6
Spatiotemporal conditions
abstraction as freedom from, V.I:224, 225
aesthetic status and, V.II:56–57
audience and, V.I:51
in conceptual art, V.I:241
as limitations, V.I:33, 37
performance art and, V.II:60
sensory information and, V.I:20–21
in *Spectator Series*, V.I:102
as subject matter, V.I:19, 20
Spatiotemporal coordinates, for self as object, V.I:261
Spatiotemporal integration, of art process and viewer, V.I:34
Spatiotemporal perspective, V.I:225
Speaking in Tongues (Talking Heads) V.I:215
"Speaking Out: Some Distance to Go. . ." (Berger) V.II:185n2
Special interest groups, passive censorship and, V.II:201
Specificity, connecting to stereotype, V.I:268
Spectator, artist as, V.I:94
Spectator Series (Piper)
Catalysis and, V.I:104
performing, V.I:103–105
planning, V.I:101–103
Spectatorship, V.I:101–102
participation vs., V.I:213
Speculation
art criticism and, V.II:23
pricing proposal and, V.II:32
Spingarn, Jim, V.I:48, 50
Spirit of Love (ConFunkShun) V.I:214
Spiritual; Spirituality
aesthetic emotion and, V.II:192–193, 194–195, 196
friendship and, V.I:57
objective judgment and quality of, V.II:196–197
quality art as celebration of, V.II:192–193
standards and, V.II:199, 200
Spy magazine, racist criticism in, V.II:163n10
Stability, tolerance for unconventional and, V.II:206
Standards, V.II:185
artist-defined, V.I:29–30
artistic, V.I:30, 33
artistic vs. moral, V.II:154–158
art market and, V.II:154–155, 156
disvaluees and, V.II:250–251
intellectual, V.II:151–152
of quality, V.II:189, 198, 199, 200
self-transcendence and, V.II:198
spiritual cultivation and, V.II:199, 200
valorization and, V.II:199
See also Aesthetics; Value(s)State, civil society vs., V.II:206
Static media, use of, V.I:137
Static nature of commitment, argument against, V.I:71
Stations of the Cross (Newman) V.II:196
Status, V.I:9
of disvaluees, V.II:250–251
ethnicity and, V.I:147, 149
family background and, V.I:147
Funk music and, V.I:204
gender and, V.I:147, 149
passing and, V.I:284
race and gender stereotypes and, V.I:xviii; V.II:xvi
racial identity and, V.I:292–293, 295, 306
schooling and, V.I:147
social class and, V.I:147
Steeh, Charlotte, *Racial Attitudes in America: Trends and Interpretations*, V.II:246n28
Steely Dan, "My Rival" (*Gaucho*) V.I:215
Stella, Frank, V.I:29, 52, 246
Stellarc, V.I:189
Stereotyping, V.II:226
of African Americans, V.I:xviii, xxi, 181, 183–185, 229–230, 253, 266–268, 267–268, E-278, 281; V.II:xvi, xix, 164–165. *See also* Stereotyping, racist
art as attack on, V.II:132, 134
in artist's use of media, V.I:249
and artwork, V.I:245; V.II:186
of colored artists as Other, V.II:186
confronting, V.I:xxi, 242; V.II:xix
connecting specificity to, V.I:268
cultural conventions and, V.II:224–225
as cultural racism, V.II:134
of CWAs, V.II:164–165, 166
definition of, V.II:229
derogatory, V.II:229–230, 232
discriminatory, inductive generalization vs., V.II:230
eliciting awareness of, V.II:130
eliminating, V.I:245–246
formation of, V.II:240–241
in *Four Intruders. . .*, V.I:183–185
higher-order political discrimination and, V.II:248
honorific, V.II:229, 230, 231–233
linguistic pigeonholing, V.II:133
monologues on, V.I:266–268
Mythic Being and, V.I:xviii; V.II:xvi
politically discriminatory, V.II:230–231, 238
pseudorationality and, V.II:222
racial identity and, V.I:268
racist, V.I:203, 277; V.II:134, 138. *See also* Stereotyping, of African Americans
in response to political art, V.I:164
roots of, V.I:246
satire of, V.I:266
shame and, V.II:231, 232–233
showing effect of, V.I:220
singularity and, V.II:230
social comfort and, V.I:xix; V.II:xvii
as subject for artist, V.I:xv; V.II:xiii
in *Vanilla Nightmares*, V.I:253
in xenophobia, V.I:248
Stockhausen, Karlheinz, V.II:193
Stone, Sylvia, V.II:52
Storr, Anthony, *The Dynamics of Creation*, V.II:18n1
Storr, Robert, "Shape Shifter," V.II:185, 185n7
Strangers
anger at, V.I:83, 84
dealing with, V.I:62, 65
fear of. *See* Xenophobia
Straub, Jean-Marie, *History Lesson*, V.I:103
Straw men, stereotypes and, V.II:134
Strawson, P. F., 248n31
The Bounds of Sense, V.II:217n6
Street performances, V.I:xxxvi, 42–51, 129; V.II:xxxiv
beginnings of, V.I:89
behavioral codes and, V.I:262
Catalysis series, V.I:262–263
of Mythic Being, V.I:137, 138, 147, 263–264
See also specific works
Streetworks, V.II:129. *See also* Performance art; Street performances
Stress, art making and, V.I:239
Strider, Marjorie, V.I:37
Structure, communication through, V.II:194. *See also* Form
The Structure of Scientific Revolutions (Kuhn) V.II:220n11
Strunk, W., Jr., *Elements of Style*, V.II:149
Strutting (Piper) V.I:147
Student revolts, V.I:227
Studio Museum, V.II:162
Stupidity, V.II:135–136
Style, as vehicle for content, V.II:150
Subjecthood
of Mythic Being, V.I:117
objecthood as, V.I:27
Subjectivity; subjectivism
in aesthetic emotion, V.II:197–198
in art criticism, V.I:xxix; V.II:xxvii, 22n2
dichotomy between cosmic and, V.II:97–98
dichotomy between universal and, V.II:94–98, 99
exploration of solipsism and, V.I:57

freedom from, V.I:224
as limitation, V.I:142
Mythic Being and, V.I:263
performance art and, V.II:101, 102, 104
self-indulgence and, V.II:95
subjective-cosmic dichotomy, V.II:97–98
transcendence and, V.I:65–66, 68; V.II:3
xenophobia and, V.II:223
Subject matter
abandonment of for abstraction, V.I:225
of analytic philosophy, V.II:149
anomalous behavior as, V.I:261
artist as, V.II:101–102, 118, 120, 129. *See also* Artist(s) as art object
assimilation as, V.I;xv; V.II:xiii
assimilation of by artist, V.I:94
as context-independent, V.II:70
of criticism, artist vs. work as, V.II:164–166
distancing from, V.II:211
documentation and, V.I:35–36
dualism as, V.I:17–18
ethical issues, V.I:189
in Euroethnic art, V.II:210–211
Greenbergian formalism and, V.II:209
hidden properties, V.I:18
human consciousness as, V.I:19
human objects as, V.I:19, 262
imagery as, V.I:121
language as, V.I:91; V.II:213
misinterpretation of, V.II:118, 120
morality as, V.I:9-10
objectified perceptions as, V.I:9
physical properties as, V.I:18
racism as, V.I:255-273
racism vs. sexism as, V.I:247, 251
as realization of idea, V.I:17–18
resistance as, V.I:xv; V.II:xiii
"riding with the material," V.I:4–5
spatiotemporal, V.I:19, 20
stereotyping as, V.I:xv; V.II:xiii
as threat to mainstream, V.II:168–169
unperceived function or process as, V.I:18
zero-sum game and, V.II:167
Subject-object dichotomy, dissolution of, V.I:50–51, 89, 90
Subject-objects, artists as, V.II:129
Subject-predicate relation, in Kantian Rationalism Thesis, V.II:217, 218, 219
Sublimation, Mythic Being and, V.I:138
Sublime, recognition of, V.II:191
Subliminal thought process, in art making, V.II:17, 18
Subversive nature of performance, V.I:155–156
Success
abdication of power required for, V.II:78–79
art world's determinants of, V.II:153–154, 167–168, 169–172
definition of for author, V.II:50
financial, V.I:239, 240
ideological definition of, V.II:78
market value as measure of, V.II:169–170
professional, V.I:239, 240
as zero-sum game, V.II:167, 169–172
Sucking in the Seventies (Rolling Stones) V.I:215
Suffering Test of blackness, V.I:276, 278, 303, 305
The Sugar Hill Gang, V.II:175
Sullivan, Kaylynn, *Unburied Treasure,* V.II:196
Superiority
self-demeaning behavior and, V.I:299
sense of, V.I:295
Support for artist
appreciation for, V.I:239
institutional politics and, V.I:xxxii–xxxiv; V.II:xxxi–xxxii
Suppression of anomaly, V.I:265
Surface, Mythic Being as, V.I:125
Surfaces (Piper) V.I:137
See also Some Reflective Surfaces
Surrealism show, in Berlin, V.II:37
Surrealists, appropriation by, V.II:183
Suspicion, V.I:230
Symbolic code, confronting, V.I:xxi, xxiii; V.II:xix, xxi
Symbolism; Symbols, V.I:xxi; V.II:xix
abstract system of, V.I:259, 261
conceptual, V.I:242
darkness, V.I:xxiii–xxiv; V.II:xxi–xxii
Symbology
in *Catalysis* series, V.I:262–263
in conceptual art, V.I:257–258, 259, 261
in *Mythic Being* series, V.I:263–264
Symbols, shared lexicon of, V.II:96
Synthesis, in dialectic analysis, V.II:18
Systematic approach, intuition vs., V.I:96
Systems
finite, construction of, V.I:5, 7
search for truth and, V.I:75, 76
Szakacs, Dennis, V.II:162n6

Tahitian art, Gauguin and, V.II:209
A Tale of Avarice and Poverty (Piper) V.I:230, 270, 283*f*
Talking Heads, V.I:200
"Making Flippy Floppy" (*Speaking in Tongues*) V.I:215
"Talking to Myself" (Piper) V.I:xvii; V.II:xv
Tannen, Deborah, *You Just Don't Understand,* V.II:224n14
Tape recordings
audio, V.I:48, 49, 141, 144
Food for the Spirit, V.I:55
as forms, V.II:6
for *Phillip Zohn Catalysis,* V.I:58–88
Tapes, aural information context for, V.II:7
Taste
aesthetic judgment and, V.II:195, 196
etiquette and, V.I:247
Tau Zero (Anderson) V.I:58–59, 60
Taylor, Joe Gray, *Negro Slavery in Louisiana,* V.I:287, 307
Tazzi, Pier Luigi, V.II:214n2
Teacher, author as, V.I:xiv, xv; V.II:xii, xiii
Teleology, V.I:142
Telephone, as aural information context, V.II:7
Television, as event context, V.II:7
"Tendenz der Zwanzigen Jahre" exhibit, V.II:37
$10.00/Hour Drawing of Pontus Hulten (Piper) V.I:188*f*
Terminology, in analytic philosophy, V.II:149
Text
as art media, V.I:49
as art object, V.I:263–264
in fictionalized family narrative, V.I:282
See also Media
Textual performance
concept of, V.II:108, 109, 111, 113
meta-art seen as, V.II:115
Theory
aesthetic emotion as resistant to, V.II:199
identification with, V.II:229
personal investment in, V.II:228
Therapy, attitude toward, V.I:111. *See also* Psychotherapy
Thesis, in dialectic analysis, V.II:18
Think About It (Piper) V.I:272, 290*f*
Third-order political discrimination, V.II:238–239
Third-personal opacity, V.II:225–226
Third-person distance, responsibility of critic and, V.II:144
Third world
cultural racism and, V.II:127
identity with, V.I:245
This Is Not the Documentation of a Performance (Piper) V.I:xix, 160*f*, 265; V.II:xvii
Thompson, Robert Farris, V.I:xiv; V.II:xii, 165n14
Flash of the Spirit: African and Afro-American Art and Philosophy, V.I:216
Thorson, Alice, "Conceptualized Conflicts," V.II:186n8
Thought, V.I:241
art as stimulus to, V.II:203
failure to perceive in Other, V.II:227–228
impact on art of, V.I:xxxi; V.II:xxix
Thought processes
in analytic philosophy, V.II:149–150
in meta-art, V.II:17
Three-dimensional objects, tracking changes in, V.I:251
Three Political Self-Portraits (Piper) V.I:228
Through the Looking Glass (Carroll) V.I:59
Timaeus (Plato) V.I:92
Time
in event context, V.II:7
sensory information and, V.I:21
See also Spatiotemporal conditions
"A Times Critic's Piece about Art Amounts to Political Propaganda" (Kramer) V.II:187n12
Tolerance
acceptance vs., V.I:245
in relationships, V.I:256
unconventional art and, V.II:205, 206
Tolkien, J. R., V.I:59

To the Max (ConFunkShun) V.I:214
Tragedy, racism as, V.I:xxiv; V.II:xxii
Training, artistic. *See* Art education
Transcendence, V.I:112
abstract subjectivity and, V.II:97
aesthetic emotion and, V.II:192–193, 194–195, 196, 198–199
Euroethnic male view of women and, V.II:168
mantras as means to, V.I:112
recognition of truth and, V.I:76, 77
self-consciousness and, V.I:55, 142–143
study of Kant and, V.I:55
and subjectivity, V.I:65–66, 68; V.II:3
Transformation
artist as art object and, V.II:100–101
artist-audience relationship and, V.II:98, 99, 100
degrees of, V.II:177
failure of, V.II:97
as self-transcendence, V.II:102–103
through experience, V.I:247–248
through familiar social content, V.II:210–211
through performance art, V.II:93–94, 95–96
Transparency, epistemic, V.II:21
Transparency. *See* Opacity
Transpersonality, in artist-audience relationship, V.II:100, 102
Transvestism, Mythic Being and, V.I:117–118
Trivial concerns, in mainstream art, V.II:45
Trombipulation (Parliament) V.I:214
Trust
friendship and, V.I:300–301
reserve about, V.I:288
Truth
commitment to, V.I:72–77, 249
Easy Listening Art and, V.II:178
epistemic insecurity and, V.I:xxxix; V.II:xxxvii
objective quality judgments, V.II:198
political art as pointer to, V.II:178, 180
postmodernism and, V.II:168–169
validity of concept questioned, V.II:161
Turnley, Peter, V.II:160*f*
Twain, Mark, *Pudd'nhead Wilson,* V.I:298, 307
Twelve-Part Grid Proposal for Dugway Proving Ground (Piper) V.I:30
"Two Conceptions of the Self" (Piper) V.II:220n10
Two-dimensional media, V.I:227

Ultra Wave (Bootsy) V.I:214
Unburied Treasure (Sullivan) V.II:196
Uncategorizable data, V.I:255
Unconventional, arguments for government support of, V.II:201–206
Unfamiliarity
aesthetic emotion and, V.II:198–199
xenophobia and, V.II:221
Unification Church, V.I:65
Unique; uniqueness
aesthetic value vs., V.II:57–58, 59
of artist, V.II:19–20, 21
of art product, V.II:19, 79–80
desire for, V.II:55
as ideology, V.II:79–80
loss of in generalization, V.II:56
of performance, V.II:60
spiritual growth through experience of, V.II:198–199
United States, contemporary art in, V.II:209–214
Unity
aesthetic emotion and, V.II:193
Funk music as means to, V.I:214
Universals; Universality, V.II:94, 97–98, 130
absurdity of demand for, V.I:251
aesthetic, subjectivity of artist vs., V.II:95, 96
artist's message in, V.I:xviii; V.II:xvi
cultural racism and, V.II:145
dichotomy between subjective and, V.II:94–98, 99
formalist constraints and, V.II:69, 70
idiolect variations and, V.II:145–146
objective, V.I:xxxi, xxxiv, xxxix–xl; V.II:xxix, xxxii, xxxvii–xxxviii
quality criteria and, V.II:196–198, 199
recognition of, V.II:89
as relative to audience, V.II:100
subjective-cosmic dichotomy and, V.II:97–98
value criteria, V.II:197
Un-self-conscious self-consciousness, V.I:114
Unsituated information contexts, V.II:7
Untitled (Judd) V.II:9*f*
Untitled Catalysis for Max's Kansas City (Piper) V.I:262
Untitled Construction (Piper) V.I:258
Untitled Drawing (Darboven) V.II:11*f*
Untitled Drawing (Piper) V.I:225
Untitled Performance for Max's Kansas City (Piper) V.I:27, 27*f*
Untitled Three-Part Painting (Piper) V.I:225
Upanishads, V.I:9
Ur-Mutter #2 (Piper) V.II:160*f*
USSR. *See* Soviet Union
Utah-Manhattan Transfer (Piper) V.I:227, 259–260
Utah-Manhattan Transfer #1 (Piper) V.I:260*f*
Utah-Manhattan Transfer #2 (Piper) V.I:260*f*
Utilitarian value of art, V.II:25
Utility, marginal utility of commodity consumption, V.II:54–55
Utopian modernism, conceptualism and, V.I:xvii; V.II:xv

Valentine, DeWayne, V.I:187
Validation
art criticism and, V.II:68
audience and, V.I:52, 53
Valorization
empowerment through, V.II:198
standards and, V.II:199
Valuees, V.II:229, 231, 234
epistemic vs. normative judgment of, V.II:233
Value(s) V.II:25, 215
aesthetic. *See* Aesthetic value
aesthetic vs. economic, V.I:121; V.II:31, 32
aesthetic vs. humanistic, V.II:25–27
in art criticism vs. meta-art, V.II:23–24
of artist's time, V.I:159
in contemporary art, V.II:169–170
creating with art, V.I:178
exchange and production, V.I:121, 159; V.II:31–32
first-order political discrimination and, V.II:245
intellectual conscience and, V.II:157–158
investment, V.I:121
motivation and, V.II:74
personal, V.II:233–237
personal vs. political, V.I:161
primary valued or disvalued properties, V.II:215
uniqueness as, V.II:57–58
universal binding criteria of, V.II:197
Van Gogh, Vincent, V.II:209
Vanilla Nightmares #3 (Piper) V.I:252*f*
Vanilla Nightmares #16 (Piper) V.II:131*f*
Vanilla Nightmares #18 (Piper) V.I:235*f*, 273
Vanilla Nightmares series (Piper) V.I:229, 245, 253–254, 273
Vedanta philosophy, cultural knowledge and, V.II:165n14
"Vehicles for Rare Color," V.II:41
Venues, alternative, V.I:45
"Vestiges," V.I:99, 100
Victimhood, rejection of, V.I:277–278, 298
Victimization, V.I:208–209
complicity with, V.II:85
Victims
of cultural racism, V.II:127–128
projection of racists' fears onto, V.I:253–254
Video tape
in *Cornered,* V.I:272–273
in *Funk Lessons,* V.I:196
use of by artist, V.I:xxi; V.II:xix
See also Media
Vietnam, V.I:177
Vietnam War, V.I:xvii, 299; V.II:xv
"On View: New York" (Heartney) V.II:186n10
Viewers, V.I:34, 37
artist's relationship with, V.I:234
Euroethnicity of, V.II:164
passive vs. active, V.I:37
See also Audience
Village Voice (newspaper)
CWA show reviewed in, V.II:162
Mythic Being series and, V.I:112n6–112n8, 113, 114, 117, 123, 137, 147, 227, 263–264
Spectator Series and, V.I:101, 102
Violation of social conventions, V.II:204
See also Conventions
Violence, *Mythic Being* series and, V.I:147
Visibility, artist's need to sustain, V.II:76, 77, 78
Vision
of audience and artist, V.I:7, 53
concretizing, V.I:94

limitations of, V.I:142
Visual culture, censorship of, V.II:213
Visual forms, V.II:6
Visual pathology, racism and sexism as, V.II:177
Visual titillation, in Easy Listening Art, V.II:177
Vocabulary, search for, V.I:xxx; V.II:xxviii
Vocational choice
socioeconomic status and, V.II:23
supplementary occupations, V.II:80
Voice
individual, V.II:100
objective declarative, V.I:xxxiv, xxxix–xl, 253; V.II:xxxii–xxxiii, xxxvii–xxxviii
Vulnerability
aesthetic emotion and, V.II:191
encounter with, V.I:93–4
as goal, V.I:143
reminders of, V.I:233

War, "Night People," V.I:181, 266
Warhol, Andy, V.I:268; V.II:157
Washington Women's Art Center, V.II:161
WASPs
black counterpart for, V.I:xviii; V.II:xvi
racism among, V.I:229, 281; V.II:232
sense of entitlement and, V.I:xviii, xxxiii–xxxiv, xxxix; V.II:xvi, xxxii, xxxvii
status and, V.I:147, 149
See also Heterosexual white males; Whites
Waterman, Richard Alan, "African Influence on the Music of the Americas," V.I:216
Waters, Maxine, V.I:299
"Ways of Seeing Adrian Piper" (Hess) V.II:134n2, 186n9
Weber, John, V.I:xxxvi, V.II:xxxiv
Webern, Anton, V.II:175
Weems, Carrie Mae, V.II:193
Welchman, John, V.II:146
Welfare system, in art world, V.II:183, 184
affirmative action and, V.II:186, 187
Welish, Marjorie, "In This Corner: Adrian Piper's Agitprop," V.II:186n10
Wells, Ida B., V.I:298–299
"Wem Gehört die Welt?" exhibit, V.II:37–38
"We Shall Overcome," V.I:279
West Berlin, author's visit to, V.II:35–38, 39
What It's Like, What It Is #3 (Piper) V.I:xxi, xxii*f*; V.II:xix, xx*f*
White Anglo-Saxon Protestants. *See* WASPs
White by Definition: Social Classification in Creole Louisiana (Dominguez) V.I:286, 289, 307; E-V.II:245n27
White, E. B., *Elements of Style,* V.II:149
Whitehead, Alfred North, *Science and the Modern World,* V.I:92
White middle-class het males, vision of parity with, V.I:246
Whiteness, assumptions about, V.II:137
Whites, V.I:206, 209
acknowledgment of mixed ancestry among, V.I:292–293
and alien other, V.I:207–208
art lovers as, V.I:xx; V.II:xviii
dance and, V.I:195
entitlement and, V.I:xviii; V.II:xvi
Funk and, V.I:195, 198–199, 200–201, 215
racial identity and, V.I:233, 272–273, 275, 278–279, 287, 288–289, 291–293, 294–295, E-298–299, 306
racism and anti-Semitism of, V.I:219, 267, 298–301
vision of parity with, V.I:246
See also Heterosexual white males; WASPs
White society, limits of assimilation into, V.I:201–202
Whitney Biennal, CWAs excluded from, V.II:161
Whitney Museum of American Art, V.I:155
Who Is Black? One Nation's Definition (Davis) V.I:284, 287, 288, 289, 291–292, 297, 307; E-V.II:245n27
"Who me?" syndrome, V.I:249
confronting, V.I:xix–xx; V.II:xvii–xviii
"Who Owns the World?" exhibit, in Berlin, V.II:37–38
Why Guess? #2 (Piper) V.II:147*f*
Wide Receiver (Henderson) V.I:215
Williams, Esther, V.I:271–272
Williamson, Joel, *A New People,* V.I:206; V.II:245n27
Wilson, Emmet, V.II:18n1
Wilson, Ian, V.I:37
Withers, Josephine, V.II:127, 146
Witness, mythology of, V.I:103
Wojnarowicz, David, V.II:163, 209
Wolff, Robert Paul, *Kant's theory of Mental Activity,* V.II:216n5
Women, V.II:240
awareness of exploitation by, V.II:86
calling card for use of, V.I:272
in Euroethnic art world, V.II:168, 170
in ideal society, V.I:245
in philosophy, V.II:150–151
as primary disvalued properties, V.II:240, 241
pseudorationality and, V.II:222
special knowledge of, V.I:299
stereotyping of, V.I:xviii; V.II:xvi, 135n7
See also Gender; Sexism; Women artists
Women artists, V.I:xxxiv–xxxvi; V.II:xxxiii–xxxiv
art world and, V.I:xxxvii; V.II:xxxv, 168
marginalization of, V.I:xxxv; V.II:xxxiii
Women's Movement, V.I:30, 227
"Woody Allen" syndrome, V.I:237
Workers, artists as, V.II:32
Working-class culture, black. *See* Black working-class culture
Workman, P. L., "Selection, Gene Migration and Polymorphic Stability," V.II:245n27
Works
artist as identical with, V.I:35–36
condition placed on, V.I:159
decision making about, V.I:119–120
documentation confused with, V.I:35, 36–37
examples of, V.I:45, 48–49
ideological restrictions on, V.I:115
marketing, V.I:270–271
ontological status of, accessibility and, V.II:98
overview of (lecture) V.I:258–273
solitary, V.I:48, 49, 51
See also Art making; *specific works*
Worth. *See* Self-worth
Writing as occupation, compared to art, V.II:33
Writing(s) V.II:xxvii
by artist on own work, V.I:xxix; V.II:xxvii
as clarification of ideas, V.I:31, 32
difficulties in, V.I:11
on performance, V.II:112–113
role of for artist, V.I:xxxix–xl; V.II:xxxvii–xxxviii, 112

Xenophobia, V.I:200, 202; V.II:233
in art criticism, V.II:143, 145, 146
of audience, V.I:268
black popular culture and, V.I:198, 199, 200, 201
cognitive discrimination and, V.II:216, 220–228
cognitive errors behind, V.II:223–228
confronting through art, V.I:234, 242
definition of, V.I:255; V.II:216, 221
failure of transformation and, V.II:97
fear of the Other and, V.II:128–129, 130
indexical present as antidote to, V.I:248
political discrimination and, V.II:216, 222
as reaction to anomaly, V.II:220, 222, 223, 226
as reaction to fear, V.II:220, 221
in relationships, V.I:256
roots of, V.I:246, 255–256
scope of, V.II:223
social context and, V.I:256
of white Americans, V.I:206
xenophobic reactions vs., V.II:228
"Xenophobia and Kantian Rationalism" (Piper) V.II:220n12

Yoga, V.I:9, 57, 261
author's feelings about, V.I:89, 90, 91
commitment to, V.I:70–71
subject-object distinction dissolved in, V.I:89, 90
Yogic system, commitment to, V.I:70–71
You Just Don't Understand (Tannen) V.II:224n14

0 to 9 (magazine) V.I:xxxvi; V.II:xxxiv
Zero-sum game
artistic success as, V.II:167, 169–172
cooperation as alternative to, V.II:173
economics and, V.II:169
Zohn, Phillip, V.I:49, 227–228
artwork on, V.I:57–88
drawing of, V.I:56*f*
Zola, Émile, *Germinal,* V.II:195